Essentials of Financial Accounting

Focus on Fundamentals, Vol-1

Panirselvam Ayadurai
Gayatri Panirselvam

notionpress.com

INDIA • SINGAPORE • MALAYSIA

ISBN 979-8-89446-033-8

Dedicated to my beloved mother and father,
Saraswathy Raju Pillay and Ayadurai Ponnusamy

You are one, and everything else is zero.

Put a zero before one, and what happens?

Nothing. Zero is zero. One is one. Put the zero after one?

Magic happens. Ten. Another zero? Hundred.

Another zero? Thousand. Another zero? Ten thousand.

Make magic happen. Put the self first.

— Prem Rawat, Lima, Peru - June 19, 2013

Contents

Foreword

My sincere congratulations to Dr. Panirselvam Ayadurai for his effort in writing this book entitled "Essentials of Financial Accounting." It is indeed an excellently written text that explains the financial accounting standards and practices in the Malaysian context.

The development and advancement of accounting knowledge has always been the primary intention of the Dr Panir. The publication of book with endorsement of very experienced accountants is thus in line with his intentions. Additionally, the release of this publication is very timely because it also addresses the accounting issues of the current practices in the accountancy profession.

The 26 chapters in the book cover such diverse topics, ranging from accounting for asset and liability items, profit and loss items, business combinations, derivatives, and financial instruments, to social and voluntary reporting practices. The author has carefully explained the application of accounting principles in each accounting standard with illustrative examples. Also, extracts of published financial statements have been included to highlight current reporting practices.

Up-to-date references have also been included in the book to provide readers with current thinking in the accountancy profession.

In my view, this book will be a very suitable text for students taking their examinations as well as for students pursuing an accountancy degree in the local universities and other professional courses. Accounting practitioners should also find this book an invaluable and useful reference because it focuses on the current development in the area of financial accounting and reporting.

I would like to take this opportunity to commend Dr. Panir. I hope that other accounting academics and professionals would also contribute their experience and acknowledge by publication in text books to increase the Malaysian accounting literature.

SEELAN CHELLIAH

C.A (M) F.C.A (ICAEW), CPA(M), F.C.T.I.(M)

Managing Partner,

Inpana & Amp; Associates,

Chartered Accountants,

Malaysia.

Preface

The authors desired this book to serve the needs of the targeted audience, while taking a comprehensive approach to students' learning, and by ensuring that the structure, content and coverage of accounting topics and concepts are relevant to the syllabus requirements. We also made sure it meets student and faculty expectation.

Essentials of Financial Accounting is our first edition; a book provides an essential study text for any accounting student. The book's accessibility is suitable for a wide range of courses in accounting. The text comes in two separate volumes with 2 Chapters, primarily intended for students doing the first and second year of an accounting and finance degree program in most Universities and Colleges. Students of accountancy undertaking professional examinations may also find the book very useful. There are others of course, who may have a desire to improve and expand their knowledge of accounting, they too can benefit from using this text selectively for many useful accounting topics. There are many published books on accounting available in the market. However, this introductory textbook reflects the current trend in financial accounting practice in Malaysia. The book's emphasis is on the essential elements of accounting practice in today's business environment. Accounting and accounting education has changed in recent years and with increasing complexity, accounting is seen crucially challenging for any aspiring students to be engaged in learning this social science so that they gain a better understanding of the world of business.

All the essential topics in accounting are covered in this text with many illustrative examples. The examples explain and show the accounting treatment given for the type and nature of business transactions. We show the application of generally accepted accounting principles (GAAPs) on these transactions undertaken by business entities. Where appropriately required, the text also discusses the application of relevant Financial Reporting Standards. Business entities are always engaged in satisfying their informational needs for strategic growth and expansion. The management of a company is more focused on financial performance and financial position which directly impacts on the share value of a company. The financial statements serve as a purpose to provide vital information for making informed economic decisions. Conventionally, the accounting process of any business entity is mutually tied-up with the value creation process.

Three chapters of the text are long. Chapter 3 on computerized accounting system, Chapter 24 on analysis and interpretation of financial statements and Chapter 25 relates to the preparation of basic consolidated accounts. Students are expected to give their attention to these areas as they are highly relevant in today's business context for any aspiring accountants.

As authors, we hope the book can immensely imbue students' interest in gaining more accounting knowledge by realising its importance to their careers.

Acknowledgments

A textbook is not the lonely effort of its author or co-author but the efforts and skills of other individuals contributing to the task. We extend our special thanks and appreciation to our reviewers particularly to B. Jayasangar, a practising chartered accountant who painstakingly reviewed most of the important chapters with valuable input and comments in the midst of his busy work schedule. We are also grateful to Paran Puvanesan, a chartered accountant and Mergers & Acquisition advisor with AKINA Deals Advisory, Shanti, a general editor who significantly contributed in sustaining our effort to complete the book on time and Rukkumani whose moral support encouraged us to stay on course.

As the main author, I (Panirselvam) would also like to take the liberty to express my special gratitude to these British chartered accountants, Keith Farmer, Francis Braganza, Navzar Tarapovalla, Dass Daruwalla, Doug Bearden and Andy Perkins who were all my gurus while studying at the Emile Woolf College of Accountancy in London, England between the years 1985 and 1992. I want to also thank Amutha and our three other children, Gnaeskandan, Vidya and Dinesh Thillainathan.

My gratitude also goes to the late Mr Narayanan Chettiar, a CPA, who was my first employer and inspired me to take up professional accountancy. Another person to whom I owe a special thanks is the late Mr Gandhi for suggesting me to take up a junior position in Narayan & Co, Chartered accountants in Ipoh which actually started my accountancy career. Of course, there are others whom I must offer my special appreciation, particularly to Anthony Goonting and Anthony Skelchy, both of whom were partners in the firms of practicing chartered accountants where I had spent many years gaining significant public accounting experience.

Authors

Panirselvam Ayadurai

Gayatri Panirselvam

April 2024

Changes in Financial Accounting Practice

The text incorporates the legislation changes in recent years that relate to a number of key developments in contemporary financial accounting practice:

- Convergence with International Financial Reporting Standards. This convergence has put Malaysian Financial Reporting Standards (MFRSs) to be in line with international financial reporting practice. Reporting Entities in Malaysia must now comply with both the MFRSs issued by MASB and the IFRSs issued by IASB. This means accounting practice in Malaysia is identical in all material respects with the ones adopted by IFRSs as a forerunner except for some minor changes or modifications to reflect on conventional practice based on local requirements of law and customs.
- Financial reporting of private entities commonly referred as SMEs in Malaysia are given special emphasis with adoption of the recent MPERS reporting framework. Private entities now have the choice of adopting the MFRS framework which is mandatory for all listed companies or to make a legal transition to the new MPERS Framework effectively implemented by 1 January 2016. This framework simplifies the reporting practice for SMEs by simply avoiding the economics of cost in terms of disclosure requirements and presentation of financial statements. MFRS and MPERS are listed in the ensuing pages for reference purposes.
- Another important development is the enactment of the new *Companies Act 2016* which effectively replaced the original *Companies Act 1965*. Amongst the changes, we saw the implementation of the *'no par value share regime'* that created the amendments and for removing both the share premium and capital redemption reserve accounts. We saw these changes in the legal requirements for redeemable preference shares, share buybacks, and distribution of profits. The 9th Schedule enshrined previously in the old Companies Act 1965 is effectively revoked. The new regime in terms of accounting requirements, presentation and disclosure is in line with the approved accounting standards issued by MASB.

A Roadmap of Chapter by Chapter Review

Every chapter in the text comes with main objectives intended for students learning outcome. An important checklist of the main topics and specific areas in accounting that students need to study. The scope for study in every chapter is briefly explained.

Students are guided by review of all the chapters contained in the textbook. The end of each chapter has a summary of essential points that can probably help students to remember important accounting issues, concepts and principles underpinning financial accounting practice.

Chapter 1 starts the introductory phase by providing the enabling student to grasp all about financial accounting and reporting in a business environment. Business entities must be aware of their financial performance and financial position if they want to know where their business stand in terms of their overall financial standing in the face of competition in the market place so that they are able to make informed economic decisions unique to their circumstances. The chapter brings out many aspects relevant to legal and institutional frameworks that governs current financial accounting and reporting practice in Malaysia.,

Chapters 2 and 4 primarily deal with the core elements of financial accounting and reporting system and the importance of financial statements. The system of double entry bookkeeping with its due emphasis on the recording of business transactions is all explained and demonstrated. The use of T-accounts and analysis framework are well demonstrated.

Chapter 3 is singled out as something more relevant and useful in the present day accounting regime because we are in the digital era where accounting systems must be computerized. Accounting information systems use sophisticated software packages to make the world of financial accounting and reporting systems more easy and speedier.

Chapters 5, 6,7 and 8 are devoted to trading activities in business where the sales and purchasing systems take center stage to show how these functions in an organization facilitates the core activities in terms of accounting. Inventory systems linked to sales and purchases are explained with the reporting outcomes determining the profitability of business entities. Cash and internal controls are business related control issues that cannot be overlooked in a system of corporate governance are discussed in these chapters.

Chapters 9, 10, 11 and 12 are all crucial chapters that deal with both tangible and intangible financial assets that form the mainstay of an entity's core business because revenue generation depends on these asset tools. Assets generally undergo depreciation, amortization, and depletion over the useful lives of the asset and as such accounting for maintaining asset values including impairments and accompanied by the revaluations of assets. All these issues are regulated by accounting standards and company policies.

Chapters 13 deals with the accruals system of accounting for timing of business transactions as income and expense are time related. This process is well demonstrated by examples. The moral hazards of doing business in a trading environment is inevitable as debts often arise in business conditions and accounting for these contingencies has become part of the system. Chapter14 deals with this situation. Financing the purchase of business assets such as motor vehicles is common to Malaysian scenarios and chapter 15 pays attention to these hire-purchase transactions.

Chapter 16 is about provisions and contingencies. Provisions are liabilities of uncertain timing and amount whereas contingencies do not relate to assets or liabilities but their relevance is important to financial reporting as users are in better position to appraise the financial effects of transactions and events. The concept of liability is explored here.

Chapters 17–26 reviewed here will be published under Volume 2

Chapters 17, 18 and 19 are focused on capital structure, issue of shares and debentures as a means of raising capital funding. Shareholders' have rights and obligations whereas debentures as debt capital are governed by covenants so that legal obligations must be fulfilled. The chapter explores several issues relating to disclosures and presentation in the financial statements.

Chapter 20 is on incomplete records interestingly written through a case scenario where records of business transactions and events apparently lacking an audit trail are accounted for by making assumptions with whatever supporting evidence are available to the preparer of accounts.

Chapters 21, 22 and 23 are final steps of the accounting cycle process that deals exclusively with preparing a trial balance, completing the accounting cycle and preparing the financial statements. Resolving a suspense account, putting through necessary final adjustments and getting the final accounts from the system becomes the main objective. With the financial statements in place, Chapter 24 covers the analysis and interpretation of accounts by using financial ratios and other available techniques to examine and report on the financial health of an organization so that management's decision-making is effectively rendered enhanced.

Chapter 25 is devoted to preparing simple consolidated financial statements. We look at the application of accounting principles involved on consolidated accounts and attempt some basic calculations relating to goodwill on consolidation, non-controlling interest, eliminating inter-group transactions with adjustments for provisions on unrealized profit on unsold inventories. With illustrated examples, we show how the equity method of accounting is applied to associated companies and showing how these results are disclosed in the consolidated financial statements.

Chapter 26 is the final chapter which focuses on ethics and corporate governance that are essentially required .in today's corporate environment. Board of directors, management and other stakeholders as guardians are bound by a code of governance that must promote best ethical practice so that accountability and transparency are culturally imbibed in all facets of corporate life.

Financial Reporting Standards (FRSs) *[Common to both Volumes 1 and 2]*

Financial Reporting Standards were generally formulated as approved accounting standards. Approved accounting standards are taken concurrently to represent both the Malaysian Financial Reporting Standards and International Financial Reporting Standards. These standards are considered to be best accounting practice that formed the basis of generally accepted accounting principles (GAAPs) in Malaysia.

Members of the profession are those employed in commerce and industry and are required through their best efforts to ensure that approved accounting standards are observed in the preparation of financial statements while those in practice are also required to ensure that their clients' audited financial statements comply with these approved accounting standards.

MASB announced the new IFRS compliant MFRSs framework effectively from 1 January 2017. These approved accounting standards are listed as follows:

MFRSs	**IFRSs**	**Title**
MFRS 1	IFRS 1	First-time Adoption of Financial Reporting Standards
MFRS 2	IFRS 2	Share-based Payment
MFRS 3	IFRS 3	Business Combinations √
MFRS 4	IFRS	Insurance Contracts
MFRS 5	IFRS	Non-current Assets Held for Sale and Discontinued Operations
MFRS 6	IFRS 6	Exploration for and Evaluation of Mineral Resources
MFRS 7	IFRS 7	Financial Instruments – Disclosures
MFRS 8	IFRS 8	Operating Segments
MFRS 9	IFRS 9	Financial Instruments
MFRS 10	IFRS 10	Consolidated Financial Statements √
MFRS 11	IFRS 11	Joint Arrangements
MFRS 12	IFRS 12	Disclosure of Interests in Other Entities
MFRS 13	IFRS 13	Fair Value Measurements

MFRS 14	IFRS 14	Regulatory Deferral Accounts
MFRS 15	IFRS 15	Revenue from Contracts with Customers
MFRS 16	IFRS 16	Leases
MFRS 101	IAS 1	Presentation of Financial Statements
MFRS 102	IAS 2	Inventories √
MFRS 107	IAS 7	Statement of Cash flows
MFRS 108	IAS 8	Accounting Policies, Changes in Accounting Estimates and Errors √
MFRS 110	IAS 10	Events after the Reporting Period
MFRS 111	IAS 11	Construction Contracts
MFRS 112	IAS 12	Income Taxes
MFRS 116	IAS 16	Property, Plant and Equipment √
MFRS 117	IAS 17	Leases
MFRS 118	IAS 18	Revenue √
MFRS 119	IAS 19	Employee Benefits
MFRS 120	IAS 20	Accounting for Government Grants and Disclosure of Government Assistance
MFRS 121	IAS 21	The Effects of Changes in Foreign Exchange Rates
MFRS 123	IAS 23	Borrowing Costs
MFRS 124	IAS 24	Related Party Disclosures
MFRS 126	IAS 26	Accounting and Reporting for Retirement Benefit Plans

MFRS 127	IAS 27	Separate Financial Statements
MFRS 128	IAS 28	Investments in Associates and Joint Ventures √ (optional)
MFRS 129	IAS 29	Financial Reporting in Hyperinflationary Economies
MFRS 131	IAS 31	Interests in Joint Ventures
MFRS 132	IAS 32	Financial Instruments – Presentation
MFRS 133	IAS 33	Earnings per Share
MFRS 136	IAS 36	Impairment of Assets
MFRS 137	IAS 37	Provisions, Contingent Liabilities and Contingent Assets √
MFRS 138	IAS 38	Intangible Assets √
MFRS 139	IAS 39	Financial Instruments – Recognition and Measurement *
MFRS 140	IAS 40	Investment Property
MFRS 141	IAS 41	Agriculture

Of the Accounting Standards listed above, the most relevant ones that are appropriate and useful to your studies at this level are based on the requirements of the syllabus. These MFRSs/IFRSs are indicated by the ticks (√). The Chapters in the text focus on the application of relevant accounting standards to those topics you will need to cover in your studies. Students need not study these standards in detail but focus on the application of required principles. The Chapters automatically explain how these standards are applied and demonstrated through illustrated examples.

Private Entity Reporting Standards

Under current practice, private entities in Malaysia need not comply with the MFRSs. They can instead apply the MPERSs framework which took effect from 1 January 2016.

A private entity is a company incorporated under the Companies Act 2016 which

a. is exempted from preparing or lodging any financial statements under any prescribed law by the Securities Commission or Bank Negara Malaysia: and

b. is not a subsidiary or associate, or jointly controlled by an entity which is required to prepare or lodge any financial statements under any law enforced by the Securities Commission or Bank Negara.

Therefore, private entities are required to comply with either:

1. MPERS in their entirety; or
2. MFRSs in their entirety.

MPERSs is a set of accounting standards that comes in 35 sections covering all the relevant areas for financial reporting by private entities. The effect of adopting the MPERS framework is to bring private entity reporting in Malaysia to be exactly the same as the IFRSs.

The following 35 sections contain the MPERS:

Section	**Title**
1	Private Entities
2	Concepts and Pervasive Principles
3	Financial Statement Presentation
4	Statement of Financial Position
5	Statement of Comprehensive Income and Income Statement
6	Statement of Changes in Equity and Statement of Income and Retained Earnings
7	Statement of Cash Flows
8	Notes to the Financial Statements
9	Consolidated and Separate Financial statements
10	Accounting Policies, Estimates and Errors
11	Basic Financial Statements
12	Other Financial Instruments Issues
13	Inventories
14	Investments is Associates
15	Investments in Joint Ventures
16	Investment Property
17	Property, Plant and Equipment
18	Intangible Assets other than Goodwill
19	Business Combinations and Goodwill
20	Leases
21	Provisions and Contingencies

22	Liabilities and Equity
23	Revenue
24	Government Grants
25	Borrowing Costs
26	Share-based Payment
27	Impairment of Assets
28	Employee Benefits
29	Income Tax
30	Foreign Currency Translation
31	Hyperinflation
32	Events after the End of the Reporting Period
33	Related Party Disclosures
34	Specialized Activities
35	Transition to the MPERS

Note:

MPERS *as applied in smaller business entities overcomes the complexity in accounting treatment of business transactions that is normally involved in bigger and listed companies where accounting requirements and rules are more complicated given by their very nature unlike in smaller entities, the transactions may appear straightforward and easier to deal with. The application of MFRSs can be a costly and complicated affair for larger listed companies whereas small entity companies can obviously avoid the expensive route altogether.*

Chapter 1

Learning Objectives

Understand the role of accounting in communicating financial information

Understand the accounting function – is about recording, analyzing business transactions and summarizing financial data.

Identify the different types of business entities – sole-proprietorship, partnership, and limited liability company.

Know their legal features and differences between these operating business modes.

Identify the main advantages and disadvantages of operating as a limited liability company and other types of business entities.

Understand the primary purpose and scope of financial reporting as meeting financial informational needs of users

Identify the users of financial statements and differentiate between their informational needs.

Understand the role of regularity system underpinning financial reporting and in particular know the role of statutory bodies involved in the regularity framework such as FRF, MASB, IASB, Securities Commission, CCM, Bursa Malaysia, etc.

Understand financial reporting standard (FRSs) and their importance.

Understand the accounting profession and the financial reporting environment

Know and understand the conceptual frameworks for financial reporting requirements.

Know the difference between 'Rules' and 'Principles' based regimes in the context of financial accounting practice.

Know the corporate governance codes and ethics, their relevance to financial reporting.

Understand the role of corporate governance in institutional settings particularly the role and duties of board of directors as a prime guardian and the importance of audit committee and the auditor's role in the governance structure

Accounting in the Business Environment

Scope

This being the first chapter, it starts the introductory phase of your financial accounting studies. You need to understand the context and purpose of financial accounting and reporting. You need to know why business entities must be aware of their **financial performance** and **financial position**. Financial information comes from financial statements and the need to interpret them accordingly. All the remaining Chapters in this textbook is geared to taking you through that process, thus building your knowledge and skills in financial accounting. This introductory chapter tells you what the accounting function is all about. **Accounting** is crucial in our information age. We discuss the **purpose and importance of accounting** in business as many corporate financial decisions are made on the basis of financial information gathered from financial statements and reports. **Users of financial statements** are business people who generally need to know where they stand in terms of their overall financial standing so that they are able to make informed economic decisions. The different types of users and their **informational needs** are identified. One of the primary features of this Chapter is some discussion on the **regulatory framewor**k which underpins the financial reporting environment. The background to financial accounting and reporting in any jurisdiction, let alone in Malaysia, is the legal and institutional regulatory framework by which the entire accounting process is set to take shape for it to function in order to fulfill business and society's needs.

We discussed the main issues of the **regulatory framework** that underpins financial accounting and reporting system and why we need a proper framework. At best, it promotes **accountability and transparency in** financial reporting practices and **a properly governed regulatory framework** has the potential to facilitate this required process as investor confidence and public interest are enhanced. We touched on the **current legal regime in financial reporting system** in Malaysia and outlined the role played by MASB/IASB in the accounting standard setting process. **Convergence** of accounting standards on a global basis to create one set of uniform standards has increasingly assumed greater importance these days in contemporary accounting practice. We then explained that financial accounting practice is governed by **generally accepted accounting principles** (GAAPs) in the form of **financial reporting standards.**

We also touched on the **Conceptual Framework** for financial reporting where we explained two **fundamental characteristics** (*relevance and faithful representation*) when presenting financial information while stressing the importance of the **enhancing characteristics** such as *comparability, verifiability, timeliness and understandability*. The four **underlying assumptions** (see underpinning the accounting process were explained before discussing the **fundamental concepts** in financial reporting practice which are the cornerstone concepts that forms the basis of accounting as a social science. We identified and described the **importance of informational needs of different type of users** of financial statements and reports. The last section in the Chapter briefly looks in context at **ethics** and a proper **corporate governance structure** being crucial to the financial reporting system particularly for those who are charged with responsibilities in the governing process. Being the last chapter in the textbook, Chapter 26 looks at the ethical framework and corporate governance practice in an organization. The Malaysian Code on Corporate Governance incorporates the principles and rules that are commonly adopted by all business entities in Malaysia and the Code conforms to international practice.

1. Business Decisions on the Basis of Financial Information

Accounting is a social science based on GAAPs, FRSs, concepts and assumptions. Business owners, managers and directors of an organization, including shareholders and potential investors make strategic decisions based on financial information. Management of a company decide on growth and expansion of their business segments, marketing decisions on pricing, products innovation and market development. Investors decide on when to buy, hold or sell their investments. These decisions include assessing profitability, efficiency, liquidity and cash flows of the company, Directors assess their stewardship role and accountability of the company's management. Big and small business owners must look at the future viability of the business, the potential for growth including their profitability and taxes. In nearly all cases, all types of businesses also need to use financial information to help decide on its available resources, its sources of funding and capital. For all these reasons, **accounting serves as a useful tool** helping businesses, their shareholders and management to make these important decisions.

In summary, it is important to note that the three primary goals of any business include:

i. Making a profit (value or wealth creation process)
ii. Creating liquidity, generating adequate cash from selling goods or services, to pay or discharge bills on time.
iii. Strategic growth and market growth.

1.1 How does the accounting function contribute to the business?

Accounting consistently ranks as the top career opportunity in business. Accounting and finance is frequently rated among the most popular courses in Colleges and Universities. Why do business owners' in industry and commerce focus **on accounting rules and regulations**? Owners' as corporate leaders wanted to understand generally what was happening financially to their companies in terms of the financial performance, financial position and the cash generating capacity of the company.

Accounting is an information and measurement system that provides these financial insights. In other words, to understand the financial dynamics of an organization, you have to know the numbers game. To sum up, accounting is the **language of business**. The better our understanding of the language, the better we can understand what is happening with our finances, our business performances and our investments.

Accounting is based on **Financial Reporting Standards (FRSs),** and mainstream concepts of business and assumptions. rules and regulations, such as **Generally Accepted Accounting Principles** (GAAPs) which take the form of **financial reporting standards,** protect those who interact with the business. The **accounting business cycle** begins setting the scoreboard by keeping track of the entity's operating activities for a period of time, usually a year. At the end of that time period, the accounting process sets the scoreboard back to zero so that the business may account for a new line of activity or expanding similar or existing activities at a start of a new financial year.

Accounting is therefore **a function** that identifies, records and measures business activities or events of an organization, processing these data into useful information which then gets communicated to users of financial statements who subsequently make informed economic decisions.

Three interrelated activities of accounting:

- It **identifies** activities or economic events relevant to its business. The production and sale of petrol by Petronas, the provision of internet mobile services by Maxis and the payment of salaries to employees of an organization are typical examples of economic events.
- Say, Maxis identifies economic events, it **records** them as financial activities. **Record-keeping** is what we refer to as a bookkeeping exercise using the double entry system. Computerized accounting systems deployed by organizations these days are doing the processing, classifying and summarizing the economic events.
- Finally, Maxis **communicates** the collected information to interested user groups by means of accounting reports and analysis, called financial statements

A crucial element in communicating economic events **is the accountant's ability to analyze and interpret** the reported financial information. Analysis involves the use of ratios, percentages, graphs and charts to highlight significant financial trends and relationships. Interpretation of accounts involves explaining the implications, meaning and limitations of reported accounting information.

Difference between Bookkeeping and Accounting

The accounting process includes the bookkeeping function. Bookkeeping usually involves only the recording of business transactions and economic events. Bookkeeping is a part of accounting, just as arithmetic is a part of mathematics. It is important to note that accounting extends to the use of information produced by bookkeeping.

1.2 Why do we need f a Regulatory Framework in Accounting?

An **accounting framework** can be regarded as a systematically structured as a coherent system with objectives that reflects fundamental characteristics and concepts all of which can lead to high quality reporting standards. The regulatory framework in accounting can be seen as the most important element for ensuring that **financial information is faithfully represented and thus meeting and serving the relevant needs of shareholders and other stakeholders** in the business.

Accountability and transparency are therefore important issues in financial reporting and a properly governed regulatory framework has the potential to facilitate this required process. Enforcement and compliance with **financial accounting standards** and **GAAPs** are crucial because without the key roles of regulators such as the accounting standard setting bodies such as the MASB in Malaysia and IASB whose overall responsibility for producing financial reporting standards and a framework of principles, the accountability process is impeded. Furthermore, without accounting regulation through the application of **accounting standards** and GAAPs, businesses would be unable to evolve in a structured and systematic way to meet the changes in current and future economic conditions.

Current Financial Reporting Regime in Malaysia

A financial accounting and reporting regime was established by the Malaysian Government when the **Financial Reporting Act 1997** was passed through Parliament. This Act created two independent bodies:

1. The Financial Reporting Foundation (FRF)

FRF serves as a governing body for the operations and activities of MASB. However, FRF has no direct influence over MASB's role to undertake or omit any particular project such as developing and implementing new accounting standards or exercise its influence on the outcome of MASB's performance.

The **primary role** of FRF is:

i. to provide its views to MASB on any matters that it decides to implement in relation to issuing, reviewing, or developing approved accounting standards;

ii. to be responsible for all the financing arrangements relating to MASB's operations including approving its budget;

iii. to perform whatsoever function the Minister of Finance may prescribe by order and published in the government gazette.

2. The Malaysian Accounting Standards Board (MASB)

MASB's primary role as an independent accounting standard setting authority is **to develop and issue accounting and financial reporting standards in Malaysia.** Other functional roles of MASB as follows:

i. issue new accounting standards as approved accounting standards

ii. review, revise or adopt the existing accounting standards as approved accounting standards

iii. issue statements of principles (SOPs) for financial reporting

iv. conduct public consultation as may be necessary to determine the content of accounting concepts, principles and standards

v. develop a conceptual framework for the purpose of evaluating proposed accounting standards.

3. Regulation of the Accounting Profession in Malaysia

The Accountants Act, 1967 sets up the mechanism for the regulation of the accounting profession under the leadership of The Malaysian Institute of Accountants (MIA). MIA provides suitably trained qualified accountants to ensure highest standards in the quality of accounting and auditing services in the corporate sector. Apart from MIA, the other prime regulators equally play a significant role in the accountability process by ensuring that a sound system of financial reporting is ever present in order to safeguard public interest.

1.3 Why do we need a Conceptual Framework for Financial Reporting?

In a broader sense, a *Conceptual Framework* can be seen as an attempt to define the nature and purpose of accounting. It lays the groundwork for resolving the emerging big issues in financial reporting. The conceptual framework basically prescribes the nature, function, and the limits or boundaries within which financial accounting and reporting operate. In other words, it must consider the theoretical and conceptual issues surrounding financial reporting. It takes a coherent and consistent approach that will underpin the development of accounting standards.

As the purpose of financial reporting is to provide useful information as a basis for economic decision making, a conceptual framework will form both a theoretical and practical basis for determining how transactions should be measured and reported – that is, how they are presented and communicated to users of financial statements.

It could be argued that the lack of a conceptual framework led to the proliferation of ***'rules-based'*** accounting systems whose main objective is that the treatment of all financial transactions should be dealt with the detailed specific rules or requirements. Such a system is very prescriptive and inflexible, but has the attraction of financial statements being more comparable and consistent. However, by contrast the availability of a conceptual framework could lead to a ***'principles-based'*** system whereby accounting standards are developed from an agreed conceptual basis with specific objectives. In other words, the objective of the *Conceptual Framework* is to create a sound platform for future financial reporting accounting standards based on **'principles'** that are consistently adopted in practice and internationally converged. The new framework builds on the existing **IASB framework**

The International Accounting Standards Board's (IASB) Conceptual Framework for Financial Reporting, mainly deals with

a. The objective of financial reporting;
   - Assist in the development of future FRS and the review of existing standards by setting out the underlying concepts.
   - Promote harmonization of accounting regulation and standards by reducing the number of permitted alternative accounting treatments.

- Assist the preparers of financial statements in the application of FRS which would include dealing with accounting transaction for which there is not (yet) an accounting standard in force.

b. The qualitative characteristics of useful information;

c. The definition, recognition, and measurement of the elements from which financial statements are constructed; and

d. Concepts of capital and capital maintenance.

However, it must be noted that the *Conceptual Framework* does not constitute a Financial Reporting Standard (FRS) and nor does it define standards for any specific measurement and disclosure issues. The Framework does not override any specific financial reporting standard whether IFRS or MASB. The Framework serves auditors, and other prime users of financial statements, and more generally help interested parties to understand the IASB's approach to the formulation of accounting standards. The Conceptual Framework was jointly published by the IASB and FASB (US's Financial Accounting Standard Setting Board).

1.4 Financial Reporting Standards (FRSs)

All the financial reporting standards adopted by MASB are effectively based on IASB's IFRS framework. As such there are **no fundamental differences in principle** when applying these accounting standards by business entities in Malaysia or elsewhere in other jurisdictions except for some minor modifications required to suit local customs and business practice wherever they are needed. Otherwise they are the same in all material respects as the **emphasis now is increasingly on international convergence**. The principal ideology is to have only one set of rules (or universal conventions) to serve a common purpose, thus eliminating all forms of confusion and clout in standard accounting practice.

1.5 Generally Accepted Accounting Principles (GAAPs)

Financial accounting practice is governed by concepts and rules known as **Generally Accepted Accounting Principles (GAAPs).** To use and interpret financial statements effectively, we need to understand these accounting principles as they can change over time in response to the needs of users. GAAPs aim to make information in financial statements *relevant, reliable* and *comparable.*

It is important to note that in countries like the UK, GAAPs is not enforced by statutory or regulatory authority unlike in the USA it is enforced predominantly by legislation. There are different views of GAAPs in different countries. However, most agree that there is a need for one set of international accounting standards to be applied universally, thus removing or eliminating any distortion emerging from differences between reporting systems internationally.

The UK view is based on UK GAAP (Ernst & Young version 5TH Edition).

"Our view is that GAAPs is a dynamic concept which requires constant review, adaptation and reaction to changing circumstances. GAAPs changes in response to changing business and economic needs and developments. As circumstances alter, accounting practices are modified or developed accordingly. We believe that GAAPs goes far beyond mere rules and principles, and encompasses contemporary permissible accounting practice."

An important consideration that needs to be taken is that '**Generally Accepted Accounting Principles'** are defined as those principles which have substantial authoritative support'. Therefore, accounts prepared in accordance with accounting principles for which there is not substantial authoritative support are presumed to be misleading or inaccurate. The effect here is that 'new' or 'different' accounting principles are not acceptable unless they have been adopted by the mainstream accounting profession, usually the standard-setting bodies and /or professional accountancy bodies. This could be much more rigid than the earlier UK views expressed.

Financial Reporting Standards (FRSs) in actual fact represents GAAPs. The accounting principles and rules are embodied in FRSs

1.6 Underlying assumptions

The accounting process is based on four main underlying assumptions.

- **Monetary Unit Assumption**: requires that companies include in their accounting records only transaction data that can be expressed in terms of money. This assumption enables accounting to measure (quantify) economic events objectively, thus giving credence to applying the cost principle.
- **Economic (Business) Entity Assumption:** An economic entity can be any organization that has a perpetual continuity. It can be a company (such as Petronas) or a government statutory body (Treasury or Khazanah). The economic entity assumption requires that the activities of the business entity be kept separate and distinct from the activities of its owner and all other entities.
- **Going Concern Assumption:** The entity is normally viewed on a going concern basis, that is, as continuing in operational existence in the foreseeable future. It is assumed that the entity has neither the intention nor the necessity of liquidation or of curtailing materially the scale of operations. If it did, then the financial statements would be prepared on a different basis usually at a liquidated basis. On a practical basis, non-going concern basis is avoided as steps would be taken by the board of directors and shareholders injecting more funds into the business with a turnaround strategy to revive the business into more profitable lines.
- **Time Period Assumption:** The operating life-cycle of a company is usually taken to be one calendar year. Useful accounting reports are conventionally prepared on this time period basis. Accounting reports can be prepared for shorter periods if necessary, for useful management purposes.

1.7 Fundamental Accounting Concepts

The accounting process deals with a number of accounting concepts fundamental to the preparation and presentation of financial statements. The relevant application of these concepts requires that the preparers of accounts to understand its intended uses and purposes for which financial statements are required. A number of these fundamental accounting concepts are discussed here as follows: -

Historical Cost Convention or Fair Value Accounting

In accounting, the historical cost basis is conventionally used in reporting economic events. Asset values are recorded at their historical cost. The cost of the asset at the time of purchase and over the time period the asset was held in business is reported at the initial acquisition price. For e.g. if a company bought a piece of land for RM 1.2 million, it is initially reported on the balance sheet at RM 1.2 million. What happens if the land value appreciates to RM 2 million in 2 years' time? Under the historical cost convention, the value of the land continues to be reported at RM 1.2 million. This is where the **anomaly** of financial reporting gets distorted as asset values do not reflect current values. Critics contend the **cost principle** is irrelevant. They argue that **market or fair value accounting** (determined by the market trends at a particular time) is more useful to financial decision makers. However, proponents of the historical cost convention counter that cost is the best measure as it can be easily verified, whereas market value is often subjective and not easily ascertainable.

Given the controversial issue, the accounting profession has modified the accounting rules by going back in recent years and allowing that certain non-current tangible fixed assets to be recorded at their fair values. In choosing between cost and market value, the **reliability of the cost figures** versus the **relevance of market value** should be weighed. It must be noted that relevance and reliability are two desirable qualitative characteristics that makes accounting information useful for decision making.

Accrual Concept

We prepare financial statements on an accrual basis which means that transactions and other economic events are recognized when they are incurred or earned in the accounting period and not when cash is paid or received. We could say accrual accounting is a more faithful representation of economic reality than cash basis accounting. Virtually all businesses apply the accrual basis of accounting as required by financial reporting standards. It must be noted that entities that use cash basis accounting do not follow generally accepted accounting principles. Their financial statements omit important information and thus are less relevant to users of financial statements.

For example, an entity has the following transactions for the year ended 30 June 2021:

1. Rent for the premises amounting to RM 5,000 was paid on 30 June 2021 for the month of April 2021 and May 2021. The June 2021 rent was paid on 31 July 2021.

2. RM 9,000 from interest income for the month of June 2021 and July 2021 were not received by the entity

Show how the amount of rent expense account and the income on interest will be reported in the Statement of Profit or Loss for the year ended 30 June 2021.

Suggested answer

Accrual basis of accounting is adopted.

1. Rent expenses recognized for the period is RM7, 500. June 2021 rent of RM2,500 was treated as an accrual adjustment as this was not paid until 31 July 2021.
2. Interest income to be recognized for the period is RM 4,500 although it was not received until after the financial year end. Income is recognized for the period not when it is received.

Prudence or Conservatism

Under the prudent concept of accounting, no entity should overestimate the amount of revenues recognized or underestimate the amount of expenses. The entity should be also prudent in recording asset values on a conservative basis while not underestimating liabilities. Another way of looking at prudence is to only record a revenue transaction or an asset when cash can be realized with certainty and record an expense transaction or liability when it is probable. Prudence would normally be exercised in the following instances:

- When setting up an allowance for irrecoverable (doubtful) debts, thus debtors' amounts are not overstated when recovery is uncertain.
- Recognizing a loss immediately when it is anticipated.
- Writing off for obsolete or slow moving inventories.

Matching Concept

Under this concept, revenues are matched with associated cost or expenses and both of which should be dealt with in the same accounting period. This process is commonly referred to as the *"matching of costs with revenues"*. For an example, if an entity earns revenue through a sale of a product which it manufactures, all the associated manufacturing costs and directly attributable expenses in earning that revenue must be matched before profit is recognized.

Consistency Concept

Consistency in accounting policy and accounting treatment of similar class of transactions or assets should be adopted by an entity in preparing and reporting its financial statements. Given the numerous methods and bases for treating similar transactions or assets, financial statements tend to result in a lack of comparability in reported information that could be misleading to users of accounts. It is important that accounting policies adopted by entities will need to be **consistently applied** to financial statements from year to year unless business conditions and circumstances warrant a significant change in an accounting policy and treatment. It is also equally important that companies operating in the same industry or business segment need to achieve comparability if the same accounting policies are adopted and applied consistently.

Materiality Concept

Financial accounting reports should disclose all items that are material enough to impact evaluations or decisions. Under the materiality concept, **financial information is material if it would change the opinion or view of the users of financial statements.** An entity normally presents separately each material class of similar items in the financial statements. An item is material when its omission or misstatement could, individually or collectively, influence the economic decision that users make on the basis of the information in the financial statements. In other words, an item is material when it has the potential to sway or change a user's decision or opinion. The concept of materiality is **relative to size and importance**. Some financial information might be material to one company but might be immaterial to another. For example, a large and material expense to a small company might be immaterial to a large company in terms of their size and magnitude relative to their revenue earning capacity.

For example, say a large company's building was destroyed by fire and after a lengthy insurance process claim, it resulted in a reported loss of RM 10,000. The company's net revenue for the period was RM 12,500,000. The loss represents 0.08% of the net income. The materiality concept states such a loss is immaterial because the average financial statement user would not be concerned with something that is less than 1% of net income. In contrast, if the company is smaller with RM 50,000 of net income, then the loss is 20% of net income. This is a substantial loss for the company and creditors would regard the RM10, 000 as a material loss by virtue of its size. By convention, a rule of thumb developed by accountants suggests that anything that exceeds 5% in size will be considered material. However, this is only a relative measure or guide at best to be judged in a particular case or circumstance.

1.8 Main Types of Business Ownership

Organizing a business undertaking generally takes one of the following forms:

i. **Proprietorship:** Only a small amount of money (capital) is necessary to start in business as a proprietorship. The owner receives any profits, suffers any losses, and is personally liable for all the debts of the business. There is no legal distinction between the business as an economic unit and the owner, but the accounting records of the business activities are kept separate from the personal records and activities of the owner.

ii. **Partnership:** A business formed by two or more persons with a view to making profits. A partnership agreement (orally or written) sets forth such terms and conditions of initial capital requirements, profit or loss sharing ratio, duties of partners and dissolution, etc. Each partner has unlimited persona liability for the partnership debts. Like a proprietorship, for accounting purposes transactions must be kept separate from the personal activities of the partners. Partnerships work well for service-oriented businesses including professional practices such as accountants, lawyers and doctors.

iii. **Companies:** Companies are incorporated as a separate legal entity and ownership is determined by shares or equity. Owners enjoy limited liability as they are not personally liable for the debts of the company. One of the main features of equity ownership is that shareholders can sell or transfer their shares to other investors at any time. Companies enjoy perpetual life.

Accounting is still an important function used in every type of business despite the different modes of running the business. While accounting requirements are the same for each type of business, the formats used in financial reporting are differently tailored to the needs of these types of business modes

1.9 Importance of Financial Reporting to Stakeholders' Needs

The prime objective of financial reporting is to provide financial information about the reporting entity that is useful to existing shareholders' and potential investors, lenders, other creditors such as suppliers, customers, employees, the government and other parties who have direct or indirect vested interests in the business. Such information may relate to the entity's resources, claims of those resources by outside parties, the operating results or financial performance including the state of its financial position, its ability to meet its liabilities as and when they fall due. The dynamics of the cash flows - how company's cash is generated from business and deployed in operations, for growth and expansion. Furthermore, users evaluate financial statements to make informed decisions as to whether or not to invest or make an additional investment by committing funds to the business or continuing supporting lines of credit or financing for the business or assessing management's performance.

The shareholders normally need to know the company's financial position and performance so that they continue with their investments to derive a steady stream of dividend income and achieve wealth maximization in terms of their shareholdings in the company. All other types of stakeholders have specific financial information needs that satisfy their **special vested interests** in the business.

1.10 Users of Financial Statements

The annual report consisting of the audited financial statements of the entity will be the main focus of many vested parties of the company. Each of these users have their specific requirements about the financial information they need in order to assess the company's overall economic position as part of the investor group relations, corporate social responsibility, governance, environmental sustainability, and state of corporate citizenship. Some of the main users and their specific information requirements are identified below:

- *Shareholders or Investors*

  Investors are concerned about getting adequate returns on their investments for the risk they are taking when they invest in the company as shareholders. Investors tend to increase, hold, or decrease by buying or selling their shares in the stock exchange. A shareholder generally expects a dividend payment and a steady appreciation of value in his/her stockholding in the company.

- *Employees*

  Employees are interested in financial information because of their job security, salary increments, compensation bonus, and their welfare, health and safety issues. A company that has declining profits or experiences losses will signal signs of job insecurity for employees and in some worse-off scenarios; retrenchment or redundancies may eventually result.

- *Suppliers of trade credit*

  Suppliers provide credit lines to their customers on the basis of regular and prompt settlements. They do this with the expectation that their invoices are settled as and when they fall due.

- *Customers*

  Customers will continue buying the company's products or services as long as the company is not experiencing financial difficulties or sustaining losses. Otherwise customers will not be satisfied as investment into research and development of the product or service quality may be lacking. In some cases, warranties will be not be supported.

- *Lenders or Financiers*

  Bankers or other financial institutions will need to determine the credit-worthiness of the customers particularly if they wish to extend credit facilities such as loans and overdrafts on the basis of the customers' ability to service the interest payments and eventually settling the loan principal. They need to be aware of the strength of the financial position of the customer and the assets that can be secured against any credit lines being granted.

- *Government and its Agencies*

  Government and its agencies are interested in the financial viability of the business entity and the various aspects of its business. For example, the Inland Revenue Board deals with tax collection and therefore it needs to pick up information from the company's audited financial statements in order to assess the amount of tax liability based on the reported profits. Certain government agencies will be also looking into the allocation of capital grants or subsidies.

- *The Public*

  Given the increasing expectations of the public on issues of corporate social responsibility, and environmental sustainability, information on the company's board and executive compensation, corporate welfare and issues such as health and safety including the environment impact of its business operations are all important to the governance of the company. Public perception of corporate citizenship of an entity can be gleaned from its annual report.

Stakeholders' Interest

The *Conceptual Framework specifically states that the general purpose financial reports (annual reports and accounts) do not satisfy all the potential information needs of financial statement users.* It must be noted that the focus is on the primary users of financial statements which includes existing shareholders and potential investors, lenders and creditors. Much of the information set that is reported and disclosed in the financial statements are geared towards the primary users. Non-primary users, such as the government regulators such the Inland Revenue Board, might find financial statements useful but it must be noted that the financial statements are not intended or directed towards them. **Financial statements are seen as general purpose documents governed by FRSs and GAAPs.**

1.11 Duties and Responsibilities of Those Charged with Governance

Corporate Governance of high standard quality helps to underpin long-term company performance. It is critical to the financial reporting environment particularly of those who are charged with responsibility for governance both internally within the company and externally.

"The Malaysian Code on Corporate Governance 2012 (MCCC) focuses on strengthening board structure and composition recognizing the role of directors as active and responsible fiduciaries. They have a duty to be stewards and guardians of the company, not just in setting strategic direction and overseeing the conduct of business, but also in ensuring that the company conducts itself in compliance with the laws and ethical values, and maintains an effective governance structure to ensure the appropriate management of risks and the level of internal control systems".

[*Source: Securities Commission of Malaysia*]

Role of Key Guardians

Board of Directors and Senior Executive Management

Board of directors' and management must be mindful of their duty to direct their efforts and resources towards the best interests of the company and its shareholders while ensuring that the interests of other stakeholders are not compromised. **Disclosure and transparency** are essential for informed decision-making. The timely availability of quality and accurate information that is faithfully representing, including the reporting of **financial performance and position are** key facets of investor protection and market confidence. Being the prime guardian, the board of directors of a company has a collective role and responsibility not only for the proper governance of a company but also delivering a management style and structure that facilitates effective control systems and establishing a framework to manage risks through the internal audit function and reporting to the audit committee within the organization.

Principle 5 of the Malaysian Code on Corporate Governance 2012 *deals with upholding integrity in financial reporting.*

Two recommendations are listed under this principle which requires the audit committee to enforce:

a. Ensure financial statements comply with applicable financial reporting standards
b. Institute policies and procedures to assess the suitability and independence of external auditors

These recommendations are emphasized more on the significant role of auditors as one of the prime guardians of corporate governance.

Other Key Guardians in the Governance Process

Their role is to effectively regulate the capital markets of Malaysia so that investor confidence and public interests are safeguarded.

1. **The External Auditors**

   The statutory auditor's role enhances the credibility of the audited financial statements.

2. **The Companies Commission of Malaysia**:

   The Commission's role is to ensure that the company law provisions and other enactments comply in all material aspects.

3. **The Securities Commission of Malaysia**

   A government agency that regulates the orderly function of the capital markets in Malaysia to ensure compliance with the approved financial reporting standards and other prescribed law enforcements on all matters relating to the securities industry.

4. **Bursa Malaysia (Kuala Lumpur Stock Exchange)**

   KLSE's Listing requirements are enforced so that the capital market system in Malaysia operates to high standards with a delivery system to ensure investor relations and public interests are upheld in the best interests at all times.

5. **Other Guardians, such as Bank Negara and Government Agencies**

   These institutions also significantly influence the governance of companies through their related enforcements.

In nearly all these cases, the financial reporting environment is the critical component in the accountability and transparency process, thereby fostering a strong culture of corporate governance in Malaysia.

Chapter Summary

The regulatory and conceptual framework of accounting

We saw the business entity's environment is governed by both the regulatory and conceptual frameworks, all of which is crucial to financial accounting and reporting. We explained the current reporting regime in Malaysia, the legal *and* accounting process by which financial reporting rules and regulation operate. Briefly we discussed the need for a **regulatory framework** of accounting by identifying the roles played by **Financial Reporting Act** which created two independent bodies – **Financial Reporting Foundation (FRF) and Malaysian Accounting Standards Board (MASB)**, the former being a governing body of the later and their respective roles. The accounting profession is regulated by **the Accountants' Act**. The **conceptual framework** speaks of two accounting regimes, the *"rules based"* and *"principle based"* determining the basis by which financial reporting is done. The conceptual framework is seen as seen as an attempt to define the nature and purpose of accounting. It lays the groundwork for resolving the emerging big issues in financial reporting. **Financial Reporting Standards (FRSs**) governs the rules of accounting treatment of business transactions and events in the financial reporting process.

Purpose and importance of accounting

Accounting is crucial in our information age. **Accounting serves an important function** in an organization by providing an **information and measurement system** that aims to identify, record, and communicate relevant, reliable, and comparable information about the principal activities undertaken by the business entity. Accounting fulfils social, economic and community responsibilities by being accountable and ensuring transparency. We spoke on **accounting concepts** such as historical cost or fair value, accruals, prudence, matching and consistency and materiality all of which are fundamental to the preparation and presentation of financial statements with some examples. We also discussed the **different forms of business ownership** and their characteristics.

Goal of financial accounting and reporting

The goal of financial accounting and reporting is **to provide useful information** for decision making. For information to be useful, it must be trusted to have the necessary qualitative characteristics as stated in the **Conceptual Framework**. It also demands ethical behavior in accounting and reporting by ensuring that information in financial statements are **relevant, reliable, and faithfully represented**. Financial accounting practice is underpinned by concepts and rules known as **generally accepted accounting principles** (GAAPs). To use and interpret financial statements, we need to understand and rely on these principles, which can change over time to meet demands of users of financial statements. Financial statements are required to reflect four **assumptions**: going concern, monetary unit, time period, and business entity. The four **enhancing qualitative characteristics** of the Conceptual Framework are comparability, verifiability, timeliness, and understandability.

Users of financial statements and their needs

Users of financial statements are both external and are internal. These users include shareholders and other stakeholders for assessing the return and risk of investments(shares**); Directors have a stewardship role in the management of the company**, Employees interested in their welfare, security and employment opportunities: Managers in controlling, monitoring and planning; Lenders interested in risk, security and return of loans.

Three major activities of a business entity (organization)

Business entities normally carry out three major activities: **operating, investing and financing**. Operating activities are those that are intended for carrying out the entity's operational business plans. Investing as an activity relates to buying and selling of assets (or resources) used in acquiring and selling of products and services. Financing relates to the entity's activity such as financing resources in acquiring land, buildings and plant and machinery to generate revenue.

Corporate governance and ethics

We identified those who **are charged with corporate governance as key guardians**, this being the board of directors and top management and as well as other guardians such as external auditors, CCM, Security Commission, Bursa Malaysia, Bank Negara, etc. We stated **how important is the Malaysian Code on Corporate Governance** in upholding integrity in the financial reporting environment, the special role of directors and the significant role to be played by auditors - all these forms a critical component in **the accountability and transparency process** thus ensuring a strong corporate governance culture.

Key Terms

Accounting

Accountability and transparency

Accountants Act 1967

Audit

Accruals concept

Business ownership

Conceptual framework of accounting

Corporate governance

Consistency concept

GAAPs

Board of directors

Ethics

Fair value accounting

Financial statements

Financial reporting standards (FRSs)

Fundamental accounting concepts

Fundamental characteristics

Enhancing characteristics

Informational needs

Prudence concept

Underlying assumptions in accounting

Sole proprietorship

Partnership

Limited liability company

Shareholders

Stakeholders' needs or interest

Informational needs of users

Users of financial statements

Malaysian Code on Corporate Governance

Guardians of corporate governance

Historical cost convention

IASB

FASB

Materiality concept

Users of financial statements

Financial performance

Financial position

MASB

Regulatory framework of accounting

Principle-based

Rules-based

Review Questions

Q1. Explain the purpose of financial accounting and reporting.

Q2. What are the three main interrelated activities of accounting?

Q3. State the primary goals of a reporting entity or any organization.

Q4. a. Explain the role of board of directors and

b. What strategic financial decisions do they usually make in their role?

Q5. The accounting process includes the bookkeeping function.

a. Explain this function

b. How would you distinguish between bookkeeping function and the accounting role?

Q6. Define and explain with reasons why we need a regulatory framework of accounting.

Q7. Identify and describe the functional roles of the current financial reporting regime in Malaysia.

Q8. How is the accounting profession regulated in Malaysia?

Q9. Explain what you understand by the term 'GAAPS'? State its importance to accounting.

Q10. Explain what you understand by the term 'FRSs'. State its prime purpose.

Q11. Explain in the context of financial reporting, the following terms:

i. Financial performance; and

ii. Financial position

Q12. The 'Conceptual Framework' (CF) is an important development in financial reporting.

a. Explain what you understand by the term *'Conceptual Framework'* and describe its primary purpose in the context of financial reporting. State some of its limitations.

b. State and explain the two types of financial reporting systems the 'CR' deals with.

Q13. Describe and identify the main issues dealt by the 'Conceptual Framework' in promoting financial reporting.

Q14. Identify and explain the four underlying assumptions governing the accounting process.

Q15. The accounting process deals with a number of accounting concepts fundamental to the preparation and presentation of financial statements. The relevant application of these concepts requires that the preparers of accounts to understand its intended uses and purposes for which financial statements are required.

Required

List and explain these fundamental accounting concepts and why they are important in the preparation and presentation of financial statements?

Q16. Discuss briefly the main types of business ownership that any business entity can operate?

Describe the distinguishing features of these ownership modes.

Q17. Explain the importance of financial reporting to users' and stakeholders' needs.

Q18. Identify the main types of users of financial statements. Briefly state their informational needs.

Q19. *Financial statements are seen as general purpose documents governed by FRSs and GAAPs. The 'Conceptual Framework' specifically states that the general purpose financial reports (annual reports and accounts) do not satisfy all the potential informational needs of financial statement users.*

Explain why is this so?

Q20 a. Briefly explain the importance of *corporate governance and ethics* in financial reporting systems.

b. Identify who are these prime guardians in the governing process and discuss their significant roles. In your discussion, you are required to exclude the Board of Directors.

Q21. Discuss briefly the stewardship role of the Board of Directors' and why they seen as a prime guardian of corporate governance.?

Multiple Choice Questions

1. All the following statements are true except one. Identify which statement is not true (false)?
   a. The professional body that creates IFRS is the International Accounting Standards Board (IASB)
   b. Bookkeeping is only a part of financial accounting.
   c. Accountants are held responsible for maintaining high standards of professional integrity and ethical conduct.
   d. Users of financial statements are limited only to shareholders of the company.
2. The definition of an asset is best described as:
   a. It has a tangible physical form that is valued at cost in the accounting records.
   b. An economic resource that is expected to benefit from future operations
   c. It is owned by any business entity that already has ready market
   d. It represents cash or the right to receive cash in the future.
3. Identify which of the following items relate to fundamental qualitative characteristics of financial information?
   a. Materiality and substance over form
   b. Cost and matching principle
   c. Relevance and faithful representation
   d. Shareholders' equity + liabilities
4. The accounting equation represents correctly which of the following expressions?
   a. Shareholders' Equity – Assets = Liabilities
   b. Assets = Liabilities – Shareholders' Equity
   c. Assets – Liabilities = Shareholders Equity
   d. Assets + Liabilities = Shareholders' Equity
5. Which financial statements relates to a period of time?
   a. Statement of comprehensive income (Income statement)
   b. Statement of financial position (Balance sheet)
   c. Statement of Cash Flows
   d. Both a and c above
6. Which items are reported in the statement of financial position?
   a. Accounts receivable
   b. Inventory (Stock)
   c. Expenses
   d. Share capital and reserves
   e. All of the above except 'c'
7. The primary objective of financial reporting is to provide information
   a. About the position, performance and the cash flows of the company.
   b. Reporting income tax expense for the period

   c. The liquidity rand profitability of the company
   d. Value of the company's share
   e. b, c, and d of the above.

8. Assets are usually reported at
   a. Current market value
   b. Modified value
   c. Historical cost
   d. None of the above

9. Debts collected from trade customers are shown in the
   a. Statement of profit or loss under sales
   b. Statement of financial position under current assets
   c. Under cash balance
   d. Under retained earnings in the statement of changes in equity

10. All of the following are current liabilities except
    a. Accounts payable
    b. Other creditors and accruals
    c. Sales revenue
    d. Tax payable

11. The financial statement that reports revenues, operating expenses and income tax expense is called
    a. Statement of financial position
    b. Statement of comprehensive income
    c. Statement of cash flows
    d. Statement of changes in equity

12. Which of the following is not an enhancing qualitative characteristic?
    a. Materiality
    b. Verifiability
    c. Comparability
    d. Understandability

13. Cash paid to acquire tangible fixed assets appears on the statement of cash flows under
    a. Operating activities
    b. Non-current assets
    c. Investing activities
    d. Financing activities

I don't think you should teach the accounting standards. I think you should teach the conceptual framework, then discuss why certain standards have followed the framework.

—Sir David Tweedie, former IASB Chairman

Chapter 2

Learning Objectives

After you have studied this chapter, you should be able to:

Identify and explain the function of the main sources of data in an accounting system

Outline the role of source documents in a trading environment for sales and purchasing functions.

Explain the steps in processing business transactions and events

Understand and apply the concept of double-entry accounting principles and duality concept

Understand and apply the accounting equation

Understand how the accounting system provides useful financial information by complying with organizational policies and deadlines

Identify main types of ledger accounts and books of prime entry, use of journals, and understand their nature and purpose or function.

Understand and illustrate the use of journal entries and their postings to ledger accounts.

Be able to write accurately the narratives to the journal entries

Understand the use of cash book and its purpose

Understand and how to balance and close a ledger account.

Know the use of a T-account to write-up ledger entries.

Analysing and Recording Transactions

1 Scope

The modern day era virtually uses developments in information technology in every facet of economic activity. Accounting systems today in a business environment are computerized using software accounting packages or one that is tailored to suit a particular business application or requirement. With relative ease, the double-entry system is facilitated with the hitting of the buttons in the keyboard. Accounting as a social science has to be learned by reasoning and logic. There are no short cuts even in the computerized accounting environment because accounting decisions on business transactions must be translated using the double-entry bookkeeping system. The accounting entries that get recorded in the **books of prime entry** in the computerized accounting system are governed by **generally accepted accounting principles** (GAAPs). Therefore, theory and practice goes together in accounting discipline.

In this chapter, we focus on the **accounting process** by applying the iterative steps in the **accounting cycle** and describe the transactions and source documents involved. We explain the analysis and recording of transactions and events. We also explain the **accounting equation** and show how the **double entry system** is linked to it. You get to understand how the double-entry system works but you must really know that it is merely a **recordkeeping** exercise based on GAAPs. You are not creating something new here other than conventionally following a down-trodden system which has been practiced successfully for a very long time by others before you. **Accountants** and **Bookkeepers** have been doing this scorecard exercise for a very long time and the computer accounting packages came into the scene by simplifying the workload, doing away with the tedious nature of the recording of accounting entries. The double-entry system has stood the test of time and it can accommodate virtually all kinds of business transactions in unlimited amounts and magnitude. The books of prime entry such as the **journals, cash book** and **general ledger** form the basis of the recording function. The use of **T-account**, **trial balance**, **debits** and **credits** are the key tools used in the accounting process. Debits on the right-hand side and credit**s** on the left-hand side are the two pillars of the accounting system that underpin the double-entry system.

Chapter 3 is also about analysing and recording but we deal with **transaction data processing** within a computer-based system environment. The treatment on *data storage, data input, data processing*, and *data output* is covered in reasonable detail there. However, the scope of this text is primarily focused on financial accounting not systems analysis. Therefore, what is needed essentially for a student's understanding is the *Accounting Information System* (AIS) that deals with these data processing concepts which ultimately can result in producing the financial statements and reports for decision making.

2. The Basic Accounting Equation

The three basic elements of a business are:

- What it owns as assets
- What it owes as liabilities; and
- Equity which is what shareholders as investors provide capital to the business.

The basic accounting equation shows the relationship among assets, liabilities, and equity.

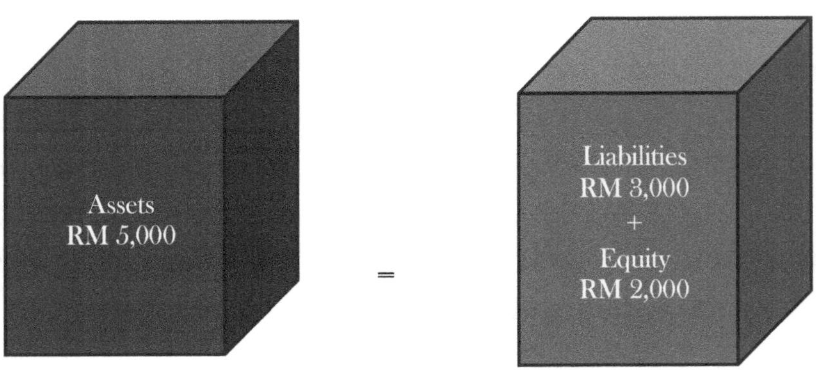

Illustration: The Basic Accounting Equation (1)

Assets = Liabilities + Shareholders' Equity

The two sides of the equation must be equal. In this example the entity's assets of RM 5,000 are financed by liabilities of RM 3,000 and equity of RM 2,000

Assets are resources a business entity owns by control. **Liabilities and shareholders' equity are** the rights and claims against these resources. Claims of those outside parties to whom the entity owes money (creditors) are called liabilities. Claims of owners are called shareholders' equity. Liabilities appear before shareholders' equity in the basic accounting equation because they are paid or discharged first if the business goes in liquidation. The term shareholders' equity refers to ownership in the business entity. The accounting equation applies all to business entities regardless of size, nature of business or form of business organization. It applies to a small proprietorship as well as to a giant company.

A second accounting equation shows how profits earned by an entity during the financial year. Profit is arrived at Income (including gains) less Expenses (including losses). The illustration shows that a profit of RM1, 375 was made from revenue of RM 7,600 and expenses of RM 6,225. When revenue exceeds expenses, the result is called net income, or net profit. When expenses exceed income, the result is a net loss.

Revenue and Gains - Expenses and Losses = Net Profit (or Loss)
RM 7,600 RM 6,225 RM 1.375

Illustration: Accounting Equation (2)

It must be noted that incomes increases equity, whereas expenses decreases equity. This is usually reflected as an increase to retained earnings for a net income or a decrease to retained earnings for a net loss. A profitable business usually pays dividends to shareholders as a return on their capital investment normally in the form of cash. **Dividends** are treated as a deduction of retained earnings in the Statement of Changes in Equity. Dividends are an appropriation of realized profits, distributed to shareholders as owners of the business. Therefore, dividend is not an expense and will never affect net income.

Components of Retained Earnings

The illustration below shows the movement in retained earnings over an accounting period.

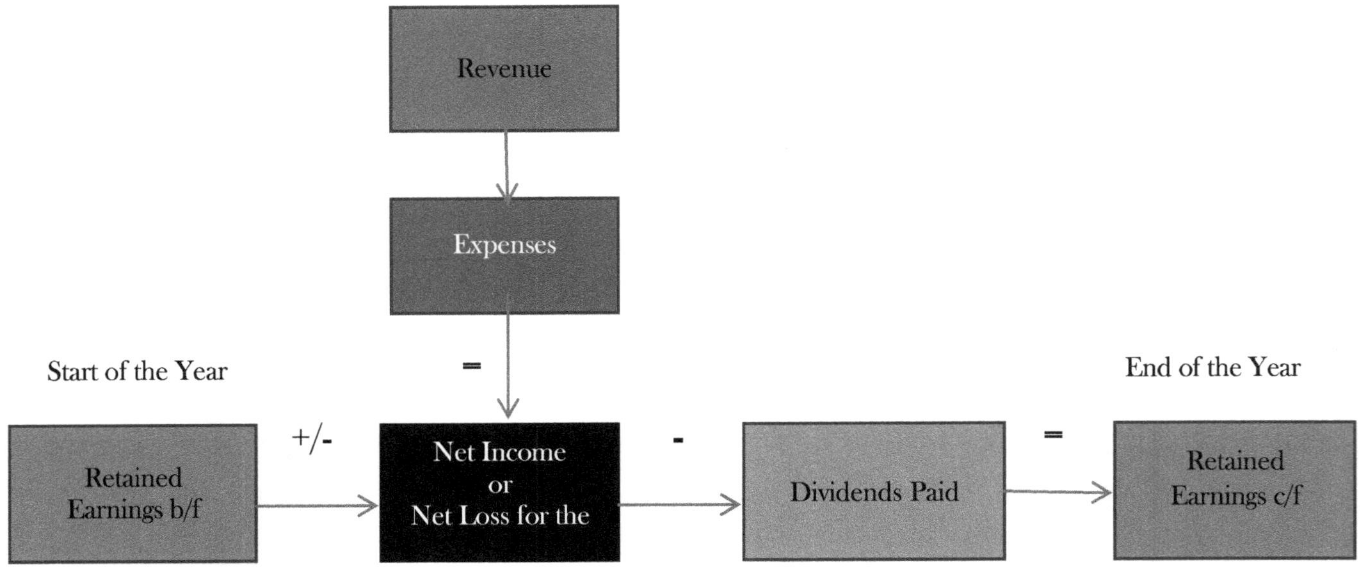

3. Analysing and Processing Transactions

The **accounting process** starts by identifying transactions and events. Relying on **source documents**, the transactions and events are analysed before recording its effects in the **accounting records** The accounting system makes use of several techniques and tools in analysing and processing transactions. These include debits on the left-hand side and credits on the right -hand side. Transactions are normally entered in the **books of prime entry** before they are posted to the general ledger. Some transactions that do not go through the books of prime entry are journalized before being posted to the general ledger system.

The accounting process begins with the processing and recording of transactions before providing useful information in reports that we call financial statements. These are made available to top management to make relevant and appropriate decisions.

The accounting process is illustrated below:

Steps in the Accounting Process

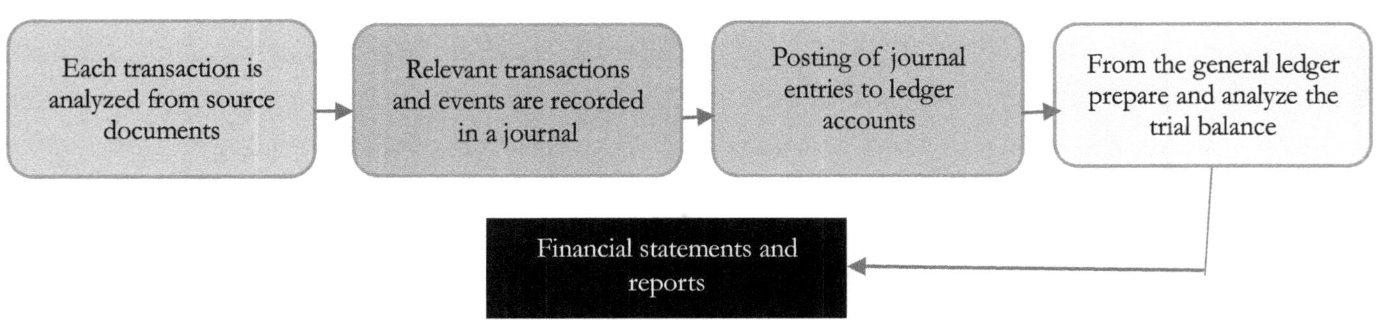

Source Documents

Third party documents are referred as **source documents**. Source documents provide documentary evidence on transactions and events which form the basis of accounting information and they can originate as hard copies or in electronic form. Examples are sales invoices, customers' orders, purchase orders and invoices, suppliers' statements, bank statements, bills and receipts, etc. The recording of transactions is done using these source documents and other related documents. Third party source documents are relied by auditors as authentic tangible audit evidence to support transactions and balances.

Use of Double-Entry System in Accounting

All the transactions of a business entity are recorded in the books of account (accounting records) using a double-entry bookkeeping system before being summarized in the financial statements, this is done at least annually. Accounting is based on a double-entry system, which records the **dual effects of a transaction** on the entity. Each transaction therefore affects at least two or more accounts. For an example, when ordinary shares are issued by a company for cash, say RM 25,000, it will increase both cash and share capital. At all times, the accounting equation: Assets = Liabilities + Shareholders' Equity, will remain in balance.

Use of T-Account

A T- account is an account that summarizes transactions. It is accounting record that shows movements (increases and decreases) of transactions in a specific asset, liability, or equity. A business entity would typically maintain separate accounts for cash, accounts receivable, accounts payable, sales and expenses such as salaries, electricity and water, insurance, etc. The T-account is used as a written record to keep track of increases and decreases whenever a transaction or economic event takes place and thus the balance of the account is maintained. For example, the cash account can appear as follows:

Cash Account

(Left side)	(Right side)
Debit	Credit

Students must note for every account, the Debit is always on the left and the Credit on the right. Every business transaction involves both a debit and a credit. In a T-account, the total debits and credits for every business transaction must be equal. This is the cornerstone of the double entry system.

Debits and Credits

In summary, what we need to know is that debits and credits provide the basis for the double-entry system of recording business transactions and economic events. This system provides a logical and methodical approach with accuracy for recording the transactions. It must be noted that the sum of all the debits to the accounts must equal the sum of all credits. It does not matter whether the transactions are big or small, it works very well for all systems of accounting.

Effects of Debits and Credits

We look at the effects of the double-entry accounting on some of the following types of transaction items:

Assets and liabilities

Taking a bank account balance as an asset

Bank Account

Dr		Cr	
	9,000		4,500
	5,000		1,200
	1,500		500
	750		1,300
	16,250		7,500
		Balance c/f	8,750
	16,250		16,250

Balance b/f 8,750 (debit)

Increases in cash are recorded as debits – an asset on the left side and decreases in cash on the right side. The illustration below summarizes the effects:

Debits	Credits
Increase assets	Decrease assets
Decrease liabilities	Increase liabilities

Shareholders' Equity

The shareholders' equity comprises the share capital, retained earnings, profit after tax, and dividends. Under the double-entry system, entities keep separate accounts to reflect on these equity items.

Debits	Credits
Decrease share capital	Increase share capital

Entities issue shares in exchange for owners' investment into the company. Credits increase the share capital account and debits decrease it. When a shareholder invests cash in the business in exchange for shares of the company's share capital, the company debits (increases the asset) cash account and credits (increases the equity) the share capital account.

Retained Earnings

Retained earnings are net income or profit after tax that is retained in the business. It represents the portion of shareholders' equity that the business entity has accumulated through the profitable operation of the business.

Debits	Credits
Decrease retained earnings	Increase retained earnings

Credits (net income) increases the retained earnings account and debits (dividends or net losses decrease it), as illustrated above

Dividends

A dividend is a Company's distribution of its realized profits to its shareholders. Basically, dividends reduce the shareholders' equity. Dividends paid is normally shown as a deduction (as a debit) of retained earnings.

Revenues and Expenses

Revenues increases shareholders' equity. Expenses have the opposite effect as expenses decrease shareholders' equity. Expenses decreases net income and revenue increases it. Therefore, increase and decrease sides of expense accounts should be the reverse of revenue accounts. Thus, debits increase expense accounts and credits decrease them. Putting all these items together, we can see how the final shareholders' equity figure is arrived at. The illustration on page 3 shows the components of retained earnings which forms part of the shareholders' equity.

4. Bookkeeping – Record keeping

The double entry process of recording the details of business transactions in the books of account is known as **Bookkeepin**g or alternatively it can be called '**Record Keeping'**

Steps in the Recording Process:

- Transactions takes place (e.g. sales, purchases, receipts and payments)
- Analyze the transactions for its effects on the accounts
- Source documents evidencing the transactions are created (Invoices, cheque stubs, etc)
- Entries relating to transaction information are made through the books of prime entry:
- (Journal entries, using computerized accounting system)
- Transfer the journal information to the appropriate individual accounts in the Ledger via postings using the double-entry system of debits and credits
- Extracting the trial balance and making adjusting entries
- Financial statements and reports are then produced

Journals

A journal is a book of prime entry. A business entity initially records business transactions in the order in which they occur, using the double-entry system. For each transaction the journal shows the debit and credit effects on specific individual accounts in the Ledger as explained below. The most basic form of journal is the general or nominal journal. The format of a journal shows the dates, account titles, explanations in narratives, references to source documents and two amount columns. For illustration of the Journal, see below.

Importance of a journal

i. It discloses the complete effects of a business transaction in one location
ii. The record of transactions are usually done in a chronological order, using dates as a reference point
iii. It assists in locating or preventing errors by identifying the debit and credit amounts for each entry as this can be compared.

The Illustration below shows the technique of journalizing using the two transactions relating to issue of ordinary shares and purchase of equipment.

General Journal

Date	Account Title and Narratives	Ref	Debit	Credit
15 July	Cash	AJE 1	25,000	
	Share capital			25,000
	(Being issue of shares by cash)			
16 July	Office Equipment	AJE 2	6,300	
	Cash			6,300
	(Being purchase of computer by cash)			

A complete journal entry will consist of:

i. The date of the transaction
ii. The accounts and amounts to be debited and credited, and
iii. A brief narrative explaining the transaction.

Adjusting journal entries (AJEs) are recorded in the journal when such transactions are not routinely taken up in the books of prime entry. Usually the reference to these AJEs is evidenced by supporting third party source documents and in some cases, self-generated internally authorized documents.

Just a word of caution – It is important to use correct and specific account description in journalizing. Each description of the account must appropriately describe the content of the account.

It is to be noted that most simple transactions involve two accounts, one debit and one credit. Some transactions due to its complex nature, could result in more than two or multiple accounts. An illustration of a **multiple journal entries** is as follows:

Date	Account Description and Narrative	Ref	Debit	Credit
17 July	Cash	CB	675	
	Accounts receivable	SL	1,325	
	Sales	GL		2, 000
	(Being sales partly for cash with balance on credit)			

Conventionally, a journal entry format requires that all debits to be listed before the credits.

Postings to Ledger

At the end the period, any journal entries created as a result of emerging transactions, must be posted to the relevant individual accounts in the ledger usually to the corresponding debit or credit of the specific account titles.

Transferring journal entries to the ledger accounts is typically called **posting**.

Ledgers

A general or nominal ledger contains the entire group of accounts that are usually maintained by a business entity. The ledger shows all the recorded movements in an account by debits and credits and for the entire set of accounts operated by the entity. Any changes in data and information will be shown in the movements of the specific account balances.

A **general ledger** maintained by an entity contains all the assets, liabilities shareholders' equity including all the revenue accounts and the various expense accounts. It must be noted several ledgers can be created depending upon the business requirements, for instance a sales ledger will solely contain records of all accounts receivable from the various customers by name description. Likewise, a purchases ledger will be maintained in a similar fashion as the sales ledger. An index of page numbers will be maintained to identify the respective customers' accounts. An important consideration is that the accounting staff normally arranges the ledger in the sequence in which they are presented in the financial statements. beginning with the balance sheet (SOFP) items, in the order of asset accounts first, followed by liability accounts, shareholders' equity accounts, revenues and expenses. An index of page numbers is listed in the chart of accounts to identify the relevant accounts. At any point in time, the ledger account balances when updated, can be reviewed and extracted as information for making useful decisions on finances.

Ledger Account

Sales Ledger Account				
Date	**ABC Sdn Bhd - Trade customer**	**Dr**	**Cr**	
1.6.15	Balance b/f	6,700		6,700
	Sales Day Book – credit sales for week 2	3,500		10,200
	Cash: proceeds from customer		6,700	3,500
	Credit note: trade discount		250	3,250
	Balance c/f - 30 6.15		3,250	

The balance in the account is determined after end of each month or it could be extended to a third column

Chart of Accounts

In today's context where business transactions are recorded using accounting software packages, the accounting process is made easier for business entities to make use of a **chart of accounts** to list all the designated accounts along with the numbers they assign to them. In this sense, accounting is consistent in that accounts are listed in the chart of accounts in the chronological order of assets, liabilities, equity (share capital and reserves) revenues and expenses.

Account numbers are identified by two or more digits indicating the type of account. Usually, if an account starts with:

- 1, it is an asset account
- 2, it is a liability account
- 3, it is a capital account or any of the equity or reserve accounts
- 4, it is a revenue account
- 5, it is an expense account

The second and third digits are an account number which indicates where the accounts fit within the category.

For example, Cash may be account number 101, the first asset account. Accounts receivable may be account number 121, the second asset account. Accounts payable may be account 201, the first liability. All accounts used by a business are numbered by this system.

The **chart of accounts** varies from business to business because every business has accounts based on its own needs and circumstances. However, further discussion on this topic is extended under **Section 5** of this Chapter related to computerized accounting information system(AIS).

Books of Prime Entry

Early writers on bookkeeping recognized that the recording process involved several steps:

a. The transactions
b. Evidencing the transactions in the form of source documents
c. Entering the details of each transaction in a primary book or journal
d. Entering the details of each transaction in the double-entry accounts.

Modern systems of accounting follow the same pattern; the only difference is that it is performed using computerized accounting packages. Books of primary entry are still the same even with computerized accounting systems. These include customary records such as:

- Sales Day Book or Sales Journal
- Purchases Day Book or Purchases Journal
- Cash Book

The general ledger is not a book of prime entry. It is a **book of final entry** because all entries from the books of prime entry are eventually posted to the ledger before the extraction of the final balances (after the adjusting entries) goes to the trial balance. The financial statements are then prepared from the trial balance.

Transactions	**Source document as evidence**
• Credit sales	Sale invoices
• Purchases and expenses made or incurred on credit	Suppliers' invoices
• Cash sales	Till rolls/Cash bill
• Receipts from customers	Bank in slips/official receipt
• Payments to suppliers of goods and expenses on credit	Official receipts/remittances
• Wages paid	Payroll/ Time sheets

Sales Day Book

Sales on credit to customers are evidenced by sending invoices to customers. A copy is retained and the invoice contains detailed information of the sale as follows:

a. The invoice number which is pre-numbered consecutively.
b. Name, address of the customer and other contact details
c. Date
d. Specification of goods sold, price, GST, and the monetary value of the invoice.

The invoices details are entered into the Sales Day Book or Sales Journal by keying the data into the computer accounting system. The sales day book, being a book of prime entry is simply a recorded list of sales invoices. It does not form part of the double-entry system but merely acts as a permanent record or journal of sales transactions recorded for the period. The double-entry is the subsequent entries in the customer accounts and the GST account while the totals are treated as part of the control accounts for the total sales done for the period in question.

A typical record is as follows:

SALES DAY BOOK

SL Folio	Date	Invoice number	Customer's name	Net RM	ST 6%	Gross sales RM
02	22/7/15	28960	John Smith Co	1,950	117	2,067
10	22/7/15	28961	Chong Trading Sdn Bhd	2,700	162	2,862
07	25/7/15	28962	Azhar Supplies.	975	59	1,034
18	30/7/15	28963	Zenith Sales Services	12,500	750	13,250
			Total	18,125	1,088	19,213

In the computerized accounting system, the column totals are posted automatically to the relevant individual accounts in the General Ledger and to the respective Sales Ledger Customer Accounts (as account receivables) in the double entry system.

Double entry postings

Net – RM 18,125 credited to Sales account

ST – RM 1,088 credited to Sales Tax account

Gross sales – RM 19, 213 debited:

i. to sales ledger control account (as accounts receivable) and
ii. to the individual debtor's account in the sales ledger

Procedures are

a. Invoices are created by the sales division as and when the sales occur
b. The sales day book is recorded on a daily basis from the copy invoices retained by the accounts division
c. The accounts receivable account of the respective customers (trade debtors)in the sales ledger is debited with the entry.
d. Monthly (weekly) sales day book is totaled and the totals are posted on the credit side of the sales account and the GST account respectively.

Note: In this section, T-accounts not ruled off.

General Ledger Accounts

Sales Account

Dr					Cr
			31.7 15	Sales day book	18,125

Goods and Sales Tax Account

Dr					Cr
			31.7.15	Sales day book	1,088

Sales Ledger Control Account

Dr					Cr
31.7.15	Sales Day Book	19,213			

Sales or Debtors Ledger (Accounts Receivable):

02 **John Smith Co**

Dr					Cr
22/7/15	Invoice 28960	2,067			

07 **Azhar Supplies**

Dr					Cr
25/7/15	Invoice 28962	1,084			

10 **Chong Trading Sdn Bhd**

					Cr
22/7/15	Invoice 28961	2,862			

18 **Zenith Sales Services**

Dr					Cr
30/7/15	Invoice 28963	13,250			

System for recording sales invoice

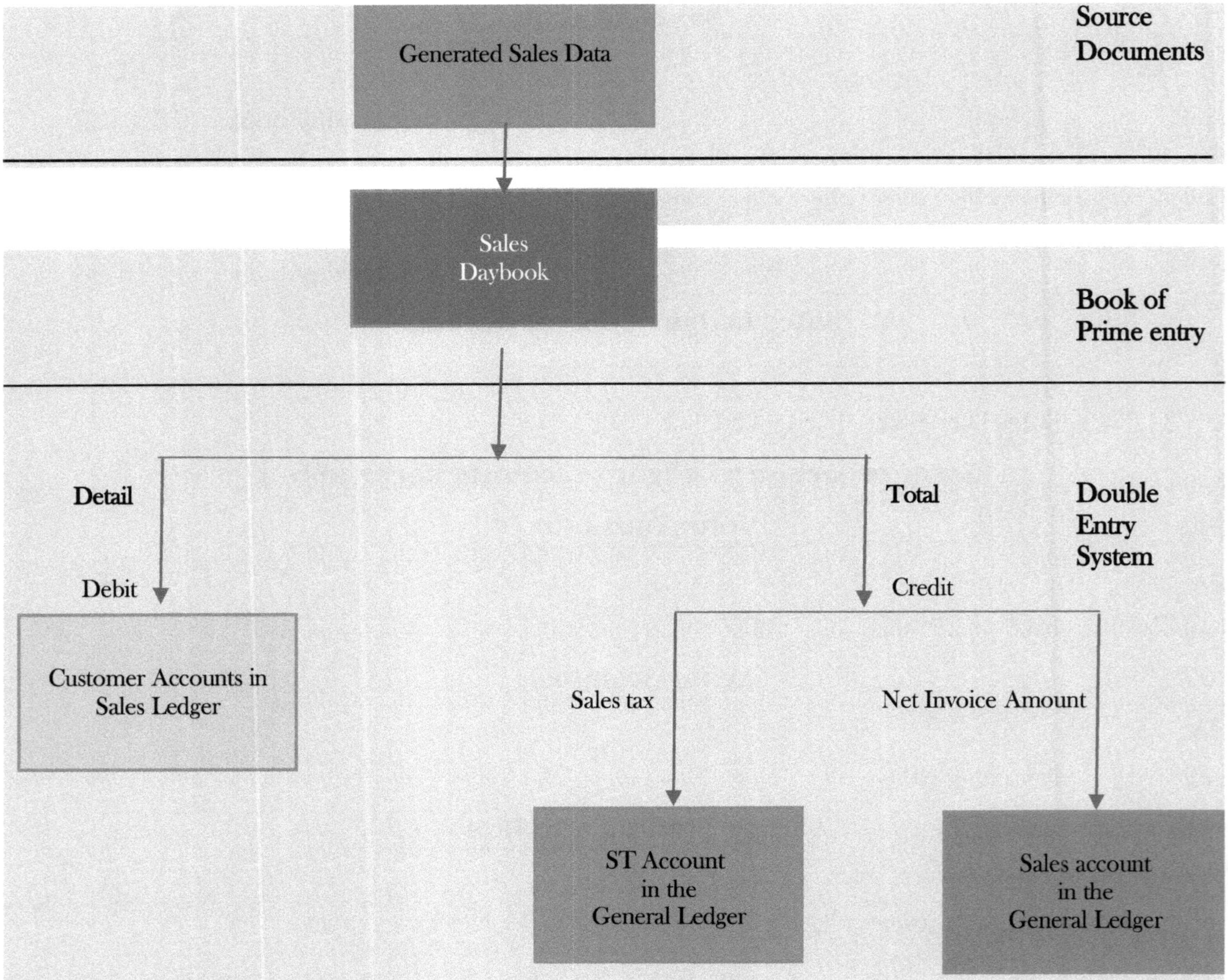

Note

The GST Account is in fact an account created to record items due to and from Customs and Excise Malaysia.

Purchases Day Book or Purchases Journal

In practice, goods and services are supplied to businesses on credit and the amount to be paid is evidenced by an invoice sent by the supplier. All incoming purchase invoices should be checked and filed together in date sequence. The recording of the purchasing system is exactly the same as for the sales transactions but the book-keeping entries using the double entry system is just the opposite of the sales system. The invoice details are entered in the purchases and expenses day book as follow:

PURCHASES AND EXPENSES DAY BOOK

Date	Supplier	Invoice No	Gross Amount	ST	Net	Purchases	Fixed Asset	Rent
28/7/15	Ah Chong	251	715	43	672	672	-	-
28/7/15	Equipment	285	990	59	931	-	931	-
29/7/15	Greentown	075	500	-	500			500
30/7/15	GT Supplies	118	385	23	362	362	-	-
31/7/15	Magnum	975	1,575	95	1,405	1,405	-	-
		Total	4,165	220	3,870	2,439	931	500

Note

Further columns will be extended if necessary, to account for other type of expenses incurred on credit.

It must be emphasized that the purchases and expenses day book is not part of the double-entry system, although it is a medium where data is recorded for the double entry postings *to the General Ledger and Purchases (Trade Creditors) Ledger.*

Postings

Accounts to be **debited** are:

ST Account – RM 220

Purchases account - RM 2,439

Fixed asset account – RM 931

Rent expense account – RM 500

Account to be **credited**:

Purchases ledger control account - RM 4,165

Purchases Ledger

The individual gross amounts listed in the purchases day book under the respective creditors' names are to be posted to the credit side of the suppliers' accounts. The approach to be taken is the same as the exercise done for the sales transactions but entries are on the opposite side.

General Ledger (Extract)

Goods and Sales Tax Account

Dr		
31/7/15	Purchases day book	220

Purchases

Dr		
31/7/15	Purchases day book	2,439

Fixed Asset Account – office equipment

Dr		
31/7/15	Purchases day book	930

Rent

Dr		
31/7/15	Purchases day book	500

Purchases Ledger Control Account

		Cr
31/7/15	Purchases day Book	4,165

Accounts Payable (Creditors' Ledger)

Ah Chong

		Cr
28/7/15	Purchases Invoice 251	718

Equipment Sales Services

		Cr
28/7/15	FA Invoice 285	990

Greentown

		Cr
29/7/15	Invoice 075	500

GT Supplies

		Cr
30/7/15	Invoice 118	385

Magnum

		Cr
31/7/15	Invoice 975	1,575

The above GL accounts are not ruled off using T- Accounts but the double entries are clear.

System for Recording Purchases and Expenses

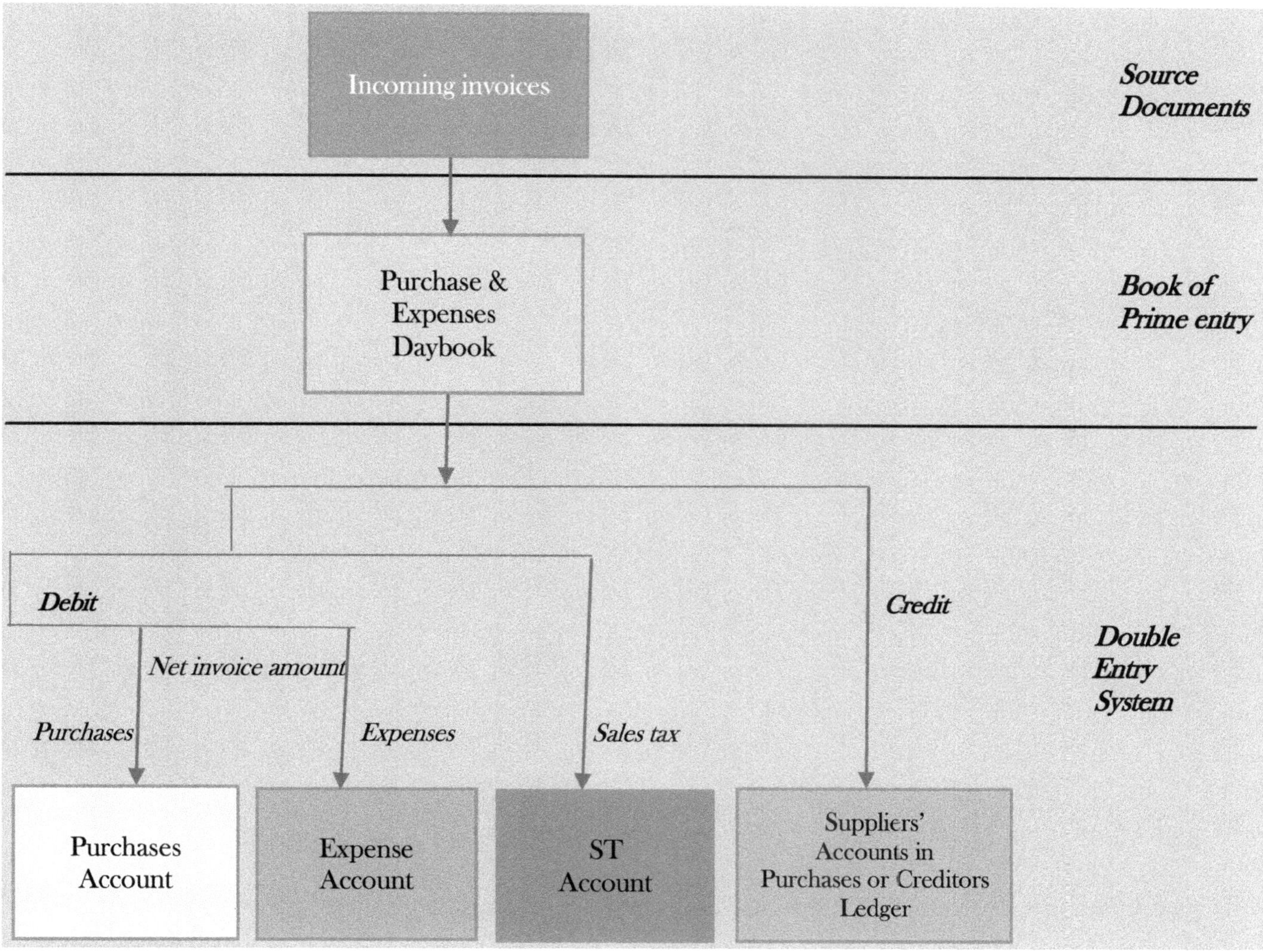

Notes

a. Purchases here, technically means goods resale or materials and components to be incorporated in a product.

b. There will be as many expense accounts as there are expense headings in the profit or loss statement.

c. Expenses will include capital expenditure

Cash Book

The third book of prime entry is slightly different in that the cash book forms both a book of prime entry and a part of the double-entry system. In practice, entities prepare the cash book with as many columns as to account for the various items of expenditure and payments. However, computerized accounting systems may not typically follow this format for the cash book unless the accounting software package is one that is tailored for the business entity. A cash book represents receipts and payments taking the form of cash inflows and cash outflows. A common format for a cash book is shown below:

Cash Book

Dr		Receipts			Payments		Cr
Date	Source	Folio	Bank Account	Date	Payee	Folio	Bank Account
1/8/15	Balance b/f		12,350				
2/8	BCG	SL 09	1,250	2/8/15	Cash – wages	GL50	850
4/8	Steven Chong	SL 15	2,705	3/8/15	Equipment	GL10	990
5/8	Loan proceeds	GL 15	25,000	5/8/15	CG Supplier	GL12	2,225
7/8	Cash sales	GL 75	895	6/8/15	Greentown	GL14	500
				7/8/15	GT Supplies	GL/PL	2,550
	(Entries on both sides of the cash book are left deliberately as Nil)						
	B/f		42,200				7,115
				31/8/15	Balance c/f		35,085
			42,200				42,200

Note

The cash book closing balance of RM35, 085 is subject to bank reconciliation.

While some transactions in the form of receipts and payments are sampled in the above cash book, the cash book do not extend to a columnar analysis of these items as some of these items tend to recur on a regular basis. However, in practice an analytical columnar cash book facilitates the double-entry posting of these items in totals to the General or Nominal Ledger.

i. Debits entries are posted to the credit side of the GL accounts (as Accounts receivable, Cash sales and to any liability account such as a loan account, etc.)
ii. Credit entries are posted to the debit side of the GL (Asset accounts or Expense accounts)

Receipts on the debit side are cash proceeds from various trade debtors (account receivables) and other sources. The banking of these cash proceeds is evidenced by the **bank-in-slips** and **official receipts** which then form the basis of recording. **Payments** are made by cheques that run into sequence. Payments are evidenced by **vouchers** and **supporting source documents** which then form the basis of recording. The folios appearing in the cash book on both sides of the debit and the credit refer to the general ledger, sales ledger and purchases ledger postings of the amounts to the respective accounts. At the end of the month or period, the cash book balance is reconciled to the **bank statements** relating to that month or period. In practice, both balances may not agree. Usually a **bank reconciliation** statement is prepared to reflect the timing of these differences at the month ending between the cashbook balance and the bank statement balance. This happens because some cheques received will not be credited yet by the bank as these may appear in the following month and in the case of payments, cheques issued by the entity will not be presented to the bank for clearance not until the next couple of days in the following month.

System for Recording Receipts and Payments in the Cash Book

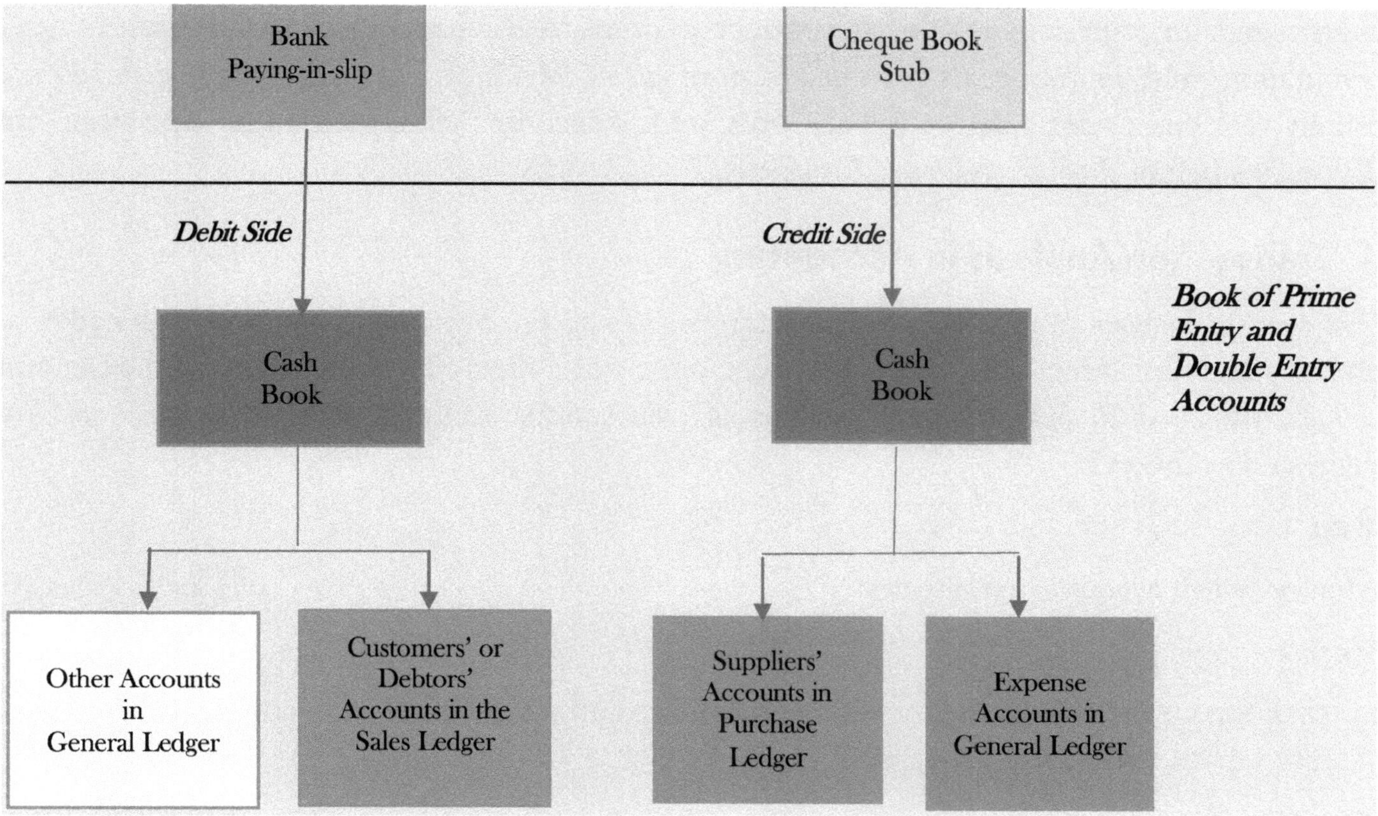

Notes

a. The cash book in which these transactions are recorded is nearly so called but it is really the Cash at Bank Accounts in the double entry system

b. The majority of cheque payments are debited to Suppliers' or Creditors' accounts. However, some payments such as wages and salaries are debited to expense accounts in the General Ledger

c. The majority of receipts are credited to customers' or debtors' accounts (accounts receivable) but a few receipts such as loan proceeds are credited to accounts in the General Ledger

d. All entries are treated as individual transactions

e. Some entries are initiated from sources other than the bank paying-in-slips and cheque book stubs. These may include direct credits from suppliers or others and debit advices such as bank interest and charges.

Now, by putting together all the transactions emerging from the books of prime entry, we are in the process of completing the bookkeeping exercise in full. However, some **adjusting journal**

entries are required to account for those transactions that do not go through the books of prime entry. Many of these transactions will come on an ad hoc basis given that some financial events occur in different times during the financial year. The accounting staff needs to identify these events prior to formalizing such entries.

Usually entries may arise as a result of more feedback such as the recovery of doubtful debts, inventories (stocks) becoming slow-moving and obsolete, accrued and prepaid expenses, adjustments for provisions relating to contract accounts, revisions required with respect to asset revaluations and depreciations or impairment of assets. Much of these **adjusting entries** are usually year end exercise before the accounts are finalized by the accountant for **approval by directors** before they are released for **audit.**

5. Transaction Analysis in Accounting

This section focuses on the transaction analysis, taking the accounting approach. In order to properly record transactions in the journals before posting them to the T-accounts in the General Ledger, we need to perform several steps of transactions analysis. The following steps are suggested as follows:

Step 1

What or which accounts are affected?

Step 2

For each account affected, what or which type of account classification is required? Is it an asset, liability, equity, revenue or expense?

Step 3

Does the affected account increase or decrease?

Step 4

Do you debit or credit the affected account?

Step 5

How does the T-account will look like after the transaction is posted or recorded?

Note, Step 1-4 deals with the analysis of the transaction involved whereas Step 5 relates to posting of the transaction from journal entries to the T-accounts in the General or Nominal Ledger All these 5 steps need to be practiced by routine. Therefore, it is important to see how this transaction analysis can be applied to a series of transactions.

Examples of Transactions

1. John Smith invested RM25,000 cash to kick start his new business venture.
2. Purchase of office equipment for RM 8,500 in cash payment

3. Borrowed cash from the bank – RM 20,000
4. Purchase supplies on credit for RM 2,250
5. A travel agency received RM 3,900 cash for travel services including air tickets.
6. Part settlement of a supplier's account for RM 1,800
7. Paid a salary to an employee at the end of the month amounting to RM 2,500
8. Paid utility bills for cash RM 285
9. Withdrawals by the owner of the business amounted to RM 1,200
10. Received cash proceeds of RM 2,750 for sale of components to a customer on credit.
11. A travel agency provided services for RM 5,500 on credit.

Note that for every transaction that takes place, there is always the **dual effect**. Let's analyse the above eleven transactions using the step approach as follows

TN	1 Accounts affected	2 Type	3 Increase (↑) /Decrease (↓)		4 Dr or Cr
1	Cash	Asset		↑	Dr
	J Smith, Capital	Capital		↑	Cr
Journal entry:					
	Cash		Dr 25,000		
	J Smith, Capital			Cr 25,000	
	(Being capital investment in the business)				
2	Equipment	Asset		↑	Dr
	Cash	Asset		↓	Cr
Journal entry:					
	Office equipment		Dr 8,500		
	Cash			Cr 8,500	
	(Being purchase of equipment by cash)				
3	Cash	Asset		↑	Dr
	Loan Payable	Liability		↑	Cr
Journal entry:					
	Cash		Dr 20,000		
	Loan Payable			Cr 20,000	
	(Being cash proceeds from bank borrowing)				

4	Purchases	Asset		↑	Dr
	Accounts Payable	Liability		↑	Cr
Journal entry:					
	Purchases		Dr 2,250		
	Accounts Payable			Cr 2,250	
	(Being purchase of supplies on credit)				
5	Cash	Asset		↑	Dr
	Sales	Income		↑	Cr
Journal entry:					
	Cash		Dr 3,900		
	Sales			Cr 3,900	
	(Being income from sales of travel services for cash)				
6	Accounts Payable	Liability		↓	Dr
	Cash	Asset		↓	Cr
Journal entry:					
	Accounts Payable		Dr 1,800		
	Cash			Cr 1,800	
	(Being part settlement on account by a supplier)				
7	Salaries	Expense		↑	Dr
	Cash	Asset		↓	Cr
Journal entry:					
	Salaries		Dr 2,500		
	Cash			Cr 2,500	
	(Being payment of staff salary for the month)				
8	Utilities	Light & Water Expense		↑	Dr
	Cash	Asset		↓	Cr
Journal entry:					
	Electricity & Water		Dr 285		
	Cash			Cr 285	
	(Being payment of utility bills)				
9	Drawings	Capital		↑	Dr
	Cash	Asset		↓	Cr
Journal entry:					

	Proprietor's Drawing		Dr 1,200	
	Cash			Cr 1,200
	(Being owner's personal drawings)			
10	Cash	Asset	↑	Dr
	Accounts Receivable	Asset	↓	Cr
Journal entry:				
	Cash		Dr 2,750	
	Accounts Receivable			Cr 2,750
	(Being cash remittance from customer for sale of components on credit)			
11	Accounts Receivable	Asset	↑	Dr
	Sales	Income	↑	Cr
Journal entry:				
	Accounts Receivable		Dr 5,500	
	Sales			Cr 5,500
	(Being sales of travel services on credit)			

Balancing the Accounts

We now turn to the final part of the bookkeeping exercise, which is the balancing of accounts. After the transactions are recorded and posted to accounts, you need to determine the T-account's balance. A balance is the difference between the account's total debits and its total credits. Every account will have a balance as shown in the following example of a T-account.:

205 Accounts Receivable			
Bal b/f	3,005 (1)		
SDB	2,690 (2)	CBK	3,695 (3)
		Bal c/f	2,000 (4)
	5,695		5,695

1. The opening balance for the period is the closing balance of the previous period. In this example, it is RM 3,005.
2. The business sold on credit RM 2,690 worth of goods to a customer during the period, this transaction is shown as a debit to reflect as accounts receivable.
3. When the customer paid a portion of the debt for RM 3,695 during the period, this amount is entered on the credit side of the account.
4. The resulting closing balance of Accounts Receivable is RM 2,000 which will appear on the list of trade debtors for the accounting period ended.

Notes

SDB – Sales day book

CBK – Cash book

Account Formats

So far, we have illustrated accounts in a **two column T-account format** with the debit column on the left and credit column on the right. This informal approach is suitable for managers in business so that they can quickly analyse transactions only using T-accounts but such routine decisions are without the benefit of a complete accounting system. Business entities usually do not actually keep records in this short-cut manner because a decision maker needs information quickly but may not have the time at his disposal to have all the bookkeeping entries such as to journalise, post to the accounts, produce a trial balance and prepare the financial statements. However, a manager who knows accounting can quickly analyse the transaction and arrive at the decision fast.

Another way of representing accounts is to adopt **a columnar format** where two further columns are extended to show the running balance for every account in the ledger system. In a computerised accounting systems, accounts are maintained and can be printed easily in columnar formats rather than T-accounts. See the **exhibit** below:

T-accounts are extensively used in exams by students as they can demonstrate transactions and balances conveniently using this approach.

Exhibit: Account using 4 Column Format

Bank account (CIMB)						**GL 39**
Date	Particulars	Debit	Credit	Balance		Notes
				Dr	Cr	
2020						
March 5	Customer Maxis	125, 000		125, 000		
10	Plant and equipment		90, 000	35, 000		
April 12	Purchases		14, 500	20, 500		
25	John & Sam	3,750		24, 250		

Note to Students

Up to this point, we have demonstrated the recording of transactions and events using the double-entry system and devoted some material that is relevant to an AIS in a computerized environment (See Chapter 3). We identified the books of prime entry and showed all the postings that usually end-up in the general ledger system under both approaches but in **economic substance** they underlie the same **accounting principles**.

We now turn to the accounting cycle and explain the related activities before closing the chapter 2.

7. The Accounting Cycle

The steps involved in the accounting cycle need to be explained here. In the first chapter we discussed the need for accountability in business. Owners and managers make decisions on the basis of financing, investing and operating activities of a business. The stewardship of the business rest with top management and these individuals have a **fiduciary responsibility** to stakeholders of the business that include shareholders and investors, suppliers or creditors, customers or debtors, employees, government agencies and others that may direct or indirect interest in the business.

Accountants use financial accounting systems to prepare financial statements that communicate the decisions made and the results derived from those decisions. The financial statements have a way of telling a story of about the business's activities.

The accounting cycle is the process of gathering financial information and preparing these financial statements. The accounting cycle is explained using several iterative steps below:

Step 1

The accountant identifies business transactions and financial events by examining source documents, contracts, and both internal and external business reports.

- Source documents are documents that represent a business transaction. For example, a sales invoice reflects sales to a customer, with delivery note indicating physical evidence of dispatch of goods to the customer. A remittance advice with a cheque reflect cash collections from the customer
- Contracts reflect contractual relationships. These documents may include a bank term loan for the business, lease or hire-purchase agreements, etc. Contracts have a legal obligation to repay the loan with interest, or pay for the use of the assets owned by the lessor or fulfill some settlement as agreed in the contractual document.
- Reports may include lists of assets used to calculate depreciation. Reports may also include payroll registers that show the salaries and other statutory deductions of employees.

Step 2

Involves the recording of the transactions through the books of primary entry or in the journal.

Step 3

Post journal entries or books of prime entry into individual accounts in the general ledger.

Note: Steps 1 through 3 takes place throughout the accounting period as the business is engaged in undertaking transactions.

Step 4

At the end of the accounting period, the accountant prepares a worksheet, or prepares a trial balance and uses this as a basis for adjusting the accounts. If the business entity prepares only a trial balance with all the year-end adjusting entries posted via the journal, then it will use this trial balance to complete the rest of the steps in the accounting cycle instead of the work sheet.

Note the trial balance contents are deliberately omitted from discussion in this Chapter 2. We will deal formally in Chapter 23 in Part 3 section of the textbook.

Step 5

The accountant (in practice) will use the worksheet to prepare the financial statements.

Step 6

Using the worksheet, the accountant puts through: -

i. Adjusting entries in the journal and posts them to accounts in the ledger.
ii. Closing entries in the journal and posts them to accounts in the ledger

Step 7

The accountant prepares a post-closing trial balance from which the financial statements are prepared for release. While the seven steps above discuss the iterative steps in the accounting cycle. In Chapter 24, we will complete the accounting cycle by accomplishing more elements in the financial reporting process.

Illustrative Summary of Accounting Cycle

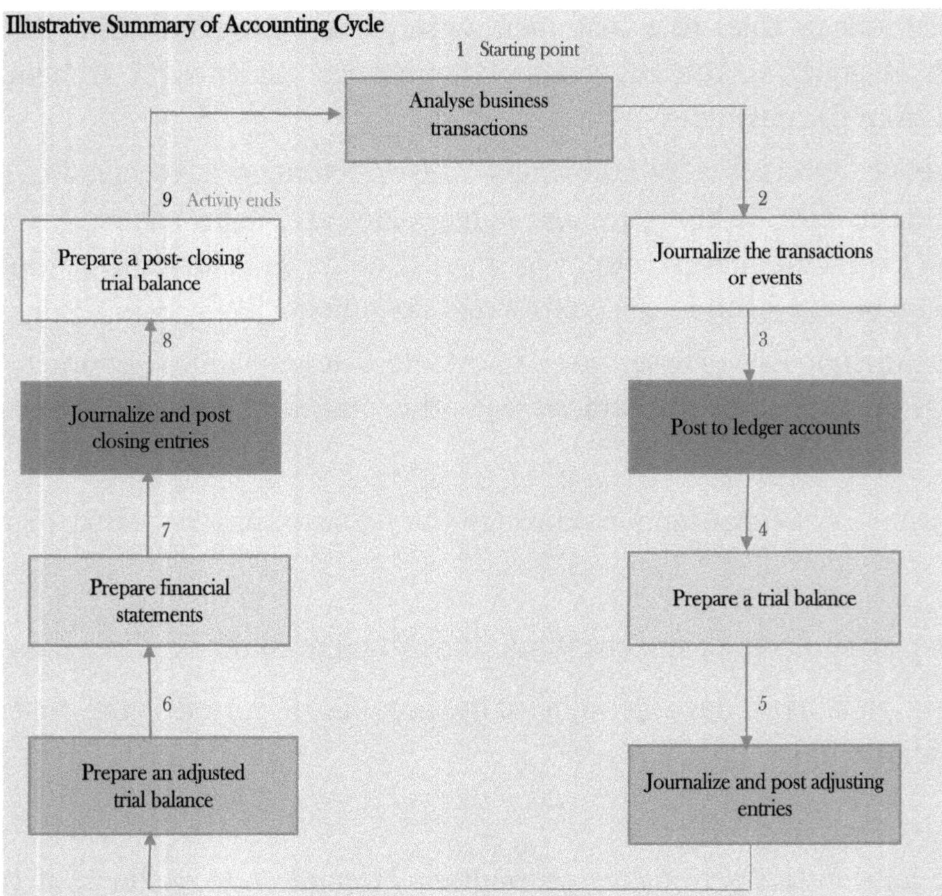

Note

Optionally, if a worksheet is prepared, steps 4, 5 and 6 are incorporated in the worksheet. In that case. only 7 steps instead of 9 steps, complete the accounting cycle. Where reversing or reclassification entries are prepared, they occur between steps 8. & 9.

Computerized Accounting Systems

In Chapter 3 that follows, we focus our attention to accounting in computerised accounting systems which increasingly has become the mainstay in today's technology driven era. Accounting systems are powered by computer software that enables speedy and efficient recording of transactions by volume. Compared to conventional accounting systems, the power of computerized systems such as ERP creates a competitive edge for business entities to leverage on this state of art and digital development because it creates value for any businesses today. Nevertheless, the conventional accounting system is still valid as you can learn and understand how the double entry works.

Chapter Summary

Steps in processing transactions

The **accounting process** identifies business transactions and events, analyzes and records their **dual effects**, summarizes with information that assist in making useful financial decisions. **Source documents** identify and describe transactions and events such as sales invoices, purchase orders, suppliers' invoices, bank-in-slips and cheque-stubs, expense vouchers and supporting third party documents, bank statements, etc. Source documents provide reliable evidence, making information more useful and objective. **Journals** are effectively used to demonstrate the dual effects of recorded transactions and events. The **trial balance** summarizes by classifying the general ledger balances into assets, liabilities, equity, revenue and expenses before they are prepared as financial statements. The **accounting cycle** outlines all these critical steps in the accounting process.

Description of an account and its purpose in recording transactions

An account is a written record that shows movements in a specific asset, liability, equity, revenue or expense. The recorded account provide information about particular transactions that can be analyzed, summarized, and reported in financial statements for decision makers.

Cash book

The cash book is a **book of prime entry** and an important one because it records all the **cash flows** of a business entity. Both incoming transactions (**cash receipts**) and outgoing transactions (**cash payments**) relating to an entity's business activities gets recorded. All these financial transactions are normally reflected in the **bank statements**. Any differences between the cash book balance and the bank statement is usually **reconciled** due to timing of deposits and withdrawals in a **bank account**.

Description of the general ledger and chart of accounts used by the entity

A written record containing all the accounts used by the business entity and their balances is referred as a **general or nominal ledger**. The chart of accounts is a list of all designated accounts in the accounting system that is uniquely identified and maintained by the entity. Each account in the ledger is assigned by a particular folio which identifies the page number and name of the account.

Double-entry accounting

Debits are on the left-hand side and credits are on the right-hand side. Debits increase assets and expenses while credits decrease them. Credits increase liabilities, contributed share capital and revenue whereas debits decrease them. In double-entry accounting, each transaction has **a dual effect**, affecting at least two accounts with one debit and a corresponding credit. Recording debits and credits under this system follows from the accounting equation in which debits must equal credits. The trial balance follows this accounting principle because all listed ledger balances must be eventually balanced.

Impact of analyzing transactions on accounts and financial statements

We can often tell what an entity did by analyzing its accounts. This is a powerful technique for a manager who knows his accounting. We analyze transactions using the concept of double-entry accounting. This analysis determines the impact or effect of a transaction on the affected accounts which normally gets recorded by a journal entry and subsequently posted to the accounts in the general ledger. All routine transactions are recorded in this way in **a journal** before being posted in the ledger. The completed ledger entries usually at the end of an accounting period provides information that is used to produce the trial balance from which financial statements can be prepared. The use and importance of a **trial balance** is explained later in Chapter 23 when the accounting cycle ends.

The Accounting Cycle

The **accounting cycle** refers to the steps taken in preparing financial statements. It is called a cycle because the steps are repeated each reporting period. We identified a series of 9 steps in the cycle, starting with analyzing transactions and ending with post-closing trial balance with adjustments for reversing entries where optionally needed. The cycle is the process of gathering financial information. Accountants use financial reporting systems in preparing these financial statements that communicate the decisions made and results derived from those decisions.

Conceptual difference between manual and computerized accounting systems

The fundamental concepts of a manual (pencil and pen) system are the same and identical to those of a computerized information systems today powered by software accounting packages that can accomplish the recording functions in an accounting environment much faster and efficient time in processing transactions by volume. Technological advances, the enabling factor that creates the competitiveness of the accounting information systems we see in the digital era.

Key Terms

Account balance

Accounting cycle

Account format

Account format

Accounts payable

Accounts receivable

Accounting process

Adjusting journal entries

Bank account

Bank balance

Bank-in-slip

Bank reconciliation

Bank statement

Record

The analyzing and recording process

Transactions

Credit note/advice

Debit note/advice

Debtors

Double entry system

Dual effect

General journal

General ledger (Book of final entry)

Invoices

Journal

Ledger

Bills
Books of prime entry
Cash book
Chart of accounts
Cheque Stubs
Columnar format
Customer's statement
Credit
Creditors
Cash receipt
Cash payments
Narration in a journal
Official receipt
Purchases day book
Purchases ledger control account
Postings
Record keeping
Sales day book
Source document
Supplier's statement of account
Sales ledger control account
Vouchers

Review Questions day

Q1. Describe the accounting process.

Q2. Explain the steps involved in processing transactions and events.

Q3. Describe the role and purpose of source documents.

Q4. Describe an account and its use in recording transactions.

Q5. How different is the accounting system using traditional recording methods from a computerized accounting system? Your answer should compare and contrast the main issues.

Q6. What purpose does a chart of accounts serve in the accounting system?

Q7. Define debits and credits in a system of double entry. Explain double-entry accounting.

Q8. Identify the books of primary entry and briefly state their function in the accounting system.

Q9. Explain why the general or nominal ledger is not a book of prime entry? Describe its role in the accounting system.

Q10. What is a journal and explain its importance in the system of accounting?

Q11. There are no exact rules for writing journal entry explanations, called narrations. An explanation should be brief and straight to the point, yet it describes why an entry is made.

a. Discuss the above statement about journal entries.

b. i. An investor receives shares in a company for investing RM 25, 000 by cash.

ii. The company invests RM 20, 000 in plant and equipment for use in the business. The payment was entered as cash book transactions when the settlement to the supplier was by a cheque payment.

Prepare the required journal entries for both transactions.

Q12. Explain the use of a T-account.

Q13. What role do postings of transactions play in double-entry accounting?

Q14. a. Receipts and payments are entered in the cash book. Explain what is the main purpose of doing these two distinct activities in the recording of cash flow transactions?

b. Explain why the role of a bank reconciliation is important to ascertaining the accuracy of a cash balance at the end of a particular period?

Q15. What types of transactions increase equity? Identify what other types of transactions decrease equity?

Q16. a. What kind of transactions can be recorded in a general journal?

b. Why does a bookkeeper prepare a trial balance?

c. Should a transaction be recorded first in a journal or the ledger?

d. Why is the general ledger is called the book of final entry?

Multiple Choice Questions

Q1. Gayavidhya received its utility bill for the current period of RM 550 and immediately settled it. Which side of its journal entry it must record this transaction?

a. Debit to cash for RM 550

b. Debit prepayment account for RM 550.

c. Debit to utility expense account for RM 550.

d. Debit to accruals account for RM 550.

e. Credit utility expense for RM 550

Q2. Rueben received shares for investing RM 200, 000 cash and acquired land and building at market value worth RM 550, 000 for his Consulting Firm. Rueben Associates. Which of the following journal entries must be recorded in his company's accounts to reflect these transactions?

a.	Cash	200, 000	
	Share capital		200, 000
b.	Cash	200, 000	
	Land and building		550, 000
	Share capital		750, 000
c.	Share capital	750, 000	
	Cash		200, 000
	Land and buildings		550, 000
d.	Share capital	750, 00	
	Assets and Liabilities		750, 000

Q3. On 1 April, Jagdish Cleaning Services collected RM 6, 000 cash from a customer in advance for six months cleaning and maintenance service. What journal entry should be recorded by Jadish for this transaction?

a. Debit to cash for RM 6, 000.

b. Debit to unearned maintenance service income for RM 6, 000.

c. Debit to prepayment account for RM 6, 000

d. Credit to unearned maintenance service income for RM 6, 000

e. Credit to share capital account.

Q4. A company has a share capital of RM 750, 000 and liabilities of RM 450, 000. Its total assets stood at RM 1, 200, 000. What is its debt ratio (or gearing ratio)?

a. 200 %

b. 67 %

c. 167 %

d. 62.5 %

e. 37.5 %

Q5. Bottom-line Results had retained earnings of RM 228, 000 at 1 October 2019. Profit after tax of RM 158, 000 was reported for the year. Dividends amounting to RM 68, 000 was declared and paid for the year. How much of retained earnings should the company report in its statement of changes in equity for the year ended 30 September 2020?

a. RM 358, 000

b. RM 415, 000

c. RM 318, 000

d. RM 328, 000

Q6. Tilly Dinesh holds cash balance of RM 12, 500 and owes RM 38, 500 on accounts payable. The company has accounts receivable of RM 43, 200, inventory of RM 36, 000, and other debtors and prepayments of RM 8, 500. The company's land and building had a reported value worth RM 185, 000. How much total assets and total liabilities will be reported by Tilly, a trading company in motor vehicle spare parts and accessories in its statement of financial position?

(Ignore other items of account)

Total assets	Total liabilities
a. RM 285, 200	RM 38, 500
b. RM 276, 700	RM 38, 500
c. RM 255, 700	RM 50, 500
d. RM 285, 200	RM 43, 200

Q7. Given the facts as in question 6 and assuming no other adjustments were put through the accounts except for sundry creditors and accruals of RM 8, 850, determine what would be Tilly's shareholders' equity (share capital and retained earnings)? (Use the accounting equation to arrive at the required solution).

a. RM 237, 850

b. RM 247, 700

c. RM 276, 700

d. RM 294, 050

Q8. Shan-Ruk Company had a shareholders' equity of RM 200, 000 at the beginning of the year and total assets stood at RM 410, 000. During the year the assets increased by RM 75,850 and liabilities went up by RM 35, 350. What figure would be reported for shareholders' equity at the end of the year?

(Use the accounting equation)

a. 230, 500

b. 240, 800

c. 240, 500

d. 250, 800

Q9. Bottom-line Results had retained earnings of RM 228, 000 at 1 October 2019. Profit after tax of RM 158, 000 was reported for the year. Dividends amounting to RM 68, 000 was declared and paid for the year. How much of retained earnings should the company report in its statement of changes in equity for the year ended 30 September 2020?

a. RM 358, 000

b. RM 415, 000

c. RM 318, 000

d. RM 328, 000

Q10. A trial balance prepared at year-end shows total credits exceed total debits by RM 975. What would have caused this discrepancy?

a. An error in recording a RM 975 increase in cash as a credit.

b. The ledger balance for accounts payable of RM 9, 750 being entered in the trial balance as RM 975.

c. An error in the journal where a RM 975 increase in accounts payable was recorded aa a RM 975 decrease in accounts payable.

d. A journal entry error where a RM 975 increase in accounts receivable was recorded as a RM 975 increase in cash.

e. The ledger balance of RM 1, 065 was entered in the trial balance as RM 90.

I define globalisation as where it is most cost-effective, selling where it is most profitable, and sourcing capital where it is cheapest, without worrying about national boundaries.

– N.R. Narayana Murthy, Founder of Infosys

Chapter 3

Learning Objectives

Understand transaction data processing cycle and how it works

Understand the concepts of data storage, data input, data processing and data output

Understand the purpose of the accounting information system(AIS)

Understand the use of computer terminology as it applies to the computerised accounting environment

Understand business activities and the related systems documentation such as source documents used in the sales or revenue,

purchasing and expenditure cycles

Understand and know how accounting information is stored in the GL system and subsidiary ledgers through the use of journals

Know and understand the purpose and importance of the chart of accounts in AIS

Understand the application of coding techniques such as bar or sequence codes that systematically assigns numbers and letters to items for classifying and organising documentation and products.

Understand the purpose of an audit trail for tracing the path of a transaction through a data processing system.

Understand the important use of a control account

Understand the use of data storage elements such as entity, attributes, fields and values as applied to transaction data.

Know the difference between transaction and master files

Know what is a database

Understand the four types of data processing activities (CRUD) and of transactions such as batch processing and online real time batch processing

Know and understand information output comes the form of reports, documents, query

Accounting in a Computerised Based System

Scope

Transaction data processing within a computer-based system environment is the main focus in this Chapter. The treatment on data storage, data input, data processing, and data output is covered in reasonable detail. This text is primarily focused on financial accounting not systems analysis. Therefore, what is essentially needed for a student's understanding is the *Accounting Information System* (AIS) that deals with the application of data processing concepts that ultimately result in producing the financial statements and reports for decision making. Chapter 3 contents although could be treated as an integrated part of Chapter 2, we did not given its special significance. We wanted Chapter 3 to be treated on its own merit to ensure that it maintains the same theme - *transaction data processing and recording* within a computer-based system environment using a computer language jargon. So, Chapter 3 now becomes an important extension to Chapter 2. Significantly, it shows how the **transaction processing cycle** works in the computerized accounting system. There is no fundamental difference in accounting principles between both systems except that the orientation now is towards **systems documentation** and the **use of computer terminology** as it applies to the computer environment. The next few pages will show how the transaction processing is done quite differently in the AIS driven by the use of computer technology concepts. **Enterprise resource planning** (ERP) **systems** increasingly has taken a centre stage approach towards integrating all aspects of an organization's operations along with a traditional AIS. Properly configured, ERP system uses a centralized database to share information across business processes, resources and coordinating activities. We cannot ignore the important role this relatively new application plays because it provides a competitive edge for an organization's business in the marketplace. The concluding pages would emphasise more on this development.

Introduction

Virtually every business entity today uses a computerised accounting system tailored to their needs to process business transactions. Depending on the accounting software used, all these transactions get systematically reported in the accounting system.

In Chapter 2, we focused on the accounting process by adopting the double entry system and T-accounts where such transactions (debits and credits) are reported in the books of prime entry (Journals, Cash book a, General ledger, etc.) before a trial balance is extracted and after the necessary adjustments, the final accounts are prepared. In contrast, the data processing of transactions in a computerised system might not be conventionally followed because the analysis and recording of transaction is done online in real time or online by batch processing. The following pages explain the data processing cycle common to a computerised accounting system where the jargon and terminology used is different from a conventional accounting system.

1. Transaction Processing: The Data Processing Cycle

One important **accounting information system** (AIS) function is to process the business entity's transactions efficiently and effectively. In a manual accounting system, the transaction data are entered into journals and ledgers maintained on paper records. In computerized accounting systems, transaction data are entered in computers and stored in **files** and **databases.** The processing of these data as input to the computer system is primarily intended to produce relevant accounting information. This is collectively referred to as the **data processing cycle.**

Accountants and other system users play a significant role in the data processing cycle. They normally interact with **systems analysts** to obtain answers to the following questions on data processing concepts such as:

i. What data should be entered and stored by the entity, and who should have access to them?
ii. How data should be organized, updated, stored, accessed, and retrieved?
iii. How can scheduled and unanticipated information needs to be met?

To answer these related questions, we must understand the **data processing concepts**.

As shown in the **Figure 2.1**, this process consists of four steps: *data input, data storage, data processing, and the information output.*

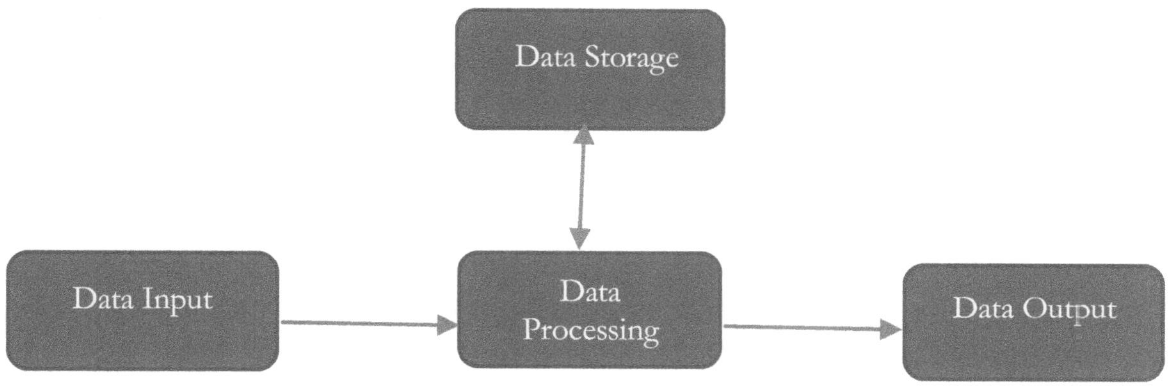

Figure 2.1 Data Processing Cycle

A detailed coverage of data processing concepts is beyond the technical scope of this accounting textbook as we are more focused on the use of transaction data and information for recording in the books of account so that the AIS can produce the required financial statements and reports for decision making by higher management in the organization. Chapter 2 content has already achieved this accounting scope. Nevertheless, we cover some essential material for you to gain some understanding and appreciation of this important function of the computerized accounting information system.

Data Input

First step in data processing input is to capture transaction data and enter them in the computer system. It is triggered by a business activity of the entity's organization. Data collection is based on each activity, the resources affecting it and the people involved in each activity. For example, the revenue cycle transaction activities (for either for cash or on credit), may provide useful data for collection about a sales transaction. Traditionally, a **source document** can provide the transaction data about the business activities which can be captured at source as input to the computer. **Table 2.1** lists some common transaction cycle activities and the associated source documents for capturing data about that event.

Table 2.1 Common Business Activities and Source Documents

Business Activity	Source Document
Sales/Revenue Cycle	
Customer order	Sales invoice/ sales order
Cash received	Goods despatch note
Deposit cash receipts	Remittance advice note
Bank-in-slip	Credit note
Purchasing Cycle	
Order items	Purchase requisition/Purchase order
Receive goods	Delivery note
Purchase of inventory	Purchase invoice
Make payment	Cheque/Electronic fund transfer

Second step in processing input is to ensure captured data are accurate and complete. Use of **source data automation devices** such as ATMs used by banks. Point of sale (POS), Bar code scanners in retail supermarkets or warehouses. Data input screens will list all the data user needs to enter. Users can improve control either by using **pre-numbered** source documents or by having the system automatically assign a **sequential number** to each new transaction. Pre-numbering simplifies verifying that all transactions have been recorded and that none of the documents has been misplaced. Imagine trying to balance a chequebook if the cheques were not pre-numbered.

Third step in the processing input is to make sure company policies are followed, such as verifying or approving a transaction. Such **internal checks** serve as part of internal audit procedures. For example, your company would not want to sell goods to a customer who was not paying the invoiced amount or to sell an item for immediate delivery that was out of stock. These problems are prevented by programming the system to check a customer's **credit limit** and payment records, as well as inventory status before confirming a customer sale on credit.

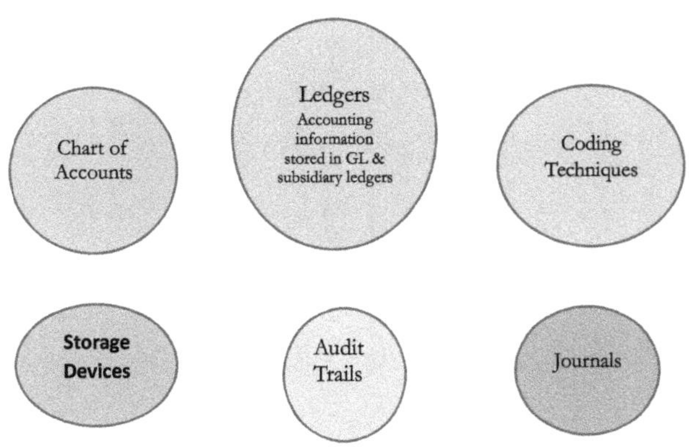

Figure 2.3 Data Storage Concepts

Data Storage

A company's data are one of its important resources. To function e to affectively, an organization must have ready and easy access to its data. Therefore, accountants or accounts preparers need to understand how data are organized and stored in an AIS and how they can be accessed. In essence, they need to know how to manage data for maximum corporate use. Just imagine how difficult it would be hard to read a textbook if it were not organized into chapters, sections, paragraphs, and sentences. Now imagine how hard it would be for a company to find an invoice if all documents were randomly dumped into file cabinets. That is why information in an AIS is organized for easy and efficient access and retrieval.

General Ledger

A ledger that contains summary-level Data for every asset, liability, equity, revenue, and expense account of the organization.

Subsidiary ledger

A ledger used to record detailed data for a general ledger with many individual subaccounts, such as accounts receivable, inventory, accounts payable.

Coding Techniques

Using coding techniques to systematically assign numbers or letters to items to classify and organize them.

Sequence codes

Items are numbered consecutively so that gaps in the sequence code indicate missing items that should be investigated. Example include pre-numbered cheques, invoices, and purchase orders, etc.

Block codes

Block of numbers that are reserved for specific categories of data, thereby helping to organize the data. An example, the following numbers are reserved for major products categories: of:

Product Code	Product Type
100000 - 199999	Electronic range
200000 - 299999	Refrigerator
300000 - 399999	Washer
400000 - 499999	Dryer

Another example is a chart of accounts. Other examples include ledger account numbers (blocked by account type), customer numbers (blocked by region, employee numbers (blocked by departments).

Control Account

The **general leger account corresponding to a subsidiary ledger is called a control** account which helps to maintain the accuracy of AIS data. It summarizes the total amounts recorded in a subsidiary ledger. For example, the accounts receivable control account in the GL represents the total amount owed by all customers (trade debtors). The balances in the accounts receivable subsidiary ledger indicates the amount owed by each specific customer.

Chart of accounts

A listing of all the numbers assigned to Statement of Financial Position(B/sheet) and Statement of Comprehensive Income accounts. The account numbers allow transaction data to be coded, classified, and entered into proper accounts. They also facilitate financial statements and reports preparation because data stored in individual accounts can be easily be **summarized for presentation.**

A chart of accounts is tailored to the nature and purpose of an organization. For example, the chart of accounts for a trading company indicates that it is a limited liability company, incorporated in Malaysia.

In contrast, a partnership would include separate capital and drawing accounts for each partner, instead of share capital and retained earnings. A retail trading company has only one type of general ledger inventory account. A manufacturing firm, in contrast, would have separate GL accounts for raw materials, work-in-progress, and finished goods inventories.

Group codes

Two or more subgroups of digits that are used to code an item. A group code is often used in conjunction with a block code. If a company uses a seven-digit product code number, the group coding technique might be applied as follows:

Digit Position	Meaning
1-2	Product line, size, style
3	Colour
4-5	Year of manufacture
6-7	Optional feature

Mnemonic codes

Letters and numbers are interspersed to identify an item. The mnemonic code is derived from the description of the item and is usually easy to memorize. For example, Dry300W05 could represent a low end (300), white (W) dryer (Dry) made by Samsung.

Journals

Transaction data are often recorded in a journal before they are entered (posted into a ledger). A journal entry shows the accounts and amounts to be debited and credited.

General Journal

A journal used to record infrequent or non-routine transactions, such as hire-purchase transactions, loan repayments and end-of-period adjusting entries and closing entries.

Specialized Journal

A journal used to record a large number of repetitive transactions such as credit sales, credit purchases, cash receipts and cash disbursements.

Table 2.2 appended below shows the chart of accounts for a typical trading Company. Each account number is based on three digits. The **first digit** represents the major account category and indicates where it appears on the company's financial statements. Thus, all current assets are numbered in the 100s, non-current assets are numbered in the 200s, and so on.

(See below for continuation)

Figure 2.2 shows how the double-entry accounting works for sales credit transactions. First, each credit sales is recorded in the sales journal. Then each journal entry is posted to the appropriate customer's account in the accounts receivable subsidiary ledger (note the arrow linking the double-entry posting) periodically, the total of all sales journal entries is posted to the both the Accounts Receivable and the Credit Sales GL accounts.
See **Chapter 5** on Sales and Receivables.

The **second digit** represents the primary financial subaccounts within each category. Again the accounts are assigned numbers to match the order of their appearance in financial statements. Thus, account 102 represents accounts receivable, and account 125 represents bank account. The **third digit** identifies the specific account to which the transaction data will be posted. For example, account 501 relates to cash sales and account 502 relates to credit sales.

Subsidiary ledger accounts often have longer account codes than GL accounts. Each account receivable will have a seven digit code. The first three digits are 102, the code for accounts receivable. The next four digits can identify up to 10, 000 individual customers.

Gaps created in the chart of accounts allows for additional accounts. For example, when the company has excess cash to invest in marketable securities, a new GL account can be created and assigned the number 116. The chart of accounts is expandable as each accounts receivable will have a seven-digit code that can represent each new store in the chain when these stores are opened in the future. It is also easier to track items in each store.

Table 2.2 Sample Chart of Accounts for a Retail Trading Company

Account Code	Account Particulars	Account Code	Account Particulars
100-199	**Current assets**	**400-499**	**Equity**
101	Inventory	400	Share capital
102	Accounts receivable	405	Retained earnings
105	Allowance for doubtful debts		
107	Notes receivable		
110	Sundry debtors		
112	Deposit - rent	**500-599**	**Revenues**
114	Deposit – utilities	501	Cash sales
118	Prepayment – insurance	502	Credit sales
120	Tax recoverable	510	Sales returns

125 Bank current account – 1
126 Bank current account – 2
130 Petty cash

200-299 Non-current assets

200 Land
210 Buildings
212 Accumulated depreciation – Buildings
215 Equipment
217 Accumulated depreciation - Equipment
218 Accumulated impairment loss - Equipment
220 Furniture and fixtures
222 Accumulated depreciation – F&F
223 Accumulated impairment – F&F
225 Motor vehicles
226 Accumulated depreciation
227 Accumulated impairment loss
230 Other assets

300-399 Liabilities

300 Accounts payable
310 Salaries payable
320 EPF payable
330 Employees' income tax payable
340 Rent payable
350 Electricity charges accrued
355 Water charges accrued
36
0 Accrued interest payable
370 Income tax payable
375 Sales tax due to Customs & Excise
380 Other sundry creditors
390 Bank term loan
395 Hire-purchase creditor
396 HP interest suspense account

512 Discounts received
515 Interest received
520 Other income
525 Miscellaneous income

600-799 Expenses

600 Purchases
610 Salaries and allowances
612 Commission expense
614 EPF contribution
616 Rent of premises
618 General expenses
620 Insurance
625 Vehicle repairs and maintenance
630 Office upkeep
635 Hire-purchase interest
640 Interest on term loan
650 Bad debts written-off (Irrecoverable debts)
655 Allowance for doubtful accounts
660 Opening Inventory
665 Freight charges
670 Transportation and handling charges
675 Travelling expenses
680 Entertainment expenses
685 Discount allowed
690 Medical expenses
701 Depreciation – Building
702 Depreciation - Equipment
703 Depreciation - F & F
704 Depreciation - Vehicles
710 Impairment loss
715 Income tax expense

900-999 Summary Accounts

Figure 2.2 Recording and Posting a Credit Sale

SALE JOURNAL **Page 5**

Date	Invoice Number	Account Name	Account Number	Folio	Amount
Nov 15	00151	Klinik Kesihatan Titiwangsa	102-035	√	785.50
15	00152	Pearl View Hotel	102-125	√	1, 250.50
15	00153	KL International Airport	102-337	√	4, 580.00
15	00154	Ng. Construction Sdn Bhd	102-085	√	3, 665.00
15	00155	Ritz Trading	102-205	√	2, 390.00
				Total Sales	12, 671.00

GENERAL LEDGER

Accounts Receivable **Account No: 102**

Date	Description	Folio	Debit	Credit	Balance
Nov 14					**85, 895**
14	Sales	SJ4	12, 550		98, 445
14	Collections	CB9		25, 675	72, 770
15	Sales	SJ5	12, 671		85, 441

GENERAL LEDGER

Credit Sales **Account No: 502**

Date	Description	Folio	Debit	Credit	Balance
Nov 14					275, 580
14	Sales			12, 550	288, 130
15	Sales			12, 671	300, 801

ACCOUNTS RECEIVABLE SUBSIDIARY LEDGER (TRADE DEBTORS' LEDGER)

Customer's Name: Ritz Trading
Account No. 102-205

Address: No. 808, Jalan Kewajipan
Subang Jaya, 47600
Selangor.

Date	Description	Folio	Debit	Credit	Balance
Oct 15	Sales	SJ3	4, 350		4, 350
Nov 03	Payment			4, 350	0
Nov 15	Sales	SJ5	2, 390		2, 390

Amount of individual sales posted to trade debtors' ledger (Subsidiary ledger)

Audit Trail

Figure 2.2 shows how the posting folios and document numbers provide an audit trail. An audit trail is a traceable path of a transaction through a data processing system from point of origin to final output, or backward from final output to point of origin. It is used to check the accuracy and validity of ledger postings and to trace changes in general ledger accounts from the opening balance to their closing balance. Observe that the SJ5 posting folio for the RM 12, 671 credit to the sales account in the GL refers to page 5 of the sales journal, it is possible to verify that RM 12, 671 represents the total credit sales recorded in November 15. Similarly, the posting folio for the RM 2, 390 debit to the Ritz Trading's account in the subsidiary accounts receivable ledger also refer to page 5 of the sales journal as the source of that entry. Furthermore, note that the sales journal lists the invoice numbers for each individual entry. This provides the means for locating and examining the appropriate source documents in order to verify that the transaction occurred and it was recorded accurately.

Figure 2.3 Data Storage Elements

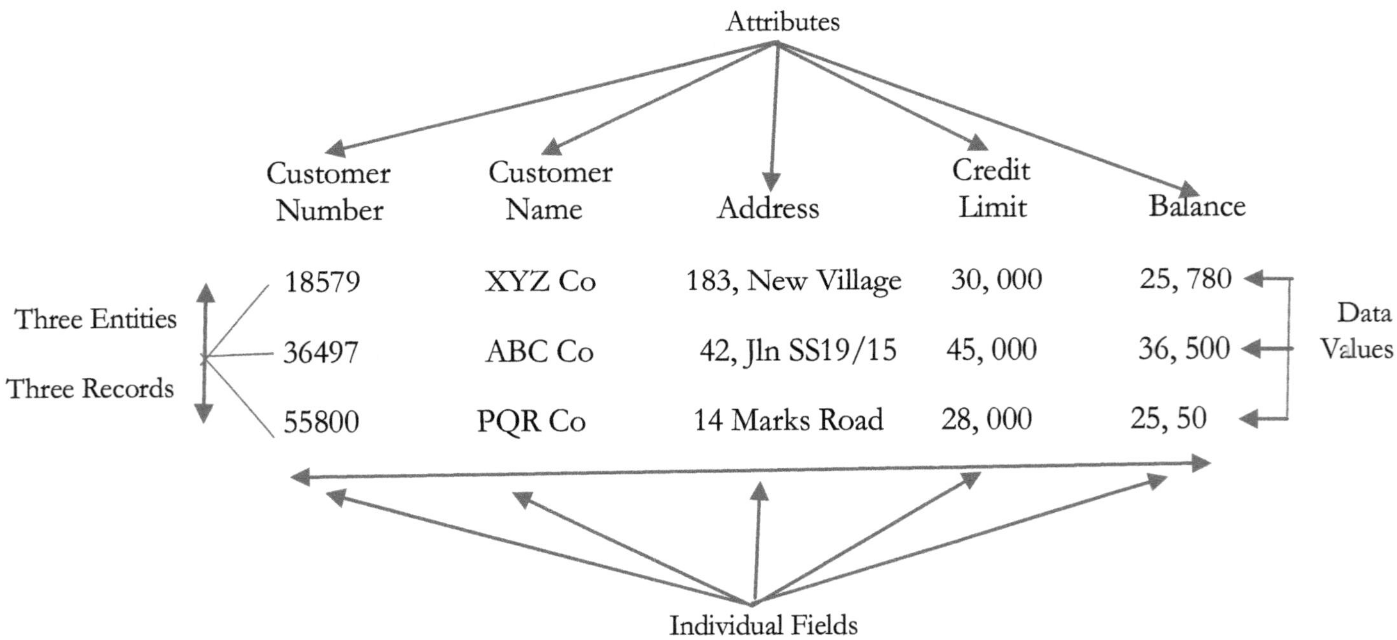

This accounts receivable **file** stores information about three separate **entities**; XYZ Co, ABC Co, and PQR Co. As a result, there are three **records** in the file. Five separate **attributes** are used to describe each customer: customer number, address, credit limit, and balance. There are, therefore, five separate **fields** in each record. Each field contains a **data value** that describes an attribute of a particular entity (customer). For example, the data value 18579 is the customer number for the XYZ Co

Computer-Based Storage Concepts

Entity

The item about which information is stored in a record. Examples include an employee number, an inventory item, and a customer.

Attributes

The properties, identifying numbers, and characteristics of interest of an entity that is stored in a database. Examples are Employee number, pay rate, name, and address.

Field

The portion of a data record where the data value for particular attribute is stored. For example, in a spreadsheet each row might represent a customer and each column is an attribute of the customer. Each cell in a spreadsheet is a field.

Record

A set of fields whose data values describe specific attributes of an entity, such as all payroll data relating to a single employee.

An example is a row in a spreadsheet.

Data Value

The actual value stored in a field. It describes a particular attribute of an entity. For example, the customer name field would contain "CBA Co" if that company was a customer.

File

A set of logically related records such as payroll records of all employees.

Master File

A permanent file of records that stores cumulative data about an organization. As transactions take place, individual records within a master file are updated to keep them current. An example is a master file, like a general ledger in a manual AIS, stores cumulative information about an organization's financial position and financial performance.

Transaction File

A file that contains records of business transactions that occur during a specific financial period. A transaction file is conceptually Similar to a journal in a manual AIS. For example, ABC Co will have a daily sales transaction file and a cash receipts file both of which will update individual customer account balances in the customer master file. Transaction files are not permanent and may not be needed beyond the current accounting period. However, they are usually maintained for a specified period for back-up purposes.

Database

A set of interrelated, centrally coordinated data files that are stored with as little data redundancy as possible. A database consolidates records previously stored in separate files into a common pool and serves a variety of users in the system and data processing applications. Databases were developed to address the proliferation of master files.

Data Processing

Once business activity data have been entered into the system, they must be processed to keep the databases current. The four different types of data processing activities, referred to as CRUD, are as follows:

1. Creating new data records
2. Reading, retrieving, or viewing existing data.
3. Updating previously stored data.
4. **Figure 2.4** depicts the steps required to update an accounts receivable record with a sales transaction. The two records are matched using the account number. The sale amount of RM 360 is added to the account balance (RM 1, 500) to get a new current balance (RM 1, 860).
5. Deleting data, such as purging the vendor master file of all vendors the company no longer does business with.

Batch processing

Updating done periodically, such as daily, is referred to as **batch processing.** Although batch processing is cheaper and more efficient, the data is current and accurate only immediately after processing. For that reason, batch processing is used only for applications, such as payroll, that do not need frequent updating and that naturally occur or are processed at fixed time periods.

Online, real-time processing

Most companies up-date each transaction as it occurs, referred to as **Online, real-time processing** because it ensures that stored Information is always current, thereby increasing its decision-making usefulness. It is also more accurate because data input errors can be corrected in real time or refused. It also provides **significant competitive advantages**. For example, **FedEx** updated its **mission statement** to include the *phrase "Positive control of each package will be maintained by utilizing real-time electronic tracking and tracing systems."* With FedEx's system, employees and customers can track the exact location of each package and estimate its arrival time.

A combination of the two approaches is online batch processing, where transaction data are entered and edited as they occur and stored for later processing. Batch processing and online, real-time processing are summarized in **Figure 2.5.**

Information Output

The final step in the data processing cycle is **information output**. When displayed on a monitor, output is referred to as "soft copy." When printed on paper, it is referred to as "hard copy". The final product of any system is **information.** Information is usually presented in one of three forms:

i. A document
ii. A report; or
iii. A query.

Documents

These are records of transaction or other company data. Some, such as cheques and invoices, are transmitted to external parties.

Others, such as receiving reports and purchase requisitions, are used internally. Documents can be printed out, or they can be stored as electronic images in a computer. For example, Toys 'R' Us uses electronic data interchange to communicate with its suppliers. Every year it processes over half a million invoices electronically, thereby eliminating paper documents and dramatically reducing costs and errors. This has resulted in higher profits and more accurate information.

Reports

System output organized in a meaningful fashion, that is used by employees to control operational activities, and by managers to make decisions and to formulate strategies, and by investors and creditors to understand a company's business activities. External users need reports to evaluate company profitability performance, judge creditworthiness, or comply with regulatory requirements. Some reports, such as financial statements and sales analyses are produced on a regular basis. Others are produced on an exception basis to call attention to unusual conditions. For example, a company could have its system produce a report to indicate when product returns exceed a certain percentage of sales. Reports can also be produced on demand. For example, a sales manager could produce a report to identify the salesperson who sold the most items during a promotional period. The need for reports should be periodically assessed, because they are often prepared long after they are needed, thus wasting time, money and resources. For example, NCR Corporation reduced the number of reports from 1, 200 to just over 100.

Query

A database **query is a request to provide the information needed to deal with a problem or answer a question that need rapid action. The specified information is retrieved, displayed by print, or analysed as requested. Repetitive queries are often developed by information systems specialists. One-time queries are often developed by users such as an audit query raised by auditors to clarify matters on internal controls over the cash payment cycle. Some companies, such as Walmart, allow suppliers to access their databases to help them better serve Walmart's needs. Suppliers can gauge how well a product is selling in every Walmart store and maximise sales by stocking and promoting items that are selling well.**

Figure 2.4 The Accounts Receivable File Update Process

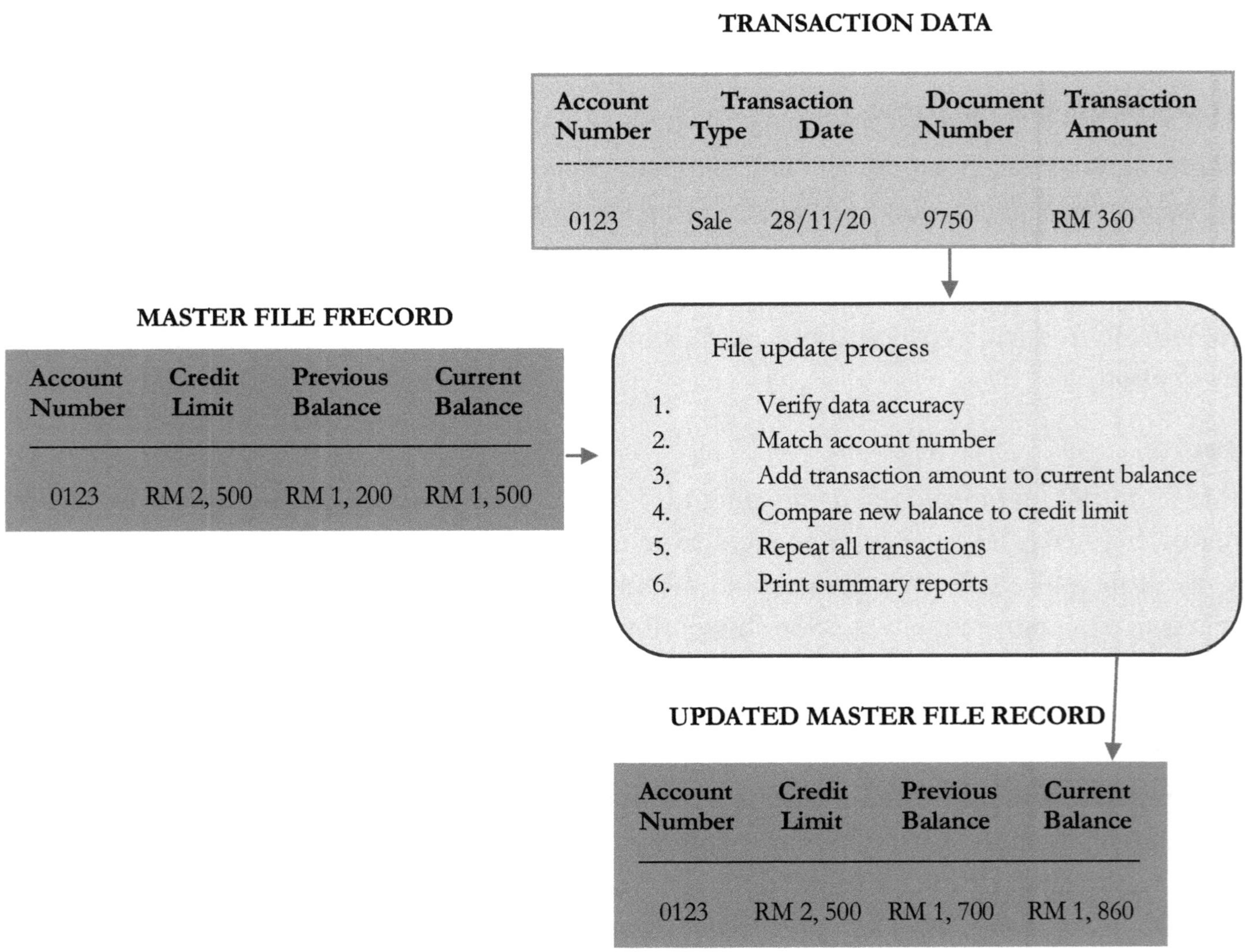

Figure 2.5 Batch and Online Processing

Batch Processing

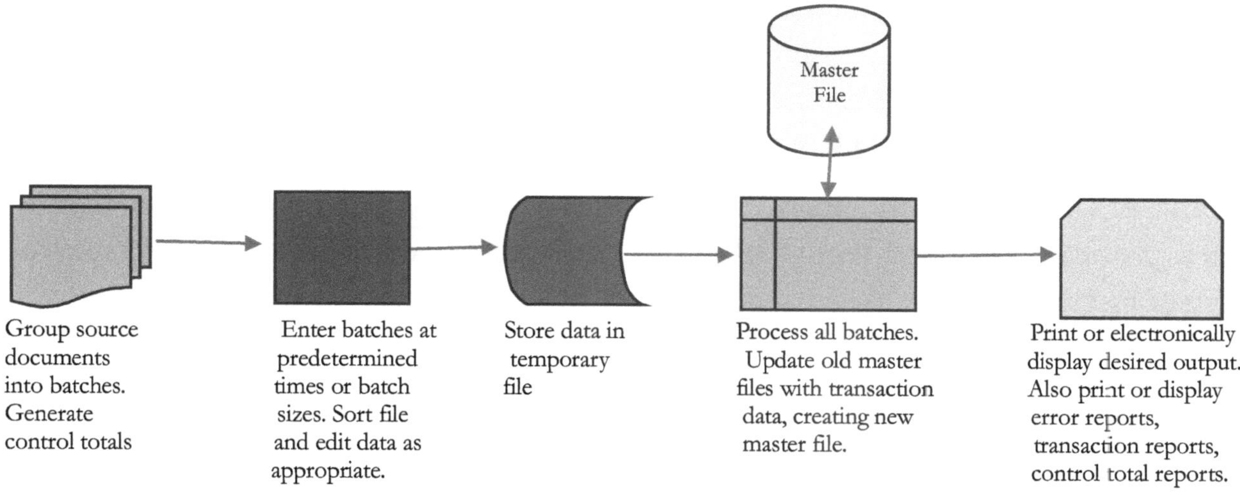

Online Batch Processing

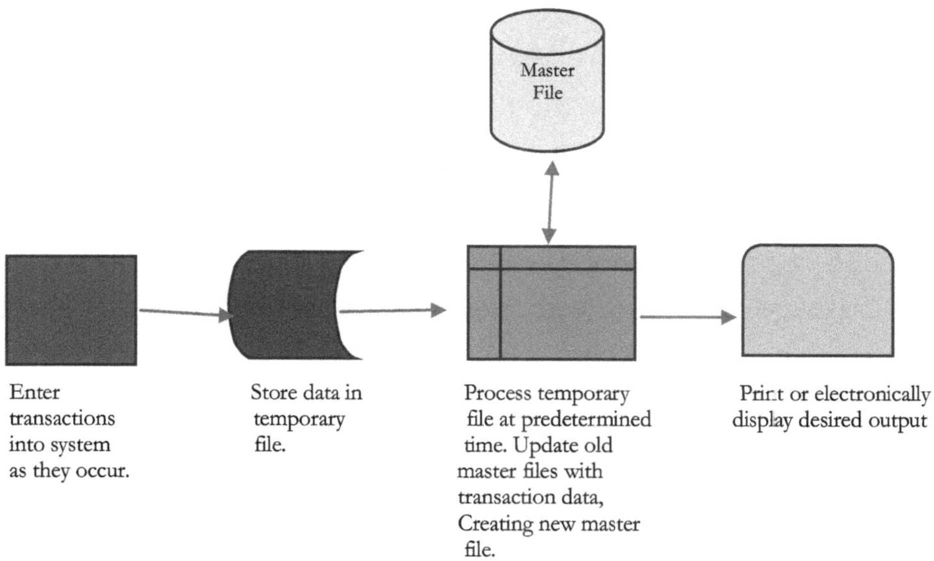

Online Real-Time Processing

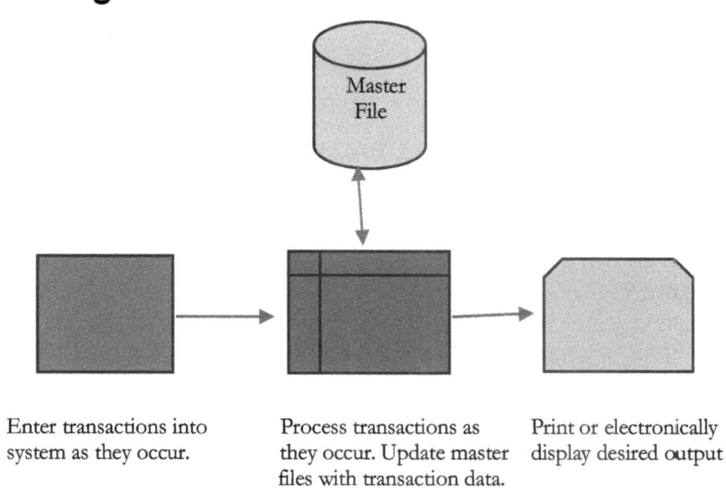

Enterprise Resource Planning (ERP) Systems

Traditionally, the AIS has been referred to as a transaction processing system because its only concern was financial data and accounting transactions. For example, when a sale took place, the AIS would record a journal entry showing only the date of the sale, a debit to either cash or accounts receivable, and a credit to sales. Other potentially useful nonfinancial information about the sale, such as the time of day it occurred, would traditionally be collected and processed outside the AIS. Consequently, many organizations developed additional information systems to collect, process, store, and report information not contained in the AIS. Unfortunately, the existence of multiple systems creates numerous problems that only results in duplication across systems but also can lead to discrepancies if data are changed in one system but not in others. The main problem is that it is difficult to integrate data from various systems.

Enterprise Resource Planning (ERP) systems overcome these problems or anomalies as they integrate all aspects of a company's operational activities such as accounting, finance, customer relationship management (sales & marketing, services and call centre support), human resources, manufacturing, inventory management and others into one system which a traditional standard AIS would not be able to do so. Most large and many medium-sized organizations use ERP systems to coordinate and manage their data, business processes, and resources. The ERP system collects, processes, and stores data and provides the information managers and external parties need to access the company.

As shown in Figure 2.6, a properly configured ERP system uses a centralized database to share information across business processes and coordinate activities. This is important because an activity that is part of one business process often triggers a complex series of activities throughout many parts of the organization. For example, a customer order may necessitate scheduling additional production to meet the increased demand. This may trigger an order to purchase additional raw materials. It may also be necessary to schedule overtime or hire temporary assistance from employees. A well-designed ERP systems therefore provide management with easy access to up-to-date information about all of these activities in order to plan, control, and evaluate the organization's business processes more effectively.

ERP systems are modular with each module using best business practices to automate a standard business process. This modular design allows businesses to add or delete modules as needed. ERP systems are complex and a costly affair that would involve more than RM 5 million to RM 10 million for midsized companies. A critical requirement is that it requires conscious effort and involvement by top management commitment to and support for the necessary changes to increase the chances of success.

Another consideration is the importance of sound internal controls in the ERP system which cannot be over emphasised. The integrated nature of ERP system means that unless every data item is validated and checked for accuracy at the time of initial entry, errors will automatically propagate throughout the system. Thus, data entry controls and access controls are essential. Most managers and employees see and have access to only a small portion of the system. This segregation of duties provides sound internal control. It is important to separate responsibility for custody of assets, authorisation of activities that affect those assets, and recording information about activities and the status of organizational assets.

An ERP system with its centralized database, provides both significant advantages:

- An ERP provides an integrated, enterprise –wide, single view of the organization's data and financial situation. Sorting all corporate information in a single database breaks down barriers between departments and streamlines the flow of information.
- Downloading data from one system to another is no longer needed.
- Management gains greater visibility into every area of the enterprise and greater monitoring capabilities.
- Employees are more productive and efficient because they can quickly gather data from both inside and outside their own department.
- The organization gains better access control. An ERP can consolidate multiple permissions and security models into a single data access structure.
- Procedures and reports are standardised across business units. This standardisation can be especially valuable with mergers and acquisitions because an ERP system can replace the different systems with a single, unified system.
- Customer service improves because employees can quickly access orders, available inventory, shipping information, and past customer transaction details.
- Manufacturing plants receive new orders in real time, and the automation of manufacturing processes leads to increased productivity.

ERP systems also have significant disadvantages:

- Cost. ERP hardware, software, and consulting costs range from RM 10 million to RM 100 million and over for a big listed company and upgrades can cost similar amount. Midsized companies spend between RM 5 million and RM 20 million.
- Amount of time required. It can take several years to select and fully implement an ERP system, depending on business size, number of modules to be implemented, degree of customisation, the scope of change, and how well the customer takes ownership of the project. As a result, ERP implementations have a very high risk of project failure.
- Changes to business processes. Unless a company wants to spend time and money customising modules, they must adapt to standardised business processes as opposed to adapting the ERP package to existing company processes. The failure to map current business processes to existing ERP software is a main cause of ERP project failures.

- Complexity. This comes from integrating many different business activities and systems, each having different processes, business rules, data semantics, authorisation hierarchies, and decision centres.
- Resistance. Organizations that have multiple departments with separate resources, profit and loss, chains of command may believe that a single system has few benefits. It also takes considerable training and experience to use an ERP system effectively, and employee resistance is a major reason why many ERP implementations do not succeed. It is not easy to convince employees to change how they do their jobs, train them in new procedures, master the new system, and persuade them to share sensitive information. Resistance, and the blurring company boundaries, can cause problems with employee morale, accountability, lines of responsibility.

Reaping the potential benefits of ERP systems and mitigating their disadvantages requires conscious effort and involvement by top management. Top management's commitment to and support for the necessary changes greatly increase the chances of success.

Figure 2.6 Integrated ERP System

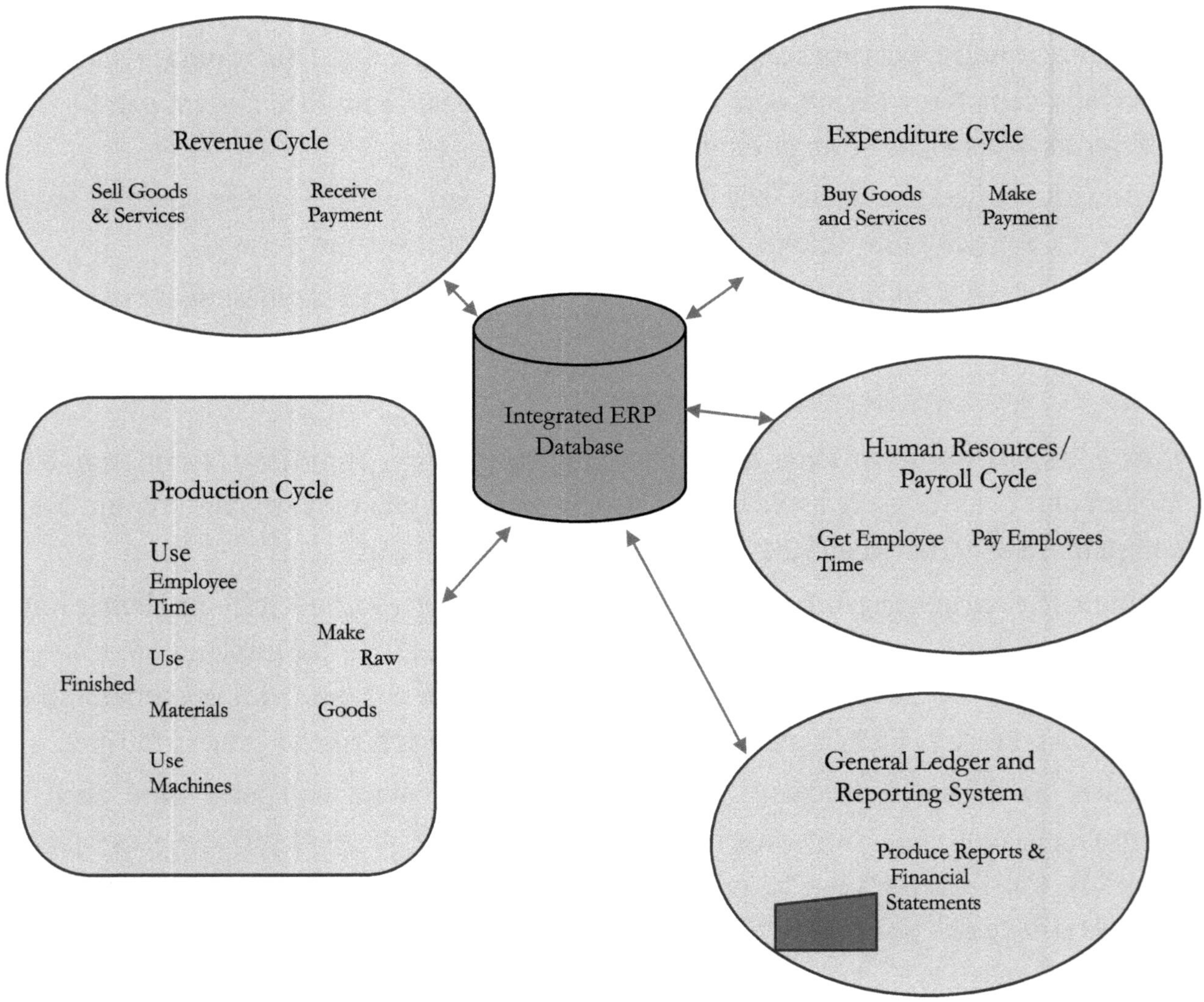

Acknowledgment

Chapter 3 contents on computerised accounting system have been more or less reproduced with some minor modifications with written permission from the publishers, Pearson, of a textbook, 'Accounting Information Systems' (14th Ed), authored by Marshall Romney and Paul John Steinbart. We gratefully acknowledge them for kindly consenting to peruse their material as part of one chapter in our textbook

Chapter Summary

- The computer based environment is one that uses an accounting information system (AIS) tailored to the needs of the organization. The **data processing cycle** and its role in organizing business activities and providing information to users is explained. It also explains how an organization captures and enter data about business activities into the entity's AIS and **how a company process data and transform it into useful and relevant information for decision making.** The data processing cycle involves four steps: data input, data storage, data processing and information output, all of which are discussed with the aid of illustrated tables and figures.
- Chapter 3 also discusses basic **data storage concepts and definitions** as it applies to the computerized accounting system, showing how data are stored for use. Finally, **information output** is discussed, including the different ways information is provided to users in the form of reports and financial statements.
- Some discussion is devoted on the role of the information system in modern organizations and introduces the concept of **an enterprise resource planning (ERP) system**. An ERP can help **integrate** all aspects of a company's operations with its traditional AIS. This section of Part 2 also highlights very briefly on significant advantages of an ERP as well as challenges that must be overcome to implement an ERP system.

Key Terms

Data processing cycle.
Source documents
Turnaround documents
Source data automation.
General ledger
Online, real-time processing
Subsidiary ledger
Coding
Sequence code
Block code
Group code

Mnemonic code
Chart of accounts
General journal
Specialized journal
Audit trail
Entity
Control account
Field
Record
Data value
File

Master file
Transaction file
Database
Batch processing
Entity
Attributes
Document
Report
Query
Enterprise resource planning (ERP) system

Review Questions

Q1. What is the purpose of source documents? What controls are embedded in source documents? Give two examples of source documents.

Q2. Discuss the guidelines for a better coding system. Explain why these guidelines are important, and what would happen if they are not met?

Q3. Some individuals argue that accountants should focus on producing financial statements and leave the design and production of managerial reports to information systems specialists. What are the advantages and disadvantages of following this advice?

To what extent should accountants be involved in producing reports that include more than just financial measures of performance? Why?

Q4. Give three examples each of the advantages and the disadvantages an ERP system with a centralized database. How you can increase the change of a successful ERP implementation?

Q5. Table 2-1 lists some of the source documents used in the revenue, expenditure, and human resource cycle. What kinds of input or output documents or forms would you find in the production cycle?

Q6. The operations performed on data to generate meaningful and relevant information are referred to collectively as the *data processing cycle*.

a. What are the four steps involved in the data processing cycle? and

b. Briefly outline on the common transactional cycle activities.

Q7. Write short notes on

a. Source documents

b. Turnaround documents

c. Coding techniques, giving two examples for each coding technique

d. Chart of accounts

e. Data storage elements

Q8. Distinguish between *a file, a master file, a transaction file, and database*

Q9. Explain what you understand by these data processing terms, *batch processing, online batch processing, and online real-time processing?*

Q10. Describe the four different types of data processing activities, referred to as CRUD.

Q11. Explain the importance of *an audit trail* through a data processing system.

Q12. Identify and describe the three forms of information output.

Q13. Write brief notes on the usefulness and importance of the ERP system. In your notes, outline at least two advantages and two disadvantages of the ERP system.

Problems and Assignments

Q6. An audit trail enables a person to trace a source document to its ultimate effect on the financial statements or work back from financial statement amounts to source documents. Describe in detail the audit trail for the following:

i. Purchase of inventory (or stocks)

ii. Sales of inventory

iii. Employee payroll

Q7. Your IT company deals with in laptops, desktops, and servers. You also sell computer parts like hard drives and motherboards.

Design a coding scheme for your company.

Q8. The chart of accounts must be tailored to an organization's specific needs. Discuss how the chart of accounts for the following organizations would differ from the one presented as a sample for a retail trading company in Table 2-2 (see earlier page).

a. University

b. Bank

c. Government agency

d. Manufacturing company

e. Expansion of the retail trading company to a chain of two stores

Q9. Raju Pillay is the controller of SDC, an automotive parts manufacturing firm. Its four major operating divisions are heat treating, extruding, small parts stamping and machining. Last year's sales from each division ranged from RM 150, 000 to RM 3 million. Each division is physically and managerially independent, except for the constant surveillance of Chet Sam, the firm's founder. The AIS for each division evolved according to the needs and abilities of its accounting staff. Pillay is the first controller to have responsibility for overall financial management. Sam wants Pillay to improve the AIS before he retires in a few years so that it will be easier to monitor division performance. Pillay decides to redesign the financial reporting system to include the following features:

- It should give managers uniform, timely, and accurate reports of business activity. Monthly reports should be uniform across divisions and be completed by the fifth day of the following month to provide enough time to take corrective actions to affect the next month's performance. Company-wide financial reports should be available at the same time.
- Reports should provide a basis for measuring the return on investment for each division. Thus, in addition to revenue and expense accounts, reports should show assets assigned to each division.
- The system should generate meaningful budget data for planning and decision-making purposes. Budgets should reflect managerial responsibility and show costs for major product groups.

Pillay believes that a new chart of accounts is required to accomplish these goals. He wants to divide financial statement accounts into major categories, such as assets, liabilities, and equity.

He does not foresee a need for more ten control accounts within each of these categories. From his observations to date, 100 subsidiary accounts are more than adequate for each control account.

No division has more than five major product groups. Pillay foresees a maximum of six cost centres within any product group, including both operating and non-operating groups. Pillay views general divisional costs as a non-revenue producing product group. He also estimates that 44 expense accounts plus 12 specific variance accounts would be adequate.

Required

Design a chart of accounts for SDC. Explain how you structured the chart of accounts to meet the company's needs and operating characteristics. Keep total account code length to a minimum, while still satisfying all of Raju Pillay's desires.

(CMA Examination, adapted)

Note to students attempting Q 9. Some cautionary advice to students from the author.

The entire case study question tests students' ability to device a chart of accounts for an automotive spare and accessories manufacturing firm. Do not let the details of this case to daunt you. Basically the examiner wants you to design and prepare a chart of accounts to suit SDC's divisions, all these divisions having a common format for a set of accounts to be designated. Follow the textbook example given in Table 2 but adapt and modify the changes required based on SDC requirements.

There is no one single correct answer to this question. Students should research a chart of accounts from otheravailable sources that could be relevant and appropriate in format.

Multiple Choice Questions

Section 1

Q1. Which of the following is NOT a step in the data processing cycle?

a. data collection.
c. data storage
b. data input.
d. data processing

Q2. All of the information (name, GPA, degree, etc) a particular student is stored in the same

a. file
c. attribute
b. record
d. field

Q3. When items are numbered consecutively to account for all of them, and the missing items

a. sequence code
c. group code
b. block code
d. mnemonic

Q4. Which of the following is most likely to be a general ledger control account?

a. accounts receivable
c. prepaid rent
b. petty cash
d. retained earnings

Q5. Which of the following documents is most likely to be used in the expenditure cycle?

a. sales orders
c. receiving report
b. credit note
d. job time sheet

Q6. The portion of a data record where the data value for a particular attribute is stored is

a. an entity
c. a field
b. an attribute
d. a record

Q7. How does the chart of accounts list general ledger accounts?

a. alphabetical order
c. the order in which they appear in financial statements
b. chronological order
d. size order

Q8. Which of the following is NOT an advantage of an ERP system?

a. better access control
c. improved monitoring capabilities
b. standardization of procedures and reports
d. simplicity and reduced costs

Q9. Records of company data sent to an external party and then returned to the system as input are called

a. turnaround documents
b. source data automation documents
c. source documents
d. external input documents

Q10. What kind of processing involves entering transaction data and editing them as they occur?

a. batch processing
b. online batch processing
c. online real-time processing
d. none of the above

Definitions

Q1. You are required to MATCH the following terms with their definitions.

Terms	Definitions
a. data processing cycle	1. Contains summary - level data for every asset, liability, equity, revenue, and expenses account
b. source documents.	2. Items are numbered consecutively to account all items; missing items cause a gap in the numerical sequence
c. turnaround documents.	3. Path of a transaction through a data processing system from point of origin to final output, or backward from final output to point of origin.
d. source data automation.	4. List of general ledger account numbers; allows transaction data to be coded, classified, and entered into proper accounts; facilitates preparation of financial statements and reports.
e. general ledger.	5. Contents of a specific field, such as "Thamby" in name field
f. subsidiary ledger	6. Portion of a data record that contains the data value for a particular attribute, like a cell in a spreadsheet.
g. control account	7. Company data sent to an external party and then returned to the system as input
h. coding	8. Used to record infrequent or non-routine transactions
i. sequence code	9. Characteristics of interest that need to be stored
j. block code.	10. The steps a company must follow to efficiently and effectively process data about its transactions
k. group code	11. An item about which information is stored
l. mnemonic.	12. Stores cumulative information about an organization; like a ledger in a manual AIS
m. chart of accounts.	13. Contains detailed data for any general account with many individual subaccounts
n. general journal.	14. Contains records of individual business transactions that occur during a specific time period

o. specialized journal.	15. Updating each transaction as it occurs
p. audit trail	16. Devices that capture transaction data in machine-readable form at the time and place of their origin
q. entity	17. Used to record large numbers of repetitive Transactions
r. attribute	18. Set of interrelated centrally coordinated files
s. field	19. Two or more subgroups of digits are used to code items
t. record	20. Updating done periodically, such as daily
u. data value	21. Systematic assignment of numbers or letters to items to classify and organize them
v. master file	22. Letters and numbers derived from the item description, are interspersed to identify items; usually easy to memorize
w. transaction file	23. Initial record of a transaction that takes place-usually recorded on pre-printed forms or formatted screens
x. database	24. Fields containing data about entity attributes like a row in in a spreadsheet
y. batch processing	25. Sets of numbers are reserved for special categories of data
z. online, real-time processing	26. The general ledger account corresponding to a subsidiary ledger, where the sum of all subsidiary ledger entries should equal the amount in the general ledger account

Q2. For each of the following scenarios, identify which data processing method (batch or online, real-time) would be most appropriate.

a. Make an airline reservation
b. Register for a university course
c. Prepare biweekly payroll cheques
d. Process an order through an e-commerce website
e. Prepare a daily bank deposit
f. Preparation of customer bills by a local utility
g. Accumulate daily costs from a production run of a single automobile part
h. Identify the replacement drill bit size for a bit broken during a production run

Q3. Which of the following actions update a master file and which would be stored as a record in a transaction file?

a. Update customer address change
b. Update unit price information
c. Record daily sales
d. Record payroll cheques
e. Change employee pay rates
f. Record production variances
g. Record sale commissions
h. Change employee office location

i. Update accounts payable balance
j. Change customer credit limit
k. Change supplier payment discount terms
l. Record purchases

Acknowledgement

The contents of this section, part 2 of Chapter 3 on computerized accounting system were reproduced, more or less, with the kind written permission from the publishers (Pearson) of the textbook – Accounting Information Systems, 14th Edition by the authors, ***Messrs. Marshall B. Romney and Paul John Steinbart.***

We are most grateful that they have consented to our request to use only relevant material from their source specific to our textbook requirements on financial accounting.

Fair trade is almost always a sneaky way of objecting to free trade.

— Jagdish Bhagvati, University Professor of economics and law at Columbia University

Chapter 4

Learning Objectives

After you have studied this chapter, you should be able to:

Understand the importance of the four primary financial statements and the notes accompanying the financial statements
Understand the elements making up the financial statements and their definitions
Know the difference between financial performance and financial position
Know the accounting equation and understand what it represents
Know profits, dividends and reserves all relate to equity
Know the formats of the statement of financial position, the statement of comprehensive income and statement of changes in equity
Know which financial statements relate to financial position, financial performance and equity
Know cash flow statement and the three type of activities that are reported in the cash flow statement
Know the links to the financial statements
Know that the notes add more information to the financial statements and which forms an integral part of the financial statements
Understand the use of financial information that for decision making
Know the limitations of financial statements

Financial Statements – Part 1

1. Scope

Chapter 4 is the first part that introduces the **four primary financial statements and the notes** to the financial statements which form the basis of financial reporting in its entirety about the **entity's financial performance, financial position and the cash flow position for the accounting period reported**. Part 2 will be dealt in Chapter 23 where all the basic preparation in drawing up the financial statements are done in conformity with the accounting standards and the provisions of the Companies Act 2016.

Chapter 4 briefly discusses the various **elements that make-up the statutory financial statements** including their definitions. The discussion focuses on financial performance and financial position of a business entity. The **accounting equation** is briefly stated to show how assets are represented by equity and liabilities. **Equity** which defines shareholders' fund constitutes retained profits (earnings), dividend distribution, contributed share capital and other reserves. **Financial performance and financial position** including the **cash flows** are disclosed and explained with reference to the financial statements where they need to be interpreted by users of such reports.

An important feature of financial reporting is that the **financial notes amplify information** for the understanding and interpreting the financial statements. Furthermore, financial statements are prepared on an **historical cost basis** and therefore it could pose a limitation in the use of financial information for **decision making** purposes. Stakeholders and other users are interested in the entity's state of affairs. Students should know strategic decision making comes more in the realm of management (or managerial) accounting and corporate finance. In addition, **non-financial indicators** such as organization's quality performance and level of customer's satisfaction are revealed and neither does it indicate environmental or social issues and other public concerns. **Financial statements are general purpose documents**. The **annual report and accounts** of an organization's primary focus is about financial information critical for users of financial statements and therefore, sparingly economic and social agenda issues of importance is ommunicated in the report. However, the reported financial statements provide crucial information about the entity's operational performance for the period under review with the **accompanying notes** to **the accounts** making-up the necessary link for understanding and interpreting key facts and figures contained in the financial statements.

2. Financial Statements and Reports

The financial statements of a business entity are normally presented as four primary statements based on summarized accounting data. These are:

1. **Statement of Profit or Loss and other Comprehensive Income (Income Statement)**: which presents a business entity's total revenues and gains and total expenses and losses, resulting in net income or net profit for a specific period of time. When expenses exceed revenues, the result is a net loss.
2. **Statement of Financial Position (Balance Sheet)**: which reports the assets, liabilities and the shareholders' equity of a business entity at a specific date.
3. **A Statement of Changes in Equity (Retained Earnings Statement):** which summarizes the changes in retained earnings for a specific period of time.
4. **A Statement of Cash Flows:** which summarizes the cash flow position in terms of inflows (receipts) and outflows (payments) for a specific period of time.
5. **Notes to the Financial Statements:** The disclosure notes that accompany the financial statements form an integral part of the financial statements. These notes provide useful and essential information that should be read in conjunction with the items appearing in the financial statements.

Financial information as reported in the four primary statements with the accompanying disclosure notes are based on legal and statutory requirements. These explanatory notes comply with the requirements of the accounting standards that are enforced by the regulatory and conceptual frameworks which were discussed earlier in Chapter 1.

3. The Elements of Financial Statements

Business transactions are broadly classified into categories so that their financial effects are shown in the financial statements. These broad classes or categories are referred as *elements of financial statements*. These elements are the building blocks on which these statements are based. An important question to ask is, **what exactly are we accounting for?** In other words, **how do we arrive at the financial statements?** This calls for a system of measurement where the accountability process takes us through. The following pages deliberate this systematically by showing us how the accounting process is achieved.

The *Conceptual Framework* lays out these elements of financial statements as follows:

Elements of Financial Statements	
Measurement of financial position in	Measurement of financial performance in
Statement of financial position	Statement of profit or loss and other Comprehensive income
Assets	
Liabilities	**Income or Revenue and Gains**
Equity	**Expenses and losses**

A process of sub-classification usually takes place for presentation in the financial statements. For example, assets are classified by their nature or function in the business to identify relevant information for users to make informed decisions.

The *Conceptual Framework* also makes another statement that in order to fulfill the *objectives of financial reporting* requirements, there are some **fundamental assumptions** preparers of accounts need to adopt.

These assumptions are covered in Chapter1 and are based on the following two premises:

Firstly, that we prepare our financial statements on **accrual basis.** What this means that transactions and other economic events are recognized when they occur within the accounting period and not when cash is paid or received. The accrual basis of accounting is explained in Chapter 1.

Secondly, in measuring and reporting accounting information, another assumption we make is that the business entity will *continue in operational existence as a* **going concern** so that it can use the existing **financial assets** – land and buildings, plant and equipment, and other tangible assets including supplies and stock-in trade for its intended purposes. The entity has neither the intention nor the need to curtail the scale of its business operations in the near future unless business circumstances or conditions warrant it. Under the going concern basis of accounting, the entity is expected to derive economic benefits from the use of the assets beyond the current accounting period. Where an entity is not continuing its business, the accounting basis would be adopted differently from one that is going concern

4. Statement of Financial Position or Balance Sheet

The management of a business entity needs to know the company's strategic position and direction in order to achieve its corporate mission. That means obtaining, allocating and using its resources to create value and what the company's obligations to third parties are.

The statement of financial position (traditionally called 'Balance Sheet') represents **resources** on one side, the **assets** and **obligations** to outside parties on the other side, **liabilities to creditors and the shareholders' equity.**

Let's represent the **accounting equation** as follows:

Resources (assets of the firm)) = Obligations to outside parties (liabilities + shareholders' equity) (Shareholders' claims)

or

Assets – Liabilities = Net assets = Shareholders' equity (net worth)

In fact, the Statement of Financial Position (or Balance Sheet) is a snapshot of the financial status and position of a business entity at a given specific point in time. To arrive at this point, regular updating of the **accounting records or books of account** are required The composition of the financial position is illustrated in **Figure 4.1** below:

Figure 4.1 Financial position

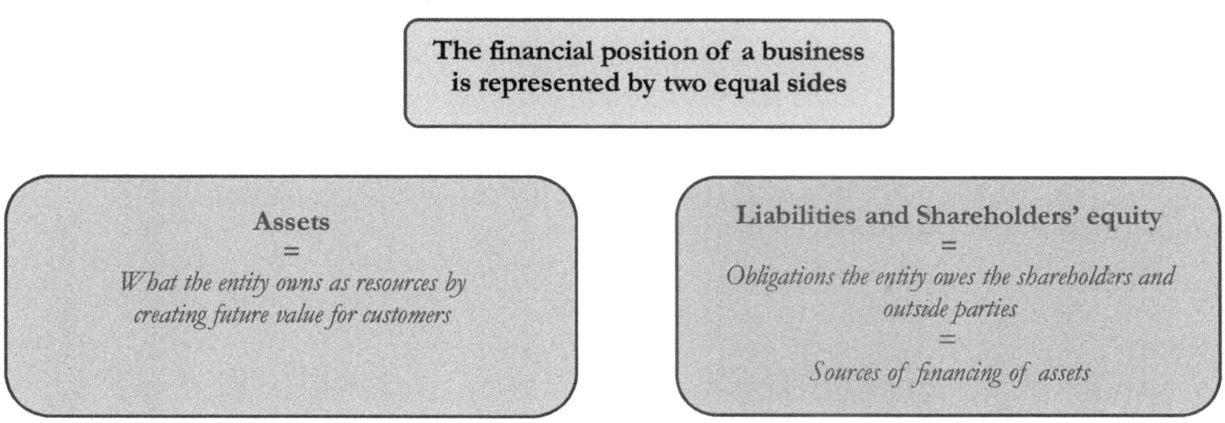

First of all, we need to **define** the three terms constituting the financial elements as listed below:

4.1 Assets

An asset is a ***resource*** *controlled by an entity as a result of past events and from which future economic benefits are expected to flow to the entity.*

Assets are usually deployed in business to generate an income stream in the production of goods and services for customers. Shown in **Figure 4.2,** are two main broad categories (or classification) of assets, *non-current assets* and *current assets*. We can define **non-current assets** as resources held on a long-term and are not supposed to be sold (or realized in cash) or potentially consumed in the normal operating cycle within the twelve months after the reporting period. **Current assets** are defined as resources potentially consumed or sold in their entirety within the normal operating period of one year.

Figure 4.2 Main categories of assets

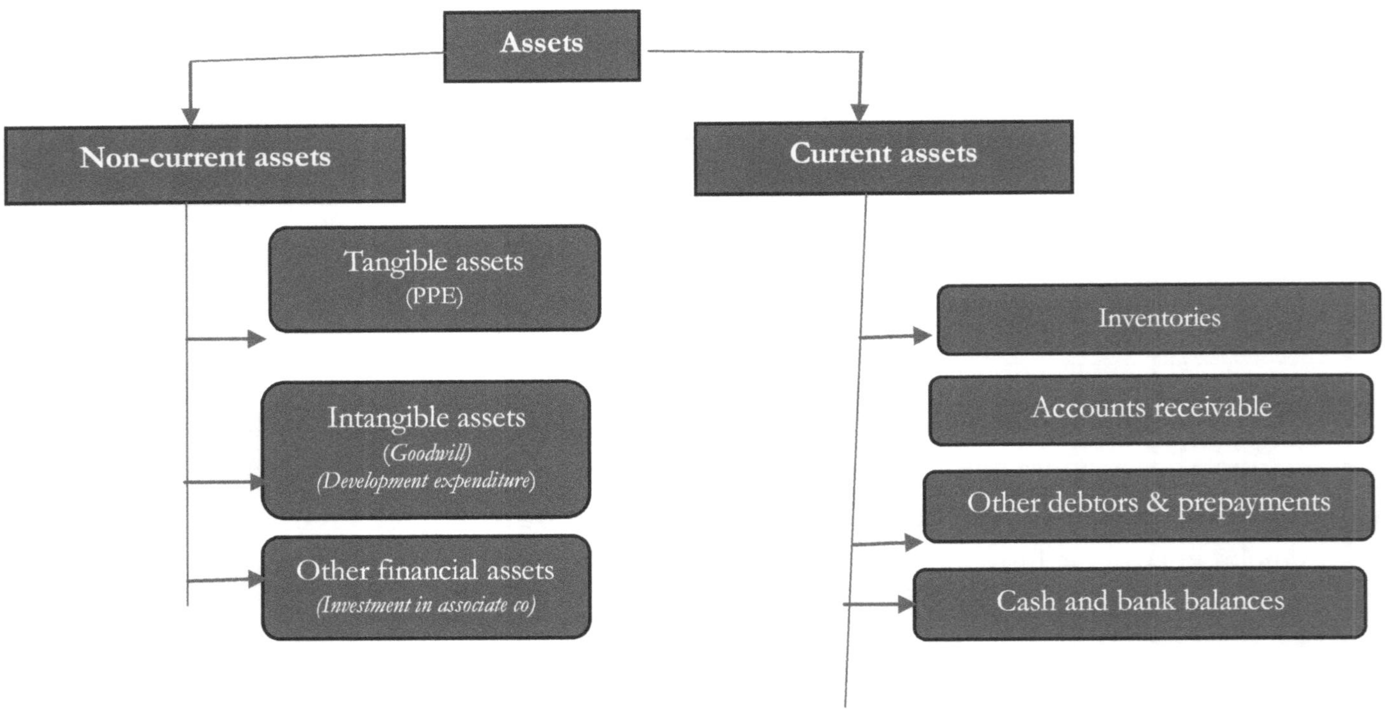

See the relevant Chapters in the text for these categories of assets where they are described comprehensively in accounting terms.

The **Statement of Financial Position** is illustrated below. The statement highlights *non-current assets, current assets, current liabilities, shareholders' equity, and long-term liabilities.* A typical balance sheet (SOFP) of a company will normally show all these items.

ABC Sdn Bhd
Statement of Financial Position as at 31 December 2021

		RM' 000
Non-current assets		
Property, plant, and equipment		
Land and buildings		3, 000
Equipment, furniture and fittings		250
Goodwill		300
Development expenditure		2, 280
Investments		1, 200
		7, 030
Current assets		
Inventories	1, 570	
Accounts receivable	2, 345	
Other debtors and prepayments	345	
Cash and bank balances	205	
	4, 465	
Less: Current liabilities		
Accounts payable	1, 270	
Other creditors and accruals	250	
Short- term borrowings	305	
Tax payable	65	
	1, 890	
Net current assets		2, 575
Net assets		**9, 605**

Financed by:		RM' 000
Equity and Liabilities		
Contributed share capital		3, 500
Reserves		
General reserve	600	
Revaluation surplus	1, 250	
Retained earnings	2, 255	4, 105
Shareholders' equity		7, 605
Long-term liabilities		
10 % Loan Notes **(secured)**		2, 000
		9, 605

We have not used comparative figures in the above illustration but in practice, however comparative figures are a statutory requirement as it compares the previous year's financial position with current year's position. Any significant variations in the figures between both years may pose serious questions for management to deliberate before considering the required remedial action. ABC Sdn Bhd's Statement of Financial Position is dated 31 December 2021. The financial position is always at a specific point in time, unlike the Statement of Profit or Loss and Other Comprehensive Income which covers a twelve-month period.

Interpreting the financial position

Let's apply the basic accounting equation to the balance sheet figures. As at 31 December 2021, ABC Sdn Bhd has **net assets** of RM 9, 605, 000 which is *financed by* **long-term liability** of RM 2 million and **shareholders' equity** of RM 7, 605, 000.

Accounting Equation [Balance Sheet Equation)

Net assets = Shareholders' Equity + Liabilities

RM 9, 605, 000 = RM 7, 605, 000 + RM 2, 000, 000

4.2 Liabilities

A liability is a ***present obligation*** *of the entity arising from past events, the settlement of which is expected to result in an outflow from the entity of resources embodying economic benefits.*

An essential characteristic of a liability is that the entity has a **present obligation**. Obligation means a duty or responsibility to act or perform in a certain agreed way. Obligations may be legally enforceable as a consequence of a binding contract or statutory requirement. Obligations also arise, however, from normal business practice, custom and a desire to maintain good business relations or act in an equitable manner. **Settlement** of a present obligation will involve the entity giving up resources embodying economic benefits in order to satisfy the claim of the party. This may be done in various ways, not just by payment of cash.

Liabilities represents what is owed to outside parties that are *not participants* in the ownership of the business and therefore *not sharing the risks* taken by the business owners. Generally known as **creditors,** they provide trade finance or loans for financing the business and other type of liabilities such as sundry creditors, amount owing in taxes and others. Liabilities are broadly classified into *current liabilities and long-term liabilities. Current liabilities* are normally discharged in the operating period within one year after the balance sheet date whereas *long-term liabilities* that may usually extend for more than twelve months or several years depending upon the nature of the liability itself.

4.3 Equity

Equity is defined as a residual interest in the assets of the entity after deducting all its liabilities.

The three elements basically make up the **accounting equation** below:

Shareholders' Equity = Assets – Liabilities

Only company's transactions with the owners are presented in the **Statement of Changes in Equity.** All other non-owner changes in equity will be presented in the **Statement of Comprehensive Income (Income Statement)** which can be reflected as a single statement. Profits that an entity generate ultimately belong to the *shareholders* of the company. Shareholders are happy when their wealth in the company maximized.

Equity represents the obligation(owed) by the company as a separate entity to the shareholders or conversely, it is the claim, a right or an interest of all the owners of the business who collectively hold over the company's present net worth and potential future wealth. Each shareholder's claim is proportional to the contributed share capital and reserves (retained earnings) and they are committed to supporting the business without a specific timeframe. **Net worth or shareholders' equity** is derived after offsetting resources (assets) and obligations (liabilities) to third parties. It is an accounting term that has nothing to do or bears any relationship with the 'market value' of the company.

Shareholders' equity as a term has three components, the *contributed share capital, retained earnings, and reserves.*

Contributed share capital represents the value of the contributions to the share capital made available through external resources by the owners of the business at the beginning and during the operational existence or life of the company. Shareholders entrust the control of this contributed capital resources to the *board of directors in their role as stewards* for the proper **governance** and **management** of the company's business.

Retained earnings represent realized profits created as a result of the company's operations and where shareholders have not decided to take out by way of cash distributions as declared dividends. This may be the case with smaller companies and when few shareholders possibly demanding a return on their investments. Instead, retained profits are ploughed backed customarily into the business as an ongoing activity of the company. Unlike share capital which remains intact until shareholders decide to increase it or contribute further to meet growth and expansion strategy, *retained earnings are used ordinarily to finance most business activities.* Where financial policy through a board decision is made to withdraw the wealth created in the form of dividends, then a formal **distribution** takes place as desired by the shareholders as returns on their investment are expected anyway. However, the norm is that listed companies by convention normally declare dividends annually to shareholders to keep them happy and also to signal the *capital markets* that the company is financially sound and on track.

There is no requirement to distinguish between retained earnings (or accumulated profits) and reserves. Both are considered **earnings** which shareholders may agree or agree not to distribute.

Figure 4.4 Components of Retained Earnings

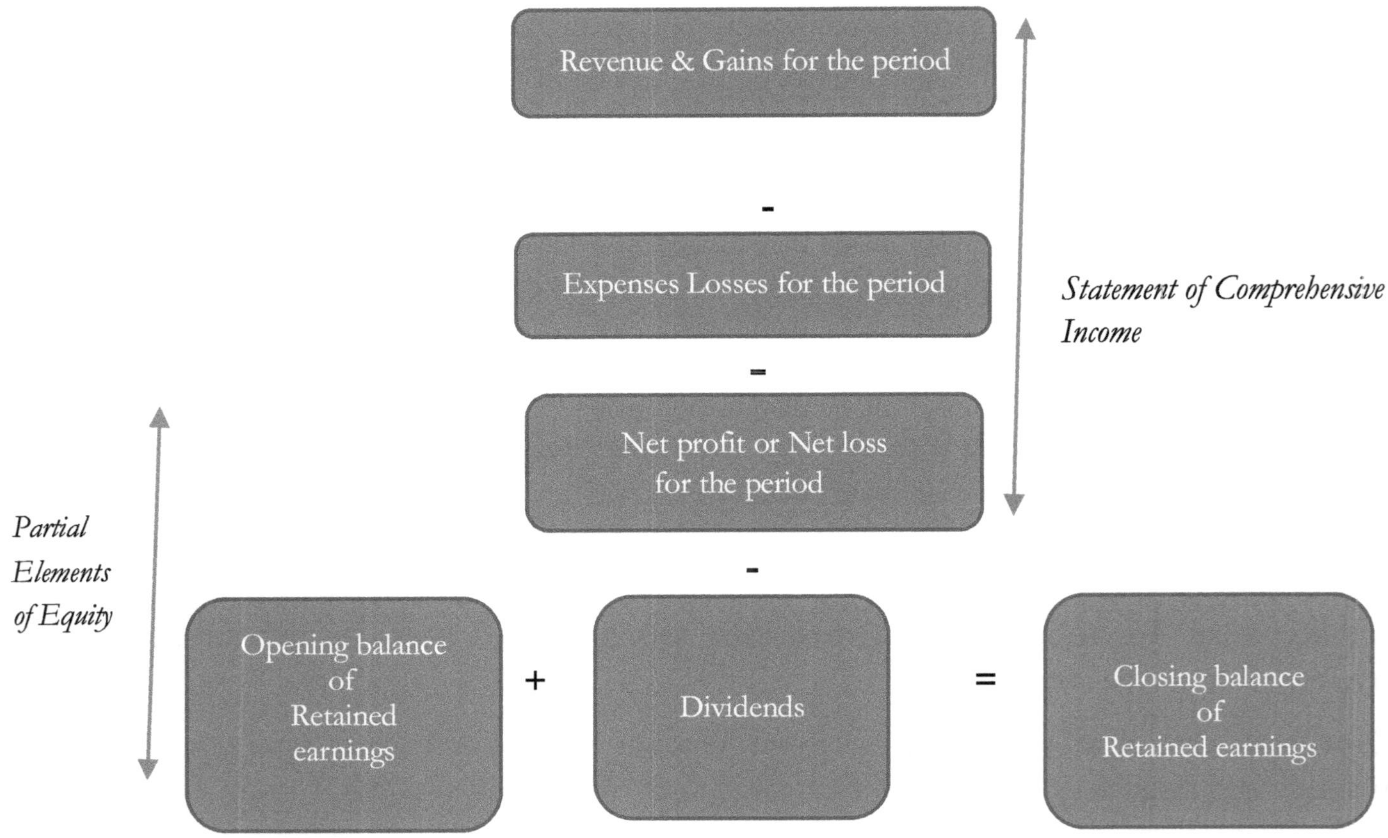

4.4 Testing Your Knowledge and Understanding

Consider the following situations, in each case, do we have an asset or liability within the definitions given by the*Conceptual Framework*? Give reasons for your answer.

a. Path-lab has purchased a patent for RM 25,000. The patent gives the company sole use of a particular manufacturing process which will save RM 5,000 a year for the next five years.

b. Uncle Sam paid Ali Khan RM 12,000 to set up a car repair shop, on condition that priority treatment be given to cars from the company's fleet.

c. A car sales company provides a warranty with every car sold.

Answer

a. This is an intangible asset. It reflects a past event, control over the manufacturing process is present with future economic benefit is to be derived.

b. This cannot be classified as an asset. Uncle Sam has no virtual control over the car repair shop because there is uncertainty over the flow of future economic benefit from the use of the asset.

   Priority condition does not constitute an outright ownership of an asset.

c. The warranty claim constitutes a liability. The business has a present and legal obligation to fulfill. A liability in the form of a provision will be recognized when the warranty is issued rather than when a claim is made.

4.5 Profits, Dividend Policy and Reserves

Net profit or net loss flows from the Statement of Comprehensive Income to the Statement of Changes in Equity. Net income or profit increases total equity and if you have any net losses, this will decrease total equity. A company pays dividends to shareholders' only *if it earns realized profits*. However, company is not obligated to pay dividends unless the Boards of Directors decide to declare them. The board's decision on this matter is highly prudent and circumstantial. Usually companies in the development stages or growth mode elect not to pay dividends, opting instead to plough back retained earnings in the company to expand operations or undertaking investments into new lines of business, or capital expenditure. **Dividends** decrease retained earnings because they represent *a distribution of a company's assets* (usually cash) to its shareholders. Dividends or other forms of distribution such as bonus shares are reflected usually in the **Statement of Changes in Equity**. Some reserves are created by statute and in other cases, general reserve is an appropriation of profits created specially by board of directors, revaluation reserve is created as a result of property valuations that give rise to a surplus in most cases and a deficit in other cases.

4.6 No Par Value Share Regime

Share premium account which is gone obsolete (no longer operative) in the accounts of companies under the *'no par value share regime'* in Malaysia following the changes enacted by the Companies Act 2016. Ordinary shares that are now issued for any value below or above par value (nominal) are simply treated as **contributed share capital** in the Statement of Changes in Equity. A listed company can issue or buy-back shares and these are usually reflected in equity. However, a company that is private limited (Sdn Bhd) do not have this privilege.

5. Financial Performance

The Income Statement which is part of the **Statement of Comprehensive Income**, reports the profitability of a company's operations over a specific period of time. Profit is used as a measure of **financial performance**. The income statement shows the revenue first, followed by expenses. When revenues exceed expenses, net income or profit results. When expenses exceed income, a net loss results. The **Statement of Comprehensive Income (profit or loss statement)** below is an illustrative format used in business to show the company's bottom line.

ABC Sdn Bhd

Statement of Comprehensive Income

For the financial year ended 31 December 2021

	RM
Sales	2,550,000
Less: Cost of sales	(1,350,000)
Gross profit	1,200,000
Selling and distribution expenses	(547,500)
Administrative expenses	(455,850)
Other operating income	32,000
Other operating expense	(38,000)
Operating profit	190,650
Finance cost	(15,500)
Profit before tax	175,150
Less: Income tax	(14,500)
Profit after tax for the year	160,650

In this case, ABC Sdn Bhd had made a *profit after tax for the year* amounting to RM 160. 650.

You will see, while most companies may have the same financial year-end date, other companies may use different year-end dates.

Revenue represents *flow of economic benefits* during the financial year arising in the course of ordinary activities of an entity when those flows result in increases in equity apart from other cash flows relating to contributions from shareholders when equity shares are subscribed by them. In other words, *revenues actually increase shareholders' equity* not only from business sources of the company from the sale of goods and services but also from gains from short-term investments. Both **revenue** and **gains** are included in the definition of income. Gains include those arising on the disposal of non-current assets.

Expenses

The definition of **expenses** includes losses as well as those expenses that arise in the course of ordinary activities of an entity. Losses will include those arising on the disposal of non-current assets such as disposal of tangible fixed assets and investments. **Losses** may or may not be in the ordinary course of business (due to natural disasters such as fire or earthquakes). **Expenses and losses** *result in decrease of shareholders' equity* during the financial period when there is an outflow of economic benefits or depletion of assets through consumption of resources. Examples of operating expenses include salaries and wages, payment of rent for use of rented premises or equipment, advertising, etc., Loses may or may

Figure 4.3 Link between profit and shareholders' equity

Statement of Comprehensive income

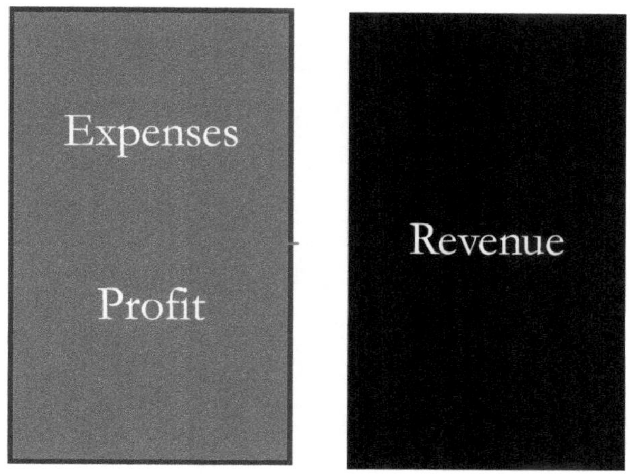

Revenue and Gains – Expenses and Losses = Net Profit (or Net Loss)

Net profit or net income [called as the bottom-line] is arrived at after deducting tax.

Net profit represent the *net difference* between the resources (*revenue generated*) resulting from the economic activity of the business entity and resources consumed (*operating* expenses*) by* the business. In essence, they represent the **profit or loss** emerging for the financial period. Net Profit has the effect of increasing owners' total equity whereas *a net loss* results in decreasing total owners' equity. Ultimately *the value of the firm is created or destroyed* through the business activity of the company.

Net profit or net loss flows from the **Statement of Comprehensive Income (SOCI)** and ends in the **Statement of Changes in Equity**

6. Cash Flow Statement

The **Statement of Cash Flows** shows a business entity's cash receipts and payments for a specific period of time. Business entities normally engage in three basic types of activities: *operating activities, investing activities and financing activities*. The Cash Flow Statement reports cash flows under each of the activities.

Operating activities: This selling of goods and services to customers which result in net income or net loss which consequentially tend to effect either an increase or decrease in cash. The Statement of Comprehensive Income shows a net profit but this does necessarily mean whether the entity has been able to generate sufficient cash flows from operating activities. In our scenario, cash generated from operating activities appeared to be only RM 190, 000.

Investing activities: Under this activity, entities invest in non-current assets such as property, plant and equipment. For example, purchases of tangible fixed assets involves an outflow of cash resources. This shows a business entity's investment in production capacity to generate a stream of income. Under this activity, cash has been absorbed to the extent of RM 52, 000 by investments.

Financing activities: Business entities need capital for funding growth and expansion strategy. This comes from financing activities. Financing comes from both equity owners and borrowings. Equity owners provide the necessary cash by taking up shares in the company. Repayment of borrowings is part of the financing activities which involves an outflow of cash. Under this activity, again the cash position has deteriorated with RM 48, 000 being absorbed by financing activities.

A summary Cash Flow Statement shown below is an illustrative format used by a typical business entity.

ABC Sdn Bhd	
Statement of Cash Flows as at 31 December 2021	RM'000
Profit for the year before tax	175
Add/less: Non-cash items	15
Net cash generated from operating activities	190
Net cash used in investing activities	(52)
Net cash used in financing activities	(48)
Net decrease in cash and cash equivalents	90
Cash and cash equivalents at the beginning of the year	105
Cash and cash equivalents at the end of the year	205

ABC Sdn Bhd's cash position for the year has increased by RM 90,000. The overall cash position however, indicates that excess cash resources were utilized by both investing and financing activities. You can trace the year ending cash balance back to the Statement of Financial Position under current assets.

7. Notes to the Financial Statements

Conventionally, the financial statements are accompanied by explanatory notes to the various items of accounts. They form an integral part of the financial statements and the information contained in these notes should be read in conjunction with the accounts as they amplify information relevant to the understanding of the accounts which is not shown elsewhere in the financial statements.

8. Relationships (or links) between the Financial Statements

The illustrative financial statements of another Company given below show the relationships and links between the financial statements. It is important to study these relationships because they apply to all business entities. We use this information in financial statements to make business decisions on the basis of economic, legal and ethical guidelines.

Illustrative Summary Financial Statements of ABC Company

Statement of Profit or Loss
For the year ended 31 December 2020

Revenues	RM 1,500,000
Less :	
Cost of sales	1,020,000
Gross profit	480,000
Selling and distribution expenses	(235,000)
Administrative expenses	(215,000)
Net profit	30,000

Statement of Changes in Equity
For the year ended 31 December 2020

	Contributed Share Capital	Reserves	Retained Earnings	Total Equity
	RM	RM	RM	RM
Balance at 1.1.2020	100,000	28,000	32,000	160,000
Net profit	-	-	30,000	30,000
Dividends paid			(18,000)	(18,000)
Balance at 31.12.2020	100,000	28,000	44,000	172,000

Statement of Cash Flows
For year ended 31. 12. 2020

Net cash from operating activities	RM 58,000
Net cash used for investing activities	(18,000)
Net cash used by financing activities	(12,000)
Net increase in cash	20,000
Cash and cash equivalents at 1.1.2020	10,000
Cash and cash equivalents at 31.12.2020	RM 30,000

Statement of Financial Position
As at 31.12. 2020

	RM
Assets	
Non- current assets	205,000
Current assets	
Cash	30,000
Other assets	65,000
Total assets	300,000
Liabilities	
Borrowings	60,000
Other liabilities	68,000
Total liabilities	128,000
Shareholders' Equity	
Contributed hare capital	100,000
Reserves	28,000
Retained earnings	44,000
Total shareholders' equity	172,000
Total liabilities and shareholders' equity	300,000

9. The Use of Accounting Information for Decision Making

What do decision makers look for when evaluating a Company's overall financial standing?

Some guidelines for users of financial statements who make informed decisions on the basis of accounting information. Suppose you are considering an investment in a company, what crucial information will be required to be evaluated by users?

Decision	**Guideline for assessing sources of accounting information**
Can the company sell its products?	Sales revenue on the income statement. are sales growing or falling?
What are the main income measures to watch for trends? (Need to see the trends over a period of 3 years)	a. Gross profit (Sales less Cost of Goods Sold) b. Operating profit Gross profit less Operating expenses Net profit before tax (Bottom line) All three income measures should be increasing over time.
What percentage of sales revenue is the profit?	Calculate net profit as a percentage of sales revenue. Examine the profit over the three year period.
How effective is the recovery from receivables?	Using the balance sheet, determine the incidence of irrecoverable debts and its provision? Any % of increase in accounts receivables to the % increase in sales. If receivables are growing faster than sales, collections may be too slow, and the risk of default in irrecoverable debts.
Can the company discharge its a. Current liabilities? b. Current and long-term borrowings?	Using the balance sheet, calculate a. Current ratio (current assets to current liabilities): ideally the ratio should be somewhat greater than two, say 2:1. b. Whether the value of total assets can more than adequately payoff the total liabilities. The liquidity of the company's assets is crucial to knowing whether company can settle its debts as and when it falls due.

Identifying where the Company's cash is generated? How cash is being used?	Cash flow Statement: Operating activities provide a major source of cash during most of the years. Otherwise the business will fail. Potential growth and expansion can be seen if investing activities shows a steady increase in capital expenditure. (property, plant and equipment)
Chapter 25 comprehensively deals with interpretation of accounts using percentages and ratios. Analysis of such financial data and related information can be useful in making decisions.	

10. Limitations of Accounting Information

Information sourced from financial reporting statements largely concentrates on accounting data that is the outcome of historical information, events and economic transactions that are based on what has already taken place in the operating period. In other words, it reflects financial decisions on past and anticipated events that gets reported in the financial statements of an entity purely on an historical cost convention. The accounting information may fail to demonstrate its future potentiality or rather what you can do in the immediate future for the company's prosperity and wealth creation. In that sense, historical financial information may not have due relevance in providing useful strategic information for decision making about the future viability of the company's survival and success in the market place. At best, annual reports and accounts tend to indicate the entity's financial position and performance, but it does reveal other bits of crucial information relating to non-financial indicators because corporate decision making is not just about only financial but relates to other business considerations which take a holistic approach of all relevant factors both local and global issues that bears on the entity's business and environmental and ethical position.

In Chapter 1, we discussed the importance of financial information to users of financial statements. We know accounting information plays a crucial role in decision-making for businesses and other users of financial statements. However, it is important to be aware that accounting does not cover every aspect of financial or business performance. While it is important to know what the accounting's role is and exactly what it achieves, it is also equally important to be aware what accounting may fail to indicate, particularly with regard to non-financial performance.

It does not provide the company with measures of quality of an organizational performance. A customer on the other hand, does provide feedback on the quality of the organization's performance and the level of satisfaction with the goods and services provided. Significantly, customers' recommendation of the company's products creates repeat sales. Secondly, accounting does not inform you of the extent of pollution, and environmental or social damage about the business entity has caused. Thirdly accounting does not provide valuation or measure of skills-base and tacit knowledge of an organization.

Qualitative measures of financial performance and financial position is another approach companies can take to inform the users of financial statements but this is beyond the entity's scope as financial reporting only covers those aspects that are pure traditional areas customarily reported. It is not just about profits.

11. What Constraints We Face in Providing Useful Accounting Information?

In providing useful financial information to users, a *pervasive constraint* we face is **cost.** Cost is incurred because of the accounting process itself which involves some activities - data collection, the cost of data processing, analyzing, verifying and disseminating the information in easy and understandable manner so that useful economic decisions can be made by management. Higher costs can lead to lower profit, hence lower returns on investments for shareholders' The important consideration for management here is one of economic benefit or cost to assess. Such assessment of whether the benefits of reporting particular information are likely to outweigh the costs incurred in providing or using the information for that purposes.

12. Preparing Financial Statements

We can prepare financial statements directly from information in the *adjusted trial balance* (ATB). An ATB (representing all year-end ledger balances) includes all accounts and balances that will end-up in the financial statements, and it is far cumbersome to work from the entire nominal or general ledger when preparing the financial statements. In practice, a working trial balance is extracted from the general ledger.

Chapter 23 deals more with the preparation of financial statements, using the prescribed formats by IAS 1/ MFRS 101. **Chapter 23** also gives a more detailed coverage of the illustrated worked examples showing how to handle the preparation of accounts from *an adjusted trial balance* (called 'accountant's worksheet). We prepare financial statements in the following customary manner: statement of comprehensive income, statement of changes in equity, and statement of financial position. It makes sense to follow a logical sequence or order since the statement of financial position uses information from the statement of changes in equity, which in turn makes use of information from the statement of comprehensive income. Finally, the statement of cash flows is prepared using the technique of *'T-accounts'*.

Chapter 21 and **Chapter 22** deal with preparing a trial balance and completing the accounting cycle respectively as these chapters provide an extensive coverage of all relevant accounting issues prior to preparing the final accounts of a business entity.

Ethics and Corporate Governance

Chapter 27 incidentally has nothing to do with financial accounting and reporting but the chapter has some useful information on ethics in decision making as well as relevant issues on corporate governance some of which underpins the financial reporting environment.

Chapter Summary

Purpose and importance of accounting

Accounting serves an important function in an organization by providing an information and measurement system that aims to identify, record, and communicate relevant, reliable, and comparable information about the principal activities undertaken by the business entity.

1. The f**our primary statements and the disclosure notes** accompanying the financial statements form the basis of financial reporting about an entity's financial performance and position for a twelve-month accounting period including the cash flows for that reporting period. These statements are statutorily referred as Statement of Comprehensive Income, Statement of Financial Position and the Statement of Changes in Equity and the Statement of Cash Flows. These financial statements comply with the accounting standards and the provisions of the Companies Act 2016. The reporting of financial information is based on historical cost basis and geared towards the informational requirements of the principal stakeholders of the business including the shareholders and other primary users.
2. Business transactions and economic events are broadly classified into categories so that their financial effect are shown and reflected as elements of financial statements. These **elements provide a measurement basis for determining the financial position and financial performance of an entity** in the form of financial assets and liabilities, equity components, revenue and gains, expenses and losses. The **accounting equation – Assets = Equity + Liability,** represents the financial position of the company. The financial position statement is always reported at a specific point in time, usually the entity's financial year end whereas the statement of profit or loss and other comprehensive income covers a twelve- month period that shows the performance of a company in the form of **value creation or value destroying**.
3. The statement of cash flows **shows the entity's actual cash position for a specific period of twelve months** and It **highlights the entity's** three basic business components – **operating, investing and financing activities**. The accompanied explanatory notes to the various items of accounts form an integral part of the financial statements, it **amplifies crucial information for readers of account**s relevant for their understanding to make informed decisions. The ensuing pages of **Chapter 4 provides an example of the various financial statements that are conventionally reported in the annual statutory accounts** together with the financial links and relationships between the financial statements. It is important to study these relationships and because they apply to all business entities. Business decisions are made on the basis of economic, legal and ethical guidelines.
4. Information sourced from financial statements largely concentrates on accounting data that is typically of historical information, events and economic transactions **based on what has already happened** in the operating period. Therefore, it reflects operating decisions using past and anticipated events purely on a historical basis and may **not reflect its relevance and future potential for useful strategic information purposes** in terms of decision making. At best, it is **record-keeping to highlight the financial position and financial performance** of a business entity. Financial reporting is all about that and nothing more. Interested users must look for other useful information outside the realm of financial reporting regime.

Key Terms

Primary financial statements

Companies Act 2016

Statement of profit or loss and other comprehensive income

Statement of financial position

Statement of changes in equity

Statement of cash flows

Income or revenue and gains

Elements of financial statements

Profit

Reserves

Revaluation reserve

No par value share regime

Current assets

Net current assets

Contributed share capital

Non-current liabilities

Associates

Operating activities

Financing activities

Non-cash items

Notes to the financial statements

Financial performance

Financial position

Assets

Liabilities

Equity

Expenses and losses

Accounting equation

Dividends

Share premium

General reserve

Non-current assets

Current liabilities

Net assets

Retained earnings

Debentures or loan capital

Joint venture

Investment activities

Cash and cash equivalents

Shareholders' equity or funds

Review Questions

1. What specific purpose does the four primary financial statements in business serve in financial reporting? Identify the four basic financial statements.
2. Define (a) assets (b) liabilities (c) equity and (d) net assets
3. Explain what you understand by these terms – financial performance and financial position.
4. Explain what events or transactions affect equity?
5. Explain what main activities are reflected in the statement of cash flows. Why is liquidity so important to a business entity?
6. What do you understand by the term 'revenue'?
7. What is net profit? Explain how it is computed?

8. Explain contributed share capital and the 'no par value' share concept.
9. How is gross profit computed?
10. Expenses and income relating to financing activities are reported as items prior to profit before tax. Give two examples of these financing items.
11. a. What are dividends?
    b. Explain why some companies do not declare and pay dividends?
    c. If dividends are paid to shareholders, where is the payment reflected in equity?
12. The cash flow statement identifies non-cash items as part of its operating activities.
    a. Explain why non-cash items are adjusted in arriving at the net operating cash flow?
    b. Give two primary examples of expense items that form part on non-adjusting items.
13. What are retained earnings or profits?
14. Explain the accounting equation and show how equity is computed? Can you agree equity represents net assets of the company? Comment.
15. Long-term liabilities represent debt or loan capital of a business entity.
    a. Explain what is debt capital and give two prime examples.
    b. What is the link between the financing costs reported in the statement of comprehensive income and debt capital?

Multiple Choice Questions

The following summarized statement of financial position of APS Sdn Bhd as at 31 December 2020.

	RM' 000
Assets	
Non-current assets	4, 600
Current assets	4, 300
Total assets	8, 900
Equity	
Contributed share capital – issued ordinary shares.	2, 000
General reserve	200
Revaluation reserve	300
Non-current liabilities	350
Current liabilities	2,150
Total equity and liabilities.	8, 900

Using the information from the above statement, answer the following questions Q1 to Q3

Q1. The figure for retained earnings is

a. 2, 800 b. 3, 600 c. 4, 900

d. 3, 800 e. 3, 900

Q2. The company's net assets

a. 6, 400 b. 4,250 c. 2, 500

d. 3, 900 e. 4 900

Q3. The company's current ratio

a. 2 : 1 b. 1 : 2 c. 2.5 : 1

d. 1.5: 1 e. 0 .8 : 1

Q4. Which of the following will not be included in the statement of profit or loss and other comprehensive income of a company?

a. Taxation b. Debenture interest c. Ordinary share dividend

d. Preference share dividend e. Interest on fixed deposits

Q5. A company's statement of statement of financial position includes the following items:

Contributed share capital	RM 1 million
Retained earnings	RM 250,000
Revaluation reserve	RM 400, 000
Authorized share capital	RM 2 million
6 % Debentures 2020-2023	RM 500, 000

What will be the company's total equity?

a. RM 3.65 million b. RM 650, 000 c. RM 1.5 million

d. RM 1.65 million e. RM 2.15 million

Q6. Which items of account is shown in the statement of profit or loss of a company?

a. General reserve

b. Auditor's fee

c. Dividends paid on ordinary shares

d. Surplus on revaluation of land

e. Allowance on irrecoverable debts

Q7. A company reported the following items in its accounts:

Gross profit	RM 289, 000
Directors' fees	RM 125, 000
Interest on borrowings	RM 25, 000
Depreciation	RM 36, 000
Legal fee and expenses	RM 4, 000
Interest received on fixed deposit	RM 3, 000
Other expenses	RM 12, 000

What will be the company's operating profit?

a. RM 90, 000 b. RM 115, 000 c. 125, 000

d. RM 140, 000 e. RM 160, 000

Q8. Syarikat Leong Rubber Traders Berhad has an authorized capital of 3,000, 000 ordinary shares of RM 2 each. The contributed share capital is RM 1, 000, 000. The directors declared and paid a dividend of 25 sen per ordinary share. Calculate what is the total amount of the dividend paid?

a. RM 150, 000 b. RM 250, 000 c. RM 125, 000

d. RM 75, 000 e. RM 100, 000

Q9. SD Investment Holdings has an authorized share capital of RM 5, 000, 000 ordinary shares of RM 0.50 each. The contributed share capital was RM 1, 500, 000. It was issued at 75 sen per ordinary share. The board of directors declared an interim dividend of 10 % to be paid to shareholders for the current year. What is the total amount of dividend payment?

a. RM 200, 000 b. RM 100, 000 c. 1, 000, 000

d. RM 50, 000 e. RM 150, 000

Q10. Which of the following items will not appear in the statement of changes in equity?

a. Revaluation reserve

b. 10% Corporate Bond 2020-2025

c. Retained earnings

d. Dividends paid to ordinary shareholders

Review Questions Part 2

Q1. i. Explain the objective or purpose of financial statements

ii. What is the purpose of accounting in society?

Q2. a. State the four primary financial statements and explain what can be obtained from each statement.

b. Discuss briefly its significance to the users of financial statements

Q3. What purpose does the notes to the financial statements serve?

Q4. Identify and briefly describe the main elements making-up the financial statements.

Q5. a. The financial position of an entity is shown in terms of assets, liabilities and equity. You are required to define these accounting terms.

b. An important recognition criterion to be satisfied for a definition of an asset

i. is the **probable flow of future economic benefit** to the controlling entity and

ii. the **economic substance over form** it must reflect. Explain these two terms.

c. An essential characteristic of a liability is that the entity has a **present obligation** to fulfill.

In what circumstances this obligation(s) can arise? Explain.

d. Explain how the **settlement of a present obligation** can be discharged?

Q6. a. In terms of the accounting equation, state how an entity's **equity** is arrived?

b. What events or transactions change equity?

Q7. Profit is used as a measure of **financial performance.**

i. Explain why shareholders or other stakeholders are interested in financial performance of a company?

ii. Briefly explain how the measurement of profit or loss is done?

iii. Revenue and expenses are matched using the accrual basis of accounting but not on a cash basis of accounting.

a. Why is the accrual basis is generally preferred over the cash basis?

b. Why the cash basis of accounting is not consistent with the matching principle?

iv. What do understand by the term *revenue*?

v. Define *net profit* and explain its computation.

Q8. Explain what you understand by **financial position** of an entity? Briefly describe the elements of making up the statement of financial position.

Q9. a. Explain the purpose of a **cash flow statement.**

b. What are the major types of business activities reported in the cash flow statement?

Q10. Describe at least three main **limitations** of financial statements.

Q11. What do **decision makers** look for when evaluating a Company's overall financial standing?

Illustrate your answer by giving at least three examples.

Q12. Explain in the context of a listed company, the importance of equity to:

a. Shareholders

b. Financial analysts as a stakeholder

Inflation is always and everywhere a monetary phenomenon.

– Milton Friedman

Chapter 5

Learning Objectives

After you have studied this chapter, you should be able to;
Understand the main activity of a trading or merchandising company
Record sales transactions in a ledger account
Understand and account for sales discounts and sales returns & allowances
Understand the general principles of operating sales and service tax (SST)
To calculate SST on transactions and record the required accounting entries
Explain accounts receivable and how it is recorded
Understand the purpose of operating a control account for accounts receivable
Understand the cost and benefit of credit facilities offered to customers
Understand control accounts as they relate to double-entry system
Prepare sales ledger control account from given information
Account for contra adjustments between trade receivables and accounts payable
Perform control account reconciliations for accounts receivable
Identify errors which would be highlighted by performing control account reconciliation
Identify and correct errors in control accounts and ledger accounts
Prepare, reconcile and understand the purpose of customer's statement of account
Understand the purpose of both credit and debit notes
Understand the purpose of operating a periodic and a perpetual system for inventories

Sales and Receivables

Scope

This chapter focuses on accounting for credit sales transactions and the associated trading environment that deals with trade and cash discounts. The recording function for the sales system is explained. The sales ledger account in the general ledger system and the subsidiary ledgers are maintained for all sales transactions on a credit system. Accounting for accounts receivables (trade debtors) is part of the sales ledger system, usually operated through a **control account**. The control account serves a useful purpose by monitoring the customers' accounts on a regular basis to ensure accuracy and completeness of all accounts receivable accounts through the subsidiary ledger system especially when the business entity has many customers' accounts to keep track. Resulting from this system, there is a need to check on the risk and incidence of doubtful bad debts arising from uncollectible accounts. **Credit control policy** and **recovery**

of debts become imperative for the business entity so as to minimize any potential financial loss. This requires the credit sales system to maintain **adequate internal controls** on a continuous basis so that proper reconciliation of customers' accounts takes place often to **avoid any potential loss of customer goodwill** resulting from **unintended accounting errors or discrepancies in the system.**

Merchandising activities

A trading company that is involved in **merchandising activities** differ from those of a service company. Merchandise often consists of tangible products or goods that a company acquires for resale to customers. A trading company earns profits by buying and selling merchandise. Merchandisers are recognized as wholesalers or retailers. **A wholesaler** acts as an intermediary by buying finished products from manufacturers or other wholesalers and sells them to retailers or other wholesalers. **A retailer** is an intermediary that buys finished products from manufacturers directly or wholesalers and sells them to customers. Most retailers like Tesco and other supermarkets like Aeon carry and sell a wide range of products and services. Companies generally institute a control system to monitor large quantities of inventories representing a wide range of stock -in-trade items as part of their trading activities.

Earning profits

Net profit for a trading company is derived from revenue obtained by selling merchandise products less cost of goods sold to customers and operating expenses for the period. Revenues from selling merchandised goods is termed as *sales or turnover.*

Figure 1 below shows how profit is made by a trading company and a service company.

	Trading Company	**Service Company**
Sales	xxx	xxx
Less:		
Cost of goods sold/Cost of sales	(xxx)	-
	_____	_____
Gross profit	xxx	xxx
Less: Operating expenses	(xxx)	(xxx)
	_____	_____
Net profit	xx	xx

Service Company

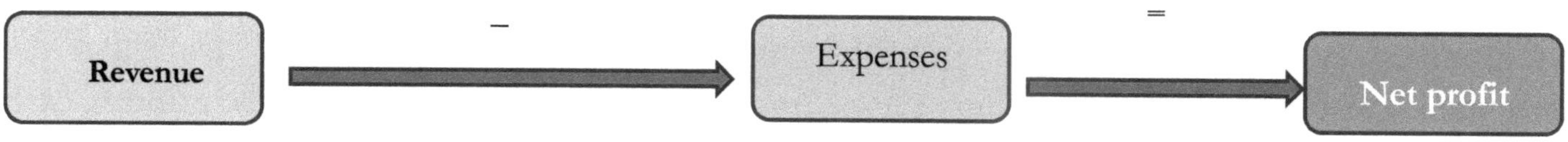

Trading or Merchandising Company

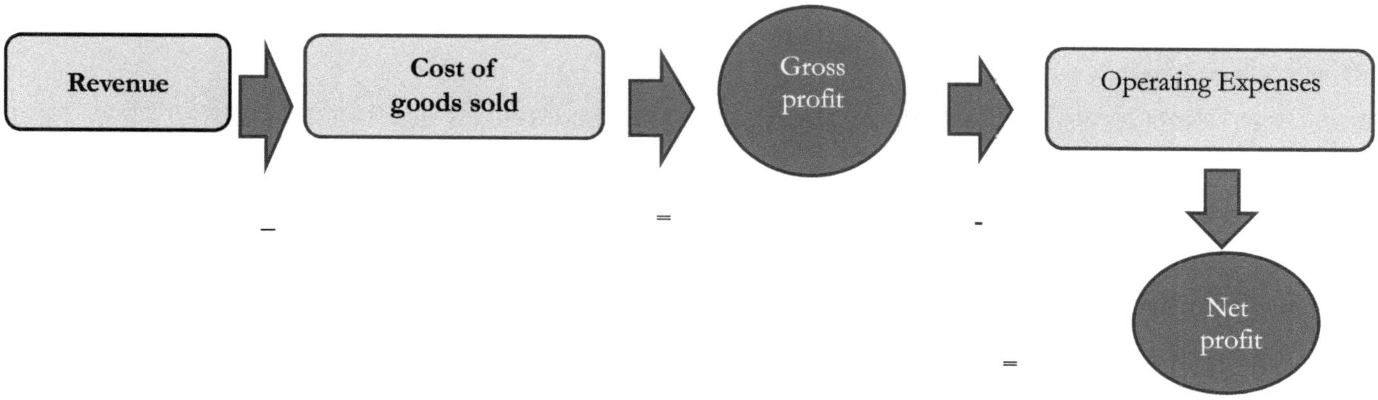

Some customers are willing to pay cash at the time of sale but others use debit cards or credit cards. While this is a common practice in retail industry, but in a trading environment, most sales transactions to customers are done on a regular basis who settle their accounts involving substantial amounts on credit.

Retail businesses work with credit card companies and banks, because they give you cash quickly and collect cash from your customers later. But you are not too sure about extending credit line to some customers particularly if they run the risk of not settling the accounts within the credit period on time and the recovery of debts may prove onerous. When this happens there can be delays in settling your own bills until cash is received. Most businesses face this situation. One advantage for extending credit to customers is expanding your customer base. More customers mean more sales with greater net income or profit. The main disadvantage, however, is to wait to receive the cash and in some cases some customers may abscond or never pay because business goes bad. This happens only in rare cases and where credit controls are stringent.

Regardless of whether the business is selling goods or services, companies find it hard to turn customers away, so they often agree to make **sales on credit**. In general, companies prefer not to do business with customers who fail to settle accounts on time. So keeping the right customers becomes a top priority, and there are internal controls to protect cash collection from customers, track amounts due from these customers.

Types of Sales

One major consideration in business is to focus on liquidity, means having enough cash to pay off liabilities as and when they fall due. Selling goods or services creates a steady cash inflow to pay for the operating expenses of the business.

Cash Sales

Cash sales are the easiest way to keep track because customers pay cash or give cheque at the point of sale. There is no necessity for keeping a sales ledger and related records of the individual customers. The accounting entries are simple and straight forward. Recording a cash sale requires increasing the cash account and increasing the sales account for the amount of the sale. It is important to note that businesses may limit their sales potential by not providing options for customers to defer payments – buy now and pay later.

Credit Card Sales

Credit card sales emerged because customers were increasingly using credit to pay for goods and services particularly when they had no easy access to cash for disbursements. Credit cards offered a convenient method for deferred payments (debt) at a certain rate of interest charge for the use of credit levied by the credit card companies, usually the commercial banks since it generated a source of revenue for them. The credit card system is widespread amongst retail businesses and transactions can be carried out in any part of the world with ease. Globalization trends have made it possible for customers to be mobile anywhere in the world they travelled where there are internet networks linking to the paying banks. Most retail and departmental stores accept credit cards such as MasterCard or Visa or others for purchases as opposed to receiving cash payments. There is no requirement for issuing an invoice except for sales receipt which confirms the transaction. The customer's bank account gets debited when the transaction is done. The downside to using credit cards is the risk of incurring unnecessary credit with customers defaulting payments on interest and principal on time, thus creating more debt trap.

Debit Card Sales

On the contrary, transactions carried out using debit cards are safer because payments are discharged instantaneously by online. Unless the customer has sufficient credit available in the account no transactions are honored by the retailing businesses. In other words, customers are more restricted in using their cash resources, thus eliminating the risk of interest-free debt. Payments immediately get debited to the customer's bank account when the card is swiped each time the transaction is made. Debit cards are more secure and faster to process compared to credit cards but it works only if the customer has sufficient funds in the current or savings account. However, the risk of debt is virtually non-existent.

Online Shopping

With improvements in **digital technology**, most merchandised transactions are done instantaneously and these transactions usually takes place via the computerized accounting system. A new trend that has emerged now is online shopping using digital technology wherever customers are located. Once the transaction goes through and accepted, online shoppers get their delivery either on their own arrangement or delivery by the suppliers.

Sales on Account (Sold on Credit)

Cash, credit card and debit card sales are common methods of sale in a retail business-to-customer environment. However, the sale of goods on credit happens more commonly in a supplier-to-retailer environment where one business is a customer to another business.

Relationship between Customers and Businesses

Let's see the common types of relationships between customers and businesses which provide opportunities for sales on account.

- Manufacturers sell to wholesalers
- Manufacturers sell to retailers
- Wholesalers sell to retailers
- Retailers sell to customers

Risk of Irrecoverable Debts (Bad Debts) arising from Uncollectible Accounts

When businesses agree to sell on credit, sales increases but so does the risk of not being able to collect what is owed as a result of these credit sales. Accordingly, companies bear the risk of bad debts or uncollectible accounts, which occur when a customer fail to pay for goods or services rendered be. So regardless of its size, a business must manage its customer relationships to avoid the incidence of bad debts. Bad debts are also known as "**irrecoverable debts**" when recovery procedures become ineffective. There could be many contributing reasons for this.

To attract customers who pay their accounts on time, a business need to consider the following two issues:

- **Choose its customers carefully.**

Establish a credit policy for accepting new customers which requires the following measures:

i. Check application
ii. Check credit risk using a credit rating agency to screen new customers
iii. Obtain credit references from businesses that sell to the new customers and banks that have accounts with the new customers.

- **Enforce a credit policy for existing customers.**

i. Explain payment terms and penalties for late payment
ii. Follow up on overdue accounts by sending statements and reminders of payments on due dates
iii. Legal action for recovery for incidence of bad debts.

Accounting for Sale of Goods

Trading companies have an obligation to report on all its trading activities. It must account for sales, sales discounts, sales returns and allowances. Using a perpetual system, it must analyze and record transactions for sales. A trading (merchandising) company such as C-Mart below, reflects these items in its trading account by showing its gross profit computation:

C-Mart Trading Sdn Bhd **Trading account for the year ended 30 September 2018**		**RM**
Sales		485, 500
Less: Discounts allowed	5, 350	
Sales returns	2, 650	(8,000)
Net sales		477, 500
Less: Cost of goods sold		(360, 900)
Gross profit		116, 600

Accounting for Sales and Cost of Goods

A trader must account for the sales transaction. This involve two parts:

i. Revenue from the sale
ii. Recognition of the cost of the goods sold to the customer.

Accounting for a sales transaction under the perpetual system requires recording the information on both parts: one for sales revenue and one for cost of goods sold.

To illustrate this, assume C-Mart sold RM 3,300 of goods on credit and the cost part of the sales transaction ensures that the inventory account reflects the cost of the merchandise available for sale. In this case, the cost of the merchandises sold by C-Mart is RM 2, 200.

The journal entries for this sales transaction and cost of goods sold are as follows:

Dr: Accounts receivable	RM 3, 300	
Cr: Sales		RM 3, 300
(Being sale of goods (merchandise) on credit)		

Dr: Cost of goods sold	RM 2, 200	
Cr: Inventory		RM 2, 200
(Being record the cost of items sold)		

However, in today's trading environment, traders must have an effective policy for bar coding and technology support systems. A trader's merchandising goal is to reduce inventories, shorten lead times and eliminate errors.

Accounting for Sales Discounts

A seller of goods can benefit from offering **sales discounts** as this can avoid potential delay in receiving cash and reducing collection efforts in future from customers. A credit sale policy will normally define the credit term period for customers to settle their accounts and take advantage of any discount offered by the trader. A seller usually does not record or account for a sales discount until a customer actually settles within the discount period.

Assume C-Mart adopts a discount policy of 10 % on credit sales if customers settle their accounts within two weeks (14 days) after sales and the credit term for full settlement is 45 days. Any delay in settlement beyond this credit period will be imposed a fine of 5 % on goods sold. To illustrate, C-Mart Trading makes a credit sale for RM 2, 000 with terms of 10/14 and 0/45.

Entry to record the revenue for this credit sale:

Dr: Accounts receivable	RM 2, 000	
Cr: Sales		RM 2, 000
Being goods sold on credit policy terms 10/14, 0/45)		

This sales transaction goes on record as if the customer will settle the full amount RM 2, 000 by waiting 45 days. In this case C-Mart will record the payment as:

Dr: Cash (bank)	RM 2, 000	
Cr: Accounts receivable		RM 2, 000
(Being payment received for sale on credit)		

The customer's other option is to pay RM 1, 800 within the 14-day settlement period if the customer wants to benefit the 10 % discount.

Entry to record the discount allowed

Dr: Cash (bank)	RM 1,800	
Discount allowed	200	
Cr: Accounts receivable		RM 2, 000
(Being payment received on sale less discount)		

Accounting treatment for sales discount is to show it as a deduction from sales as a **contra** on revenue.

Where a late penalty is imposed on non-settlement beyond the credit term period, that is, when the customer fails to settle the amount due, the imposed fine is treated as a penalty income. Such income is normally treated as part of sales revenue. However, the penalty income is maintained initially as a separate account in the general ledger before it is transferred and subsequently credited to the sales account.

Accounting for Sales Returns and Allowances

Sales returns relate to items sold that customers return to the trader after a sale. Usually in this case, traders allow customers to return the goods for a full refund. Sales allowances on the other hand relate to reductions in the selling price of goods sold to customers. This happens with damaged goods or defective merchandise that a customer is willing to purchase with a reduction in the selling price. Sales returns and allowances may lead to a possible loss of customers in the future due to quality issues, with a potential for lost sales revenue. To avoid this possibility, traders should monitor the situation with feedback from dissatisfied customers.

Sales Returns

To illustrate, C-Mart's earlier sale of merchandise for RM 2, 000 had cost RM 1, 400. Assume that the customer returns part of the merchandise and the return items can sell for RM 1, 000. and cost RM 700. The sales revenue will be adjusted downwards when the customer returns the goods. Usually, a c**redit not**e will be raised to reflect this price decrease for goods returned.

The adjusting journal entry to reflect the sales return is:

Dr: Sales returns	RM 1, 000	
Cr: Accounts receivable		RM 1, 000
(Being goods returned by customer with a full refund)		

If the returned merchandise in not defective or damaged, it can be resold to another customer. C-Mart returns these goods to its inventory. The adjusting entry to restore the cost of such goods to the inventory account is:

Dr: Inventory	RM 700	
Cr: Cost of goods sold.		RM 700
(Being goods returned added to inventory)		

However, if the goods returned are defective or damaged, the above entry changes. In this case the inventory account will be adjusted to reflect the estimated value, not its cost. Let's assume the defective goods returned is estimated to be worth RM 450, then the following adjusting entry will be made:

Dr: Inventory	RM 450	
Dr: Loss on defective goods	RM 250	
Cr: Cost of goods sold		RM 700
(Being adjustment for defective returned inventory to store)		

Sales Allowances

To account for sale allowances, let's assume that RM 1, 000 of the goods C-Mart sold is defective but the customer decides to keep it because C-Mart offers a reduction of RM 150 on the original selling price. The price reduction is treated as an allowance and C-Mart will adjust its records as follows:

Dr: Sales returns and allowances	RM 150	
Cr: Accounts receivable		RM 150
(Being adjustment to record sale allowance on defective goods)		

Similarly, as for sales returns a credit note will usually be raised by C-Mart to confirm the price reduction offered to the customer on the defective goods retained. The credit note is a written record notifying the customer of a credit adjustment to its accounts receivable.

Accounts Receivables (Trade Debtors)

Sales on account create receivables. Accounts receivables are shown as current assets that reflect the amounts due from customers for credit sales of goods or services. Businesses normally keep a subsidiary ledger of receivables due from each customer. The accounts receivable in the general ledger serves as a **control account** because it summarizes, or controls the total of the receivables from all customers. The individual customer accounts in the subsidiary ledger allows information for preparing the monthly statement of accounts. In principle, the total of the customer account balances in the subsidiary ledger should equal the balance of the account receivable control account in the general ledger. If not, an error exists in the records. Such bookkeeping errors should be investigated and rectified.

Irrecoverable Debts Write-Off

When certain accounts receivables become uncollectible after the credit term period have expired and despite **some** concerted efforts on recovery procedures (including legal and other administrative means), these bad debts will be classified as irrecoverable. When this happens, companies have no choice but to write-off them as irrecoverable debts beyond recovery. The accounting treatment to deal with these cases of delinquent accounts is explained in Chapter 14 – *Accounting for irrecoverable debts*.

The Allowance Method

Some receivables become doubtful for collection in the usual credit period because payments tend to be slower in some circumstances. In these known cases, it is prudent on the part of management to provide for an allowance of some percentage (%) to these delayed accounts as a form of insurance. This allowance method for providing for doubtful debts provision is explained in Chapter 14. The accounting aspects are discussed there, so refer to them.

Sales Ledger

In Chapter 2, we dealt with books of primary entry, one of which is the **sales day book** from which entries relating to sales transactions on credit are recorded and posted to the individual customers' account in the subsidiary sales ledger and to the sales account in the general ledger. The subsidiary sales ledger is also referred to as trade debtors' ledger. The individual customers' accounts appearing in the sales ledger are also known as accounts receivables. This is the usual terminology used in the financial statements today.

Reporting of Sales

All sales on credit in whatever mode it is transacted, recording the journal entry is the same.

Example:

A car retail sales company raised an invoice for the sale of spare parts and accessories to a regular customer for a sum of RM 8,900. Based on its latest product pricing list, it subsequently raised a credit note for RM 900 as the item qualified for a price discount.

Required:

Show the journal entries relating to this transaction:

Journal entries:	Folio	Dr	Cr
1. Accounts receivable	SL 55	8,900	
Sales account	GL 39		8,900
(Being sales of spare part and accessory)			
2. Discount on sales account	GL 58	900	
Accounts receivable	SL 55		900
(Being adjustment for a price discount on sale of spare part and accessory)			

The journal entries will be posted to the sales account in the General Ledger and the customer's account receivable in the Subsidiary Sales Ledger

Sectional Balancing Using a Control Account

A computer accounting software program can record many thousands of transactions in the double entry system. Error detected by a difference on the trial balance may pose a practical problem in finding and rectifying the source of the error. **Breaking the system into sections will facilitate the discovery of errors.**

In large accounting systems, the bulk of the entries basically fall into two broad areas:

a. Credit Sales

b. Purchases and Expenses incurred on credit

Therefore, it becomes necessary to keep the sections separate from the rest of the system particularly for these broad two areas. In a double entry system where there is a large volume of credit customers' accounts, the individual accounts of the credit customers are kept together in the *Subsidiary Sale Ledger,* of course, the sales ledger system is highly computerized today and in some cases back copies are maintained for security reasons.

Illustration of the Sales System

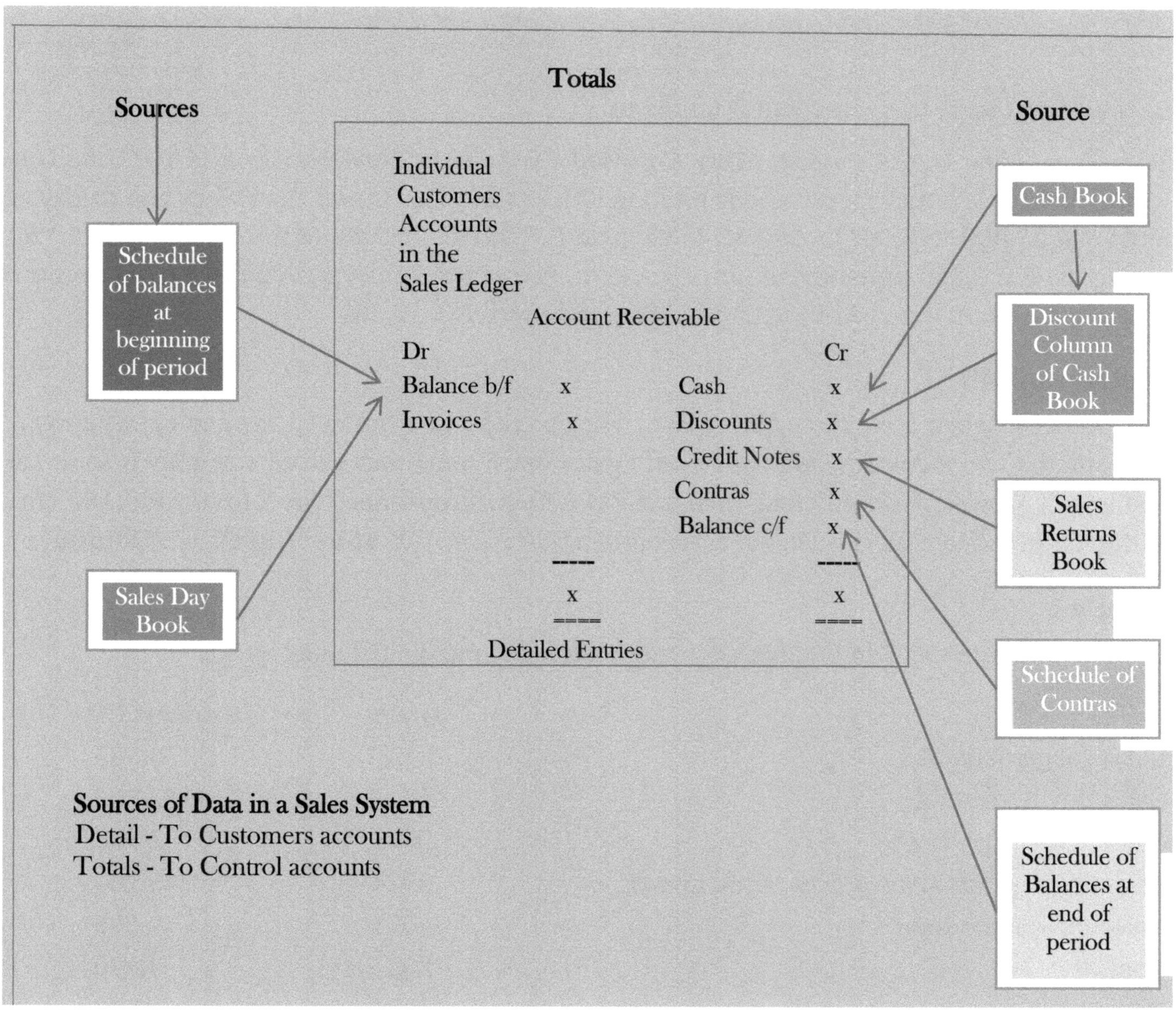

Chapter 7 on inventories will have some discussion about periodic inventory system and perpetual inventory system respectively on their relevance and usefulness.

Illustrated Example

A typical sales ledger account (accounts receivable) with respect to Misty Co, may appear like this in the books of a trading company, CG Sales & Services Sdn Bhd.

Misty Co Account

		RM			RM
1.8.21	Balance b/f	2,550	3.8.21	Cash	2,050
5.8 121	SDB:		3.8.21	Discount	250
	Goods per invoice	3,450	12.8.21	Credit note	2,000
12.8.21	Goods per invoice	2,650	20.8.21	Contra adjustment	1,820
25.8.21	Goods per invoice	14,750	31.8 21	Balance c/f	17,280
		23,400			23,400

Let's see what story of the account is telling us:

At the beginning of the August, Misty Co owed CG Sales & Services Sdn Bhd RM 2,550. In August, Misty Co bought more goods totaling RM 20,850. This meant that Misty had to pay or settle RM 23,400 in total. In August, Misty paid RM 2,050, was allowed discount RM 250 for paying the RM 2,050 promptly, returned goods valued at RM 2,000, settled RM 1,820 in contra, total RM 6,120. At the end of the month Misty still owed RM 12,280

Contras (set-off)

Contras occur when a credit customer also sells on credit to a business. Instead of exchanging a cheque the two indebtedness's are set off against each other and one cheque only is sent. For example, if X owes Y RM 450 and Y owes X RM 300, it is convenient for X to pay RM 150. The setting off of indebtedness is shown as a contra adjustment. **[(X 450– Y 300) = 150 due]**.

Example 1

CG Sales and Services Sdn Bhd has accounted the following figures in its books:

	Date	Amounts (RM)
Sales Ledger balances	1.1.21	18,525
Sales Day Book total	2021	182,760
Sales Return Day Book	2021	2,590
Cash Book – customers' proceeds (SL items)	2021	85,300
Discount column total	2021	1,895
Contras	2021	3,690
Irrecoverable debts written off	2021	790

Required

Prepare the Sales Ledger Control Account to show what the Sales Ledger balances should be at 30.9.2021.

Answer

In the books of CG Sales and Services:

Sales Ledger Control Account – at 30.9.2021

Balance b/f 1.1.2021	18,525	Sales Return DB – credit notes	2,590
Sales Day Book	182,760	Cash	85,300
		Discount	1,895
		Contras	3,690
		Bad debts written off	790
		Balance c/f 30. 9. 2021	107,020
	201,285		201,285

Now, the next stage is to extract a list of the individual sales ledger accounts. Suppose this came to RM 107,960, clearly some errors have occurred and an extensive search has shown:

i. Two balances were omitted from the list; RM 1,360 and RM 2,400
ii. The sales day book was under casted by RM 1,000
iii. A sales invoice for RM 620 in the sales day book was posted in error to two customers' accounts.
iv. An invoice for RM 460 correctly entered in the sales day book, was posted to the customer's account as RM 640.
v. A discount of RM 200 correctly entered in the customer's account was omitted from the discount column of the cash book.
vi. A contra of RM 1,000, included in the list had not been entered on the customer's account
vii. A customer had overpaid by RM 1,000 and a cheque had been sent to reimburse him. This had been correctly entered in his account.
viii. A customer had paid his account and subsequently been given a credit note. His account was in credit by RM 550 and this had been wrongly put on the list as a debit balance

Required

a. Prepare the revised sales ledger control account and

b. What should be the correct list of balances in total?

There are two sorts of error here:

i. Errors that affect the control account (errors in the books of prime entry), and
ii. Errors that affect the individual ledger accounts and hence the list of balances.

Tutorial note

It can be a daunting task to sort out any differences between control account balance and sales ledger balances. In practice, sectional balancing can be very useful in maintaining accuracy provided periodic checks are carried out on a regular basis particularly if a large system of accounts receivables is a normal feature of the business entity. Students are required to practice more exam-style questions.

Answer:

a. The revised sales ledger control account should show:

Sales Ledger Control Account – at 30. 9 .2021

Balance b/f 1.1.2021	18,525	Sales Return DB – credit notes	2,590
Sales Day Book (ii)	183,760	Cash	85,300
Credit balance (viii)	550	Discount (v)	2,095
Cash overpaid	1,000	Contras	3,690
		Bad debts written off	790
		Balance c/f 30.9.2021	109,370
	203,835		203,835

b. The list of balances in total should be:

As per original list		107,960
Add: (i) 1360 +2,400 =		3,760
		111,720
Less: Adjustments		
iii. posting error	620	
iv. posted error (640 – 460)	180	
vi. contra adjustment	1,000	
viii. 550 x 2 =	1,100	2,900
As per revised list		108,820

Reconciliation

Revised list of sales ledger individual customer's accounts in total		RM 108,820
As per Sales Ledger Control Account:		
Debit balance	109,370	
Credit balance (viii)	(550)	RM 108,820

Example 2

The following control account has been prepared by a trainee accountant:

Receivable/(Sales) Ledger Control Account (in RM)

Opening balance	308,600	Cash	147,200
Credit sales	154,200	Discount allowed	1,400
Cash sales	88,100	Interest charged on overdue accounts	2,400
Contras	4,600	Irrecoverable debts written off	4,900
		Allowance for receivable	2,800
		Closing balance	396,800
	555,500		555,500

Required

What should the closing balance be when all the errors made in preparing the receivable ledger control account been corrected?

a. RM 395,200
b. RM 304,300
c. RM 309,500
d. RM 307,100

Answer

	RM	
Closing balance as per control account	396,800	
Add: Interest charge on overdue accounts	4,800.	posted on wrong side
Allowance for receivable	2,800	should be dealt under separate a/c.
	404,400	
Less: Cash sales	(88,100)	cash sales should not be posted to control account.
Contras	(9,200)	posted on wrong side
	307,100	

Answer is (d)

Chapter Summary

1. **Sales and Receivables**

   We explained the different types or modes of sales that take place in a trading environment and the circumstantial reasons for their preferences. In a trading situation where the bulk of sales is done on a regular basis, sales transactions are often undertaken on **credit** terms. A credit system where it is necessary to maintain a **sales ledger** or subsidiary ledgers as they are called, becomes necessary to keep track of individual customers' accounts known as **accounts receivables**, a term used in financial statements.

2. **Trading or Merchandising Activities**

   We described trading (or merchandising) activities and identified the profit components for a trading entity.

   Traders buy and resell goods or products from manufacturers, wholesale suppliers and large retailers. The financial statements of a company report's their **sales or turnover** and the related cost of goods sold for the period in the trading account. **Gross profit** is arrived by matching the revenue earned from trading with the associated cost of goods sold. **Cost of goods sold** equals opening inventory + purchases for the period - closing inventory. Accounting for sales discount, sales returns and allowances were demonstrated by way of illustrated examples. Published accounts normally will not report these items because they are netted off as a contra adjustment on revenue or sales. However, for internal management accounts, these items are reflected with their impact on sales.

3. **Analyzing and Recording Transactions for Sales**

   A trader records sales at list price less any trade discounts. The cost of goods sold is transferred from inventory. Refunds or credits given to customers for defective items are recorded in **sales returns and allowances**, a contra account to sales. If goods returned and restored to inventory, the cost of this merchandise is removed from cost of goods sold and transferred back to inventory. When cash discounts from the sales price are offered and customers settle within the discount period, the trader records **discounts**, a contra account adjustment to sales.

4. **Explaining the Sales System in Accounting**

   Explained with the aid of an illustrated diagram how the **sales system** works in a trading environment, using accounting terminology and the double-entry system to account for the sales transactions. **Accounts receivable** in the general ledger, the use and purpose of **control accounts** and the **sales day book,** together with the **subsidiary ledgers** were discussed as part of the overall sales system. with illustrated numerical examples. We also explained **irrecoverable debts** and why it occurs, including the **allowance method** to account for doubtful debts as a method of provisioning.

Key Terms

Accounts receivable	Cash discount	Cost of goods sold	Credit note
Credit period	Credit terms	Debit note	Discount period
Gross profit	Inventory	List price	Merchandise
Merchandiser	Periodic inventory system	Perpetual inventory system	Retailor
Sales discount	Subsidiary ledgers	Sales returns	Contra account
Irrecoverable debts (bad debts).	Trade discount	Sales allowances	Sales day book
Wholesaler	Turnover	Trading account	

Review Questions

Q1. Rebecca Ferguson is a sole trader who does not keep full accounting records. The following details relate to her transactions with credit customers and suppliers for the financial year ended 30 September 2021.

Trade receivables, 1 October 2020	130,000
Trade payables, 1 October 2020	60,000
Cash received from customers	686,400
Cash paid to suppliers	302,800
Discounts allowed	1,400
Discounts received	2,960
Contra between payables and receivables ledger	2,000
Trade receivables, 30 September 2021	181,000
Trade payables, 30 September 2021	84,000

Required

a. What figures should appear for sales and purchases on Rebecca's statement of profit or loss for the year ended 30 September 2021

b. (**Hint:** Both sales and purchases will be balancing figures in the control accounts)

c. What should be the adjustment for irrecoverable debts arising from certain uncollectible accounts in the trade receivables ledger? Assume irrecoverable debts amounted to RM 2,550. Revise the figure for the closing trade receivables on 30 September 2021.

Q2. Explain the different types of sales transactions that can take place between the customer and the seller.

Q3. Explain a sales ledger receivable control account. What is the advantage of operating this account?

Q4. Discuss briefly why a contra adjustment is required to an accounts receivable account?

Q5. Distinguish between irrecoverable debts and an allowance for doubtful debts.

Q6. What two types of errors that can occur in the sales ledger system?

Q7. Briefly state the steps that should be taken to control credit sales from delinquent accounts?

Q8. Describe trading activities and identify profit components for a trading or merchandising company.

Q9. Explain how you would be reporting a profit between a trading (merchandising) company and a service company?

Q10. Describe how do arrive at a trader's cost of goods sold?

Q11. What is gross profit for a trading or merchandising company?

Q12. Explain why use of the perpetual inventory system has dramatically increased?

Q13. Explain what is a trade discount and how would a cash discount is distinguished from a trade discount? Give an example of each type of discount.

Q14. Why are sales discounts and sales returns (returns inward) and allowances recorded in contra revenue accounts instead of directly in the sales account?

Q15. Under what conditions are two entries necessary to record a sales return?

Q16. When merchandise or goods is sold on credit and the seller (vendor) notifies the buyer of a price allowance.

i. Does the seller prepare and send a credit note or debit note?

ii. Explain the purpose why a trader creates a credit note and a debit note?

Q17. a. Show how the cost of goods is done under the periodic system?

b. How the computation of gross profit is arrived?

Q.18 What account is used in a perpetual inventory system but not in a periodic system?

Multiple Choice Questions

Q1. A company has RM 195, 690 in gross profit and RM 575, 000 in net sales. This means its cost of goods sold equals

a. RM 745, 000
b. RM 357, 310
c. RM 379, 310
d. RM 195, 310
e. RM 379,340

Q2. A company purchased RM 4, 500 of goods on June 1 with terms of 2/10, n/30. On June 7, it returned RM 250 of that goods. On June 9, it paid the balance owed for goods, taking any discount it is entitled to. The cash paid on June 9 is

a. RM 4, 300
b. RM 4, 160
c. RM 4, 250
d. RM 4, 165
e. RM 4, 410

Q3. A company's net sales are RM 695, 000, its cost of goods sold are RM 486.500, and its net profit is RM 75, 550. Its gross profit margin equals

a. 30 %
b. 70 %
c. 48 %
d. 10 %
e. 32 %

Q4. A company has cash sales of RM 75, 000, credit sales of RM 325, 000, sales returns and allowances of RM 14, 700, sales discounts of RM 5, 000. Its net sales equals

a. RM 380, 300
b. RM 396, 000
c. RM 375, 000
d. RM 300, 300
e. RM 339, 700

Q5. Which statement is true?

1. The sales invoice is the purchaser's request for collection from the customer.
2. Gross profit is the excess of sales revenue over the cost of goods sold.
3. The sales account is used to record only credit sales (sales on account).
4. A service company purchases products or goods from suppliers and then sells them
5. Net profit is arrived after deducting operating expense from sales revenue.

Q6. Sales discounts should appear in published financial statements

1. As a deduction from sales
2. Among the operating expenses
3. As an addition to opening inventory amount
4. As an addition to sales
5. As part of finance cost

Q7. How is inventory classified in the financial statements?

1. As an expense
2. As a contra account to cost of goods sold
3. As a revenue
4. As a liability
5. As an asset

Q8. The closing inventory of Kubera Traders, is RM 58, 500. If opening inventory was RM 68,500 and goods availed totalled RM 118, 000, the cost of goods sold is

a. RM 60, 000 c. RM 99, 000 e. None of the above

b. RM 49, 500 d. RM 68, 500

Use the following information for questions 9-11

Digital Sales and Services Company had a RM 32, 000 opening inventory and a RM 36, 000 closing inventory. Sales were RM 187, 000, purchases, RM 95, 000, sales returns and allowances, RM 7, 000, freight and handling charges RM 2, 800. (This last item should be added to cost of goods sold before arriving at the gross profit).

First step is to compute the trading account

Q9. Cost of goods sold for the period

a. RM 98, 000 c. RM 96, 000 e. None of the above

b. RM 86, 000 d. RM 81, 000

Q10. What is Digital Sales and Services' gross profit percentage (rounded to nearest %)?

a. 52 % c. 48 % e. None of the above

b. 18 % d. 45 %

Q11. What is Digital Sales and Services' s rate of inventory turnover?

$$\text{Rate of inventory turnover} = \frac{\text{Cost of Goods sold}}{\text{Average inventory}}$$

a. 5. 2 times c. 2.3 times e. None of the above

b. 2.5 times d. 3.0 times

Q12. Opening inventory RM 115, 000, purchases are RM 250, 000 and sales amounted to RM 480, 000.

The normal gross profit margin is 35 %. Using GP margin, how much is the closing inventory?

a. RM 88, 000 c. RM 105, 000 e. None of the above

b. RM 130, 000 d. RM 53, 000

Q13. An overstatement of closing inventory in one period results in

1. An understatement of net profit of the next period.
2. An understatement of the opening inventory of the next period
3. An overstatement of net profit of the next period.
4. No effect on net profit of the next period.
5. None of the above.

Q14. Interpret the result to question 11 above and comment.

Mathematics is not about numbers, equations, computations, or algorithms: It is about understanding.

— Srinivasa Ramanujan

Chapter 6

Learning Objectives

After you have studied this chapter, you should be able to:

Analyze and record transactions for purchases using a perpetual system
Record purchase transactions in the purchase day book or journal before posting to ledgers
Record purchase discounts received and account for purchase returns and allowances
Identify all costs incidental to purchases
Identify and explain accounts payable to be recorded in both the general and subsidiary ledgers
Understand the purpose of control accounts for accounts payable
Understand how control accounts relate to the double entry system
Prepare purchase ledger control account from given information
Account for contras between accounts payable and accounts receivable
Perform control account reconciliations for accounts payable
Identify errors emerging by performing control account reconciliation
Identify and correct these errors in control accounts and ledgers using journal entries.
Prepare, reconcile and understand the purpose of supplier statement of accounts
Prepare a list of closing balances for all accounts payable from the subsidiary ledgers

Purchases and Payables

Scope

This Chapter focuses on accounting for **purchases and payables**. What we are doing here is just the opposite of sales and receivables that was a subject of accounting in Chapter 5. Business entities need to **account for all forms of purchasing transactions as part of its trading activity**. The trader's **operating circle** depicts a trading environment which begins with **purchase**s becoming **inventory** (stock-in-trade), converting them into **credit sales** and **accounts receivable**s before **cash collection**. Cash collection from accounts receivable is based on **credit terms** negotiated on arm's length basis. Analyzing and keeping records of both trade and cash purchases is part of the mainstream accounting process. The **cost of goods sold** comprising some breakdown figures is reported in the trading account. (See illustration given in item 2 of Chapter summary) The **trading account reflects what the sales revenue was and the associated cost of goods sold to arrive at the gross profit amount before operating costs** of the business. **Various cost elements making up the purchasing function are explained** in the form of **purchase returns**, **allowances**, **discounts** (trade and cash). **Freight charges** and their shipping FOB terms are also explained. The **source documents** accompanying the various purchasing activity are **used** as a basis **for recording the accounting transactions and events**. The **control accounts** relating to sales ledger (accounts receivable) and purchases ledger (accounts payable) are the mirror image of sales and purchases respectively. The **control account simply acts as a detection and correction tool to keep track of account balances free of errors** that may wrong in accounting. The **use of sectional balancing of control accounts and their reconciliations can serve as an effective device.** The ending pages gives an illustration of how control accounts is maintained.

Operating Cycle for a Trader

A trading company dealing with merchandise usually has an operating cycle that begins by purchasing goods and ends by collecting cash from selling the merchandise (or stock-in-trade). The operating cycle period differs across the different types of business. Supermarkets or departmental stores normally have operating cycles that range between two to six months. Others like grocery traders usually have shorter periods ranging between two weeks to six weeks. Retailers in electrical and electronic items may have longer periods that take months or a year or more time.

Figure 5.1 illustrates an operating cycle for a typical trader operating with credit sales.

The cycle begins from purchases to inventory for sale to credit sales to accounts receivable to cash collection. Companies tend to keep their operating cycle short because to avoid too much of working capital being tied-up in inventory and receivables that are not productive. The main purpose is to convert inventory into sales before cash collection. Cash sales obviously shorten operating cycles as cash collection is instantaneously realized.

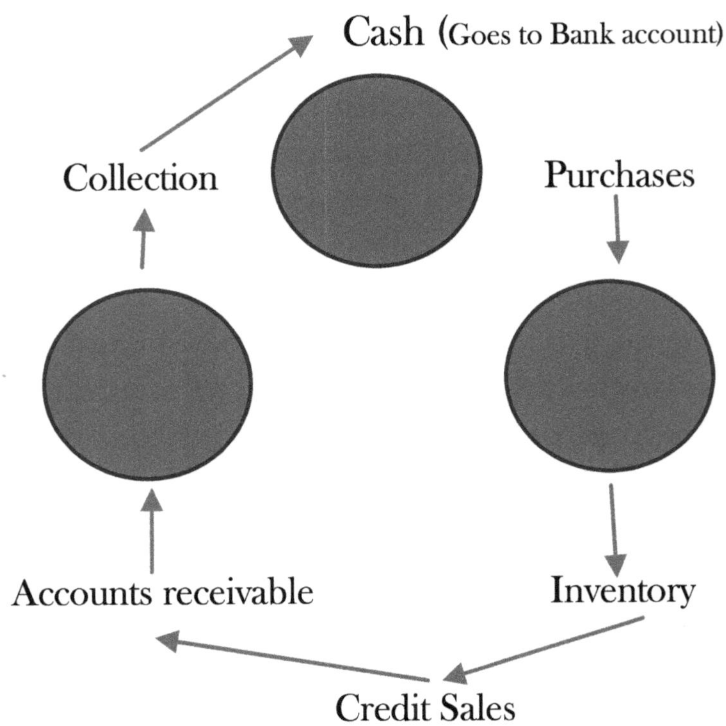

Figure 5.1 Trader's operating cycle

Purchases

Business entities in retail industry or in other business operating segments make purchases for resale. All these purchases of stock-in-trade are treated as part of the **perpetual inventory system.** The perpetual inventory system is operated by the majority of business entities in various industries. The system tracks all inventory movements of purchases and makes use of a computer system to keep a running record of inventory on hand and what has been sold. This system provides better information and control over the inventory for companies. In a perpetual inventory system, all credit purchase transactions are tracked and accounted for using the purchase day book or journal as part of the accounting system. The system of recording purchases is continuously updated as transactions occur throughout the accounting period. The use of **accounting software package** facilitates this process and recording.

Accounting for Purchases and Inventories

The cost of goods purchased for resale is recorded in the **purchases accoun**t with a corresponding entry in the **accounts payable**. Both these accounts are recorded in the general ledger. However, the **inventory asset account** is automatically recorded for the purchases done in a perpetual system, but the inventory account is not part of the double-entry system because inventories are recorded physically in quantities to keep in a running track**. Inventory valuation** takes place at the end of the reporting period using **the cost valuation method.** Refer to details in **Chapter 7** for the basis of valuation as prescribed by the accounting standard.

To illustrate, C-Mart records a RM 2, 200 credit purchase of goods as follows:

Dr: Purchases	RM 2,200	
Cr: Accounts Payable		RM 2,200
(Being goods purchased on credit from Aachi Traders)		

The purchases ledger for this supplier – Aachi Traders gets credited via posting from the purchases day book., using the perpetual system.

A **purchase requisition note** is usually raised for every credit purchase by the trader. The trader obtains an original **purchase invoice** and the supplier (seller) keeps a copy. This invoice indicates the total purchase price and other related information. The purchaser uses the copy of the sales invoice sent by the seller as a **source document** to record the purchases. The amount recorded for merchandise (goods) includes its *purchase cost, freight and handling charges, and any other incidental costs* necessary to bring the goods to its present location in the warehouse or stores.

Transportation Costs (Freight Charges) and Ownership Transfer.

The contract between the seller and the purchaser should indicate who – the seller or the buyer – is to pay for transporting the goods to the buyer's location of business. Usually transporting of goods is by a common carrier and can take several modes such as trucks or containers, by road, rail, or airline. The carrier prepares a freight bill based on the agreed terms of the contract.

The trader (buyer) and the supplier (seller) must agree on who is responsible for paying any freight charges and who bears the risk of loss or damage during transit for merchandising transactions. This arrangement essentially determines at which point ownership transfers from seller to buyer. The point of transfer is called the **FOB** (*free on board*). Freight terms are expressed as FOB *shipping* or FOB *destination*. Accordingly, *FOB shipping* means that the seller agrees to put the goods on board the carrier, and the buyer pays for the freight charges. Conversely, FOB *destination* means that the seller puts the goods free on board to the buyer's location of business and the seller pays for the freight. The **Table** below illustrates ownership transfer and transportations costs when goods are in transit.

	Ownership Transfers	**Transportation Costs**
	When goods passed to	**Paid by**
FOB Shipping point	Carrier	Buyer
FOB Destination	Buyer	Seller

Accounting for Freight Costs

Freight charges are accounted for as part of the cost of purchase, but some businesses may choose to keep track of the costs separately before adding it to the cost of goods sold at a later period when the financial statements are prepared. This practice is common as it allows a business to track and monitor how much shipping or delivery charges it incurs.

Purchase Returns and Allowances

When the goods received appears damaged or defective, or of inferior quality, or fails to meet the purchaser's specifications, the purchaser may be dissatisfied. In such cases, the purchaser may return the goods to the seller for credit if the transaction was made on credit or for a cash refund if the purchase was made in cash. This transaction will be referred as a **purchase return.** Alternatively, the purchaser may choose to keep the goods if the seller is willing to offer a price reduction from the original purchase price which in this case it is referred as **purchase allowance.**

Purchase Discounts

The **credit terms** of the purchase contract may allow the buyer to obtain a **cash discount** for prompt payment. The buyer will treat this as **discount received** on purchases. This policy on discounts allows both parties an advantage. The buyer saves money, and the seller is able to shorten the operating cycle by converting the accounts receivable more quickly into cash. Credit terms specify the amount of **cash** or **trade discount** and time period in which it is offered. **Credit terms** for purchases often reflect an industry's practices. **Figure 5.2** illustrates credit terms. The amount of time allowed before full settlement is due is called the **credit period.** Any cash or trade discount granted by the seller is usually reflected as credit terms in the purchase invoice.

Figure 5.2

Credit Terms		Credit period *(n/30)*	
		Discount period *(n/10)*	
	Date of invoice		
Time			
Amount		Due: Invoice price	Due: Invoice price
Due	Less discount *		

* Discount refers to a purchase discount for a buyer and a sales discount for a seller.

Trade Discounts

When a manufacturer or wholesaler prepares a catalog of items it has for sale, it usually gives each item a list price (or catalog price). However, an item's intended selling price equals list price less a given percentage (%) called a **trade discount**. The amount of trade discount usually depends on whether a buyer is a wholesaler, retailer, or final consumer. A wholesaler buying in large quantities is often given a larger discount than a retailer buying in small quantities. A buyer records the net amount of list price less trade discount. When sellers require payment within 10 days after the end of the month of the invoice date, the invoice will indicate credit terms as *n/10.,* and when sellers require payment within 30 days after the invoice date, the invoice will indicate credit terms of n/30 which means for net 30 days. For an example, C-Mart buys goods, the merchandise was listed in the seller's catalog at RM 2, 000 and C-Mart was entitled to a 30 % trade discount. This meant that C-Mart's purchase price RM 1, 400, computed as RM 2, 000 – (30 % x RM 2, 000).

Recording a Purchase Transaction

Example: Simon Chong, who runs a retail business, ordered goods for resale from a manufacturer of cloth garments. He was able to negotiate a bulk discount 8% for his purchases and a payment term of 30 days. The invoice received from the supplier showed a total purchase price of RM 3,600 (after bulk discount). Freight charges amounted to RM 250.

Simon has a choice of recording the transaction in either of the following journal entries:

Option 1	Journal entry:	Dr	Cr
	Purchases	RM 3,850	
	Account Payable		RM 3,850
	(Being purchase of cloth garments, including freight charges)		
Option 2	Journal entry	Dr	Cr
	Purchases	RM 3,600	
	Freight charges	RM 250	
	Account Payable		RM 3,850
	(Being purchase of cloth garments, including freight charges)		

If Simon uses option 2, at the end of the accounting period, the freight inwards account should be separately added as part of the cost of sales figure. In practice, Option 1 is not adopted although freight and handling charges form a part of the purchase costs, a preferred practice is to keep separate accounts for cost management purposes.

Recording Purchases Returns and Allowances

Sometimes, there will be instances where specifications are not met. For example, if Simon might have ordered a dozen of black blazers of certain size but blue ones were delivered instead, or in the wrong sizes and the items were defective. Depending on the terms of the contract, Simon may be able to ask for either a cash refund or a further discount. A **purchase return** is a reduction in price since the customer is returning the goods to the supplier or vendor. A **purchase allowance** is also a price reduction because the buyer acquired defective or unacceptable merchandise. Buyers often keep defective but still marketable merchandise if the seller gives an acceptable allowance. When a buyer returns or accepts an allowance on goods acquired, the buyer issues a **debit note** to inform the seller of a debit adjustment to the seller's account (accounts payable) in the buyer's records. In some situations, the seller issues a **credit note** to indicate a price reduction for defective merchandise when the buyer returns the affected items.

In a perpetual system, the inventory records are adjusted accordingly to reflect the goods returned to the warehouse or the store. But in the case of defective items, they are treated as obsolete inventory possibly ear-marked to be non-marketable. However, in such cases, the inventory valuation sheets reported at the year-end will show an allowance or a provision for **obsolescence** which renders those items at **net realizable value** if it can be **marketable below market price.** In some cases, these stock items will be **written-off** in the stock valuation sheets if no reliable value can be determined.

Some sellers or vendors will revise the original purchase invoices to reflect these returns and allowances. Suppose Simon returned RM 600 worth of products to his supplier and the seller has agreed to reduce the amount due which in this case, the following journal entry would be recorded:

Journal entry:	Dr	Cr
Account Payable	RM 600	
Purchases		RM 600
(Being returned defective goods to seller)		

Recording Purchase Discounts

As we know, Simon makes his purchases from various suppliers on credit. **Credit terms** could be 30 days which indicate that the buyer has to settle the full amount within 30 days. Occasionally, the seller or vendor gives a settlement discount of 2 % to the buyer for early payments say within 10 working days, otherwise the invoiced amount is due within 30 days. The discount is based on the amount of goods purchased and excludes other incidental charges such as delivery or handling costs.

Suppose Simon ordered another line of lady garments from a different supplier amounting to RM 2,500. This supplier offers a 3 % settlement discount and 30-day credit period with free freight and handling charges. When the goods were received, Simon records the transaction as follows:

Journal entry:	Dr	Cr
Purchases	RM 2,500	
Account Payable		RM 2,500
(Being purchase of lady garments on 3% settlement discount and 30-day credit)		

If Simon decides to take advantage of the early settlement discount, he would pay RM 2,425 to settle his invoice amount of RM 2,500. The journal entry would be as follows;

Accounts Payable	RM 2,500	
Cash		RM 2,425
Discount received*		RM 75
(Being payment for purchases with 3% settlement discount)		

*Discount received will have the effect of reducing the cost of sale figure

Putting together all these transactions, let's determine the cost of purchases using the following example as an illustration

Example:

Caxton Press purchased large quantity of rolls of paper from one of its major suppliers amounting to RM 395,000 for printing works. Caxton paid RM 2,800 for the delivery and handling charges to get the shipment to the store. However, due to incorrect specification details, the company returned some of these rolls of paper with the supplier raising a debit note for RM 13,500. The supplier also extended an allowance for price revision of certain types of paper amounting to RM 3,000. Caxton took advantage of early settlement of a discount scheme offered by its

Required:

What is Caxton Press's net cost of purchases?

	RM
Cost of Purchases: (to the buyer)	
Purchase price	395,000
Freight and handling charges	2,800
Purchase returns	(13,500)
Allowance for price reduction	(3,000)
Cash discount for early settlement	(10,000)
Net cost	365,700

Tutorial note

Some business entities maintain separate accounts for purchase discounts, returns and allowances, freight or transportation and handling costs. These accounts are then transferred to ***the cost of goods sold*** *as part of the purchases cost at the period-end, this represents a hybrid of perpetual and periodic systems. The inventory cost is updated on a perpetual basis but only for purchases and cost of goods sold.*

Purchases Ledger

If you have understood the sectional balancing of the sales ledger, then the sectional balancing of the purchases ledger will present no difficulties as it is the mirror image of the sales ledger. Simply, the entries relating to the purchases ledger control account go on the opposite side of their counterparts on the sales ledger

A common examination style question which combines knowledge of both sales and purchase ledger control accounts is presented here.

Illustrative Question

Sun-Moon Sales and Services include the following items in their books for 2021

Balances at 31.7.2020	RM
Dr. Sales Ledger	160,220
Cr. Sales Ledger	1, 400
Cr. Purchases Ledger	600,310
Sales day book	1,101,005
Purchases day book	520,666
Sales return day book.	10,040
Contras	10,551
Irrecoverable debts (Bad debts) written off	20,150
Cash Book Debit	
Sales ledger items	960,484
Purchase ledger items	1,052
Cash Book Credit	
Purchase ledger items	490,200
Sales Ledger items	14,000
Dr. Discount column	19,200
Cr. Discount column	8,670
Purchase ledger Dr. balance 31.8.21	650
Sales Ledger Cr. balance 31.8.21	2,440

Required: Prepare the control accounts for the sales ledger and the purchases ledger, showing clearly the closing balances as at 31.8.21

Sales Ledger Control Account - y/e 31.8.21

	RM		RM
Balance at 31.7.20	160,220	Balances at 31.7.20	1,400
Sales	1,101,005	Sales return	10,040
Cash	14,000	Contras	10,551
Balance at 31.8.21	2,440	Bad debts written off	20,150
		Cash	960,484
		Discounts	19,200
		Balance 31.8.21	255,840
	1,277,665		1,277,665

Purchases Ledger Control Account - y/e 31.8.21

	RM		RM
Contras	10,551	Balances at 31.7.20	600,310
Cash	490,200	Purchases	520,666
Discount	8,670	Cash	1,052
Balance at 31.8.21	613,257	Balance 31.8.21	650
	1,122,678		1,122,678

Tutorial notes: *Large accounting systems need to be broken down into manageable sections to facilitate the detection of errors The most useful way to manage sectional balancing is the creation of sales ledger sub-system and the purchase ledger sub-systems, using control accounts. Students should scrutinize the entries to ensure they understand the double-entry accounting for both types of ledger control*

Chapter Summary

1. **Analyze and record transactions for trade purchases**

   Purchase of merchandise for resale is reported net of **trade and cash discounts**. Purchase returns and allowances are deducted from purchases in the trading account. They are accounted for as separate accounts in the general ledger. However, when computing for cost of goods sold at the end of reporting period, these items are shown net of purchases. **Cost of purchases** include its original costs (list price less both trade and cash discounts) less any amount for returns and allowances plus incidental costs such as freight (shipping), handling and transporting charges to bring the acquired merchandise or goods to its present location for resale. The individual cost components are accounted separately.

2. **Cost of goods sold reported in the trading account of a business entity**

   The **cost of goods sold** is arrived by adding and subtracting opening inventory and closing inventory costs respectively. In the trading account, however, the cost of goods sold is added to other incidental costs that is incurred as part of the total trading costs. However, in practice, published accounts like **the statement of comprehensive income** rarely discloses **purchase discounts**, **purchase returns** and **allowances**. Only net purchases get reported as a disclosure requirement. Do you know why? Figure it out.

   The computation is shown below:

Calculation of Cost of Goods Sold and Other Incidental Costs

			Internal Reporting	Published Accounts
Opening inventory			xxx	xxx
Purchases	xxx			
Less:				
Discounts		(xx)		
Returns and allowances		(xx)		
Net purchases			xxx	xxx
Cost of goods available for sale			xxx	xxx
Less:				
Closing inventory			(xxx)	(xxx)
Cost of goods sold			**xxx**	xxx
Add:				
Freight charges			xx	xx
Transportation charges			xx	xx
Total trading cost			xxx	xxx

A trader's costs in the **statement of comprehensive income** include cost of goods sold. *Gross profit = Sales – Cost of goods sold.* Closing inventory is the remaining stocks in hand, valued at the close of the reporting period and shown as a **current asset** in the **statement of financial position.**

3. **Accounting for Purchases Returns and Allowances.**

   Where **specifications** are not met by quality standards, traders would normally return the merchandise to the supplier or seller. These specifications may include quality issues, wrong description of items and in some cases defective goods were shipped to the stores. In all such cases, the trader or buyer would normally return the goods, this is called **purchase returns** and in some other cases, the goods received by the buyer can be defective or faulty and would be either returned for replacements by the seller or the buyer would keep the items if they are marketable merchandise (and sold later at lower prices) but may negotiate for price reduction. This is called **purchase allowances**. Purchase returns and allowances is a normal feature of trading or merchandise activity.

In all these circumstances, the buyer would raise a **debit note** to inform the seller about price reduction for such merchandise and where the seller's account is adjusted in the buyer's books. Where the seller issues a **credit note**, a similar adjustment will be done to the buyer's account in the seller's books. In practice, either party can prompt the required action to correct the anomaly. Both credit and debit notes are **source documents** evidencing returns and allowances.

4. **Purchase Ledger and Control Accounts**

   A business entity that engages in heavy trading of merchandise will need to keep an accounting system that maintains proper records to account for all kind of purchases whether for cash or on credit. The use of books of prime entry becomes essential because in a **perpetual inventory system**, the updating and tracking of transactions is done on a continuous basis. This necessitates the use of **subsidiary ledgers** to keep track of all **accounts payables** and the operation of c**ontrol accounts** to ensure an error-free accounting system. There must be adequate procedures for **reconciliation** if bookkeeping errors occurring in accounting, particularly in accounts payable (trade creditors) where balances may be wrong or inaccurate. The detection and correction of such errors can be time consuming and a costly affair. The use of **sectional balancing** of control accounts and their reconciliations can be effective if regular scrutiny or internal checks are done on a regular basis.

5. **Transportation and Ownership Transfer**

   Companies engaged in trade usually negotiate with suppliers and customers on **freight cost**. Two alternative points of transfer are identified. (i) **FOB** *shipping point* and (ii) **FOB** *destination point*. FOB *shipping* means the buyer or customer accepts ownership when the goods depart the seller's place of business. The customer is then responsible for paying shipping costs and bearing the risk of loss or damage when goods are in transit. The goods in transit becomes part of the buyer's inventory as ownership of title passes to the buyer (customer). FOB *destination* means ownership of goods passes to the buyer only when it arrives at the buyer's place of business. The seller is responsible for paying shipping charges and bears the risk of loss or damage during transit. The seller does not record revenue from this sale until the goods arrive at the customer's destination or place of business, at which point the transfer of ownership title passes to the customer.

Key Terms

Accounts payable
Cash discount
Credit note
Discount period
Gross margin
List price
Paid on account
Purchase discount
Obsolescence
Sales discount
Trade discount

Payment on account
Cost of goods sold
Credit terms
FOB Shipping
Gross profit
Merchandise (Goods)
Periodic inventory system
Purchase requisition note
Retailer
Sectional balancing
Wholesaler

Control account
Credit period
Debit note
FOB Destination
Inventory
Merchandiser
Perpetual inventory system
Reconciliation
Subsidiary ledgers

Review Questions

1. Describe merchandising activities of a trading company. Show the profit components for a trading company that is engaged in buying and selling goods
2. Explain what is a wholesaler, a retailer and distinguish their activities.
3. Describe a trading company's cost of goods sold.
4. How is gross profit determined for a trader or a merchandising company?
5. Explain how accounting is done for merchandise purchases by cash and on credit?
6. How would you analyze and record transactions for purchases using a perpetual system? Explain which books of prime entry is used for recording and postings to the ledgers?
7. Explain what you understand by trade discounts and cash discounts? Is the amount of trade discount on purchased merchandise recorded in the accounts?
8. Why do companies offer a cash discount?
9. What items appear in financial statements of trading (merchandising) companies but not in in the financial statements of service companies?
10. a. Explain what are purchase returns and allowances. Under what circumstances they occur?
    b. How would a trader account for these transactions in the records?
11. What source documents are used for credit purchases in accounting? Specify what information is recorded in the purchase invoice? Explain the purpose of using a purchase requisition note?
12. Explain what is the importance of maintaining an accounts payable? What accounting records are used to account for all outstanding balances of individual trade creditors.
13. a. Explain the purpose of operating control accounts in the purchases ledger system, particularly when a merchandising company has a large volume of trade with numerous suppliers.
    b. Describe the benefits of using control accounts in the purchases ledger system.
14. Traders normally negotiate purchase contracts with suppliers. What type shipping terms should a trader attempt to negotiate to minimize freight costs or charges?
15. Explain the meaning of these terms (i) FOB, (ii) FOB *Shipping,* (iii) FOB *Destination*
16. Explain the importance of these terms, (i) Debit note, (ii) Credit note, and their accounting adjustments in the records.
17. Explain the accounting entries for defective merchandise. What happens when cash is refunded?
18. Suppose C-Mart Trading purchases RM 1, 000 of merchandise on July 1 with terms 2/10, n/30. Two days later, C-Mart returns RM 100 of goods before paying the invoice. When C-Mart later pays on July 11, it takes advantage of the 2 % discount only on RM 900 remaining balance of the invoice.

Required

a. Explain the credit terms, 2/10 and n/30.

b. Show the required journal entries to reflect on these transactions.

Multiple Choice Questions

1. A company reported RM 580, 000 in net sales and its cost of goods sold amounted to RM 359, 500. What was the gross profit for the reporting period?

   a. 745, 000 b. RM 545, 000 c. RM 230, 000
   d. 195, 000 e. RM 220, 500

2. A company net sales are RM 675, 000, its cost of goods sold are RM 459, 000, and its net profit is RM 74, 250. Its gross profit margin equals

   a. 32 % b. 68 % c. 48 %
   d. 12 % e. 35 %

3. A company reported cash purchases of RM 75, 000, credit purchases of RM 335, 000, purchase returns and allowances of RM 14,400 and purchase discount of RM 6, 000. Its net purchases equal

   a. RM 389, 500 b. RM 385, 000 c. RM 375, 500
   d. RM 300, 30 e. RM 339, 900

4. A company has RM 650, 000 in sales. Sales discounts were RM 15, 000 and its sales return and allowances amounted to RM 35, 000. Its gross profit reported to be RM 198, 000. This means its cost of goods sold equals

   a. RM 443, 000 b. RM 550, 000 c. RM 355, 000
   d. RM 283, 000 e. RM 402, 000

5. A company purchased RM 4, 500 of goods on 1 April with terms of 2/7, n/30. On 6 April, it returned RM 250 of that merchandise. On 8 April, it paid the balance owed for merchandise, taking any discount it is entitled to. What cash was paid on 8 April?

   a. RM 4, 500 b. RM 4, 250 c. RM 4, 160
   d. RM 4, 165 e. RM 4, 410

6. Purchase discounts should appear in the financial statements

   a. As a deduction from purchases b. As an operating expense
   c Among the current liabilities d. As an addition to sales
   e. As a deduction to inventory

7. Which of the following statements is true?

   a. The invoice is the purchaser's requisition for collection of goods from the seller.
   b. Gross profit is the excess of sales revenue over cost of goods sold.
   c. The sales account is used to record only credit sales.
   d. Cost of goods sold is deducted from closing inventory to show the gross profit.

8. The closing inventory of C-Mart Traders is RM 57, 000. If the opening inventory was RM 68,000

   Goods available for sale amounted to RM 117, 000. The cost of goods sold is

   a. RM 60, 000. b. RM 120, 000 c. RM 65, 000
   d. RM 48, 000

9. Keith Farmer is a British chartered accountant who runs residential courses in Financial Reporting and has many students in Malaysia. His revenue is made up of fee collections from conducting these courses and he reports RM 100, 000 as his income. Farmer's operating expense are RM 36, 000. Ignoring his resident status, what will be his operating profit?

   a. RM 70, 000. b. RM 54, 000 c. RM 64, 000
   d. RM 66, 000 e. RM 74, 000

Using the following information, answer the question 10 – 11.

Fair Trading Company's net sales were RM 153, 000, purchases, RM 94, 000, purchase returns and allowances, RM 7, 000 and freight costs, RM 4, 000. The company's opening inventory and closing inventory were RM 28, 000 and RM 35, 000 respectively.

10. Cost of goods sold for the period is

    a. RM 69, 000 b. RM 94, 000 c. RM 84, 000
    d. RM 68, 400 e. RM 86, 600

11. What is the gross profit margin?

    a. 60 % b. 55 % c. 45 %
    d. 42 % e. 44 %

    Some adjustments are required as a result of audit findings relating to accounting errors. Net sales were understated due to omission of two invoices totaling RM 2, 000. Purchase returns were overstated by RM 450 due to clerical error. Freight charges wrongly computed by the forwarding company, the correct amount should have been RM 4, 350. Audit checks showed the closing inventory figure had several counting errors in the stock sheets that overvalued the amount by RM 1, 800. **What impact do these adjustments will have?**

12. On the actual cost of goods sold for the period, correctly stating the amount.

    a. RM 69, 000 b. RM 94, 000 c. RM 84, 000
    d. RM 68, 400 e. RM 86, 600

13. On the gross profit amount?

    a. RM 69, 000 b. RM 94, 000 c. RM 84, 000
    d. RM 68, 400 e. RM 86, 600

14. On the GP margin (%) by restating to nearest whole number

    a. 60 % b. 55 % c. 45 %
    d. 42 % e. 44 %

Unless the derivatives contracts are collatarised or guaranteed, their ultimate value depends on the credit worthiness of the counter parties to them. In the meantime, though, before a contract is settled, the counterparties record profits and losses - often huge in amount - in their current earnings statements without so much as a penny changing hands. The range of derivatives contracts is limited only by the imagination of a man (or sometimes, its madmen).

— Warren Buffet

Chapter 7

Learning Objectives

Recognize the need for adjustments for inventory in preparing financial statements
Be able to record opening and closing inventory
Be able to identify the items making up the inventory
Be able to identify the costs of merchandise inventory
Understand and apply the accounting standard's requirement for valuing inventories
Be able to identify alternative methods of valuing inventory
Be able to recognize which costs should be included in valuing inventories
Be able to analyze the effects of inventory methods for both financial and tax reporting, particularly on profits and on assets.
Be able to analyze the effects of inventory errors on current and future financial statements
Be able to compute the value of closing inventory in a perpetual system using methods of specific costs, FIFO, weighted average cost.
Be able to compute the value of closing inventory in a periodic system using the methods of specific costs, FIFO and weighted average cost.
Be able to understand and apply inventory estimation methods such as retail inventory method
Be able to compute the lower of cost and net realizable value and understand why inventory is measured this way.
Understand the impact of accounting concepts on the valuation of inventory
Understand and know the matching principle in inventory valuation.
Understand and apply ratios such as inventory turnover, days' sales in inventory as part of analysis of inventory management.

Inventory

Scope

Earlier in chapters 5 and 6, we focused on merchandising activities using both the sales and purchasing systems. We showed how these activities are reported in accounting and their impact on the financial statements. This chapter's primary focus is on accounting for inventories. We apply the accounting principle of **lower of cost** and **net realizable value** as the basis for valuing inventory, this being the requirement of the accounting standard. We describe the different methods involved in assigning the costs to inventory and show the components and costs making up the inventory for financial reporting purposes. The different methods of estimating and measuring inventory were also discussed using examples and their valuation effects on profits and on assets. We discuss both the **perpetual** and **periodic systems** used in inventory. The widespread use of computing and related technology such as the Enterprise Resource Planning (ERP) systems has dramatically increased the use of perpetual inventory system. The **matching convention** in inventory valuation is also explained. The chapter outlines a **standard accounting policy** used as part of the disclosure notes in financial statements. We described the **stock-taking procedures** involved in physical counting of stock items at the end of accounting period and their valuation for financial reporting purposes. It is important to note that the perpetual recording system and the physical inventory sheets might produce valuation figures that are different owing to such factors like **obsolescence, shrinkage or pilferage,** etc. It is worthwhile noting that inventories reported for a typical merchandising entity and a manufacturing concern are virtually different as the chapter reveals.

Introduction to Inventory Systems

Merchandise sold to customers represents the cost of goods sold during an accounting period. The quantified amount is often the single most trading expense reported in the statement of comprehensive income. **Inventory** refers to a range of products or goods a merchandising company owns and expects to sell to customers in the ordinary course of business operations. Figure 7.1 illustrates a company's goods available for sale. It begins with opening inventory and what is purchased for the trading period. The goods available is either sold (making up the cost of goods sold) and whatever inventory is left or kept for future sales (representing the closing inventory).

Figure 7.1 Cash flow for a trader's operationfor a single time period

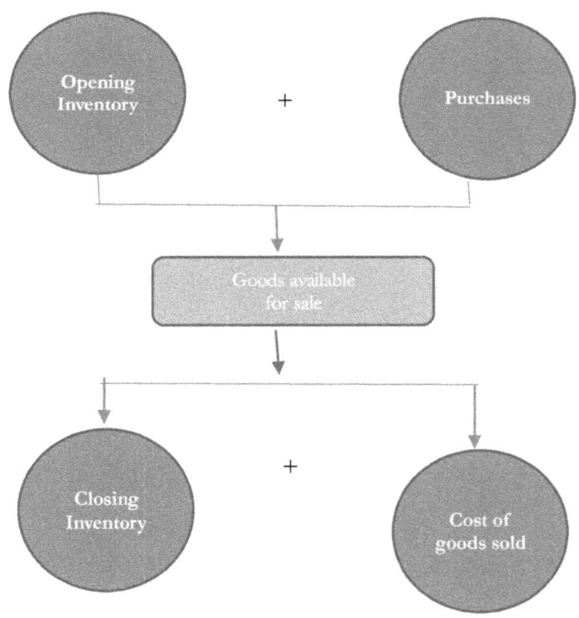

Two alternative inventory accounting systems are used to gather information relating to the cost of goods sold and cost of inventory: *perpetual system and periodic system.*

i. The **perpetual inventory system** continually updates accounting records for trading transactions – specifically for those records of inventory available for sale and goods sold.
ii. The **periodic inventory system** updates the accounting records for trading transactions only at the end of a reporting period.

Companies have an option of adopting one of these two systems. Most companies have resorted to using the **periodic system** in the past because the recording function had been a time-consuming process and a costly affair. Although the practice still prevails, **technological advances** and the widespread use of computing has dramatically increased the use of **perpetual inventory system**. The perpetual system gives managers immediate access to detailed information on sales, purchases and inventory levels, where they can strategically respond to sales trends, cost information changes, consumer tastes and lifestyles, etc. Some companies use a hybrid system where the perpetual system is used for tracking available stock items and the periodic system is used to calculate the cost of goods sold.

The **accounting standard** however, **specifies physical contact with inventory counting of stock items** as this reflects the actual reality particularly where physical condition of stock items or inventory can be readily ascertained. Auditors would normally be present during the physical stock-taking session at the reporting year-end period to confirm the inventory position for financial reporting purposes. Usually, the perpetual system will show **inventory valuation** at a stated amount based on record keeping but the physical inventory valuation sheets may show another accounting estimate. Of course, there bound to be some differences in reporting these valuation figures and depending on the materiality, some reconciliation adjustments may be necessary to arrive at the final acceptable valuation. A number of factors can be attributed for the differences, these could be the result of *counting errors, obsolescence, shrinkage or pilferage*, etc.

The basic concept of accounting for inventory (or stock-in-trade) can be best explained with reference to an illustrated example below.

Suppose a retailer has in stock seven units of notebooks of a particular brand that cost RM 750 each. The retailer sells four units for RM 990 each:

i. The inventory asset account reveals three units that the retailer still hold in inventory
ii. The statement of comprehensive income reports the cost of the four notebooks sold, as shown below.

An accounting assumption we make here is that inventory cost is constant.

Inventory and Cost of Goods Sold

Statement of Financial Position		Statement of Comprehensive Income	
	RM		RM
Current Assets		Sales	
Closing stock (3 units @ RM 750)	2,250	(4 units @ SP of RM990 each)	3,960
Accounts receivable	-	Less: Cost of goods sold	
Other debtors and prepayments	-	(4 units @ Cost of RM750 each)	3,000
Short-term investments	-	Gross profit	960
Cash at bank	-		

Inventory is the heart of a retailing business, and the cost of sales is the most important expense item for the retailor. Gross profit is the difference between sales and cost of goods sold. This is the basic concept of how we identify inventory as an asset, and the cost of goods sold as a trading expense. The cost of the goods sold shifts from asset to revenue expense when the retailor delivers the stock items, in this case the notebooks to the customer.

Inventory is a **financial asset** which is usually classified as a current asset.

Inventories or Stocks of retailing industry comprise mainly of finished goods for resale unlike entities in the manufacturing sector, carry their stocks or inventory as *raw materials, work–in-progress and finished goods*. For manufacturers, inventory is handled in much the same way as a retailor, the difference being that manufacturers purchase raw materials (accounted for as raw materials stock) that they work on (as work in progress) until it is converted into finished goods for resale (finished goods stock). Whatever costs and attributable overheads they incur during the production process is added or allocated to the work in progress inventory.

For inventory accounting, measuring the quantity and value of this asset is a difficult process as they are highly subjective to differing methods or basis of valuation, time consuming and there is much potential for committing errors. *Stocks or inventory has a direct impact on the level of company profits reported in the financial statements.*

The treatment of inventories is discussed under a number of headings which are as follows:

i. Stock and the matching convention

ii. Categories of inventory (or stocks)

iii. Inventory cost

iv. Net realizable value

v. Accounting policies for inventory

vi. Inventory systems

vii. Methods for inventory valuation

viii. Financial effects of inventory valuations

ix. Stocktaking procedures

x. Illustrated exercises given in appendices

FRS 9 covers the valuation of stock and work-in-progress. The accounting principles relating to treatment of inventories are discussed under the respective headings.

Inventory and the Matching Convention

When you consider the accounts of a retailer and a manufacturer in the illustration, the matching principle can be both simple and complicated in application. The objective in each case is to match the cost of the goods sold with the sales made for the year. The cost of any unsold or unconsumed stocks (or inventory) will have incurred in anticipation of future revenue. Closing inventory is included in the accounts in order to remove the costs of those costs which should be matched with sales of the following year. The issue here is which costs relate to the following period and accordingly this is taken out by the inclusion of closing inventory in the accounts.

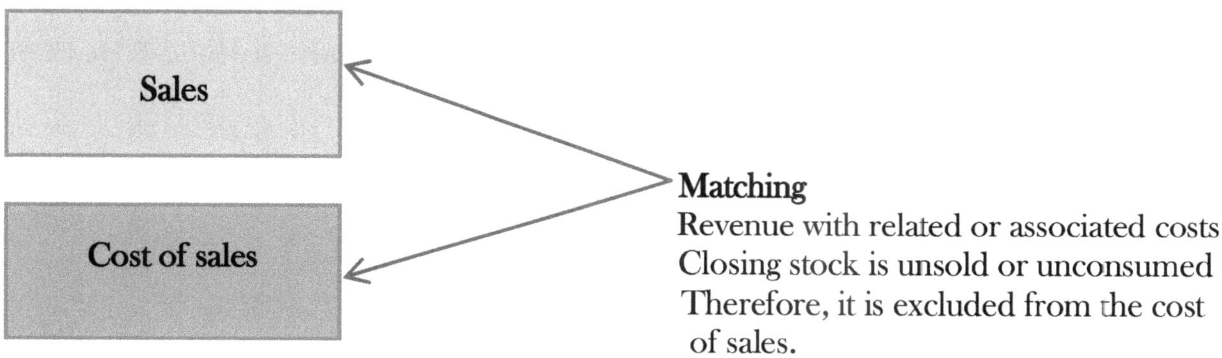

Retailing and Manufacturing Operations

We need to show how the financial statements of retailers such as Tesco, differ from those of manufacturing entities such as Nestle. The financial statements highlight how manufacturing entities differ from retailers.

XYZ Traders

Trading Account for the year ended 31 December 2020		**RM**
Sales		155,875
Less: Cost of sales or goods sold		
Opening stock	24,500	
Purchases	96,580	
	121,080	
Closing stock	(27,595)	(93,485)
Gross profit.		62,390

In the retailer's case, the cost of unsold stock is relatively straight forward. The inventory takes out that portion of purchases which relates to as unsold stock as part of the closing inventory. However, the treatment is more complicated with a manufacturer because costs of manufacturing, work in progress, and finished goods are not simply the bought in cost of goods but include prime cost and some proportion of the indirect production overheads. The idea to grasp is that closing inventory comprises raw materials, closing work in progress and finished goods:

i. Taking out those costs included in prime cost and indirect production overheads which relate to incomplete or unsold goods which can then be *matched* with the sales of the following year.
ii. Treat the sales of this year to be matched with the costs of producing the goods sold this year.

ABC Industries

Manufacturing and trading Account for the financial year ended 31 Decembers 2020

	RM
Sales	431,275
Materials consumed	65,800
Direct labour costs	75,400
Prime cost	141,200
Indirect production overheads	155,800
	297,000
Add: Opening work in progress	67,500
	364,500
Less: Closing work in progress.	(93,700)
Cost of finished goods output	270,800
Add: Opening stock of finished goods	105,750
	376,550
Less: Closing stock of finished goods.	(145,550)
Cost of goods sold	(231,000)
Gross profit	200,275

Overview of Inventory for Manufacturers

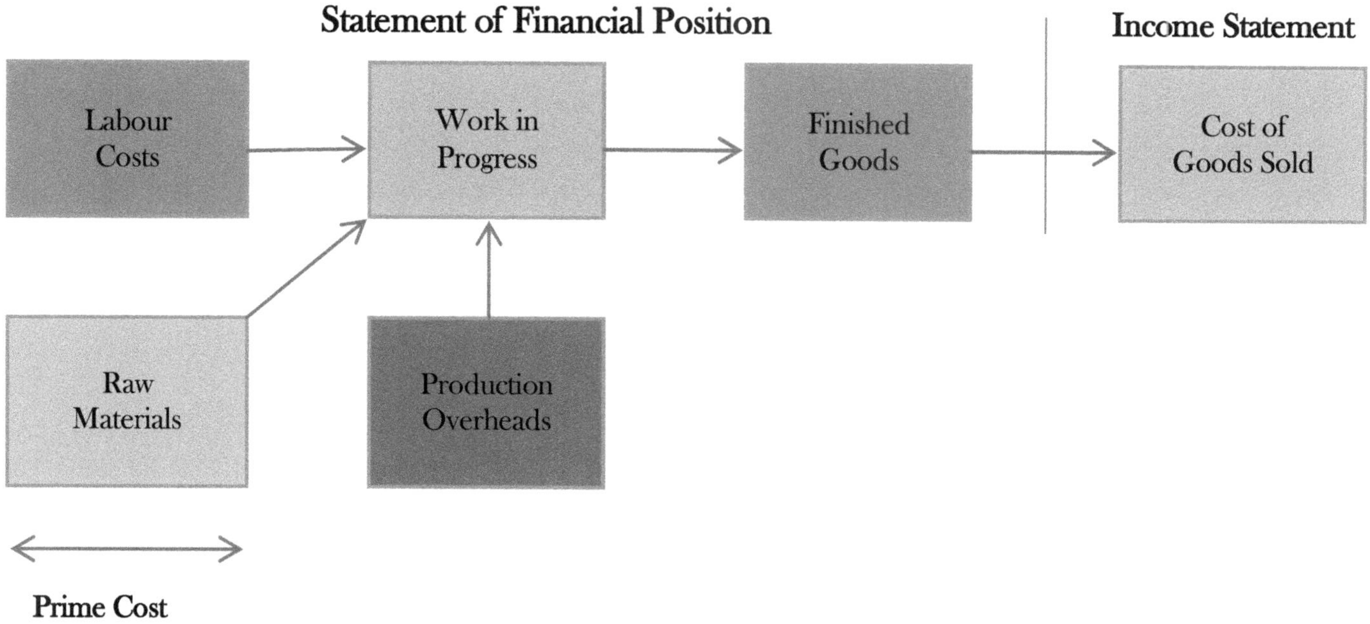

The important thing to note is that a retailer is more likely to have finished goods in its inventory, whereas a manufacturer may have inventories at various stages of completion – from raw materials, labour cost to finished goods or products.

Categories of Inventory

Inventories can be categorized as:

i. Finished goods held for sale
ii. Goods purchased for resale
iii. Work-in-progress
iv. Raw materials and components purchased to be incorporated into products for sale
v. Consumables – lubricants, cleaning materials, fuel, spare parts, etc.

These categories are classified according to stage of production or movement in the ordinary course of business such as trading activity in the case finished goods held for sale or goods purchased for resale and those going through different stages in manufacturing process and other types used for consuming in the business.

Note the present accounting regime no longer uses the term 'Stocks' but instead uses the international term 'Inventory'. Stocks were predominantly referred by the British accounting profession.

Certain inventory items require special consideration, including goods in transit, consignment goods and goods that are damaged or gone obsolete.

Goods in Transit

The purchaser's inventory may include goods in transit from the supplier. This depends if the title to ownership of goods has passed to the purchaser, which in that case, the goods will become part of the purchaser's inventory. Again, the shipping terms will need to be reviewed to determine who is responsible for paying the freight charges: FOB *destination* of FOB *shipping point*. If the purchaser is responsible for settling the freight, ownership automatically passes when the goods are loaded on the transport vehicle. If the seller is responsible for paying freight, ownership passes when goods arrive at their destination.

Goods on Consignment

These goods are shipped by the *consignor* (the owner) to another party, called *consignee*. The consignee under contract sells the goods for the owner. The consignor continues to own the goods and reports them in owner's inventory while the consignee holds the goods in custody over which ownership is not exercised

Goods Damaged or Obsolete

Goods that have damaged or gone obsolete (or deteriorated) are not accounted (counted) for in inventory if they cannot be sold. If these goods can be sold at a reduced price, they are included in the inventory at an estimate of their **net realizable value (NRV).** NRV is the estimated selling price in the ordinary course of business less the estimated costs of completion, and the estimated costs necessary to make the sale. The period in which the damage or obsolescence (or deterioration) occurs, the loss in value will be reported for that period. The valuation sheets of inventory will normally include such a provision for damaged goods and obsolescence.

Inventories or stocks reported in the statement of financial position should be analyzed into categories to be shown as a single combined item figure and usually disclosed in a note in the financial statements.

Inventory Costs

Stocks or inventories are valued *at **lower of costs or at net realizable value***. The term **"cost"** needs a precise definition. According to FRS No 9, cost is defined as:

"That expenditure which has been incurred in the ordinary course of business in bringing the product or service to its present location and condition."

Cost should include:

i. The cost of purchase including import duties, transport and handling charges and any other directly attributable costs less trade discounts, rebates and subsidies.

ii. Cost of conversion

Cost of conversion comprise:

i. Costs which are specifically attributable to units of production (i.e. direct labour, direct expenses (e.g. royalty payable on production) and sub-contracted work.
ii. Production overheads
iii. Other overheads (e.g. of administration), if any, attributable to the particular circumstances of the business to bringing the product or service to its present location and condition. In practice, few of these associated costs are ever included.

Production overheads are overheads or expenses incurred for production, based on the normal level of activity. Overheads to be included are all those related specifically to production (e.g. rent of factory, depreciation of plant and machinery used in production, wages of factory staff) not withstanding that may accrue wholly or partly on a time basis.

This means that expenses such as rent which accrues strictly on a time basis can be taken out of production overheads by inclusion of part of the cost in the value of work in progress of finished goods.

Operating expenses

Once the finished goods or products are ready for sale, other costs such as advertising, and sales commissions, are *not* included as the cost of inventory. Advertising, sales commissions, and delivery costs are selling and distribution expenses that go into the **statement of comprehensive income** as operating expenses.

Net Realizable Value

So far, all our discussions have focused on the cost aspect of inventory. Regardless of which cost method of inventory valuation is used, there is however, one additional basis of inventory valuation that is equally important. The accounting standard requires inventories to be measured (or stated) at **the lower of cost and net realizable value (NRV)**. In other words, you need to compare and evaluate the cost (as originally determined using specific valuation method, FIFO or the average cost method) to its net realizable value (NRV). **Net realizable value** *is the estimated selling price in the ordinary course of business less the estimated costs of completion and the estimated costs necessary to make the sale.*

This comparison of **Cost** versus NRV is required because an entity may not be able to recover the cost of inventory if the goods are damaged or have gone obsolete, or if their selling price has declined below costs due to adverse market conditions. If an inventory is written down to an NRV below cost, the write-down is recognized immediately as an **expense** in the period of the write-down. This is necessary because of the **prudence concept** which specifies any such *anticipated losses* are to be written-off. If there is going to be a subsequent reversal, any such subsequent reversal is recognized as a reduction in the cost of goods sold

The following example below illustrates the concept of **lower of *Cost and* NRV**

On 23 March 2020, John purchased stocks for resale amounting to RM 2,850. On 31 December 2020, the financial year-end, RM 1,500 of these stocks were sold, and the cost of the remaining stocks in the storeroom is RM 1,350. Let say, due to adverse market changes some of these stock items have gone obsolete and becomes no longer suitable for normal sale. John estimates the NRV of these stock items to be RM 550. John has to account the value of these stocks at NRV. Before any NRV effect, cost of goods sold is RM1, 500.

An NRV write-down decreases closing inventory value and correspondingly increases cost of goods sold as follows:

	Cost	NRV	Reduction in Value
Closing Stock	1,350	550	800

Journal entry:	Dr.	Cr
Cost of goods sold.	800	
Closing inventory		800
(Being write-down of closing inventory to net realizable value)		

If the NRV of John's stock had been above cost, there is no requirement for adjustment to NRV and the actual cost figure would be reported in accounts.

The effects of NRV for statement of financial position and statement of comprehensive income purposes are shown below. However, in later pages, we will also examine on valuing inventory at Lower of Cost and NRV and their effects of inventory errors.

Net Realizable Value Effects on Inventory and Cost of Goods Sold

Statement of Financial Position (Extract)	
Current assets	
	RM
Closing stock, net realizable value	
(Which is lower than RM 1,350 cost)	550
Accounts receivable	xxx
Other debtors and prepayments	xxx
Short-term investments	xxx
Cash and bank balances	xxx
	xxx

Statement of Comprehensive Income (Extract)	
Sales revenue	XXXX
Less:	
Cost of goods sold	
(RM 1,500 + RM 800)	2,300
Gross profit	XXXX

Significant Accounting Policies on Inventory

A typical **accounting policy disclosure** on inventories for a manufacturing firm in the notes to the financial statements will read as follows:

Notes to the Financial Statements – An Extract

Inventory	2020	2019
	RM 000	RM 000
Finished goods	1,575	1,550
Raw materials and components	365	395
Work-in-progress	175	183
	2,115	2,128

Inventories are stated at the lower of cost and net realizable value. Cost comprises all costs of acquisition, conversion and other costs incurred in bringing the inventories to their present location and condition. Cost is calculated using the FIFO basis and includes cost of materials consumed, labour and manufacturing overheads. The cost of inventories is adjusted downwards when cost exceeds net realizable value. Net realizable value of an item is defined as the amount which the item can be disposed of without creating either profit or loss in the year of sale. It is estimated proceeds of sale less all further costs to completion and less all costs to be incurred in marketing, selling, and distributing directly related to the item.

An accounting policy for a retailer group where disclosure is made with regard to inventory obsolescence, in notes to the financial statements will read as follows:

Inventory Obsolescence (Extract from notes)

The management reviews the aging analysis of stocks of the Group at each SOFP or balance sheet date, and makes an allowance for obsolete and slow-moving stock items identified that are no longer suitable for normal sale. Allowance is made on the basis of management's prudent judgment and estimates. Physical count of all stocks is carried out on a periodic basis in order to ascertain whether allowance will be necessary in respect of any obsolete and slow-moving stock items identified. The

Group carries out an inventory review at the end of each reporting period and makes allowances against obsolete and slow-moving items.

Inventory Systems

Basically two types of inventory accounting systems are maintained, these being:

i. The periodic inventory system
ii. The perpetual inventory system.

Earlier pages of this chapter discussed the two types of inventory systems that can be operated by an entity.

Periodic Inventory System

The periodic inventory system is more confined and typically used for inexpensive stocks where the inventory record keeping practically would be rather cumbersome and time-consuming. For example, a clothing or garments store or automobile repair workshop would not keep an elaborate running record of every needle, threads, buttons for every fabric used or nuts and bolts or tools and equipment for repairs. The stores would instead physically count their inventory periodically to ascertain the quantities on hand. Other types of businesses such as restaurants and florists may also use a periodic inventory system to record their inventories as this would not make sense to keep track of the precise amount of dry and wet items such as meat, vegetables, cooking oil, and other items used in producing the food for customers. Under the periodic inventory system, the idea behind the difference between quantity of stocks or inventory on hand and the accounting records is simply considered used or sold. The cost-benefit approach is adopted here.

Accounting under the Periodic Inventory System

Under this system, the business entity keeps no physical record of the stocks involved. Instead at the end of the accounting period, the business does physical count of the stocks and applies the unit costs to ascertain the value of the closing inventory. The closing inventory figure is reported in the SOFP (or balance sheet) and the unit cost is used to calculate the cost of goods sold.

Throughout the period in the periodic system, the inventory account shows the opening balance brought forward from the previous period. During the period, the purchases are recorded in the **purchases account**. Only sales revenue from inventory sale is recorded in the general ledger. At the end of the period, the purchases are added to the inventory account. A physical stock-take is carried out to arrive at the closing inventory balance. Any stock that is not present is assumed to be sold and charged to the cost of goods sold account under the **matching principle**.

The cornerstone of the periodic inventory method is therefore the physical inventory amount or value – always measured at the reporting date of the statement of financial position. The balance shown in the inventory account in the ledger is only changed when a new physical inventory is taken. The recording of the final inventory amount in the general ledger is done by a closing journal entry at the year-end. This amount or value is normally attested by the external auditors once their audit checks on the physical stock-take is completed.

Using T-accounts and journal entries, accounting for inventory in a periodic system is illustrated as follows:

TJ Salas started the period with an opening balance of RM 120,000. During the year TJ sales made purchase on credit, amounting to RM 690,000. TJ Salas's total sales for the year was recoded at RM1,050,000, all on credit. A physical stock-take at the end of the year showed that TJ Salas has an inventory ending balance of RM 145,000.

Reporting Entries for the Periodic Inventory System

TJ Salas

1.	Purchases	690,000	
	Accounts payable		690,000
	(Being purchase of stocks on account)		
2.	Accounts receivable	1,050,000	
	Sales account		1, 050,000
	(Being sale of inventories on account)		
	Year-end closing entries to update inventory and record Cost of Goods Sold		
3.	Inventory	690,000	
	Purchases		690,000
	(Being transfer of purchases to inventory)		
4.	Cost of Goods Sold	665,000	
	Inventory		665,000
	(Being closing inventory based on physical stock-take)		

The following T-Accounts reflects the transactions and year-end closing entries:

Purchases

	RM		RM.
PDB	690,000	Transfer	
	=======	to Inventory	690,000

Inventory

	RM		RM
Balance b/d	`120,000	COGS	665,000
Purchases	690,000	Balance c/d	145,000
	810,000		810,000

Cost of Goods Sold

Inventory	665,000		

Inventory Account

Opening balance	120, 000	Transfer to TB	120, 000*
Closing balance	145, 000	* consumed (assumed)	

Closing inventory (measured at year end.

	RM
Opening stock	120,000
Purchases	690,000
	810,000
Closing stock	(145,000)
Cost of Goods Sold	665,000
	========

(Shown as part of the trading account in SOCI)

Most business entities conventionally tend to keep the purchases and inventory accounts separate until the year-end reporting date when they are transferred and shown individually in the trial balance. These final balances are then taken-up and shown in the trading account when the final accounts are prepared.

Perpetual Inventory System

Under this system, unlike the periodic inventory system, *a computer system is typically used to keep a running track all inventory movements showing record of inventory on hand, goods sold, and bought*. This system creates a better information and control over inventory for business entities. Hyper supermarkets s such as Tesco, Carrefour and others use this inventory system. The use of bar codes facilitates scanning of the products being sold and it is more likely that a perpetual inventory system makes use of a bar code system in operation in hyper retail stores. The bar code on the product label holds critical information for the optical scanner to read and the computer system automatically records the sale and updates the inventory records. Most trading companies with large stores or warehouses maintain a perpetual inventory system to account for their inventory. The perpetual inventory system is used for all types of goods.

According to FRS on Stocks and Work-in-Progress, the a**nnual physical counting of stocks on hand** is still operative even with a perpetual inventory system. The physical stock count is still relied for accurate record of closing inventory at the year-end for financial reporting purposes.

The system also serves as a moral check on the perpetual records maintained by the entities. Any discrepancy may signal the presence of any pilferage or theft of inventory or obsolescence and in some situation it could be due to bookkeeping errors. Pilferage is common in retail industry, usually committed by employees and others like shoplifters in the departmental stores of a hyper market

Accounting under the Perpetual Inventory System

All inventory movements relating to transactions are tracked and accounting records are updated in real-time under this system. This updating is a continuous process which ensures that at any one point in time, the cost of sales account and inventory account are reflected correctly. Decision making is easily facilitated.

Let's examine **how the perpetual inventory system works?** Say, a business entity operates an online boutique shop for lady's clothes and apparels. The shop source from various suppliers or manufacturers of lady's clothing, placing orders for selected styles and designs in bulk purchases and then sells the clothing to customers through the shop's internet advertised website. The shop selected and ordered a number of clothing items from a garments manufacturer. A negotiated bulk purchase discount of 10% with 30-days credit period settlement was arranged. When the goods arrived, an invoice accompanied showing a total purchase price of RM 3,300 (after trade discount and GST) and freight, handling and shipping charges of RM 300. Freight charges is treated as part of the cost of inventory but some businesses may keep track of it separately before adding to the overall cost of inventory at a later point. If adopted, this will allow a business to track and monitor how much of handling and shipping charges it incurs.

Journal entries			
Option 1	Inventory	3,300	
	Accounts payable		3,300
	(Being purchases of inventory, inclusive of freight charges RM 300)		
Option 2	Inventory	3,000	
	Freight-inwards	300	
	Accounts payable		3,300
	(Being purchase of inventory and freight charges RM 300)		

If the business entity uses option 2, then at the end of the accounting period, the freight-inwards should be transferred to the inventory account as part of the closing entry process.

Inventory	300	
Freight-inwards.		300
(Being transfer of freight-inwards to inventory cost)		

In so far as inventory sales, purchase returns, and settlement discounts are concerned, the related accounting entries will be journalized in the normal way as they are dealt with and discussed in Chapter 5 and Chapter 6 respectively.

Methods for Inventory Valuation

Inventory as **an asset** requires an accounting method by which it should be measured or valued for financial reporting purposes. The cost of an item in stock should be measured at historical cost or approximately close to the actual cost of the particular item. Managers need to decide which accounting method is appropriate to use as there are several methods available for stock valuation purposes. This is because the method selected for valuation purposes affects the profits to be reported, the amount of income tax to be paid and including the values of the financial ratios to be derived from the financial statements. The important thing to remember here is that the *inventory costing methods can have very different effects on reported profits in the statement of income and the statement of financial position*. Therefore, an entity's management must select the inventory method that should be most suited to their appropriate circumstances and condition of the business. An example to illustrate the choice of these methods for selection purposes is demonstrated below:

Suppose, in a shop, physically there are in stock 175 units of a particular item. The most recent purchases of these units were:

October,	5	150 units @ RM 25 each
	12	18 units @ RM 27 each
	29	90 units @ RM 30 each.

The price of these items of stock has steadily gone up due to market demand and supply.

How much did the 175 units cost?

The answer clearly depends on which consignment the individual units arrived in and this may not be known as the units are undifferentiated one from another as the units all look alike. Perhaps, identification tags can help. In practice, entities tend to use one of the following methods of stock rotation for actually with stock.

a. The oldest are used up first – this is essential for perishable items like foodstuffs.
b. The latest arrivals are used first – this seems unlikely but if the goods are stacked in a container as:

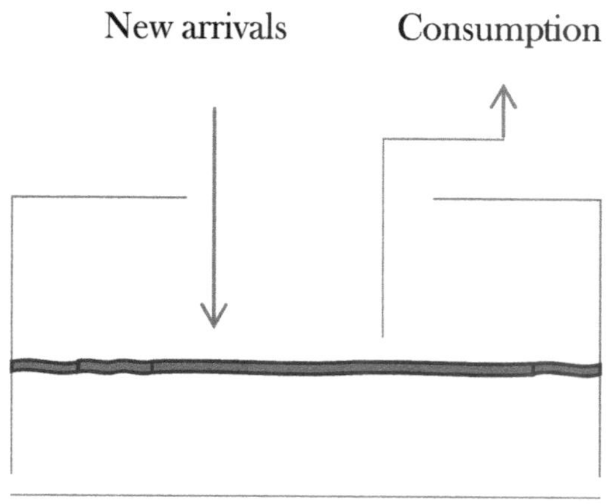

It will be seen that this can occur.

c. Consumption is from old and new stocks selected randomly. This happens with liquids as old and new stock mix up completely and selection for consumption must be of the mixture. It can also happen with solid items that are stacked randomly so that it is not known which is old and which is new unless identification tags are inserted. In practice this may appear rather cumbersome.

So, for the year-end stock valuation purposes, a method is selected which approximates to (a), (b) or (c). The method chosen may not actually follow precisely the reality but it should do so as nearly as possible.

The methods described above correspond with (a), (b) and (c) are:

a. FIFO – *First in, first out*
b. LIFO – *Last in, first out*
c. Weighted Average cost – AVCO

Retail Inventory Method

The accounting standard also allows for the *Retail Inventory Method* which is commonly used in most retail supermarkets given the large and massive numbers of rapidly changing stock items with similar margins which they carry in their cash and carry business. **This method is permitted provided it closely approximates the cost.** The cost of the year-end inventory is ascertained by reducing the sales value of the inventory by the appropriate percentage gross margin. The percentage used takes into account inventory that has been marked down to below its original selling price. This industry specific cost formula applies to some specialized industries in retail trading.

Companies use the **retail inventory method** to estimate cost of goods sold and closing inventory in order to avoid the time-consuming and expensive process of taking a physical inventory each month, or quarter or half yearly. Some companies may even use the retail inventory method to prepare the financial statements annually provided the external auditors have suitably tested this method and accepted the basis. In some circumstances, a company may also estimate inventory when inventory is damaged or destroyed as a result of natural disasters like fire or floods or even war.

Let's examine how this basis of inventory valuation works. The retail inventory method adopts a three-step process to estimate the closing inventory. We need to establish:

i. The amount of inventory a company had at the opening period both in terms of cost and retail amounts. The cost of inventory is already known from records. The retail amount of inventory is measured using selling prices of inventory items.
ii. The net amount of good purchased (minus returns, allowances and discounts) in the period, both cost and retail.
iii. The amount of net sales at retail.

The 3-step process is illustrated below:

Step 1	Goods available for sale at retail	–	Net sale at retail	=	Closing inventory at retail
Step 2	Goods available for sale at cost	÷	Goods available for sale at retail	=	Cost – to – retail ratio
Step 3	Closing inventory at retail	×	Cost to retail ratio	=	Estimated closing inventory at cost

The reasoning behind the retail inventory method is that we can get a good estimate of the **cost-to-retail ratio**, we can multiply closing inventory at retail by this ratio to estimate closing inventory at cost. Let's **illustrate** by an example, how these steps can be applied to estimate closing inventory for a typical small-sized retail supermarket. We find RM 500, 000 of goods at retail selling prices were available for sale at the supermarket. RM 375, 000 (75 %) of these goods were sold, leaving RM 125, 000 (25 %) in retail value of merchandise in closing inventory. The cost of these goods sold is 65 % of the RM 500, 000 retail value. Since cost for these goods is 65 % of retail, the estimated cost of closing inventory is RM 81, 250 (65 % x 500, 000 = 325, 000 x 25 %).

		At Cost	At Retail
		RM	RM
	Opening inventory	112, 125	172, 500
	Purchases	212, 875	327, 500
	Goods available for sale	325, 000	500, 000
Step 1	Less net sales at retail		375, 000
	Closing inventory at retail		125, 000
Step 2	Cost to retail ratio: (RM 325, 000/500, 000) = 65 %		
Step 3	Estimated closing inventory at cost (RM 125,000 × 65 %).		(or 25 % x
		81, 250.	RM 325,000)

Tutorial Notes

There are two possible reasons or circumstances why inventory requires estimation:

1. *Companies often require interim financial statements; these financial statements are prepared for accounting periods of less than a year, usually for a quarterly or semi-annually period, but only annually take a physical count of inventory for financial reporting purposes. For example, interim reports are required by KL Stock Exchange.*
2. *Companies may require an inventory estimate particularly when a casualty such as fire or flood makes it impossible to take a physical inventory count.*

   Estimates are usually required for companies that use the periodic system. Companies using perpetual system would presumably have updated inventory records.

FIFO Cost Method

Under the FIFO method, the first costs into inventory are the first costs assigned to cost of goods sold, hence, the name *first in, first out.* The following example illustrates how to compute FIFO cost of goods sold and closing inventory

Stock item.	**- Units**
Stock at 1.10.15	- 25 @ RM 5 each
Purchases	
9.10.15	- 30 @ RM 6 each
Consumed*	
12.10.15	- 40
18.10.15	- 10

*Consumed means used in production or sold but never use the sale price in these calculations.

Inventory (@ FIFO cost)

Opening balance:	25 @ RM5	= RM 125	**Cost of goods sold (50 units)**		
Purchases	30 @ RM6	= RM 180	25 units @ RM5	= RM 125	
			15 units @ RM6	= RM 90	
			10 units @ RM6	= RM 60	RM 275
Closing balance: 5 units @ RM6 = RM30					

Notes

i. *The account balances as to quantity: 25 + 30 – 40 – 10 = 5 units and cost value (RM): 125 + 180 – 125 – 90 – 60 = 30*

ii. *When the 40 Units were consumed, the oldest stock (25 @ RM 5) was assumed to be used first and the balance must have come from newer stock*

iii. *The method is cumbersome in that the cost of an item sold is a mix of different prices and individual stock items may have different prices.*

iv. *Stock is valued at the latest price (RM 6)*

Under FIFO, the cost of closing inventory is always based on the latest price or cost.

LIFO Cost Method

We will use same data as above, for LIFO costing. LIFO is the opposite of FIFO. Under LIFO *(Last in First out),* the last costs into inventory go immediately to cost of goods sold. For illustration of this method, we will use same data as above.

Inventory (@ LIFO Cost)

Opening balance:	25 units @ RM5 = RM125	**Cost of goods sold** (50 units)	
Purchases	30 units @ RM6 = RM180	30 units @ RM6 = RM 180	
		5 units @ RM5 = RM 25	
		15 units @ RM5 = RM 75	RM 280
Closing balance: 5 units @ RM5 = RM25			

Notes

i. *The account balances as the quantity: 25 + 30- 35-15 = 5 and cost value (RM) 125 + 180 – 180 – 25 – 75 = 25*

ii. *When the 35 units were consumed, the newest stock (30 @ RM6) were assumed to have been used and the balance only came from earlier purchases.*

iii. *The method is cumbersome in that consumption and stock can be at multiple prices.*

iv. *Stock is valued at the earliest price (RM5)*

v. *In time of inflation, LIFO method gives a lower value to stock.*

Under LIFO, the cost of closing inventory is always based on the earliest price or cost. In times of inflation, LIFO gives a lower value to inventory. However, given the merit of this method, both the Inland Revenue Board (IRB) and the accounting standard strictly prohibits the use of this valuation method. Look for explanation later in the page below.

Weighted Average Cost

Assuming the same data as above, we calculate using the average cost method.

Inventory (@ AVCO)

Opening balance:	25 units @ RM5 = RM 125	**Cost of goods sold** (50 units)	
Purchases:	30 units @ RM6 = RM 180	40 units @ RM 5.55 = RM 222	
		10 units @ RM 5.55 = RM 56	RM 278
Closing balance:	5 units @ RM5.55 = RM28		

Notes

i. *On the purchase at 9.10.15. a weighted average cost is calculated by dividing the total cost (RM125 + RM180 = RM305) by the number of items in stock (25 +30 = 55). This gives a cost of RM5. 55 per unit which is a middle value given the weighting between RM5 and RM6.*

ii. *The calculations of average cost occur only at the purchases although in practice issues are much more frequent than purchases*

iii. *Issues and closing stock are at one price.*

iv. *All the stock is valued at the same average price.*

In times of inflation, weighted average cost gives a stock valuation and profit, between that of LIFO and FIFO

Why both FRS and IRB prohibit the use of LIFO?

LIFO is **not allowed** by Inland Revenue Board (IRB) as a valuation method for inventories and the accounting standard equally also **prohibits the use of LIFO formula** to measure the cost of inventories. It is already established that by using the latest prices in stock valuation, it gives a better measure of income and, on the other hand, older prices tend to result in more meaningful and appropriate inventory values for balance sheet presentation.

The *Conceptual Framework* also prefers the balance sheet approach. Changes in asset values and liabilities determine income and net worth of a business. However, LIFO gives more importance to income measurement over asset values and liabilities and results in stating inventories on the statement of financial position, amounts that bears little relationship to the cost of inventories. LIFO can also distort when inventory reaches low levels as much older prices (the inventory could have been there for years) could are used, thus creating unrealistic profits.

According to FRS, *"it is not appropriate to allow an approach that results in a measurement of profit or loss for the period that is inconsistent with the measurement of inventories for balance sheet purposes."*

Furthermore, the accounting standard also indicates the concept of selling newer items first before older ones is not a reliable or faithful representation of actual inventory flows. Accounting standards interestingly is determined at the highest level. As FRS uses the *Conceptual Framework* to determine what should be the most appropriate accounting treatment for the items on the financial statements. The rationale behind IRB's stand is also somewhat similar in their policy contention.

Effects of FIFO, LIFO and AVCO on the Cost of Goods Sold, Gross Profit and Closing Stock

It is important to note that as unit cost of inventories change, either increasing or decreasing, the different inventory methods will produce different income effects. Let's examine these income effects below.

Assuming stock prices are rising (RM5 to RM6)

	FIFO	LIFO	Average Cost
Sales revenue 50 units @ RM10	500	500	500
Less: Cost of Goods Sold	275 *lowest*	280 *highest*	278
Gross profit	225 *highest*	220 *lowest*	222
Closing stock (balance sheet)	30 *highest*	25 *lowest*	28

When inventory costs are increasing

	Cost of Goods Sold	**Closing stock**
FIFO	COGS is lowest because it is based on the oldest prices which are low. Gross profit is therefore the highest.	Closing stock is highest because it is based on the most recent prices, which are high.
LIFO	COGS is highest because it is based on the most recent prices which are high. Gross profit is therefore the lowest.	Closing stock is lowest because it is based on the oldest prices, which are low.

Under both methods, the Cost of Goods Sold and Closing Stock will produce exactly the opposite results as we observed in the above matrix.

When inventory costs are decreasing or increasing

When purchase costs regularly rise, the weighted average cost method yields the higher cost of goods sold and lower profit as it averages the recent higher costs with earlier lower costs. When costs regularly decline, the weighted average cost then gives the lower cost of goods sold, thus yielding higher gross profit and net profit.

All three inventory methods are acceptable but as we know the restrictions imposed by IRB and FRS, only FIFO, AVCO, and Specific Cost methods end-up as accounting policies in the financial statements.

Cost Effects of Valuation Methods

When purchase prices do not change over time, each inventory valuation method assigns the same cost amounts to inventory and to cost of goods sold. When prices are different due to demand and supply conditions, the methods always result in different cost amounts. We have seen these differences in our illustrated examples above.

Next we consider the tax effects on valuation methods.

Tax Effects of Valuation Methods

We can examine the tax effects on valuation methods using the income statement of a company XYZ as follows:

XYZ Company

For month ended 30 June 2020

	Specific Cost Unit	FIFO	Weighted Average Cost
Statement of Comprehensive Income	**RM**	**RM**	**RM**
Sales	7, 560	7, 650	7, 560
Less:			
Cost of goods sold.	(5, 725)	(5, 700)	(5, 750)
Gross profit	1, 835	1, 950	1, 810
Less: Expenses.	(960)	(960)	(960)
Profit before tax	875	990	850
Less Income tax expense (@27 %).	(236)	(267)	(230)
Net profit	639	723	620
Statement of Financial Position			
Current assets			
Closing inventory	RM 1, 739	RM 1, 796	RM 1, 709

The **SOCI** shows income tax expense is at the rate of 27 % applicable to a SME company. Inventory costs obviously affect net profit and potentially has an effect on taxes. The weighted average cost method results in a lower tax advantage.

Consistency in using Valuation Methods

The Conceptual Framework states that *comparability* is an enhancing qualitative characteristic of financial information. **Comparability** allows users to identify and understand differences and similarities among items reported in the financial statements. **Consistency** in accounting treatment is related to comparability; the use of the same method or basis for the same items, from period to period within a reporting entity or in a single period across business entities. *Consistency helps to achieve comparability as a goal.*

Sometimes management of an entity tend to change from applying one method to another method to suit their circumstances and conditions of business in order to improve its financial reporting performance. Where such change is needed or justified, the *entity must disclose the type and nature of change, the reason and effects on profit* in the notes to the financial statements.

Effects of Inventory Errors

There is a need for business entities to ensure that it exercises caution in both taking a physical count of gross profit, net profit, thus affecting current assets and equity. Errors also causes misstatements in the next period's accounts because closing inventory of one period is the opening inventory of the next accounting period. Let's recall the inventory relation:

Opening inventory + Purchases – Closing inventory = Cost of goods sold

Effects on Statement of Comprehensive Income

The Table below shows the effects of inventory errors in cost of goods sold and net profits in the current and next periods' in the *statement of comprehensive income.*

	Year 1		Year 2	
Closing inventory	Cost of Goods Sold	Net Profit	Cost of Goods Sold	Net Profit
Understated	Overstated	Understated	Understated	Overstated
Overstated*	Understated	Overstated	Overstated	Understated

When you look at row 1 and year 1. We see that *understating closing inventory has the effect of overstating cost of goods sold.* By subtracting a smaller closing inventory amount in computing cost of goods sold, then a higher cost of goods sold produces a lower profit. Now look at year 2 of row 1, you already know closing inventory for year 1 becomes opening inventory for year 2. Based on this inventory relation, we can see if opening inventory is understated, then the cost of goods sold is understated. This is because we are starting with a smaller value. Therefore, a lower cost of goods sold results in higher profit.

On *overstatement of inventory*, let's look at row 2 and year 1. If closing inventory is overstated, the effect on cost of goods sold is understated. A lower cost of goods sold yields a higher profit to be reported in the statement of comprehensive income. As we know, the closings inventory for year 1 becomes the opening inventory for year 2. If opening inventory is overstated, the cost of goods sold then becomes overstated. A higher cost of goods sold yields a lower profit.

* Overstatement is less likely to happen under a perpetual system. This is because more inventory is recorded (given less shrinkage). A number of factors can contribute to inventory shrinkage such as loss, physical damage, deterioration, defective items and pilferage or theft. Corrective action by management to address these errors should be undertaken in order to minimize the impacts on accounts.

Let's consider how an inventory error can be illustrated using the case of company with a sale of RM 150, 000 for each of the years 2018, 2019, and 2020. Assuming the company maintains a constant RM 30, 000 inventory level throughout this 3-year period. Also assume purchases for each of these years are RM 90, 000 and its cost of goods sold is RM 100, 000 and its gross profit is RM 50, 000 each year.

Year 2018

The company makes an error by understating its closing inventory in year 2018 by an amount of RM 6, 000. Thus, reporting the closing inventory to be RM 24, 000 instead of the correct amount of RM 30, 000. This error has the effect of **overstatin**g the cost of goods sold by RM 6, 000 with a consequential RM 6, 000 **under statement** in both gross profit and net profit in 2018. We can see that these effects match the effects predicted in the Table on the statement of comprehensive income.

Year 2019

The 2018 understated closing inventory becomes the 2019 understated opening inventory. This obviously causes an understatement in 2019 cost of goods sold and a RM 12, 000 over statement in both gross profit and net profit for 2019. From here you can see how an accounting error committed in one year has an impact on the profit performance in following year. The effect is doubled as both gross profit and net profit becomes RM 12, 000 (2 x RM 6, 000) given the profit shifting of RM 6, 000 from year 2018 to 2019'

Year 2020

The **Figure 7.2** clearly indicates that the 2018 closing inventory error affects only that period and the next. It does not affect 2020 results or any period thereafter. An inventory error is said to be self-correcting because it always results in an offsetting error in the next accounting period (**2019**).

Figure 7. 2 Shows the effects of inventory errors for a three-year period

Statement of Comprehensive Income			
	2018	**2019**	**2020**
	RM	**RM**	**RM**
Sales	150, 000	150, 000	150, 000
Less:			
Cost of goods sold			
Opening inventory	30, 000	24, 000	30, 000
Purchases	90, 000	90, 000	90, 000
Goods available for sale	120, 000	114, 000	120 000
Closing inventory	(24, 000)	(30, 000)	(30, 000)
Cost of goods sold	96, 000	84, 000	90, 000
Gross profit	54, 000	66, 000	60, 000

Less:			
Operating expenses	(15, 000)	(15, 000)	(15, 000)
Net profit	39, 000	51, 000	45, 000
Analyzed as follows:			
Year 2018 understated net profit shifts to 2019		6, 000	
Year 2019 net profit		45, 000	
Reported as net profit		51, 000	

Accounting errors like this is unintentional. Fundamentally, the accounting standard calls for a prior year item adjustment.

Effects on The Statement of Financial Position

Closing Inventory	Assets	Equity
Understated	Understated	Understated
Overstated	Overstated	Overstated

Effects on the Statement of financial position relating to inventory errors:

Assets = Equity + Liabilities.

So, by understating closing inventory, both current and total assets are also understated. An understatement in closing inventory also has the same effect of understating equity (as a result of understating the net profit). The effects are shown in the above Table for the current accounting period's Statement of Financial Position.

Disclosures in Financial Statements

Disclosure of inventory valuation policy in the notes to the financial statements may vary between reporting entities. According FRS, the following minimum information on stocks and work-in-progress need to be disclosed:

1. Accounting policies adopted in measuring inventories, including the cost basis. MFRS 102/IAS 2. (See earlier pages on disclosure of accounting policies).
2. Total carrying amount of inventories (CA). CA by classification appropriate to the reporting entity.
3. Carry amount of inventories carried at fair value less selling costs (applicable to retail or wholesale Trading).
4. Amount of any write-down of inventories (due to obsolescence, etc.) recognized as an expense in the period.

5. The amount of any reversal of any write-down that is recognized as a reduction in the amount of inventories recognized as an expense in the period.
6. The circumstances or events that led to the reversal of a write-down of inventories; and
7. The carrying amount of inventories pledged as security for liabilities.

Just a **digression**, a knowledge of these *inventory effects on profits* has become a well-known phenomenon amongst the accounting fraternity and some users of financial statements. By overstating or understating the closing value of year-end inventories, profits can be manipulated recklessly to meet a desired objective. A number of financial corporate scandals involving the manipulation of profit (well-known documented cases) are appended below.

1. *The Kingston Cotton Mill (1896) (UK)*

   Auditors failed to detect overstatements of the amounts of inventories
2. *McKesson and Robbins Inc., (1939) (USA)*

   The directors of the company created fictitious records of trading, sales, purchases, and inventories, including accounts receivables and bank accounts so that the assets were overstated by over $ 20 million.
3. *Allied Crude Vegetable Oil Refining Corporation of New Jersey (1963) (USA)*

   In this scandal, methods were used to fool auditors who were present at the stocktaking session.
4. *Re: Thomas Gerard & Sons Ltd (1967) (UK)*

   This was a cotton spinning and manufacturing company where the manager and a principal shareholder

   1. *Post-dated purchases invoices received before the year end; and*
   2. *Ante-dated sales invoice copies in the new year to dates prior to the year end.*

   This was done quite openly for five half year periods for bigger sums each time, thus turning losses into profits and causing the company to pay income tax and dividends. The auditors discovered the alterations, asked questions and were put off by answers such as 'these were year-end adjustments' The judge awarded damages against the auditors on the grounds that once their suspicions were aroused they had a duty to satisfy to probe the matter to the bottom. Auditors have a duty to satisfy themselves as to the validity of stock and work in progress and this cannot arise solely out of assurances from management, however trustworthy in appearance.
5. *Re: Long Pharmacy Bhd,*

   A local Malaysian pharmacy company with hundred stores used creative accounting in the form of phantom increases in inventory costs, using issued fake invoices for merchandise purchases, made fraudulent journal entries to increase inventory and decrease cost of goods sold, over-counted and double-counted inventory items.

6. *Re: The Crazy Eddie, Inc., Fraud. USA*

   A consumer electronics retail company had 43 consumer sale outlets. By end of 1989, the company had filed for bankruptcy, closed all stores, and liquidated all assets at a huge loss to investors. Investigation by regulatory authorities found extensive financial fraud, the most important being a US $65 million overstatement of inventory. Naturally the question arose as to why the auditors failed to uncover the fraud in their annual audit. The defense used by the auditor was the difficulty of uncovering the well-conceived fraud. The parties involved colluded or who knew of the fraud included the acting controller, the director of internal auditing and the director of accounts payable. One example of fraud was the shipment of inventory from store to store immediately before the auditor arrived to count the inventory. Another was the destruction of documentation to conceal inventory shortages at various locations. The auditor argued that it almost impossible to uncover fraud when there is extensive collusion. The suit against the audit firm and other defendants were settled out of court in 1993.

Nearly all these reported legal cases involved the manipulation of closing value of inventories in the financial statements because it is one of the most convenient way to **window-dress the profit performance of reporting entities**. It is for this reason that **auditors** are required to have **physical contact in order to verify the value and existence of inventories (or stocks) being reported** in the annual financial statements. It is also equally the responsibility of management to ensure proper controls are instituted for the physical custody of inventories and their valuation while controls in other critical areas must be also seen to be operating.

Ethics and Corporate Governance

Obviously, **integrity, ethical thinking and behavior** were completely lacking in all these fraudulent cases. It is not the systems and operating rules per se but rather **human nature taking the form of uncontrolled greed or avarice** is to be blamed for all these corporate scandals. It is a **moral hazard** that organizations must overcome this tendency to commit fraud on the part of individuals holding responsible positions of authority. **Corporate governance codes** alone cannot or will not overcome **irregularities and fraud** in an organization because of the uncertain involvement of the human element. Of course, moral and ethical training can resolve the issue to a large extent in these cases provided a **system of internal controls** relating to the **human level conscience** is given more consideration by management. Some members of top management more often than not, are the real culprits in perpetrating fraud who should be watched closely of their actions particularly where the **collusion element** could be present in their decision making process. The real problem is that it can be difficult to identify who are these individuals bent on committing fraud. **Internal audit checks** on a regular basis can scrutinize the most critical areas where irregularities and fraud potentially might take place.

Stocktaking Procedures

Business entities who maintain stocks for trading purposes will need to carry out at least an annual stock valuation exercise in order to ascertain the value of the closing inventories in hand at the year end. A physical stock-take achieves this requirement for financial reporting purposes. In practice, stock is difficult to determine both as to quantity and to value. We assume the company has already established an ongoing inventory control system for this purposes. In stocktaking, errors are easily made and therefore, specifically we to establish proper procedures for a physical stock-take. This might entail:

a. Identifying accurately each items of stock by description
b. Procedures for counting, weighing or measuring accurately
c. Entering the details or specifications on stock sheets
d. Ensuring all stock sheets are controlled for inclusion
e. Determining cost for each item
f. Extending 'quantity x price' accurately to give value
g. Identifying and valuing items which need to be valued at net realizable value(NRV)
h. Summing up the values
i. Ensuring accurate cut-off procedures

A well-organized stocktaking procedures would include the following:

a. Careful planning of the stock-taking operation
b. Issue and discussion of stock-taking instructions to staff
c. Division of the stock into manageable areas for control purposes
d. Proper instructions for counting, weighing, measuring and checking
e. Two persons to be involved in counting each item
f. Procedures for marking items which have been counted
g. Control movements during the stock-take
h. Establishing clear cut-off procedures
i. Procedures for identifying damaged, obsolete and slow moving stock
j. Identification of stock on the premises owned by third parties and of stocks held by outside parties
k. Control over the issue of blank sheets and the return of completed and unused stock sheets.

While all these procedures are primarily intended for a proper physical stock-take, computerized systems for control and movement of stocks in the warehouse or storerooms will need to be studied to ensure that stocktaking procedures within these domains are easily facilitated. However, physical observation is crucial to a physical stock-take as it may reveal any anomalies that need to be addressed and remedied before the actual valuation amount is reported in the financial statements.

MFRS 102/IAS 2 on Stocks and Work-in-Progress requires inventories to be stated *at a lower of cost and NRV.*

The physical stock-take (of inventories) is still required conventionally to establish the existence, physical conditions of the inventories being counted. Distortions in estimation may occur if inventories are found to be defective, have gone obsolete due to slow-moving, deterioration in quality, theft or pilferage, etc. Under these physical conditions, inventory valuation amounts may not be accurate or reliable for financial reporting purposes, thus, giving rise to misleading estimates that may cast a doubt on the accountability process. The **under or over stating of inventory valuation has consequential effect on profit reporting**, thus **impairing the true and fair view of f operating performance.** Taxable profits, earnings per share and dividends are affected adversely if financial reporting systems fails to provide quality assurance on the equitable position of the reporting entity. Given its magnitude and size, inventory is a significant value item in the statement of financial position that **needs to be accounted correctly at its fair value.**

It is for this primary reason, inventory valuation and its material effect on the financial statements cannot be dispensed easily if corporate governance policies on this type of issue is compromised. **Internal controls** must be seen to be working optimally to produce reliable financial outcome that represents faithfully the state of affairs of a business entity however big or small.

The appendices below are intended to provide further illustrative examples on the computation of closing inventory value and cost of goods sold under both perpetual and periodic systems.

Appendix 1

Inventory Valuation Under Perpetual System

JPS Trading Enterprise uses a perpetual inventory system for one of its product. The company's opening inventory, purchases, and sales for the year ended 2020 are as follows:

Date	Transaction	Units at Cost	Units Sold at Retail Price	Inventory Units
Jan 1	Opening inventory	500 units @ RM 15 =RM 7, 500		500 units
Jan 21	Sale		200 units @ RM 30	300 units
Feb 10	Purchases	200 units @ RM 15 = RM 3, 000		500 units
Mar 1	Sale		250 units @ RM 30	250 units
Apr 15	Purchases	250 units @ RM 17= RM 4, 250.		500 units
May 12	Purchases	250 units @ RM 18= RM 4, 500.		750 units
July 25	Sale		350 units @ RM 36	400 units
Sept 21	Purchases	150 units @ RM 20= RM 3, 000		550 units
Dec 5	Sale		100 units @ RM 36	450 units
	Total	1,350 units	900 units	

Additional information for specific cost method:

January 14 Sale 250 units @RM15 March 5 Sale 200 units @ RM 16 July 25 Sale 250 units @ RM 15 & 100 units @ RM 17 Nov 12 Sale 150 units @ RM 17 Dec. 1 Sale 150 units @ RM 20.

Required

a. **Calculate the cost of goods available for sale**

b. **Using the three different methods of inventory valuation, determine the closing inventory and cost of goods sold under each method.**

c. **Calculate the gross profit earned by JPS Trading Enterprise for each of the methods in (b)**

d. **State the inventory amount to be reported on the statement of financial position for each of the methods.**

In preparing financial statements for the year 2020, the accountant had in mind to use FIFO but failed to apply the method and instead computed cost of goods sold according to weighted average cost.

e. **You are required to determine the impact on year 2020's profit from the error. Also determine the effect of this error on year 2021's profit.** Ignore income tax.

The company's management wants a report that shows how changing from FIFO to another method would change net profit.

f. You are also required to prepare a table showing:

i. The cost of goods sold amount under each of the three methods;

ii. The amount by which each cost of goods sold is different from the FIFO cost of goods sold; and

iii. The effect on net profit if another method was adopted instead of FIFO.

Solution

JPS Trading Enterprise

a. Cost of goods available for sale

Date.		Units	Unit Cost	Cost
Jan 1	Opening inventory	500	15	7, 500
Feb 10	Purchased	200	15	3, 000
Apr 15	Purchased	250	17	4, 250
May 17	Purchased	250	18	4, 500
Sept 21	Purchased	150	20	3, 000
Total cost of goods available for sale		1, 350		22, 250

Note: The total amount is the same for all valuation methods.

b. Inventory valuation using all the three costing methods.

i. FIFO perpetual method.

Date	Goods purchased	Cost of goods sold	Inventory balance
Jan 1	Opening inventory		500 @ RM 15 = RM 7, 500
Jan 21		200 @ RM 15 = RM 3, 000	300 @ RM 15 = RM 4, 500
Feb 10	200 @ RM 15 = RM 3,000		300 @ RM 15 = RM 4, 500
			200 @ RM 15 = RM 3, 000
Mar 1		250 @ RM 15 = RM 3, 750	50 @ RM 15 = RM 750
Apr 15	250 @ RM 17 = RM 4, 250		200 @ RM 15 = RM 3, 000
May 12	250 @ RM 18 = RM 4, 500		250 @ RM 17 = RM 4, 250
July 25		250 @ RM 15 = RM 3, 750	250 @ RM 18 = RM 4, 500
		100 @ RM 17 = RM 1, 700	150 @ RM 17 = RM 2, 550

Sept 21	150 @ RM 20 = RM 3, 000		150 @ RM 20 = RM 3, 000
Dec 5		100 @ RM 17 = RM 1, 700	50 @ RM 17 = 850
			250 @ RM 18 = 4, 500
Total cost of goods sold		RM 13, 900.	RM 8, 350

Note: Cost of goods available for sale = Cost of goods sold + Closing inventory RM [22, 250 = 13, 900 + 8, 350]

Alternative Ways of Computing FIFO numbers

1. FIFO Alternative 1

Calculating the cost of goods sold first		RM	RM
Cost of goods available from sale (from *part a*)			22, 250
Cost of goods sold			
Jan 21	Sold (200 units @ RM 15)	3, 000	
Mar 1	Sold (250 units @ RM 15)	3, 750	
July 25	Sold (250 units @ RM 15)	3, 750	
	Sold (100 units @ RM 17)	1, 700	
Dec 5	Sold (100 units @ RM 17)	1, 700	(13, 900)
Closing inventory			**8, 350**

2. FIFO Alternative 2

Calculating closing inventory first.

		RM	RM
Cost of goods available from sale (from part a)			22, 250
Closing inventory			
Sept 21	Purchased (150 units @ RM 20)	3, 000	
Dec 5	Purchased (50 units @ RM 17)	850	
Purchased (250 units @ RM 18)		4, 500	(8, 350)
Cost of goods sold			**13, 900**

Since FIFO assumes the earlier costs are the first to flow out, we calculate ending inventory by assigning the most recent costs to the remaining stock items.

Tutorial note

Once we calculate the cost of goods available for sale, then we can determine the amount for either (a) *cost of goods sold* or (b) *closing inventory* – whichever is preferred. **Alternative 2** is adopted in practice to determine the cost of goods sold to be matched against sales revenue to produce the gross profit figure.

ii. Weighted Average Cost Method

Date	Goods purchased	Cost of goods sold	Closing inventory
Jan 1	Opening balance.		500 @ RM 15 = RM 7, 500
21		200 @ RM 15 = RM 3, 000	300 @ RM 15 = RM 4, 500
Feb 10	200 @ RM 15 = RM 3, 000		300 @ RM 15
			200 @ RM 15
			500 @ RM 15 = RM 7, 500
Mar 1		250 @ RM 15 = RM 3, 750	250 @ RM 15 = RM 3, 750
Apr. 15	250 @ RM 17 = RM 4, 250		250 @ RM 17 = RM 4, 250
			500 @ RM 16 = RM 8, 000
			(Avg. cost is RM 16)
May 12	250 @ RM 18 = RM 4, 500		250 @ RM 18 = RM 4, 500
			500 @ RM 16 = RM 8, 000
			750 @ RM 16.67 = RM 12,500
			(Avg. cost is RM 16.67)
July 25		350 @ RM 16.67= RM 5,835	400 @ RM 16.67 = RM 6,668
Sept 21	150 @ RM 20 = RM 3, 000		400 @ RM 16.67 = RM 6,668
			150 @ RM 20 = RM 3,000
			550 @ RM 17. 58 = RM 9,668
Dec 5		100 @ RM 17.58 = RM 1, 758	450 @ RM 17. 58= **RM 7,911**
Total cost of goods sold		**RM 14, 343**	

The cost of goods sold (RM 14, 343) plus closing inventory (RM 7, 911) appears to be more than the goods available for sale (RM 22, 250) by RM 4 due to rounding difference.

iii. Specific Cost Method (Using the information in the Question)

Date	Goods purchased	Cost of goods sold	Closing inventory
Jan 1	Opening balance		500 @ RM 15 = RM 7, 500
Jan 14		250 @ RM 15 = RM 3, 750	250 @ RM 15 = RM 3, 750
Feb 10	200 @ RM 15 = RM 3, 000		450 @ RM 15 = RM 6, 750
March 5		200 @ RM 15 = RM 3,000	250 @ RM 15 = RM 3, 750
April 15	250 @ RM 17 = RM 4, 250		250 @ RM 17 = RM 4, 250
May 12	250 @ RM 18 = RM 4, 500		250 @ RM 18 = RM 4, 500
July 25		250 @ RM 15 = RM 3, 750	All sold @ RM 15 = Nil
		100 @ RM 17 = RM 1, 700	150 @ RM 17 = RM 2, 550
			250 @ RM 18 = RM 4, 500
Sept 21	150 @ RM 20 = RM 3, 000		150 @ RM 17 = RM 2, 550
			250 @ RM 18 = RM 4, 500
			150 @ RM 20 = RM 3, 000
Nov 12		150 @ RM 17 = RM 2, 550	All valued @ RM 17 = Nil
			250 @ RM 18 = RM 4, 500
			150 @ RM 20 = RM 3, 000
Dec 1		150 @ RM 20 = RM 3, 000	All valued @ RM 20 = Nil
			250 @ RM 18 = RM 4, 500
Total cost of goods sold		**RM 17, 750**	**RM 4, 500**

Costing of units is strictly based on identification of specific cost.

	FIFO	Weighted. Average Cost	Specific Cost
	RM	RM	RM
Statement of Comprehensive Income			
Sales	29, 700	29,700	36, 900
Cost of goods sold.	(13, 900)	(14, 343).	(17, 750)
Gross profit	15, 800.	15, 357	19, 150
Statement of Financial Position			
Current assets			
Closing Inventory	8, 350	7, 911	4, 500

Workings

Sales	200 units @ RM 30 = RM 6, 000		
	250 units @ RM 30 = 7, 500		
	350 units @ RM 36 = 12, 600		
	100 units @ RM 36 = 3, 600		
		RM 29, 700	FIFO & WAC
Sales	200 units @ RM 36 =	7, 200	
		RM 36, 900	Specific Cost

e. By an oversight error, using weighted average cost instead of FIFO, this has the effect of overstating cost of goods sold in year 2020 by RM 443. Therefore, profit in 2020 gets understated by RM 443. In year 2021, gross profit is overstated because opening inventory amount gets understated by (RM 8, 350 – RM 7, 911 = RM 439). The inventory difference of RM 4 (443 – 439) in the inventory figures is due to rounding off.

f. The statement shows the analysis of effects of using alternative costing methods.

	Cost of goods sold	Difference using FIFO Cost of goods sold	Effect on Net profit if adopted instead of FIFO
FIFO	**13, 900**	-	-
Weighted average cost	**14, 343**	**443**	**443 lower**

Note: The RM 3, 850 difference between using FIFO and Specific cost methods appears to show a large difference in the amount of cost of goods sold because of more sale units were reported under the specific cost method unlike the other two methods the sales amount were the same. The closing inventory figure of RM 4, 500 is lower because more units were sold under this valuation method. See workings above.

Appendix 2

Inventory Valuation Under Periodic System

Both the perpetual and periodic systems have the same objective in assigning costs to inventory and cost of goods sold. All the three methods are used to assign the costs under both systems: FIFO, Weighted Average Cost and Specific Cost. We are ignoring LIFO completely here because as mentioned earlier, this valuation method is not accepted by both IRB and FRS, therefore it serves no real purpose in financial reporting.

We use the information for sales and purchases given in the table to show how to assign costs using these three methods with a periodic system.

Date	Transactions	Units at Cost.		Units Sold	Inventory Units
Sept 1	Opening inventory	12 units @ RM 90 = RM 1, 080			12 units
Sept 5	Purchases	18 units @ RM 105 = RM 1, 890			30 units
Sept 15	Sales			20 units @ RM 130 = RM 2, 600	10 units
Sept 20	Purchases	20 units @ RM 110 = RM 2, 200			30 units
Sept 28	Purchases	15 units @ RM 120 = RM 1, 800			45 units
Sept 30	Sales			25 units @ RM 145 = RM 3, 625	20 units
	Totals	65 units		RM 6, 970	45 units

Specific Cost Method

We use the above given data on sales and purchases and the specific cost method to assign the costs to units sold and closing inventory. The company's internal data further reveals additional information on specific unit sales:

- **Sept 15 Sold 8 units costing RM 90 each and 12 units costing RM 105 each**
- **Sept 30 Sold 3 units costing RM 90 each, 6 units costing RM 105 each, 15 units costing RM 110 each, and further one unit costing RM 120 each.**

Required

a. Explain how the FIFO method is applied in valuing the closing inventory?

b. Using FIFO, compute the cost of goods sold and cost of inventory.

c. Explain how the Weighted Average Cost method works?

d. Using the weighted average cost method, determine the closing inventory value and the cost of goods sold.

e. **Applying the Specific Cost Method and using the information on purchases and sales, prepare a computation to show the**
   i. **Total cost of goods sold, and**
   ii. **Closing inventory value.**

f. **Prepare the required journal entries for the transactions on sales and purchases under periodic system.**

g. **Show the effects of the three methods on the financial statements on reported profits and closing inventory. Comment on the differences. Assume expenses totaled RM 550 and Income tax is 25 % on profit before tax.**

Solution

a. **FIFO** – The first-in, first-out method of assigning costs to inventory assumes that inventory items are sold in the order acquired. When sales take place, the costs of the earliest units acquired are charged to cost of goods sold. Thus, the costs from the most recent purchases goes into closing inventory. The order in which this happens will remain consistent under this basis.

			RM
b.	Total cost of 65 units available for sale (from the given table)		6, 970
	Less; Closing inventory using FIFO		
	15 units from Sept 28 purchases @ RM 120 each	1, 800	
	5 units from Sept 20 purchases @ RM 110 each	550	
	Closing inventory		**(2, 350)**
	Cost of goods sold		4, 620

The computation starts with RM 6, 970 in total units available for sale. Applying FIFO, 20 units in closing inventory will be reported at the cost of the most recent 20 purchases. We assign costs to the 20 units in closing inventory as follows: RM 120 cost to 15 units and RM 110 cost to 5 units. This gives 20 units costing RM 2, 350 in closing inventory. We then subtract this RM 2, 350 in closing inventory from RM 6, 970 in cost of goods available to obtain RM 4, 620 in cost of goods sold.

Closing inventory reported in the statement of financial position is RM 2, 350, and its cost of goods sold reported in the statement of comprehensive income is RM 4, 620. These amounts are the same as those computed using the perpetual system. This always happens because the most recent purchases are in the closing inventory under both systems.

c. **Weighted Average Cost** – The weighted average cost method of assigning cost requires that we use the average cost per unit of inventory at the end of the period.

$$\text{Weighted average cost per unit} = \frac{\text{the cost of goods available for sale}}{\text{the number of units available}}$$

d. The method involves 3 steps: the first two steps are shown below:

Step 1:		
	12 units @ RM 90 = RM	1, 080
	18 units @ RM 105 =	1, 890
	20 units @ RM 110 =	2, 200
	15 units @ RM 120 =	1, 800
	65	RM 6, 970

Step 2: RM 6, 790/65 units = RM 107.23 weighted average cost per unit

The third step is to use the weighted average cost per unit to assign costs to inventory and to the units sold as shown below:

Step 3:	Total cost of 65 units available for sale	RM 6, 970
	Less:	
	Closing inventory valued @ weighted average cost basis:	
	20 units @ RM 107.23	(2, 145)
	Cost of goods sold.	RM 4 825

The closing inventory reported in the statement of financial position is RM 2, 145, and its cost of goods sold reported in the statement of comprehensive income is RM 4 825 when using the weighted average cost under the periodic system.

An important point to note is that **weighted average cost** usually tend to produce different results for the perpetual and the periodic systems. This is because under a perpetual system it recalculates per unit cost prior to each sale, whereas under a periodic system, the cost per unit is calculated only at the end of a period.

e. **Specific Cost Method –** We use the information on sales and purchases and the specific cost method to assign costs to closing inventory and units sold. We prepare a schedule as before and apply specific cost method using the information n above. You need to study carefully the schedule (or table) to see the flow of costs both in and out of inventory. Each unit, whether sold or remaining in inventory, has its own specific cost attached to it.

Date	Goods Purchased (Goods in)	Cost of Goods Sold (Goods out)	Inventory Balance (What's left)
Sept 1	Opening inventory		12 @ RM 90 = RM 1, 080
Sept 5	18 units @ RM 105 = RM 1, 890		18 @ RM 105 = 1, 890
			30 RM 2, 970
Sept 15		8@ RM 90 = RM 720	4 @ RM 90 = RM 360
		12@ RM 105 = 1, 260	6 @ RM105 = 630
		** 20 RM 1, 980	10 RM 990
Sept 20	20 units @ RM 110 = RM 2, 200		4 @ RM 90 = RM 360
			6 @ RM 105 = 630
			20 @ RM 110 = 2, 200
			30 RM 3, 190
Sept 28	15 units @ RM 120 = RM 1, 800		4 @ RM 90 = RM 360
			6 @ RM 105 = 630
			20 @ RM 110 = 2, 200
			15 @ RM 120 = 1, 800
			45 RM 4, 990
Sept 30		4 @ RM 90= RM 360	
		6 @ RM 105= 630	
		14@ RM110= 1, 540	6 @ RM 110 =RM 660
		1 @ RM120= 120	14 @ RM 120 = 1,680
		25 RM 2, 650	20 **RM 2, 340**
Total cost of goods sold		**RM 4, 630**	

*** for 20 units sold on Sept 15, the entity specifically identified that 8 units of those had cost RM 90 and 12 had cost RM 105.*

 # for 25 units sold on Sept 30, the entity specifically identified each unit sold and its acquisition cost from prior purchases.

Using specific cost method, the entity's cost of goods sold reported in the statement of comprehensive income totals RM 4, 630 (RM 1, 980 + RM 2, 650) from the third column in the computation schedule and the closing inventory reported in the statement of financial position is RM 2, 340 which appears in the final column of the computation schedule.

The assignment of costs to the goods sold and inventory using specific cost method is the same for both the perpetual and periodic systems.

f. **Journal entries**

All purchases and sales are made in credit. The journal entries are the same for all three methods except that an adjusting entry is required to show the opening inventory balance in the reported figures under each method because it is included in the closing inventory amount.

Purchases			
Sept 5	Purchases	1, 890	
	Accounts payable.		1, 890
Sept 20	Purchases	2, 200	
	Accounts payable		2, 200
Sept 28	Purchases	1, 800	
	Accounts payable		1, 800
Sales			
Sept 15	Accounts receivable	2, 600	
	Sales		2, 600
Sept 28	Accounts receivable	3, 625	
	Sales		3, 625
Adjusting entries			
FIFO			
Sept 30	Closing inventory	2, 350	
	Retained earnings		1, 270
	Opening inventory		1, 080
Weighted Average			
Sept 30	Closing inventory	2, 145	
	Retained earnings		1, 065
	Opening inventory		1, 080
Specific Cost			
Sept 30	Closing inventory	2, 340	
	Retained earnings		1, 260
	Opening inventory		1, 080

g. **Effects on Financial Statements**

Company's Financial Statements
For Month Ended September 30

	FIFO	Weighted Average Cost	Specific Cost
Statement of Comprehensive Income			
	FM	**FM**	**RM**
Sales	6, 225	6, 225	6, 225
Less:			
Cost of goods sold.	**(4, 620).**	**(4,825)**	**(4, 630)**
Gross profit	1, 605	1,400	1, 595
Less:			
Expenses.	(550).	(550).	(550).
Profit before tax	1, 055	850	1, 045
Less: Income tax @ 25 %.	(264).	(138)	(261)
Net profit	**791**	**712**	**784**
Statement of Financial Position			
Current assets			
Closing inventory	**2, 350**	**2, 145**	**2, 340**

The important thing to note is that when purchase prices do not change (remain stable), each inventory method assigns the same cost amounts to inventory and to cost of goods sold. When purchase prices are different (fluctuating), the methods always assign different cost amounts. We have shown these cost differences in the above financial statements.

The financial statements reveal two important results.

1. When purchase costs *regularly rise*, as in the above case, the following issues can be observed:
   - FIFO assigns the lower amount to cost of goods sold, thus resulting in higher profit and net profit
   - Weighted average cost results in higher cost of goods sold (RM 4,825) and lowest profit as it averages the recent higher costs with the earlier lower costs.
   - Specific cost always yields results that depend on which units are sold.
2. When costs *regularly decline* (which seldom happens these days). The reverse occurs for FIFO and weighted cost.
   - FIFO gives the higher cost of goods sold, thus yielding the lower profit and net profit. Weighted average cost results in lower cost of goods sold, thus giving higher gross profit and net profit.

MFRS 102/IAS 2 on Stocks and Work-in-progress accepts all three valuation methods. However, the Standard requires entities to disclose the inventory method used. See earlier pages for accounting policies on stocks and work-in-progress.

There are certain advantages attached to each method as follows:

- FIFO assigns a value to inventory in the statement of financial position that approximates current costs;
- Weighted average cost tends to smooth out fluctuating or erratic changes in costs;
- Specific cost exactly matches the cost of inventory items with the revenues they generate;

The retail inventory method is a special case for the stated reasons explained in earlier pages. It obviously serves the special needs of certain companies .

Appendix 3

Use of Ratios in Inventory Management

Inventory management puts an important emphasis for both manufacturers and trading companies. In order to perform well, these companies must both plan and control inventory purchases and sales. Two crucial ratios useful in evaluating a company's short-term liquidity: *current ratio and acid-test ratio.* A merchandising entity's ability to settle(pay) its short-term obligations also depends on how speedily it sells and converts its inventory into accounts receivable before realizing cash.

Inventory turnover is one such ratio used to assess this and is defined as follows:

$$\text{Inventory turnover} = \frac{\text{Cost of goods sold}}{\text{Average}}$$

$$\text{Cost of goods sold} = \text{Opening inventory} + \begin{matrix}\text{Purchase of goods or}\\ \text{raw materials or cost of}\\ \text{goods manufactured}\end{matrix} - \text{Closing inventory}$$

This ratio reveals how many **times** a company turn over (sells) its inventory during a period. If a company's inventory significantly varies within a year, average inventory amounts can be calculated from interim periods such as quarters or months.

Users apply inventory turnover to help analyze short-term liquidity and to assess whether management is performing well controlling the amount of inventory available. A low ratio compared to that of a rival competitor suggests inefficient use of assets. The company may be holding more inventory (too much capital) than it needs to support its sales volume. Similarly, a very high ratio compared to that of its competitors suggest inventory might be too low to meets sales demand. This can cause lost sales if customers must back-order merchandise. There is no stated rule for inventory turnover except to say *a high ratio is preferable provided inventory is sufficient to meet customers' demand.*

Days' Sales in Inventory

For better interpretation of inventory turnover, many users particularly measure the adequacy of inventory to meet sales demand. Days' sales in inventory is a ratio that reveals how much inventory is available to interpret the number of days' sales. This is interpreted as the number of days an entity can sell from inventory if no new items are purchased. This ratio is often seen as a precautionary measure to avoid out-of-stock inventory and is useful in evaluating liquidity of inventory (how fast inventory is converted into sales). It is defined as follows

$$\text{Day's sales in inventory} = \frac{\text{Closing inventory}}{\text{Cost of goods sold}} \times 365 \text{ days}$$

The ratio estimates how many days it will take to convert inventory at the end of a period into accounts receivable or cash. Days' sales in inventory focuses on closing inventory whereas inventory turnover focuses on average turnover

Cautionary advice

1. *It is important to take care when comparing turnover ratios across companies that use different valuation methods such as FIFO and Weighted Average cost.*
2. *Industries such as foods and other perishable products will normally have a higher inventory turnover and a lower days' sales in inventory.*

Chapter Summary

1. **Know what is inventory**

   Merchandise inventory refers to purchased goods owned by a company and held for sale (as stock-in-trade) in the ordinary course of business, in the process of manufacturing for such sale; or in the form of raw materials, purchased components and supplies to be consumed in the production process or in rendering of services. As long as a product (finished good) has not been sold, all costs attached to it are not released in the statement of comprehensive income but essentially stored in the inventory account. Inventories not consumed or sold are financial assets (potential source of future economic benefits) classified under current assets in the statement of financial position.

2. **Categories of inventory – what items constitute as inventory**?

   Inventory is categorically identified as goods purchased for resale without transformation (commercial activity), finished goods available for sale, raw materials used in production process, and work-in-progress (manufacturing activity). Three types of classification of goods require special attention: Goods in transit are reported in inventory of an entity that holds ownership rights. Goods on consignment are reported in the consignor's inventory. Goods damaged or obsolete are reported in inventory at their net realizable value.

3. **Cost of inventory**

   The FRS on stocks and work-in-progress states: the cost of inventories shall comprise all costs of purchase, cost of conversion and other attributable costs incurred in bringing the inventories to their present condition and location.

Inventory and its classification must be disclosed and its accounting treatment on valuation or costing explained as part of the accounting policy adopted in measuring inventories.

4. **Inventory equation**

   The fundamental inventory equation is: Cost of goods sold = Opening inventory + Purchases – Closing inventory. Opening inventory plus purchases represent goods available for sale. As inventories represent a large in the value of shareholders' equity.

5. **Inventory recording systems**

   Two systems most commonly used in reporting inventory movements whether they are related to purchase of goods or raw materials or goods to be consumed in the manufacturing process and sales activity (outflow of inventory) are the perpetual and periodic systems. A perpetual inventory system is a continuous record of changes in inventory movements (additions and withdrawals) whereas the periodic inventory system relies on the required periodic (annual) physical counting to establish and value the quantities in the closing inventory to be reported in the statement of financial position. These two practices impact differently on the profit and the closing inventory. Inventory items carried in inventory are either so large, so valuable and/ or so specific that they cannot be considered perishable, (a basic assumption common to both perpetual and periodic inventory systems) and therefore kept in inventory and accounted for under the specific cost method.

6. **Computing the lower of cost and net realizable value (NRV)**

   Inventory is reported at NRV

7. **Inventory valuation methods**

   Inventory valuation and costing methods have a great impact on reported net profit. There are four methods for valuing or costing of closing inventory: FIFO (first-in, first –out), Weighted average cost, LIFO (last-in, first-out) and Specific cost method. FRS no longer allows the use of LIFO method for financial reporting purposes nor does the IRB. The reasoning behind this restriction is well- explained in the pages of the chapter.

8. **Analyze the effects of inventory methods for both financial and tax reporting**

   When purchase costs are rising or declining, the inventory costing methods are likely to assign different costs to inventory. FIFO assigns an amount to closing inventory closely approximating current cost (using latest prices). Weighted average cost smooths out cost changes. Specific cost method exactly matches costs and revenues. These cases are well demonstrated through the use of our illustrated examples.

9. **Analyze the effects of inventory errors on financial statements**

   An error in the amount of closing inventory affects assets, net profit (cost of goods sold) and equity for that period. Since closing inventory is next period's opening inventory, an error in closing inventory affects next period costs of goods sold and net profit. Inventory errors in one period are offset in the next period. Again, we have made use of illustrative examples to show the financial effects. On this note, one should be cautioned against irregularities and fraud that can recklessly take place through improper manipulation of closing inventory and its adverse impact on profit performance. The chapter reveals a number of documented cases on fraud.

10. **Inventory management using financial ratios**

    Financial analysts are mainly concerned with coherence between the current or actual level of inventory of a business, appropriate to the entity's business's environment and strategy. Their measures to evaluate this coherence are through the use of ratios: (1) preferably a high **inventory turnover** (number of times the inventory 'turns' during the accounting period provided that goods are not out of stock and customers are not turned away; and/or (2) **average days of sale** in inventory available so that the entity can serve customer needs and provide a buffer for uncertainties.

Chapter Summary

1. **Know what is inventory.**

   Merchandise inventory refers to purchased goods owned by a company and held for sale (as stock-in-trade) in the ordinary course of business, in the process of manufacturing for such sale; or in the form of raw materials, purchased components and supplies to be consumed in the production process or in rendering of services. As long as a product (finished good) has not been sold, all costs attached to it are not released in the statement of comprehensive income but essentially stored in the inventory account. Inventories not consumed or sold are financial assets (potential source of future economic benefits) classified under current assets in the statement of financial position.

2. **Categories of inventory – what items constitute as inventory.**

   Inventory is categorically identified as goods purchased for resale without transformation (commercial activity), finished goods available for sale, raw materials used in production process, and work-in-progress (manufacturing activity). Three types of classification of goods require special attention: **Goods in transit** are reported in inventory of an entity that holds ownership rights. **Goods on consignment** are reported in the consignor's inventory. **Goods damaged or obsolete** are reported in inventory at their net realizable value.

3. **Cost of inventory**

   The FRS on stocks and work-in-progress states: the cost of inventories shall comprise all costs of purchase, cost of conversion and other attributable costs incurred in bringing the inventories to their present condition and location. Inventory and its classification must be disclosed and its accounting treatment on valuation or costing explained as part of the accounting policy adopted in measuring inventories.

4. **Inventory equation**

   The fundamental inventory equation is: Cost of goods sold = Opening inventory + Purchases – Closing inventory. Opening inventory plus purchases represent goods available for sale. As inventories represent a large in fairly the value of shareholders' equity.

5. **Inventory recording systems**

   Two systems most commonly used in reporting inventory movements whether they are related to purchase of goods or raw materials or goods to be consumed in the manufacturing process and sales activity (outflow of inventory) are the **perpetual and periodic systems**. A perpetual inventory system is a continuous record of changes in inventory movements (additions and withdrawals) whereas the periodic inventory system relies on the required periodic (annual) physical counting to establish and value the quantities in the closing inventory to be reported in the statement of financial position. These two practices impact differently on the profit and the closing inventory. Inventory items carried in inventory are either so large, so valuable and/ or so specific that they cannot be considered perishable, (a basic assumption common to both perpetual and periodic inventory systems) and therefore kept in inventory and accounted for under the specific cost method.

6. **Inventory valuation methods**

   Inventory valuation and costing methods have a great impact on reported net profit. There are four methods for valuing or costing of closing inventory: FIFO (first-in, first –out), Weighted average cost, LIFO (last-in, first-out) and Specific cost method. FRS no longer allows the use of LIFO method for financial reporting purposes nor does the IRB. The reasoning behind this restriction is well- explained in the pages of the chapter.

7. **Analyze the effects of inventory methods for both financial and tax reporting**

   When purchase costs are rising or declining, the inventory costing methods are likely to assign different costs to inventory. FIFO assigns an amount to closing inventory closely approximating current cost (using latest prices).

Weighted average cost smooths out cost changes. Specific cost method exactly matches costs and revenues. These cases are well demonstrated through the use of our illustrated examples.

8. **Analyze the effects of inventory errors on financial statements**

   An error in the amount of closing inventory affects assets, net profit (cost of goods sold) and equity for that period. Since closing inventory is next period's opening inventory, an error in closing inventory affects next period costs of goods sold and net profit. Inventory errors in one period are offset in the next period. Again, we have made use of illustrative examples to show the financial effects. On this note, one should be cautioned against irregular-ities and fraud that can recklessly take place through improper manipulation of closing inventory and its adverse impact on profit performance. The chapter reveals a number of documented cases on fraud.

9. **Asses inventory management on the basis of financial ratios**

   Financial analysts are mainly concerned with coherence between the current or actual level of inventory of a business, appropriate to the entity's business's environment and strategy. Their measures to evaluate this coherence: (1) **inventory turnover** (number of times the inventory 'turns' during the period; for a given industry preferably the higher the turnover ratio, the more likely the management of inventory flows is efficient. In the case of 'just-in-time' relations between suppliers and customers, the ratio of 26 (an inventory sufficient to meet 2 weeks of average demand or sales are not uncommon in automobile industry or the assembly of electrical or electronic items. (2) **average days of inventory available** to interpret the number of days' sale without having to purchase any new products or materials.

10. **Computing the lower of cost and net realizable value**

    Inventory is stated at NRV when NRV is lower than recorded cost, that is at the lower of cost and NRV. NRV is the estimated selling price in the ordinary of business less estimated costs of completion and estimated costs necessary to make the sale. Lower of cost and NRV should be applied separately to each item or to major categories of items.

11. **Inventory management using financial ratios**

    Financial analysts are mainly concerned with coherence between the current or actual level of inventory of a business, appropriate to the entity's business's environment and strategy. Their measures to evaluate this coherence are through the use of ratios: (1) preferably a high **inventory turnover** (number of times the inventory 'turns' during the accounting period provided that goods are not out of stock and customers are not turned away; and/or (2) **average days of sale** in inventory available so that the entity can serve customer needs and provide a buffer for uncertainties.

12. **Disclosure requirements of inventory reporting in financial statements**

    Know the statutory requirements on disclosures on inventory to be reported in the financial statements. What are those requirements and why the need for such disclosure?

Key Terms

Average cost

Cost

Consignee

Consignor

Days' sales in inventory

Damaged (or defective) goods

First –in, First-out (FIFO)

Interim financial statements

Inventory turnover

Last-in, First out (LIFO)

Net realizable value (NRV)

Obsolescence

Retail inventory method

Specific cost method

Shrinkage

Weighted average cost (WAC)

Review Questions

Q1. a. Explain what you understand by the term 'Merchandise Inventory'?

b. Identify the different elements of cost that make-up purchase cost.

Q2. Which accounting standard governs the presentation, disclosure, and accounting treatment of inventories in financial statements?

Q3. State and explain the accounting principle that treats inventory in the financial statement. Give an example to illustrate how it is dealt in the accounts.

Q4. i. Identify the categories of inventory that is reported in the notes to the financial statements.

ii. Where is the closing inventory is shown in the statement of financial position?

Q5. Explain the terms – Goods-in-transit, Goods on-consignment and Goods damaged or obsolete.

How these types of goods are accounted for in the inventory account?

Q6. i. Explain and identify the costs of inventory.

ii. Why incidental costs such as freight, import duties, storage, and insurance added to the cost of inventory?

Q7. What components that make-up the cost of goods sold? Identify the cost elements that make-up cost of goods available for sale.

Q8. Perpetual and periodic inventory systems are the main two systems of inventory adopted in accounting. Explain in your answer, the main difference(s) between these two inventory systems.

Q9. Emphasis is laid on physical stock count under the periodic system Why are the auditors present during physical stock-take that takes place annually.?

Q10. Inventory valuation is done by a number of costing methods. What the methods applied in

valuing inventory for financial reporting purposes?

Q11. i. Briefly explain the use of FIFO, LIFO, Weighted average cost and Specific cost as the main methods used to assign costs to cost of goods sold and closing inventory.

ii. Explain the main effects of these methods on financial statements.

Illustrate by way of numerical examples

Q12. Explain why the LIFO method is not accepted by the MFRS/IAS and Inland Revenue Board?

Q13. Explain why the accounting standard requires inventory be reported at the NRV when NRV is lower than cost.

Q14. Describe one advantage for each of the inventory valuation methods; FIFO, Weighted average cost, and Specific cost.

Q15. i. When costs are rising, which method reports higher net profit – FIFO or Weighted average cost?

ii. When costs are rising, what effect does Weighted average cost have on the statement of financial position compared to FIFO?

Q16. A company uses the retail inventory method to estimate the closing inventory value.

1. Explain under what circumstances is this method permissible for financial reporting purposes?
2. What three step process is used to estimate the closing inventory? You may use your own example to numerically obtain the closing inventory figure.

Q17. Can a company change its inventory method each accounting period? Explain.

Q18. A company takes a physical count of inventory at the end of 2020 and finds closing inventory is understated by RM 9, 000. Can this error cause cost of goods sold to be overstated or understated in 2020? If so, by how much?

Q19.

Product	Units	Unit cost	Unit NRV
		RM	RM
A	25	7	6
B	40	10	8
C	12	12	14

Required: Use lower of cost and NRV applied separately to the above individual items to calculate closing inventory.

Q20. A company reports the following opening inventory and purchases, it ends the reporting period with 45 units in inventory.

Opening inventory	105 units @ RM 15 cost per unit
Purchased	42 units @ RM 17 cost per unit
Purchased	20 units @ RM 18 cost per unit

Required: Compute (a) Cost of goods sold, (b) Closing inventory using FIFO periodic system.

Q20. Estimate the closing inventory using the retail inventory method and the following data:

Cost.	**Retail**	
RM.	**RM**	
Opening inventory	365, 000	575, 000
Cost of goods purchased	205, 000	345, 000
Net sales		330, 000

Q21. When a trader in merchandise uses a perpetual inventory system, why it is necessary to adjust the inventory account balance with an adjusting entry?

Multiple Choice Questions

Select the right answer (only one possible answer unless otherwise stated).

Q1. Raw materials, work-in-progress and finished goods are included in

1. Expenses
2. Non-current assets
3. Cash and bank balances

4. Current assets
5. Cost of purchases

Q2. In the statement of financial position, the item 'inventories' may be subject to

1. Amortization
2. Depreciation
3. Provision
4. Depletion
5. None of the above

Q3. The following inventory costing method provides a value for closing inventory which approximates most closely its current cost

1. FIFO
2. LIFO
3. Weighted average cost
4. Specific cost
5. None of the above.

Q4. An audit reveals that the opening inventory at 1 January X1 had been overstated by RM 1, 800 and the closing inventory at 31 December X1 was overstated by RM 800. As a consequence, the cost of goods sold for X1 was

1. Overstated by RM 1, 800
2. Understated by RM 1,800
3. Overstated by RM 1, 000
4. Understated by RM 1, 000
5. Overstated by RM 800

Q5. In periods of steadily decreasing prices, the following costing method will give the highest closing inventory value (assuming quantities purchased exceed quantities sold).

1. FIFO
2. Weighted average cost
3. LIFO
4. Specific cost
5. None of the above

Q6. The retail inventory method is used to value closing inventory under what circumstances?

1. When there are no other alternative methods of valuing closing inventory.
2. Closing inventories are destroyed by fire or floods
3. It is an estimated method that gives a close approximation to actual cost and it is accepted by the MFRS/IFRS.
4. Because the tax authorities allow the retail inventory method under some extenuating circumstances.
5. None of the above.

Q7. The average days' sales in inventory available is defined as (Cost of goods sold/Average inventory) × 365 days.

1. True
2. False

Use the following information from No Stock-Out Company (NSOC) for month of December to answer questions 8 to 11

Dec 1	Opening inventory	75 units @ RM 25 each
5	Purchase	365 units @ RM 28 each
9	Sale	300 units
18	Purchase	250 units @ RM 29 each
23	Sale	285 units

Q8. Assume that NSOC uses a perpetual FIFO inventory system. What is the value of its closing inventory?

a. RM 1, 160 c. RM1, 625 e. RM 2, 005
b. RM 1, 285 d. RM 1, 150

Q9. Assume that NSOC uses a periodic FIFO inventory system. What is the value of its closing inventory?

a. RM 1,160 c. RM 1, 625 e. RM 2, 005
b. RM 1, 285 d. RM 1, 150

Q10. Assume that NSOC uses a perpetual specific cost method inventory system. Its closing inventory consist of 25 units from opening inventory, 42 units from December 5 purchase, and 45 units from the December 18 purchase. Determine what will be its closing inventory value?

a. RM 2, 940 c. RM 2, 625 e. RM 2, 840
b. RM 2, 685 d. RM 3, 106

Q11. What is the net profit of the company if its total sales amounted RM 32, 175 and its operating expenses were RM 9,800 under the perpetual FIFO system? (Ignore tax).

a. RM 5,100 c. RM 6, 050 e. RM 6, 090
b. RM 6, 100 d. RM 6, 010

Q12. A company's cost of goods sold is RM 105, 000 and its closing inventory is RM 23, 000. Calculate its days' sales in inventory. Assume its opening inventory value is RM 21, 000. Use average inventory for your calculation.

a. 49 days c. 47 days. e. 76.5 days
b. 60 days d. 77.3 days

Chapter 8

Learning Objectives

Be able to record cash transactions in a cash book (manually as well as in a computerised system).

Be able to understand and apply internal controls over cash receipts and cash payments.

Be able to prepare a bank reconciliation and understand why the need to do so.

Understand the need to record petty cash transactions under an impress system and know the supporting documents used.

Cash and Internal Controls

1. Scope

Cash as "King"

Cash is the life force of every business activity without which all forms of business transactions comes to a virtual halt or standstill. Cash is referred to as the 'King' because it drives everything that a business does in its pursuit of wealth maximizing goal. Among other current assets as reported in an entity's balance sheet, cash and cash equivalents is the most liquid asset prone to wider fluctuations than any other financial asset. The cash scenario changes every time when business transactions take place because cash is used as the main medium of exchange. Equally, as cash is frequently seen as the most vulnerable asset that is susceptible to theft and misappropriation through fraudulent activities, we need to implement a proper system of internal controls to monitor and check the validity of cash receipt and cash disbursement processes. For all these reasons, accounting for cash therefore becomes a crucial element of internal control in a business.

This chapter begins with the accounting aspects of cash first, then with a discussion on fraud and its financial impact. Then we discuss internal controls as a primary measure to detect and prevent such fraudulent activities and any other unintentional financial statement errors. Although these later topics are purely an auditing aspect beyond the scope of this textbook, we still need to see their link as relevant to the accounting aspects of cash and cash equivalents.

We look at a case scenario first before we consider control of cash.

Case Scenario

Nestles, a Swiss multi-national company is the world's leading nutrition, health and wellness company. Nestlé's product range is wide and carries a large portfolio of over 80-90 brands in many product categories. Given its financial statements for the year ended 31 December 2014, Nestlé's largest current assets are its trade receivables and cash and cash equivalents respectively. Together, they form over half of Nestlé's current assets. The big question is how does the accounting of these important assets is done? As a student of accounting, figure out!

Control of Cash

Earlier we said cash as "King" as every business entity sees it as a necessary liquid asset to be dispensed. Most companies carry in their current assets cash equivalents (defined below), which are assets having similar characteristics as cash. **Cash and cash equivalents** are the most liquid of all assets that can be easily moved and used in the business. Given its relative importance, there is an obvious need to have an effective system of internal controls to safeguard or protect these tangible assets. Basically there are three key issues taken as guidelines for cash management:

- *Physical custody and handling of cash is separate from recordkeeping of cash.*

  This requires segregation of duties to prevent fraud and irregularities. When duties are separated, two or more persons can be prevented from their intention to collude to steal cash and their action to conceal from the accounting records.

- *All cash receipts are promptly deposited into a bank account.*

  This requires immediate or prompt is of all cash receipts so that a timely reporting of all cash proceeds to be accounted independently as a record of cash received. This action also prevents the possibility of theft (resulting in loss) and the risk that employees could personally be using the money before depositing into the bank account (a process called 'teeming and lading').

- This requires all payments to be made only by cheque so that cash disbursements can be checked and reported independently using the bank records.

  Essentially, the exact procedures to be used to achieve control of cash resources depends on a number of factors such as company size, volume of transactions, sources of cash, and the number of employees in the organization. This varies between companies and their complexity of operations.

Cash management

Companies that manage their cash resources will be able to successfully manage its business well. When companies fail, one of the most common causes is their inability to manage cash. One major consequence of companies failing is the inability to manage its liquidity. **Liquidity** refers to a company's ability to discharge its obligations (debts) in the short-term as and when they fall due.

The proper timing of receipts and payments is part of a good planning system in cash management. Companies should **plan cash inflows (cash receipts) to meet cash outflows (cash**

payments) to avoid liquidity problems. The other important consideration is to **keep a minimum level of cash resources** necessary to operate and meet whatever contingencies that might arise.

Effective cash management is about the following key issues:

- **Prompt collection of receivables**

  Credit policies to be enforced strictly so that customers and others can settle their accounts more quickly and companies can use the money

- **Delay payment of liabilities**

  It is good business practice for a company to delay in paying others as it has the advantage of more time to use the money. Companies can post-phone paying their bills until the last possible due date. This policy has a drawback as it affects the company's credit standing.

- **Only keep necessary level of assets**

  For an example, a company could adopt *'just-in-time'* inventory. This means planning for inventories to be available just in time to meet orders, some companies may lease out excess warehouse space to generate income, others may rent out assets such as equipment instead of buying outright. The less capital is tied up in idle assets, the more money is available to invest in productive assets.

- **Spent only whatever is necessary**

  Expenditure outlays should be undertaken or spent only when money is available.

- **Invest excess cash available to generate income**

  Excess cash resources earns no income unless it is invested in short-term investments. For an example, excess cash can be placed in time deposits to earn interest income or invested in short-term fixed income securities such as government treasury bills, etc.

2. Using a Bank Account as a Control Procedure

Cash is easy to hide and relatively easy to steal. As a result, most businesses apply specific controls for cash. The use of a bank account helps control cash because banks have established custodial practices for safeguarding customers' money. The following documents are used as a control feature as part of the documentation process for operating a bank account:

- An authorized signature
- A pay-in-slip or deposit slip
- Cheques
- Bank statement
- Bank reconciliation statement

Authorized Signature

Banks require authorized signatories to sign cheques and other documents to operate the bank account. Authorized signatures prevent any form of forgery.

A pay-in-slip or deposit slip

Banks operate standard printed forms for customers to filling up details of cash or cheques for deposits into the bank account. These slips act as documentary proof of the transaction which a customer must retain as deposit receipt.

Cheques

In order to disburse cash for payments, the customer write and issues a cheque which instrucks the bank to pay the designated party a specific amount. There are three parties to a cheque:

- The drawer who issues and signs the cheque (authorized signatory to the bank account);
- The payee, to whom the cheque is paid;
- The bank on whose name the cheque is drawn.

Bank Statements

Banks send monthly statements to customers. A bank statement reports what the bank did with the customers' cash. It shows a record of beginning and ending balances for the month together with the deposits and withdrawals including some other bank related transactions where it applies.

Electronic funds transfer (EFT) moves cash by electronic communication by incurring less cost to pay without having to use or mail a cheque. This way, many customers could settle their mortgage, rent, utilities and insurance by EFT. Digital economy makes it possible to do transactions with relative ease.

3. Bank Reconciliation

Two records to consider about the entity's cash:

1. The bank account as reported in the general or nominal ledger. The ending cash balance for a particular month or period is shown; let's say it is RM 3,690.
2. The bank statement for that particular month or period shows the **receipts** (credits) and **payments** (debits) that have been transacted through the bank. The ending cash balance shown by the bank statement is, say RM 5,450.

Obviously the cash book and the bank statement will show different cash balances. A difference of RM 1,760 arises because of a timing lag in the recording of these transactions. This chapter explores these differences and shows how additional entries need to be recorded in order to reconcile the difference and this is done by preparing a **bank reconciliation statement.**

Some explanation may help to understand the time lag here:

- When a cheque is written, it is recorded as a payment in the cash book but the bank does not debit your account until the bank pays the cheque a few days later, after the payee presents the cheque for clearance to his or her own bank which may be different from your bank. At the same, any deposits may be added to the cash receipt side of your cash book in the ledger but it may take a day or two or even longer before the bank credits your current account.
- Your EFT payments and receipts may be directly deposited by your customers and recorded by the bank before you learn of them normally through a credit or debit advice issued by your bank.

To ensure consistency in accurate record keeping, the cash book should be updated to reflect these ad hoc transactions either online or after you receive the bank statement. The result of this updating process creates the bank reconciliation statement which you must prepare. The bank reconciliation explains all differences between your cash book and the bank statement. This is conventionally the banking system as it has been for a longer time. However, times are changing rapidly with innovative technology as most transactions are done electronically by online mode and using the digital technology.

4. Preparing and Recording Bank Reconciliation

It is important to understand that certain recurring items will appear on bank reconciliation. These items frequently cause the difference between the cash book balance and the bank statement balance.

Bank Statement

Items which will appear on the bank side of the reconciliation include the following:

- **Deposits in transit** – These are outstanding deposits recorded but the bank has not credited yet. You need to add these deposits in transit on the bank reconciliation statement.
- **Outstanding cheques** not presented for clearance. Entries in the cash book would be recorded but the bank has not yet honoured them. You need to subtract these outstanding cheques.

Cash Book Side

Items which will appear on the book side of the reconciliation include the following:

Bank collections are cash receipts that the bank has credited your account but you haven't recorded the cash receipts yet in your cash book. These entries arise because some customers directly pay into their bank. For example, the bank is collecting an account receivable for you. You need to add these entries to your bank reconciliation statement.

Electronic funds transfer – Banks may receive or pay cash on behalf of their customers, using the EFT system. Add EFT receipts and Subtract EFT payments.

Interest charges and Interest revenue – Banks automatically deduct interest charges on any outstanding loan or overdraft facilities. Subtract interest charges. Where interest revenue is earned on certain types of bank accounts, such interest income is usually credited to your current amount. Add interest revenue. Bank statements normally reflect on these items.

Service charges – banks charge a fee or commission for processing transactions. Subtract service charges.

Cheques not covered by sufficient funds – Cash receipts from some customers may not be covered by sufficient funds. Such bounced cheques will need to be debited by showing as contra payments. Subtract such bounced cheques.

Cost of printed cheque stubs – Banks automatically charge their customers for newly printed cheque books. Such items are treated as service charges which need to be subtracted.

Bookkeeping errors – These are book errors that result from clerical oversights. Instead of recording a RM 380 cheque, you wrote it as RM 830 on the payment side of the cash book. So, you need to correct this kind of error on the book side of the reconciliation.

5. Bank Reconciliation Illustrated

Here is the cash book of Recon Traders for month of September 2021:

CASH BOOK

2021	Receipts	RM	2021	Payments	RM
Sept 2	Peter Chong	164	Sept. 1	Balance b/d	2,005
3	Johar Sales	347	2	Mat Saleh	49
3	Rosemah Cik	163	4	Cash	615
5	Cash sales	25	7	Leong Sports Shop	89
12	Muthu Oils	825	9	Najib Stationers	715
14	Dr Willis	900	10	Noel	237
18	Arunasalam	45	18	Rebecca Nona	630
25	Low Kit Yat	1,028	21	Wee's Mill Flour	90
25	Babas	105	26	Jeyasingam	15
29	Chow	450	28	John	328
30	Kum Kum	235			
30	Balance c/d	486			
		4,773			4,773

The Bank Statement for the same month showed:

CIMB Bank Bhd

Recon Traders
Account Number: 7003261133. (All in RM)

Date		Debit	Credit	Balance
1.9.21	Balance			2,005 OD
3.9.21	105295	49		2,054
5.9.21	105296	615		2,669
8.9.21	Cash and Cheques		699	1,970
10.9.21	ATM	50		2,020
11.9.21	105298	715		2,735
15.9.21	Sound Beat	77		2,812
16.9.21	Cheques		1,725	1,087
17.9.21	105299	237		1,324
20.9.21	Dividend Sime Darby		25	1,299
22.9.21	Cheque		55	1,244
23.9.21	105300	630		1,874
24.9.21	251332	80		1,954
27.9.21	Cheque		1,028	926
28.9.21	Cheque		105	821
30.9.21	Charges	36		857
	Interest	68		925. OD

OD Overdrawn Balance

You will note that:

i. *The balance is given after each transaction*
ii. *The entries are on the reverse side to the cash book*
iii. *Payments into the account are not detailed*
iv. *Cheques are distinguished by numbers only – information not often explained in the cash book.*

Procedures

a. **You are required to compare the entries in the cash book with those in the bank statement by ticking them. You should find that unticked items are:**

Location	Item		Reason and action to be taken
Cash Book	Arunasalam	45	Error in amount, presume bank is correct -
Bank Statement	Cheque	55	Alter cash book
Cash Book			
-do-	Leong Sports	89	Time lag

-do-	Wee's Mill	90	Time lag
-do-	Jeyasingam	15	Time lag
-do-	John	328	Time lag
Bank statement	ATM	50	Enter cash book
-do-	Dividend SimeDarby	25	Enter cash book
-do-	251332	80	Error by bank – time lag
-do-	Charges	36	Enter cash book
-do-	Interest	68	Enter cash book

Update the Cash Book

CASH BOOK (All in RM)

2021	**Receipts**		**2021**	**Payments**	
Sept 20	Dividend Sime Darby	25	Sept 30	Balance b/d	486
			10.	ATM	50
18	Arunasalam (55-45)	10	15.	Sound Beat	77
30.	Balance c/d		30.	Bank charges	36
	(1corrected**).**	**682**		**Bank interest**	**68**
		717			**717**

b. Reconcile the differences between the adjusted cash book balance and the bank statement balance

Notes:

i. Outstanding lodgements' are those banking of customers' cheques' that may take at least a working day or two to clear.

ii. Company's cheques presented to the bank for clearance should also take a day or two unless the creditor (recipient) keeps the payment for extended period before crediting to their bank account.

The bank reconciliation statement used below follows the standard norm.

Bank Reconciliation Statement as at 30 September 2021

		RM
Balance as per bank statement.		(925) OD*
Less: Outstanding lodgements' not credited yet		
Chow	450	
Kum Kum	235	685
		(240)
Less: Bank error – adjusted in October		80
		(160)

Add: Unpresented cheques		
Wee's Mill	90	
Jeyasingham	15	
John	328	(522)
Balance as per Cash Book		(682) OD
OD = Bank overdraft		

Timing Difference

The adjusted balance of the cash book is the balance which should be included in the **Statement of Financial Position** (balance sheet). Thus, the figure at 30 September 2021 "bank overdraft RM 682 is the correct balance to be reported in the statement of financial position and not the balance of RM 925 according to bank statement on reporting date. This has the effect that all transactions effected with the bank by the year end are reflected in the bank balance, despite the fact that the bank may not have recognized them by that date. This difference arises because of the timing of credits and debits in the bank account statement. A second effect is that for example, the cheque drawn in favour of John is reflected as part of the bank balance and therefore must be reflected in the account of John to complete the double entry. It is important to note that the **primary purpose of the bank reconciliation** is to determine whether the bank or the company has made any errors and at the same time to ensure that the bank has entered any transactions affecting the account that the customer has not recorded in the cash book. The omission of any transactions can cause discrepancies that may affect the accuracy of the bank balance at the reporting date.

Use of Documentation and Verification to Control of Cash Disbursements

The transactions involving various type of disbursements and their reporting in both the cash book and petty cash records make use of a **voucher system.** A voucher system is set of accounting procedures and approvals designed to control cash disbursements and acceptance of obligations. The voucher system of control relies on several important documents (both internal and third party documents) including the voucher and its supporting files. A key factor in this system is that only approved departments (or divisions) and individuals (staff) are authorized to incur certain obligations. The use and purpose of documentation for cash disbursements have been discussed in the foregoing pages.

In today's business context, every commercial transaction and in fact the majority of business transactions between entities and their customers are settled by cheque or other medium. The only significant cash (notes and coins) movement in business is in retail sales and even there, payment by credit or debit cards is important but increasingly a new trend using online mode is gaining popularity (we are in digital era).

6. Petty Cash Book

The Impress System

It must be noted that cash received from retail sales is usually banked intact and hence becomes in effect, a bank transaction. For example, Tesco's supermarket system ensures all the retail sales transactions are done through cash and credit or debit cards. However, in practice most businesses have a basic need to make small cash payments for such petty claims, as staff travelling expenses, casual wages for cleaning, stationery, tea or coffee, etc. These so-called petty transactions are recorded through a petty cash book. This specific system is commonly is known as the **impress system** which means – *'to lend'*. In order to operate, the impress system requires the following procedures:

a. Need to appoint a person (petty cashier) who is responsible for maintaining the petty cash system.
b. Need to allocate a cash float of fixed sum (say, RM 300) to the petty cashier drawn from a cash cheque. This is called the *'impress or float'*.
c. All petty transactions must be accompanied by vouchers which must be authorized and approved.
d. All these transactions must be recorded in date sequence in the petty cash book, which is both a book of prime entry and a part of the double entry system.
e. At intervals the cashier will examine the supporting evidence for the payments, take away and file this evidence and draw from the bank the total amount of payments matching all disbursements. Thus, if disbursements totaled RM 285, then the cash remaining should total RM 15 and further cash will be given to the cashier of RM 285 making up the float or impressed up to RM 300 again.
f. At random intervals, an internal auditor or senior official should do a spot check of the petty cash book, vouchers and balance. The petty cashier should always have a total of RM 300 in cash or in approved vouchers supported by receipts and source documents as evidence

Space left deliberating blank

Illustrated analytical petty cash book (Credit side)

A typical petty cash book ruling is shown in the illustrated figure. (Spreadsheet)

Date Oct 21	Disbursements.	V/No	Amount **RM**	Travelling expenses	Sundry expense	Casual wages	Cleaning	Petrol	Newspapers & periodicals	Office expense
1/9		84	15					15		
3/9		85	25			25				
9/9		86	12	12						
10/9		87	20		20					
12/9		88	25			25				
15/9		89	10				15			
16/9		90	19	9	10					
18/9		91	12	12						
19/9		92	15					15		
20/9		93	28						28	
21/9		94	25			25				
25/9		95	8						8	
28/9		96	7	7						
29/9		97	24		14		10			
30/9		98				25				
	Total expenses		275	40	44	100	25	30	36	
	Balance c/f		25							
	Total		300							
	GL Folio			205	210	215	211	212	213	

Note: The debit side the petty cash book is not shown here since only one entry is required for re-imbursement of RM 300 in cash drawn by a cheque.

Postings from petty cash book

The petty cash book is a double entry account. The credit side items (disbursements) will be posted as debits to the general ledger relevant accounts. GL Folio are pages of GL accounts where postings are done. Shown below is a typical sample of items that gets reported in a petty cash book operated by an accounts department.

	RM
Traveling expenses A/c	40
Sundry expenses A/c	44
Wages	100
Cleaning	25
Petrol and toll charges	30
Newspapers and periodicals	36
Total petty cash expenses	275
Balance in hand	25
Float amount	300

The **float amount** is maintained at RM 300 and any balance remaining (RM 25) is carried forward to the next period. The amount disbursed for petty cash expenses in this case totalled RM 275 and this will be reimbursed by a cash cheque drawn on the bank account. Petty cash transactions totalling RM 275 must be evidenced by supporting documents such as authorised vouchers, bills, official receipts, invoices, etc. Internal audit procedures may carry out these checks to ensure control over the petty cash receipts and disbursements.

Cash Over and Short

Sometimes a petty cashier fails to get a receipt for payment or overpays for the amount due. The petty cash total transactions for the period plus the cash remaining in the box will not equal the float balance. When this happens, this mistake causes the float money to be *short*. This shortage is recorded as an expense in the reimbursing entry with a debit to the *cash over* and *short account*. The reverse could happen with an overage in the petty cash float with an adjustment recorded with credit to *cash over* and *short* in the reimbursing entry. Now, using the same example as illustrated, we prepare an entry with RM 300 petty cash float when its total payment shows RM 267 in petty cash disbursements and RM 25 cash remains.

Required journal entry	Dr	Cr
Petty cash expenses	267	
Cash over and short	8	
Cash		275
(Being cash float reimbursement		

The petty cash account balance always equals it fund balance (float), in this case RM 300. Usually this account balance does not change unless the fund is increased to accommodate increased petty cash transaction needs or the float could be reduced. Depending on the needs of the business from time to time, the amount of float money carried can be varied due to change of business circumstances.

For larger organizations, petty cash systems may be operated by the different divisions or departments. The accounting manager may keep an overall track of the petty cash systems in these divisions or depts.Internal audit checks will assist in the monitoring of these divisions by carrying out periodic internal checks and reporting the outcomes to management.

The petty cash impress system

Bookkeeping entries	*Actions*	*Source Documents*
Dr. petty cash book	Float	
Dr. to expense accounts in General Ledger Cr. petty cash book (disbursements)	↓ Expenses paid by Cashier	Petty cash expense vouchers
Dr. petty cash book Cr. cash book	↓ Cash from bank = total expenses	
	↓ Float again	

Cash Management

Days' Sales Receivables

A significant part of cash management involves the monitoring of receipt of cash from receivables. If customers and others who owe money to a company delay in their payment beyond the credit period, then the company may find itself in a difficult position to honour its obligations on date when they fall due. A company's customers are key partners in its cash management. Companies attract customers by selling to them on credit terms. It is therefore important to ensure that cash receipts from customers are not delayed beyond the normal credit period. Accounts receivable should be collected the sooner it is better.

One measure of how quickly a company can convert its accounts receivable into cash is the **days' sales receivables (or uncollected).** This ratio is calculated by dividing the current balance of receivables by net credit sales (after discounts and allowances) for the reporting period just ended and then multiplying by 365 days. Since net credit sales usually are not reported in published accounts, the net sales (or revenues) figure is commonly used in the computation as follows:

$$\text{Day's sales receivables} = \frac{\text{Accounts receivable}}{\text{Net sales}} \times 365$$

We use days' sales receivables to estimate how much time is needed before the current amount of accounts receivable is realised in cash. It is necessary for evaluation purposes, we compare this estimate between current and prior periods. It will be also useful to make comparisons between this estimate and to that of other companies within the same industry.

To illustrate, we select data from the annual reports of two companies listed in the main board without disclosing their names. Both companies are in the same operating segment.

		2018	2019	2020
Company X	Accounts receivable	1, 785	1,908	1, 987
	Net sales	16, 227	15, 265	15, 705
	Days' sales receivable	40.2	45.6	46.2
Company Y	Accounts receivable	705	714	785
	Net sales	4, 320	4, 355	4, 300
	Days' sales receivable	59.6	59.8	66.7

Company X's Days' accounts receivable is calculated as (1, 987/15, 705 x 365 days = 46.2 days. This translates the collection period on average for year 2020 in the case of Company X to be approximately 46 days before cash is collected from the year end receivables. A number of factors could explain Company X's ability to collect receivables. It also reflects the Company's financial health, its strategy to make payments on time, and issues such as discount terms. One curious factor to be noted is the collection period for the 3 years is showing an increasing trend for the Company X but the level of sales turnover and accounts' receivable for the 3-year period appears to be reasonably consistent. In contrast, Company Y's collection period for receivables for the same 3 years is showing an increasing trend. For 2020, Company Y has taken 66.7 day on averages before cash collection is done, a worrying feature because the credit period appears to be exceeding two months of the operating cycle. What is the normal credit period allowed for credit customers' in the case of Company Y? No information is available to assist in further analysis. It may have a bearing on its cash flow position causing the Company possibly some financial stress in its ability to fully satisfy settling creditors' payments when it falls due. Credit control and debt recovery procedures should be reviewed aggressively to improve the working capital position.

Chapter Summary

1. **Cash Balances**

   Cash is critical to every business activity without which all forms of business transactions comes to a virtual halt or the business becomes paralyzed. Cash is considered as 'King' because it drives everything that a business does to survive in its pursuit to of wealth maximizing goal. In accounting, cash and its equivalents are treated tangibly as the most liquid asset prone to a wider fluctuation. Cash is classified under current asset. Accounting for cash becomes a critical component of internal control in a business as it is susceptible to fraud and manipulation.

2. **Cash and Cash Equivalents**

   Cash includes currency, coins, and cheques, to be deposited into the current and saving accounts. Cash equivalents are short-term, highly liquid investment assets such as bank deposit accounts and bearer bonds that are readily convertible into in cash amount and sufficiently close to their maturity date. The market value of these items (except cash) can be subject to changes in interest rates. Cash and cash equivalents are liquid assets because they are readily converted into other assets or it can be used to settle for goods or services and liabilities.

3. **Internal Control Procedures over Cash**

   Management pays particular attention to all significant documentation used in the recording and control aspects of cash. **One regular control feature over the reporting of cash balance is the periodic checks done on bank reconciliations and bank statements.** Internal control of cash receipts ensures that all cash received is properly recorded and deposited. It is important to note that there are two types of cash receipts: over-the-counter and by mail. Good internal control for over-the–counter cash receipts includes the use of a cash register, review of customer accounts, use of official receipts, and a permanent transaction record (cash book), and separation of the custody of cash from its record-keeping. Good internal control for cash receipts by mail includes at least two accounting staff assigned to open mail and a listing of each customer's name, amount, and any relevant information. Good to mention here: Banks offer several related services that promote the control and security over cash. Issues of authorization over cash transactions, the handling and custody of cheques are all too important because of the risk of theft or embezzlement or misappropriation of cash funds. Issues such as cash and bank collections, EFTs, bank interest and bank service charges, and the safe custody of cheque books (or stubs) are attended with care by authorized staff in the accounting department. This function involves the segregation of duties amongst the reporting staff.

4. **Preparation of a Bank Reconciliation**

   One regular control feature over the reporting of cash balance is the periodic checks done on bank reconciliations and bank statements. A bank reconciliation proves the accuracy of the customer's and

   The bank's records. The bank statement balance is adjusted for items such as outstanding lodgements (unrecorded deposits) and unpresented cheques made on or before the bank statement reporting date but not reflected on the statement. The cash book balance is adjusted for items such as service and interest charges, bank collections for the depositor (with standing instructions) and any interest earned on the account. With this updating, the bank reconciliation exercise will be completed to reflect what the actual cash book balance should be reported in statement of financial position under current assets.

5. **The Use of Documentation and Verification to Control Cash Disbursements**

   A voucher system makes use of administrative procedures and approvals to control cash disbursements with obligations accepted on the part of employees. The voucher system of control relies on several important documents, including vouchers and its supporting invoices and receipts, etc. Only authorized departments or sections heads are authorized in their obligations to approve transactions for disbursements.

6. **The Position of Petty Cash Account**

   Petty cash is necessary and is of no exception to any business. As such, petty cash transactions are taking place routinely almost every day in the business. The very nature of transactions is so petty that it is operated by a voucher system properly authorized and thus obviates the need to issue separate cheques as the recording function can be too tedious to be maintained. The use of the impress system becomes crucial for the disbursement of petty cash transactions for the business. However, control is exercised through regular the check and balance mechanism and use of cash float.

Key Terms

Authorized signature
Cash
Cash book
Cash equivalents
Cash payments
Cash receipts
Bank overdraft (OD)
Bank reconciliation statement
Cheque
Drawer
Drawee
Bank error
Bookkeeping error
Invoice
Impress system
Credit note
Cash float
Unpresented cheques.
Bank service charge
Bank interest charge
Petty cash book
Petty cash balance
Payee
Pay-in-slip (or deposit slip)
Petty cash float
Internal control system
Balance and check mechanism
EFT
Voucher
Voucher system
Days' accounts receivable
Liquid assets
Bank statement
Debit note (or debit advice)
Bank lodgements

Review Questions

Q1. Explain the term 'Cash' in accounting

Q2. What are cash and cash equivalents?

Q3. Explain what you understand by the bank statement balance and cash book balance?

Q4. Why it is necessary to prepare a bank reconciliation statement and briefly state the items that reported in the statement?

Q5. Explain why the bank always produce bank statements to its clients?

Q6. What is the purpose of the cash book as a book of prime entry?

Q7. Explain the purpose of petty cash book and the impress system used to maintain it.

Q8. What is cash float?

Q9. Explain how petty transactions are posted to the general ledger system?

Q10. Describe some of the key documents used in cash accounting and their importance.

Q11. What are some impacts of computer technology on internal control?

Q12. Why must a company hold liquid assets?

Q13. i. Why does a company hold cash equivalent assets in addition to cash?

ii. List at least two liquid assets that are classified as cash equivalents.

Q14. Why it is necessary for a company to use a voucher system for disbursements either by cheque or cash?

Q15. Why do we reconcile the bank statement balance of cash and the company's (depositor's)cash book balance of cash?

Q16. a. List at least two items affecting the bank balance side of a bank reconciliation and indicate whether the items are added or subtracted.

b. List at least three items affecting the *book balance* side of a bank reconciliation and indicate whether the items are added or subtracted.

Practice Questions

Q17. The following is a summary of the petty cash transactions of XYZ Traders for the December 2021

December			RM
1.	Received from Cashier RM 300 as petty cash float		
2.	Stamps and postages		25
3.	Traveling		18
4.	Cleaning services		30
5.	Petrol for delivery van	20	
6.	Traveling		25
7.	Printing & stationery		16
8.	Postage	18	
9.	Traveling		9
10.	Stationery		10
11.	Delivery van 3,000 kilometer service charges		24
12.	Petrol and toll charges	15	
13.	Newspapers & periodicals		12
14.	Casual wages	12	
15.	Sundries		7

Required

a. Rule up a suitable petty cash book with analysis columns for expenditure on cleaning, motor expenses, postage, stationery, traveling, sundries and wages.

b. Enter the month's transactions.

c. Enter the receipt of the amount necessary to restore the impress and carry down the balance for the start of the following month.

d. State how the double entry for the expenditure is completed.

(ACCA)

Q18. JPS Trading Enterprise, a limited company provides the following information for purposes of reconciling the company's cash book balance with its bank statement balance as at 31 December 2020. The company's financial year end is 31 December 2020.

i. After all postings is complete on 31 December 2020, the company's cash book balance is reported to be RM 17, 440 debit balance, but its bank statement shows a RM 40, 430.

ii. Cheques No. 3202025 for RM 4, 550 and No. 3202028 for RM 6, 000 are outstanding.

iii. By comparing the cancelled cheques on the bank statement with the entries in the accounting records, it is found that cheque No. 3202027 in payment of rent is correctly drawn for RM 1, 100 but is erroneously entered in the accounting records as RM 900.

iv. The 31 December deposit of RM 18, 750 was deposited in the night after banking hours on that date, and this amount does not appear on the bank statement.

v. In reviewing the bank statement, a cheque written by APS Trading Services in the amount of RM 360 was erroneously drawn against JPS's account.

vi. A credit note enclosed with the bank statement indicates that the bank collected a RM. 32, 000 and RM 1, 000 related to interest on JPS's behalf. The transaction was not recorded by JPS Trading Enterprise prior to receiving the bank statement.

vii. A debit advice for RM 1,200 list a RM 1, 200 PSK cheque received from a customer, Rebecca Wong. JPS Trading had not recorded the return of this cheque before for receiving the bank statement.

viii. Bank service charges for December total RM 50. These charges were not recorded by JPS Trading Enterprise before receiving the statement.

Required

a. Show what should be the corrected cash book balance for JPS Trading Enterprise.

b. Prepare a bank reconciliation statement for JPS Trading Enterprise for month of 31December 2021.

c. Prepare the adjusting journal entries for the company.

Tutorial notes

- *You need to update your cash book entries prior to preparing the bank reconciliation.*
- *Examine each item (i) through (viii) to determine whether it affects the cash book or the bank balance and whether it should be added or subtracted from the bank or book balance.*
- *After all items are analyzed, complete the reconciliation and arrive at a reconciled balance between the adjusted cash book balance and the bank statement balance.*

Suggested answer

Q18. We need to correct the cash book balance first for JPS Trading Enterprise due to bookkeeping errors.

a. Adjusted Cash Book Balance

	RM	RM
As per cash book balance		17, 440
Add:		
Credit note issued by bank for collection from customer……	32, 000	
Interest credited	1, 000	
		33, 000
		50, 440
Less:		
Customer's (Rebecca Wong) cheque issued for PSK		
was credited by error (as per bank's debit advice)	1, 200	
Correction of recording error (3202027) [1, 100 – 900]	200	
Service charges	50	
		(1, 450)
Adjusted cash book balance as at 31December 2021		**48, 990**

b. Bank Reconciliation Statement as at 31 December 2021

		RM
Balance as per bank statement	40,430	
Add:		
Outstanding bank lodgements not credit yet		
Deposit	18, 750	
Bank error (APS Trading)	360	19, 110
		59, 540
Less:		
Unpresented cheques		
Cheque No. 3202025	4, 550	
Cheque No. 3202028	6, 000	(10, 550)
Balance as per cash book as at 31 December 2021		**48, 990**

c. Adjusting Journal Entries for JPS Trading Enterprise

	Dr	Cr
Cash	33, 000	
Notes receivable		32, 000
Interest received		1, 000
(Being record of collection of note with interest)		
Accounts receivable – Rebecca Wong	1,200	
Cash		1, 200
(Being reinstatement of account due on PSK cheque)		
Rent expense	200	
Cash		200
(Being correction of recording error on cheque no. 3202027)		
Bank service charges	50	
Cash		50
(Being record of bank service charges)		

Multiple Choice Questions

Q1. Procedures of internal control suggest that:

a. Responsibility for a series of related transactions such as placing orders, receiving and paying for merchandise (goods), should be assigned to one employee;

b. Responsibility for individual tasks should be shared by more than one employee so that one serves as an internal check on the other; or

c. Employees who handle considerable cash and easily transferable assets should be bonded.

Q2. Good internal control procedures for cash include which of the following?

a. All cash disbursements, other than those for very small amounts, are made by cheque;

b. One employee counts cash received from sales and promptly deposits cash receipts;

c. Cash receipts by mail are opened by one employee who is then responsible for recording and depositing them.

Q3. A company had net sales of RM 284,500 and accounts receivable of RM 35, 700. Its days' sales receivable (uncollected) is

a. 30 days
c. 130 days
e. 62.5 days
b. 18.4 days
d. 45.8 days

Q4. The following information relates to Halpern Trading Company:

a. The 31 December bank statement show a RM 1, 895 balance.

b. The cash book shows a RM 1, 742 balance at 31 December.

c. A RM 795 deposit placed in the bank's night depository on 31 December does not appear on the 31 December bank statement.

d. Unpresented(outstanding) cheques amount to RM 638 at 31 December.

e. A customer's RM 335 note was collected by the bank in December. A fee of RM 15 was deducted by the bank and the difference deposited in Halpern account.

f. A bank service charge of RM 10 is deducted by the bank and appear on the 31 December bank statement.

Q5. How will the customer' s note appears on Halpern's 31 December bank reconciliation?

a. RM 335 appears as an addition to the bank balance of cash.

b. RM 320 appears as an addition to the cash book balance.

c. RM 320 appears as a deduction from the cash book balance.

d. RM 320 appears as an addition to the bank statement balance.

e. RM 320 appears as a deduction from the bank statement balance.

Q5. Using the information from question 4, what is the reconciled balance on Halpern's 31 December bank reconciliation?

a. RM 2, 052.

b. RM 1, 895.

c. RM 1, 742.

d. RM 2, 201.

e. RM 1, 184

Q6. A company needs to replenish its RM 500 petty cash account. Its petty cash box has RM 75 cash and petty cash receipts of RM 420. The journal entry to replenish the account includes

a. A debit to cash for RM 75

b. A credit to cash for RM 75

c. A credit to petty cash for RM 420

d. A credit to cash over and short for RM 5

e. A debit to cash over and short for RM5

*All the contents below will be shifted to **Chapter 28** as a separate topic.*

Ethics in Business and Accounting Decisions

We covered some essential literature on ethics relating to business and accounting in an earlier chapter. We now need to extend some further discussion here on the same topic as we are dealing with an important element in accounting that is **cash**.

Fraud

Fraudulent activities relating to cash goes unnoticed in many business environments particularly in situations when plenty of cash transactions are involved or where access to cash resources is easily available. There could be situations where internal controls on cash monitoring are simply too weak. The decision to engage in fraud is an act that has implications in terms of economic, legal and ethical. As we know perpetrators of fraud usually do so for their own short-term financial gains. This has the effect of incurring *financial or economic losses* that could be far injurious to the business entities as cash assets are eroded as these gains are made by these fraudsters.

Fraud is considered **illegal** and those who are caught and found guilty ultimately face penalties which in some severe cases include imprisonment and monetary damages. It is important to note that Fraud violates the rights of the many for the psychological enjoyment or betterment of a few and certainly for the ultimate betterment of no one. Business entities become the victims of these corporate losses and in this sense, fraud is seriously an unethical act in business.

Internal Controls

The most effective way that fraud and irregularities can be prevented, detected or corrected in an organization is by having a proper system of internal controls. An internal control system which is properly designed can achieve the following objectives:

1. *Safeguard assets of the company*
2. *Employees of the organization can adhere to Company policy, rules and procedures*
3. *Promote operational efficiency*
4. *Ensure accurate, reliable accounting records*
5. *Comply with legal requirements*

The question is how important are internal controls? They are absolutely essential to maintaining the integrity of systems but more importantly in most jurisdictions, guardians of corporate governance, particularly the boards of directors and/or auditors are required to examine and assess the effectiveness of internal controls, particularly of listed companies. For example, the annual report of a Malaysian listed company on the main Board makes the following statement:

Extracts from the Notes to the Financial Statements

Internal Control Procedures

Separation of duties

Compliance and Comparisons

Maintenance of Adequate Records

Authorization and Proper Controls

Limitations of Internal Controls

Internal Controls over Cash

Cash receipts over the counter

Cash receipts by mail

Internal Control over Cash Payments

Payments by cheques

Illustrated diagram

A preamble to Chapters 9,10 & 11

Non-Current Assets

Scope and Overview

The accounting for non<urrent assets or long-term assets has important implications for a business entity's reported results in terms of its financial position and performance. Ellie recogiition and measurement criteria for non-current assets is explained with reference to the application of cost l)linciple to property, plant and equipment, such as land and buildings and other categories of plant and equipment, including the depleting nature of natural resources. We also describe the common methods of depreciation that entities may use to allocate an asset's cost over its useful economic life. In addition, we discuss accounting for expenditures incurred during the useful life of assets, distinguishing between capital and revenue items. We also show the ledger entlies to account for the acquisition and disposal of non-current assets, including profits or losses to be reported on disposals. Finally, the accounting topic on asset revaluation of a noncurrent asset is discussed with ledger accounts to record the entries, and its reporting in the statement of profit or loss and other comprehensive income and in the statement of financial position.

Nature and Characteristics of Non- Current Assets

First of all, let's identify the categories or types of non-cunent assets that are reported by entities in their financial statements. categories and types of non-current assets are listed as below:

Table 1 Categories of non-current assets

Tangible Fixed Assets (PPE).	Intangible Assets	Financial Assets
Determining the cost of PPFs	Accounting for intangibles	Construction contracts in progress
Depreciation	Goodwill	Trade investments
Dealing with capital expenditure	Research and development costs	Investment properties
Disposal of assets	Brands, trade-marks and patterns	Non-current assets held for sale
Revaluation and de-recognition	Software	Biological assets
Natural resources IOil and reserves, mines and quarriesl		
Depletion		

Comparison of PPE, Intangible and Financial Assets

All the three categories of non-current assets as the term implies are long-term Ilong livedl assets, their lives extend beyond several accounting periods. Of the categories, property, plant and equipment (PPE) sometimes called fixed assets, are tangible in nature with a physical substance. Intangible assets on the other hand, lack physical substance. By comparison, some financial assets as listed above are tang$ble in nature whereas others lack physical substance. However, all the three categories of non-current assets are used by entities in the operations of their business Iproduction, sale and distribution ofgoods and servicesl and arc not normally acquired or intended for sale.

Except for land, PPE items have finite life and therefore decline in their service potential over their useful lives. PPE being consumption based tangible assets; they are subjected to a systematic cost allocation process of depreciation and adjusted for impairment when appropriate. Natural resources included in the classification of PPE items and being in the nature of wasting assets that have no terminal value after use, they go through a process of depletion and not depreciation. Intangible assets with finite useful life such as development cost, patents, copyights, franchises and software are subjected to a policy of amortization and those with indefinite useful life such as brands, trademarks and goodwill have no systematic cost allocation but they may be adjusted for impairment when appropriate. Financial assets are not systematically subjected to any depreciation but they may be adjusted for impairment when appropriate.

Accounting issues in reporting PPE

Normally, accounting issues relating to the reporting of a tangible fixed asset can be broken down into three distinct stages of an asset's life. The diagram [Figure 1] below highlights the reporting of these accounting issues in the books of account over the asset's life-cycle.

The accounting issues emerging from the three stages will be dealt using the double-entry bookkeeping system in later part of the chapter sections. Most of these issues will be demonstrated through relevant examples.

Before considering the issues, we need to understand where these non-current assets are presented and reported in the statement of financial position. For the itemized assets, refer to the excerpt given below after Figure 1:

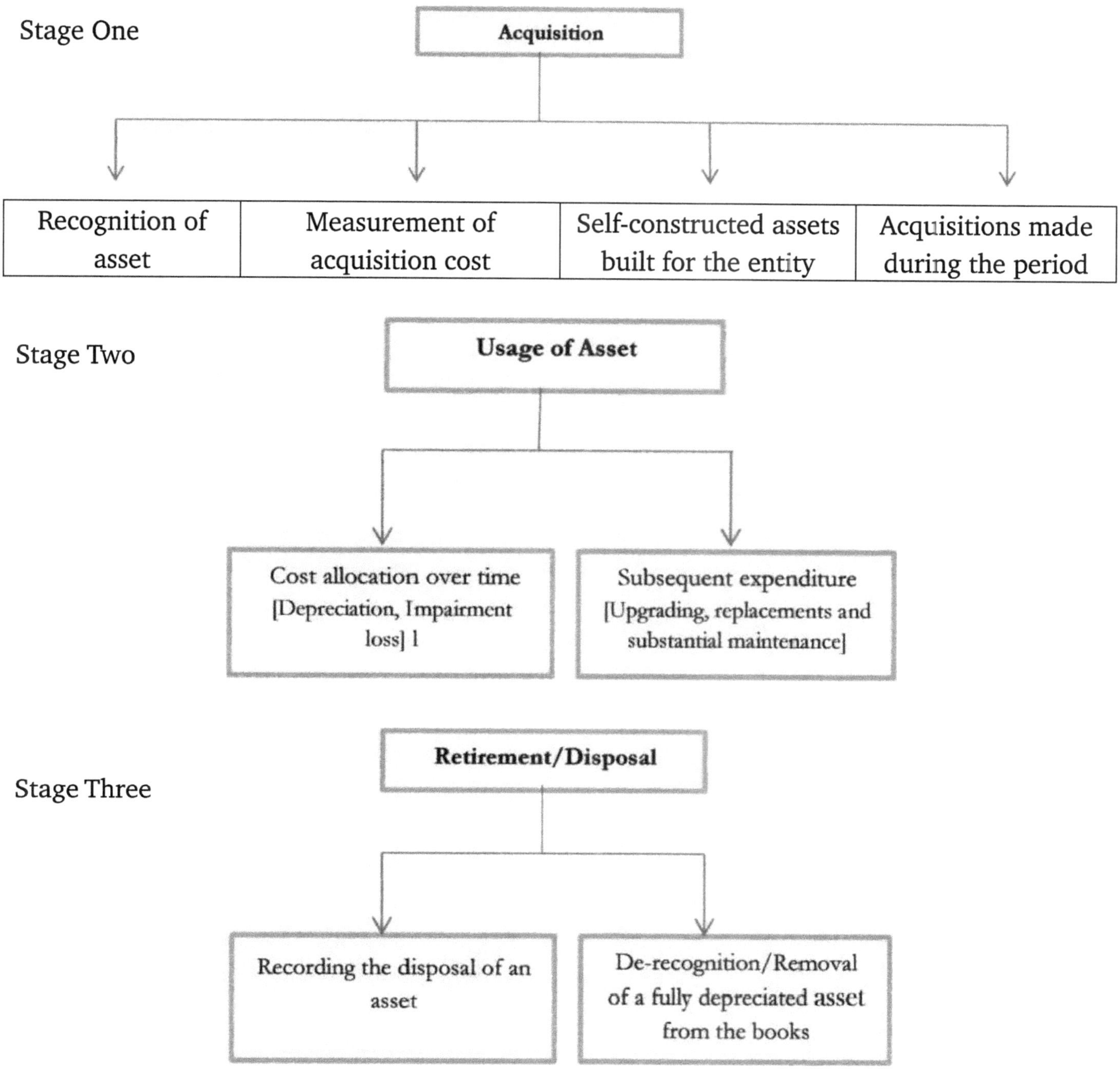

Figure 1 Accounting issues in reporting PPE

The three stages as depicted in the diagram represent the life-cycle of tangible non-current assets from acquisition to retirement phases where the accounting issues emerging in each stage or phase will have to be dealt with. The three sections written on this long chapter will discuss the process by illustrating the related accounting aspects comprehensively on the reporting requirements of this important component of the financial statements.

Reporting of Non-Current Assets in Statement of financial Position

There reporting of non-current assets by categories is shown below in the statement of financial position:

Excerpt

Statement of Financial Position

Non-Current assets: (Categories without figures)

Tangible assets

PPE

Natural resources

Intangible assets

Goodwill

Trade marks

Patents licenses

Copyrights

Development costs

Brands

Franchises

Software and infonnalion systems

Trade Investments

Invesünent properties

Non-current asseG held for sale

You will observe a detailed description of the type and classification of non-current assets that are normally reported in the statement of financial position [balance sheet]. The disclosure of information is primarily intended to show comprehensively what gets reported in a typical balance sheet but in actual practice companies only reflect those assets which specifically apply to their own operating businesses.

We will cover the content and organization of Property, Plant and Equipment [PPE] in three separate Chapters:

Chapters

9. Property, Plant and Equipment [PPE]
10. Depreciation
11. Revaluation of Assets and De-recognition

Chapter 12 will cover Intangible Assets.

As some topics in Financial Assets are not within the scope of an introductory accounting course, these will be dealt in my forthcoming textbook in the series, titled **'Financial Reporting,** *a contemporary practice* which is catered for accounting students at a higher level.

Chapter 9

Learning Outcomes

Afteryou have studied Chapter 9, you should

- *Understand the scope, definition and nature of PPE*
- *Understand the recognition criteria and initial measurement of PPE*
- *Determining the cost of PPE*
- *Undetstand how to account for subsequent capital expenditure*
- *Understand additional issues related to accounting for PPE*
- *Accounting for natural resources and depletion*
- *Reporting PPE items in cash flow statement*
- *how non-current asset balances and movements are presented and disclosed in financialstatements*
- *Understand the purpose and function of an asset register*

Property, Plant and Equipment

MFRS 116/IAS 16 covers all aspects of accounting for Property, Plant and Equipment [PPE]

The standard deals with initial measurement of PPE and the mechanics of accounting for depreciation, revaluations, de-recognition and disposal of non-current assets.

Definition of PPE

PPE is defined under the standard as tangible fixed assets of material value that are:

- Held for use in the production or supply of goods or services
- For rental to others, or for administrative purposes and
- Expected to be used during more than one accounting period.

The allocation of a PPE's cost over its useful life is called depreciation and the amount that has been allocated over the years is called accumulated depreciation. Depreciation is generally covered in Section Two of this chapter. The difference between the cost of a PPE item and its accumulated depreciation is called the carrying amount or net book value. Other useful definitions and terminology of PPE is listed in the appendix at the end of the chapter.

Entities carry several types of PPE in their statement of financial position [balance sheet] with their accompanying detailed notes to the accounts. Given the different type and nature of operating businesses and their industries, entities classify their PPE items into different categories to suit their purposes and requirements including the end-users of financial statements.

Table 2 Categories of PPE classification in annual audited accounts of Malaysian Companies

Land, freehold and leasehold properties

Buildings [stores, factories, warehouses, office complexes]

Construction work in progress [self-constructed assets]

Leasehold assets

Plant and machinery

Aircrafts

Ships

Motor vehicles

Furniture, fixtures and fittings

Computer systems

Office equipment

Other capital expenditure and improvements

All these PPE items are accompanied by relevant notes which form an integral part of the financial statements. These notes provide detailed information and data on tangible fixed assets including the accounting policies related to assets, depreciation and impairment of assets. Where certain types of PPE such as land and buildings are pledged as security for long-term borrowings, information is clearly disclosed in the notes to the financial statements.

Aircrafts and ships as separate classes of tangible fixed assets are not examined at this level of your studies. The scope for depreciation particularly for some components of these assets may fall within different rates of depreciation based on the useful lives of these component assets. Chapter 10 provide examples of this treatment.

MFRS 116 deals with PPE items except in some cases where other accounting standards allow different accounting treatment. The specified standards below deal with the following classes of assets:

- MFRS 5 Non-current Assets Held for Sale (discontinued operations)
- MFRS 140 Investment Property
- MFRS 141 Agriculture on bearer plants
- MFRS 6 Exploration for and Evaluation of Mineral Resources

These accounting standards are outside the scope of your studies and they are given only for information purposes.

Recognition

Recognition as property, plant and equipment in the business entity's accounts must fulfill the required two criteria conditions. The accounting standard stipulates that before a tangible non-current asset is capitalized in the entity's accounts.

[a] It is probable that future economic benefits associated with the asset will flow to the entity

[b] The cost of the asset to the entity can be measured reliably.

Consequence of recognition

PPE is a significant item reported in the statement of financial position at substantial amounts, thus affecting the presentation and disclosure of an entity's financial position and its financial performance through depreciation and profitability. It is also important to note that if an asset is wrongly classified as an expense and taken to profit or loss, the financial results can be distorted adversely as a consequence, particularly if the amounts involved are substantially material. Likewise, the consequence of treating erroneously an expense as an asset has a similar adverse impact on the reporting results of an entity's financial statements, again depending upon its size and magnitude.

An example of a real scenario would be WorldCom's financial statement fraud, one of the biggest frauds in US corporate history. It is a classic case of improper accounting classification of revenue related expenditure that was window dressed recklessly and treated expeditiously as capital expenditure so as to give a misleading:

i. Financial position by deliberately overstating assets; and
ii. Emancial performance by understating operating expenses [line costs] and overstating the profit figures over a five quarter period stretching between two years.

Table 3 below gives an interesting episode on the scenario that happened to WorldCom

Table 3

Accounting Fraud in WorldCom

The US WorldCom case which created one of the largest accounting frauds in corporate history also serves as a reminder of how bad accounting practice in corporate institutions can seriously go wrong for shareholders and other stakeholders with vested financial intensts if transparency and the accountability process go unchecked especially when fraud and irregularities take place. WorldCom reported the discovery of US 7 billion in expenses improperly classified as capital expenditure, a creative accounting gimmick that boosted profits over the live quarter periods between 2001 and 2002. If these line costs or expenses had been accounted properly under GAAPs, WorldCom [considered a giant telecommunication service provider and successful stock market star perförmer or the 1990s,] would have reported a net loss for 2001, as well as for the fist quarter in 2002. Instead, WorldCom reported a profit US$ 1.4 billion for 2001 and US$ 130 million for the list quarter of 2002. Given the sheer size and magnitude of the linancial fraud which led eventually to massive problems, WorldCom declared bankruptcy, much to the dismay of its investors and creditors.

Important lesson to learn

The potential for manipulation and falsification of accounting entries in financial wponing simply cannot be overlooked complacently. The important lesson here is that major and material transactions that may have a favorable or adverse impact on the financial position and performance must be independently verified and subjected to internal audit scrutiny and checks before the entries are authorized to be recognized in the accounting records.

Enactment of Sarbanes-Oxley Act, 2002-

Following the financial scandals of WorldCom and Emon [another case of massive fraud in US] the US Govemment in response to the widespread public concerns over the failure of corporate governance and the accountability process in US corporations, introduced a tough legislation to serve both as a legal and moral-safeguard to protect the interests of shareholders and investors by enacting the **Sarbanes-Oxley Act** *which came into force in July 2002. This US law laid down- stringent rules for corporate institutions, auditors and other individuals that have a responsible role to play in the governance and management of companies. This piece of legislation had far reaching implications for all those involved in corporate gorernance and accountability process of companies that are listed in the stock exchanges. Soon enough, the ptovisions of the Act came to be adopted by almost every corporate organization in various countries in the world that saw the importance of enforcement or these provisions for their own internal governance structures and policies. This single legislation has in fact changed the financial landscape in the area of financial reporting regime particularly on the duties of directors reporting to the board, other important guardians of corporate governance, and where disclosure policies and requirements have become more transparent in the accountability process.*

Students should refer more on the document fraud cases on their own. By understanding and knowing the provisions of the SOX, students will be better informed of corporate governance and how this process affects financial reporting.

Assignment questions for the student to facilitate in their study:

1. Identify by listing out the main provisions of the Sarbanes-Oxley Act, 2002
2. Explain the purpose with reasons why this piece of legislation is seen to be important to corporate organizations.
3. Discuss in what areas of corporate governance you think the provisions of the Act are more relevant in application?

There are no standard answers given for these questions but students are expected to check and verify their suggested solutions with the lecturers who are instructing on the subject.

Future economic benefits

The flow of economic benefits associated with an asset or group of assets to be used in the business should be assessed to ensure a higher degree of certainty is attached. The evidence should be assessed to ensure a higher degree of certainty is attached. The evidence should be ascertained when the assets were initially acquired at the date of purchase. The assessment of benefits to be received and the risks it will incur normally happens when the title to the assets have actually passed to the owner. Until then, the asset should not be recognized in the accounts.

Cost measured reliably

Assets acquired initially are easy to measure the cost as the purchase consideration for the asset is known and usually evidenced by the supplier's invoice or other documents of title. In the case of self-constructed assets, the cost can also be easily measured with supporting source documents for materials, labour and other related overheads from outside parties when payments are settled.

Initial measurement of PPE

MFRS 116/IAS 16 requires that if an item of property, plant and equipment fulfills the recognition criteria as a qualifying asset, it will be initially measured at 'Cost'.

Components of cost

The cost of an item of PPE comprises:

- Purchase price, net of any trade discount or rebate
- Import duties and non-refundable purchase taxes [GST]
- Directly attributable costs of bringing the asset to working condition for its intended use.

Direct attributable costs in the case of self-constructed assets such as buildings, include:

- Cost of site preparation
- Initial delivery and handling costs
- Installation, construction, or initially testing of the asset
- Professional fees: legal, surveyors', engineers' or architects'

Where these directly attributable costs are incurred over a period of time, such costs can be included in the cost of PPE when the period ends and the asset is made ready for use, even if the asset is not brought into use until a later date. Where an asset is capable of operating as soon as it is available, it can be ready for use. Sometimes, due to the level of demand which has not yet built up, the asset may not be able to operate at normal levels immediately, in such circumstances further capitalization of costs during this period is not justified ona prudent basis. Any such costs [for example, wasted materials] will be classified as abnormal and therefore cannot be treated as part of the cost of PPE. Such amounts will be written off as revenue expense.

Costs subsequent to acquisition

Costs incuned subsequent to acquisition are based on the recognition criteria we discussed earlier, that the cost of an item of property, plant and equipment should be recognized as an asset if, and only if:

a. It is probable that future economic benefits associated with the item will flow to the entity; and
b. The cost of the item can be measured reliably.

The accounting standard frequently refers to this stated rule to distinguish, among costs incurred after acquisition, between those that must be capitalized and those that should be treated as revenue expense.

Obviously, costs incurred subsequent to acquisition of an asset, such as additions, enhancements or improvements, or replacements, are to be added to the asset's depreciable cost base if they provide evidence of future service potential to generate revenue, and extend the useful life of the asset or otherwise they are recognized as revenue expenditure.

Examples of improvements or replacement expenditure that result in future economic benefits are:

i. Aircraft interior structures such as passenger seats and galleys which may require replacement several times during the lifespan of the aircraft. Capital expenditure of this nature tends to increase the asset's capacity or extend its economic life. The cost of such replacements is fully recognized when it is incurred and added to the carrying amount of the asset. These assets are depreciated over its expected life, which may be different from the expected life of the other components of the asset. The carrying amount of the old aircraft interiors being replaced will be de-recognized [removed from booksl when the replacement takes place.
ii. Upgrading nrachine parts to achieve a substantial improvement in the quality of output and level of efficiency in production time.
iii. Relining of a blast furnace required after a specified number of hours of use
iv. New production processes resulting in substantial reduction of bottlenecks and lowering of operating costs.

The Standard also states that an entity should not recognize expenditure that forms part of the normal and regular 'repairs and maintenance' of PPE. This is written-off or charged as revenue expense to the profit or loss statement when incurred.

Thus, a major decision in accounting for PPE is whether to capitalize or to expense off. The decision is often made on the basis of materiality although minimum threshold amount can be preset. This is a matter of accounting policy that could be determined by an entity's management. Most entities often for tax reasons opt out for immediately writing-off expenditure that falls below the established threshold. Doing so has the following advantage:

- Taxable income or profit for the year of acquisition will be much reduced [resulting in a minimum tax liability with a higher immediate cash flow for the entity] by an amount which is higher than the capital allowance available for the depreciation expense adjustment in the tax computation.

In most cases, GAAPs and tax legislation could be a good source for consultation to facilitate the distinction between expensing off and capitalizing the amount as an asset.

Capital and Revenue expenditure

An asset is defined by the accounting standard

a. As a resource controlled by an entity as a result of past events; and
b. From which future economic benefits are expected to flow to the entity.

Unless the expenditure falls within this definition of an asset, and the recognition criterion Idealt earlier) the expense is treated as a normal revenue item which gets reported in the profit or loss statement. Ellie focus is on capital expenditure because such expenditure is normally capitalized as PPE in the statement of financial position and depreciated over its estimated uselill life with adjustments for impairment losses.

The table below summarizes the distinction between capital and revenue expenditure.

Table 4 Capital and Revenue Expenditure

Nature of Expenditure.	Objective/Purpose	Accounting Treatment	Subject to Depreciation
Capital	Expenditure incuncd for the purpose of generating future economic benefits	Recorded as assets	Yes
Revenue	Expenditure that results in consumption of resources purposes Of generating revenue — "lliese include for short-term usage or nonnal repair and maintenance, costs of production, cost of marketing, selling and distributing the product or services, including costs of administrating.	Charged as expense when incurred, using 'cost and matching' principle	No

Capital expenditure is recorded as PPE whereas revenue expenditure is incurred in creating, sustaining and satisfying demand and as such, is recognized as expenses.

Complex assets

These are assets which are made up of separate components. Fach component is separately depreciated over its estimated useful life.

An example of a complex asset is an aircraft (or an electrical train coach) could be made up of several interrelated components such as following

	Cost (RM' 000)	Useful lifé
Engine	60, 000	12, 000 flying hours
Undercaniage	25, 000	1, 500 landings
Fuselage	90, 000	18 years

Depreciation of these components is based on average of 120 flights totaling 500 flying hours.

Required

Calculate the depreciation charge for a typical year end for this type of aircrafL

Workings

	RM' 000
Engine: [60, 000 × 500/12, 000]	2, 500
Undercaniage: [25, 000 120/1, 500]	2, 000
Fuselage [90, 000/18]	5, 000
Total charge	9, 500

The overall depreciation charge is approximately 5% on the total cost of the aircraft excluding other capital expenditure incidental to the aircraft.

For an example, China manufactures modern speed trains that run on electricity using electronic technology. KTM has invested in this type of speed trains (ETS). The journey takes about 4 hours to travel from KL Central to Butterworth, something that normally takes 8 hours for the conventional train system mode of travclling in the past.

Other types of complex assets

An entity will acquire individual assets which cannot be identified as smaller items such as tools, dies and moulds. Sometimes these items are classified as inventory and written off as an expense. However, since they are not meant for resale and given its size and magnitude, these are major components or spare parts which should be recognized as PPE. Particularly for large and specialized items, the single asset should be broken down into its component parts where the different parts have different useful lives and different depreciation rates are applied to each part. For e.g. an aircraft, where the body and engines are separated as they have different useful lives. See the example of a computation done above.

Worked Exercises

Two worked examples where the capitalization principle is applied for classification of PPE. Other review questions are given later in the chapter for student practice sessions

Example 1

On 1 July 2020, Nirpani Company bought from Capital Equipment, an item of plant and equipment under the following terns for use in the manufacturing process:

	RM
Price of plant and equipment	108,000
Import duty	2,150
Delivery and handling charges	3,000
Installation costs	10,400
Testing for pre-production trials	6,090
Purchase of a 5-year maintenance contract with the vendor	8,000

Nirpant secured a trade discount of 10 % on the list price of the asset and a settlement discount of 5 % if payment for the item was settled within a month of purchase. The company paid for the plant and equipment on 28 July 2020.

Required

Using the information given, show how the asset is accounted for in the financial statements?

Solution

All costs required in bringing an asset to its present location and condition for its intended purpose should be capitalized according to the Standard.

Therefore, the initial purchase price of the plant and machinery should be:

Vendor's list price	108,000
Trade discount 10%	(10,800)
	97 ,200
Import duty	2,150
Delivery and handling charges	3,000
Installation costs	10,400
Testing - preproduction trials Total amount capitalized	6090

The plant and equipment's initial cost price of RM 118,840 will be capitalized in the accounting ledger on I July 2020. However, the maintenance contract of RM 8, 000 is treated as a revenue expense under the regular repairs and maintenance account and should therefore be mitten off to the profit or loss statement over a five-year period. Under the accruals concept, the cost is spread each year to match against the revenue generated by the use of this asset over the contract period.

The settlement discount received amounting to RM4, 860 × RM 97,2001 will be shown as 'Other Income' in the profit or loss statement. Ellie settlement took place within a month of purchase.

Example 2

Construction of a new store for Starbuck in a prime shopping complex commenced on I March 2019.

The items of expenditure were incuned on the construction work at the shopping mall:

	RM'OOO
Freehold land.	6,280
Architect's fees	680
Site preparation.	1 ,800
Materials.	8,400
Direct labour costs	11,800
Legal fees	3,300
General overheads	1,750

The construction work was completed on I December 2019. fie store was brought into use following its gmnd opening on I March 2020. Starbuck issued a RM35 million unsecured debenture (long-term loan) on I March 2019 to finance the construction of the new store. "Ille loan carried an interest ratc of per annum and is repayable on I March 2021.

Required

[al Determine the amount to be Gipitalized for the new store as PPE

[bl State what impact the above information would have on the profit or loss statement [if anyl for the year ended 28 February, 2020 and year ended 28 February 2021 ?

Solution

This exercise relates to a self-constructed asset.

Again, all costs to get the store to its present location and condition for its intended business use should be capitalized in accordance with MFRS 116. With the exception of general overheads, all the other items of expenditure listed in the question would qualify for capitalization.

Capitalization of borrowing costs

The interest on the loan should also be capitalized from I March 2019 as it is a qualifying asset under the provisions of MFRS 123/IAS 23 Borrowing casts. The recognition criteria for capitalization is also met as the activities to prepare the store for its intended use are in progress, expenditure for the store is being incurred. Borrowing costs are being incurred. However, capitalization of the interest on the loan should cease when the store is ready for operational use, i.e. I March 2020. Any remaining interest incun•ed for the period should be charged as finance cost in the profit or loss statement for year ended 28 February 2021.

Property, plant and equipment Store

	RM'OOO
Freehold land	6,280
Architect's fees	680
Site preparation	1 ,800
Materials	8,400
Direct labour costs	11,800
Leg-al fees	3,300
Borrowing.	
Total amount to be capitalised 35,060	2 800

Borrowing cost relating to the unsecured debenture commenced on I March 2019. The asset (store) was brought to intended use on I March 2020 when the 2, 80store was opened for business. Bon-owing cost ceased at this date. Interest capitalization is for lyear. RM 35 m x x I year = RM 2. 8 million.

The standard requires that capitalization of borrowing costs ceases when substantially all the activities necessary to prepare the qualifying asset for its intended use or sale are complete. The cut-off point for capitalization is when the asset is ready for its intended use or sale for occupancy on I March 2021. Interest capitalization to the store building ceases on that.

We are not using the benchmark treatment that borrowing costs to be recognized as an expense in the period in which they are incur-red. MFRS 123, like the revised IAS 23, removes the benchmark treatment of expensing borrowing costs incuned on qualifying assets.

Impact on profit or loss statement

The profit or loss statement should be charged with:

- General overheads of RMI ,750,000
- Interest for period 1 March 2020 — 28 Feb' 2021 which is to be treated as finance cost IRM35 million x 896 x I year RM 2.8 millionl in the statement of profit or loss. For year ended 28 February 2020, interest as borrowing cost is capitalized as part of the asset cost of the store.
- Depreciation of the store. ne store has not been brought into use until 1 March 2020. However, the Standard states depreciation of an asset begins when the asset is available for its intended use. i.e. after this date when it is in the location and condition necessary for it to be capable of operating in the manner intended by management. However, depreciation of the store cannot be calculated in this situation as the information on its useful economic life [or depreciation rate] has yet to be given by Starbuck's management. This note is only for illustrative purposes. Depreciation is covered later in Chapter 10.

Asset Registers

Entities, particularly those who are operating large businesses, the tangible fixed assets deployed for various activities may be located physically in many different site locations or departments rather than being housed in its central warehouse or building premises for the sake of convenience. For example, firms whose main activities are manufacturing will have plant, equipment, and loose tools and consumables items in large quantities and of varying sizes that need to be controlled and maintained in proper custody before and after use. The movement of these PPE items may pose administrative problems if no proper documentation or written records are kept for control and information purposes. Sometimes these assets can be misplaced, lost through improper handling or even stolen.

While the accounting of these tangible assets as far as the books of accounts are concerned, they may appear intact but physically it may be an arduous task for management to keep track of every PPE item that gets reported in the accounting system. The main issue here is maintaining an adequate system of control and custodial rights where the movement of these assets is easily facilitated by the use of a fixed assets register. The importance of asset registers cannot be over-emphasized as tangible asset management becomes an onerous task.

Asset registers serves the following useful purposes and functions:-

- Management needs to control the physical movement of PPE items so that some form of accountability becomes important
- Assets are continuously being added and retired in businesses on a periodic basis and therefore need to be accounted for, particularly on disposals when asset conditions need to be assessed for estimating the scrap or salvage value.
- The repairs and maintenance of these assets can be easily facilitated and controlled as the presence of a tracking system exists.

- Annual review exercises are easily facilitated for the following purposes:
  i. Assets are needed to be examined for the incidence of impairment and other factors
  ii. Revising estimating useful lives of assets for depreciation purpose
- Record of depreciation history of assets is known.

A major exercise for proper maintenance of an asset register is to update the records on a regular basis particularly when information on changes to asset conditions occurs. These conditions on asset changes may take several forms such as revaluation of assets, new acquisitions and disposals of assets, including retirements as well.

Another important function is the reconciliation exercise between an asset register and accounting records to ensure the accuracy, completeness and ownership of assets is intact. This must be an on-going part of a control system on asset management.

Proude an extract of the audited financial statements on PPE of a quoted company in Bursa Malaysia. Include the related accounting policy as well. Provide real case scenarios to confirm this: PETRONAS, Maxis and Air Asia

Chapter Summary

1. Non-Current Assets are classified between categories of long-tenn assets used in business with a functional purpose. are both tangible and intangible assets and also distinguished from other financial assets. Some concrete examples are shown and how they are disclosed in the statement of financial position. While Chapter 9 primalily deals with tangible fixed assets (non-current assets), Chapters 10, Il and 12 focuses on other aspects of non-current assets such as depreciation and intangible assets, accounting for revaluation of assets and de-recognition.
2. Property, Plant and FAuipment (PPE) are tangible fixed assets of substantial value held and used as long-term business assets to generate income. PPE is used in the production or supply of goods or services, held for rental and their useful expected lives to be longer for more than one accounting period. PPE are reported at cost when acquired, cost includes all related expenditure necessary to bring the asset to its l)lesent location and ready for its intended use The allocation of a PPE's cost over its useful life is called depreciation and the amount that has been allocated over the years is called accumulated depreciation. "Ihe difference between the cost of a PPE item and its accumulated depreciation is called the canying amount or net book value.
3. Recognition as a Tangible Fixed Asset (PPE) in the business entity's accounts must fulfill the required two criteria conditions. Ellie accounting standard stipulates that before a tangible non-current asset is capitalized in the entitys accounts. It is probable that filture economic lwnefits associated with the asset will flow to the entity; and the cost orthe asset to the entity can be measured reliably.
4. Costs incurred on Subsequent Measurement should be on the same Recognition Criterion. The Standard requires that if an item of property, plant and equipment fulfills the recognition criteria as a qualifying asset, it will be initially measured at 'Cose. Ellie cost of an item of PPE comprises: purchase price, net of any trade discount or rebate, import duties and non-refundable purchase taxes IGSTI and directly attributable costs of blinging the asset to working condition for its intended use Costs incurred subsequent to acquisition are based on the standard recognition criteria that the cost of an item of property, plant and equipment should be recognized as a qualifying asset if, and only if it fulfills probable Tuttuc• economic benefits and its cast can be measured reliably.

5. Distinguishing between Capital and Revenue Expenditure The accounting standard refers to this stated rule to distinguish, among costs incurred after acquisition, between those that must be capitalized and those that should be treated as revenue expense. Obviously, costs incurred subsequent to acquisition of an asset, such as additions, enhancements or improvements, or replacements, are to be added to the asset's depreciable cost base if they provide evidence of future service potential to generate revenue, and extend the useful life of the asset or otherwise they are recognized as revenue expenditure. Some examples are given above. Thus, a rnqjor decision in accounting for PPE is whether to capitalize or to expense off. "Illis is a matter of accounting policy that could be determined by an entity's management.
6. Complex assets nrse are assets which are made up of separate components. Fach component is sepamtely depreciated over its estimated useful life. Some useful worked examples are provided for students' understanding and knowledge. Other types of complex assets are briefly discussed with illustrative examples as well.
7. Capitalization of Borrowing Costs are explained and the criterion used to identify borrowing cost as qualilS'ing to be treated as part the asset. Wc showed an illustrative example how borrowing costs is recognized and subject to the capitalization process.
8. Asset Registers is dealt as the final part of this chapter. Large companies may have many fixed assets that could be located physically in different parts of the organintion, particularly in manufacturing and other industrial applications. Elliere is a need for these used tangible assets to be kept in Guck and registers become a useful record in controlling the whereabouts and physical condition of these assets. Depreciation calculation is easily facilitated given the age and usage of these assets. Repairs and maintenance of assets can be undertaken on a timely basis particularly when an updated asset register provides the necessary information on the condition of the assets.

Key Terms

Accumulated depreciation
Asset register
Capitalization of borrowing costs
Carrying amount of an asset
Complex assets
Depletion
Development cost or expenditure
Goodwill
Impairment loss
Freehold land
Licenses
Net book value (or carrying amount)
Patents,
Residual mlue
Software and information systems
Trade mark (or brand name)

Asset
Cost
Capital expenditure
Copyrights
I) epreciation
De-recognized assets
Economic useful life
Franchise
Intangible assets
Iæasehold land
Natural resources
Non-current assets
Property, plant and equipment
Revenue expenditure
Tangible fixed assets
Wasting assets

Review Questions

1. Outline the main differences in the charactefistics between the categories of non-cunent assets.
2. What are the main stages involved in reporting of accounting issues on PPE? Explain what are these main accounting issues in reporting?.

3. Define PPE and provide at least five examples of categories of PPE items normally reported in the statement of financial position.
4. Explain the required criteria conditions to be fulfilled in recognition of a tangible fixed asset before it is capitalized in the accounts.
5. State the consequences of recognition of a qualifying asset. Explain what happens if:
   i. An asset is wrongly classified as an expense or
   ii. An expense is enoneously treated as an asset.
6. Briefly discuss why the Sarbanes-Oxley Act, 2002 was enacted? Outline at least three main provisions of this law and its importance to financial reporting in the annual audited accounts of entities.
7. i. Identify the main components of 'cost'in the initial measurement of an item of PPE;
   ii. Explain what you understand by the term 'direct attributable costs', and under what circumstances these costs are related and included in an item of PPE?
8. Costs incurred subsequent to acquisition are based on the same recognition criteria of IAS 16 and the standard frequently refers to this stated rule to distinguish, among costs incun•ed after acquisition, between those that must be capitalized and those that should be treated as revenue expense.
   i. Identify the purpose and nature of subsequent costs that are normally included in the canying amount of the asset. Provide three main examples that can be listed as subsequent expenditure.
   ii. Explain the conditions under which subsequent expenditure is treated as part of the can-ying amount of an asset that is already capitalized under the initial measurement rule for PPE?
9. Distinguish between capital and revenue expenditure and give reasons why such distinction is necessary'?
   a. What is the difference between costs on ortlinary repairs and those that increase or extends the useful life of an asset or improves the type or amount of service potential an asset provides?
   b. How should these costs be accounted or recorded?
11. Briefly discuss the importance of maintaining a fixed asset register?
12. What is the process of allocating the cost of natural resources to expense as they are consumed?
13. What lessons can we learn about WorldCom? Do you think scandalous cases like this will not repeat again in the corporate world as men's greed is insatiable?

Chapter Summary

1. Non-Current Assets are classified between categories of long-term assets used in business with a functional purpose. They are both tangible and intangible assets and also distinguished from other financial assets. Some concrete examples are shown and how they are disclosed in the statement of financial position. While Chapter 9 primarily deals with tangible fixed assets (non-current assets), Chapters 10, Il and 12 focuses on other aspects of non-current assets such as depreciation and intangible assets, accounting for revaluation of assets and de-recognition.
2. Property, Plant and FAuipment (PPE) are tangible fixed assets of substantial value held and used as long-term business assets to generate income. PPE is used in the production or supply of goods or services, held for rental and their useful expected lives to be longer for more than one accounting period. PPE are reported at cost when acquired, cost includes all related expenditure necessary to bring the asset to its present location and ready for its intended use. The allocation of a PPE's cost over its useful life is called depreciation and the amount that has been allocated over the years is called accumulated depreciation. The difference between the cost of a PPE item and its accumulated depreciation is called the carrying amount or net book value.

3. Recognition as a Tangible Fixed Asset (PPE) in the business entity's accounts must fulfill the required two criteria conditions. The accounting standard stipulates that before a tangible non-current asset is capitalized in the entitys accounts. *It is probable that future economic benefits associated with the asset will flow to the entity; and the cost of the asset to the entity can be measured reliably.*
4. Costs incurred on Subsequent Measurement should be on the same Recognition Criterion. The Standard requires that if an item of property, plant and equipment fulfills the recognition criteria as a qualifying asset, it will be initially measured at 'Cost'. The cost of an item of PPE comprises: purchase price, net of any trade discount or rebate, import duties and non-refundable purchase taxes [GST] and directly attributable costs of bringing the asset to working condition for its intended use Costs incurred subsequent to acquisition are based on the standard recognition criteria that the cost of an item of property, plant and equipment should be recognized as a qualifying asset if, and only if it fulfills *probable future economic benefits and its cost can be measured reliably.*
5. Distinguishing between Capital and Revenue Expenditure. The accounting standard refers to this stated rule to distinguish, among costs incurred after acquisition, between those that must be capitalized and those that should be treated as revenue expense. Obviously, costs incurred subsequent to acquisition of an asset, such as additions, enhancements or improvements, or replacements, are to be added to the asset's depreciable cost base if they provide evidence of future service potential to generate revenue, and extend the useful life of the asset or otherwise they are recognized as revenue expenditure. Some examples are given above. Thus, a major decision in accounting for PPE is whether to capitalize or to expense off. This is a matter of accounting policy that could be determined by an entity's management.
6. Complex assets These are assets which are made up of separate components. Each component is sepamtely depreciated over its estimated useful life. Some useful worked examples are provided for students' understanding and knowledge. Other types of complex assets are briefly discussed with illustrative examples as well..
   1. Capitalization of the interest on the loan should cease when the building is ready for intended operational use
   2. Any remaining interest incurred for the period should NOT be charged as finance cost in the profit or loss statement.

QB. You are given the following information on Hill-top property lots:

Category	Sale price per Lot
10 Hilltop lots	RM 585, 000
10 valley lots	RM 380, 000

You buy land for RM 3, 000, 000 and spend RM l, 200, 000 to develop the property. You then divide the land into lots as follows:

How much did cach Hilltop lot cost you?

a. RM 246,000 c. RM 234, 284

b. RM 420, 000 d. RM 415, 00

Exercises

QI. Thillai Company., a spare parts and accessories dealer, bought conveyor-belt machinery.

Required

Classify each of the following expenditure as a capital expenditure or an immediate expense related to the machinery:

i. Sales tax paid on the purchase price

ii. Purchase price

iii. Freight charges and insurance while machinery' is in transit from seller to buye (iv) Installation

iv. Training of workers for initial operation of the machinery

v. Special reinforcement to the machinery platform

(Income tax paid on income eamed from sale of spare parts manufactured by the machinery

Major overhaul to extend the machinery"s useful life by three years

Ordinary repairs to keep the machinery' in good working order (x) Lubrication of the machinery' before it is placed in service (xi) Pefiodic after the machinery is placed in service.

Q2.1. Identify the following as cither revenue or capital expenditure:

a. Completed an addition to an ollicc building for RM 250, 000 cash

b. Paid RM 9()() for the monthly cost of replacement filteß on an air-conditioning system

c. Paid RM 250 cash per 5-ton lony for the cost or their annual tune-ups

d. Paid RM 45, 000 cash to replace a compressor on a refrigeration system that extends its useful

2. Prepare journal entries to record tmnsactions (a) and (d) of part I

There are two times in a man's life when he should not speculate:
Where he can't afford, and when he can.

– Mark Twain

Chapter 10

Learning Objectives

After you have studied this Section Two, you should

Understand and explain the purpose of depreciation

Understand the causes of depreciation

Understand and learn useful definitions relating to depreciation

Calculate the charge for depreciation using straight line and reducing balance methods

Understand and identify the circumstances where different methods of depreciation would be appropriate.

Calculate the depreciation adjustments where changes are made in the estimated useful life and/or residual value of a non-current asset.

Illustrate how depreciation expense and accumulated depreciation are recorded in ledger accounts

Understand the accounting for natural resources and the depletion process

Understand the concept of impairment loss

Understand the accounting for acquisitions and disposal of assets.

Know how PPE items on disposal are reflected in cash flow statements

Be able to write an accounting policy on PPE items and depreciation (refer to annual reports of published accounts)

Able to record depreciation in the profit or loss statement and statement of financial position

Accounting for Depreciation

Non-current assets

We discussed earlier in Chapter 9, about the categories of non-current assets as being long-lived assets that have finite or limited useful lives. PPEs or commonly known as tangible fixed assets in UK [FRS 15]. These are revenue generating assets owned and controlled by the business entity and extends over more than one accounting period. Every non-current asset eventually through the passage of time and business usage, wears out over time. Therefore, it becomes necessary to apportion the depreciable amount of the asset over its economic useful life. The only exception is land held on freehold or on very long leasehold which does not normally depreciate because of unlimited useful life endowed by nature.

Types of PPE (as Tangible Fixed Assets)

Land

Buildings

Plant and machinery

Fixtures and Fittings

Assets held under leases

Motor vehicles

Other assets

When a business entity acquires a non-current asset, it will:

1. Keep the asset for use in the business until it becomes completely worn out, turning obsolete or worthless;
2. Sell it or scrap off at the end of its useful life;

Sometimes due to technological changes or industrial innovation, the entity may find it necessary to invest in new assets to improve production efficiency and be able to generate more revenue for the business.

Reporting of PPEs in financial statements

PPE items are reported in the statement of financial position at their ***carrying amounts or net book values***.

Carrying amount of a PPE item = Cost – Accumulated depreciation – Accumulated impairment losses

Notes

i. Impairment of assets is beyond the scope aand syllabus of this course.

ii. Impairment losses will be covered as a separate topic in Financial Reporting, a forthcoming textbook by the same authors.

Depreciation

The Accounting Standard that governs depreciation is IAS 16. MFRS 116 adopted the provisions of IAS 16 in entirety and therefore compliance is common to both Standards.

IAS 16 requires *the depreciable amount of a depreciable asset to be allocated on a systematic and rational basis to each accounting period during the useful life of the asset.*

Explaining the concept of depreciation

A tangible fixed asset has a cost and a finite useful life. Over a passage of time the economic value and usage of the asset eventually declines through probable causes resulting from wear and tear, technological obsolescence or other physical factors, Consequently, it makes commercial sense that an expense should be charged to profit or loss to reflect the flow of economic benefits to the entity as a result of consuming the asset in the business. Cost allocation enables business entities to properly match expenses with revenue under the cost and matching principle. This act of provisioning or charging an expense (allocation of cost) is called **depreciation**

The need to depreciate PPE arises from the application of the accruals concept of accounting to determine profits. Where cash resources are invested to acquire tangible fixed assets, then the amount expended must at some point in time be charged against profits. If the asset is one which contributes significantly to an entity's revenue and profits over a number of accounting periods, a suitable method of depreciation appropriate to the condition and use of the asset must be determined for allocating the cost of the asset over its accounting period. Putting in other words, depreciation is seen as a means of **spreading the cost or value** of an asset over its **useful economic life**. It is matching the cost against the accounting period during which it earns revenue and profits for the business This concept of depreciation as a process of allocating the cost of an asset over several accounting periods is the view adopted by IAS16/MFRS 116.

Causes of depreciation

In the preceding statement, we explained the economic and accounting rationale for depreciation of PPEs. However, we need to understand some common and natural causes of depreciation:

- **Assets undergo physical deterioration**

  Wear and tear

  Assets automatically tend to wear out over a period of time through regular usage. Examples, Plant and equipment, fixtures and fittings and motor vehicles eventually wear out after extended usage, some last few years and others last many years. Buildings last longer periods but they still wear out particularly if they are not physically maintained or neglected through lack of proper attention.

  Erosion, rust, rot and decay

  Land may be eroded or wasted away through natural environmental causes such as rain, wind or excessive heat from the sun or other elements of nature such as earthquakes, hurricanes, and tsunami. Despite these natural causes, there is no economic justification for depreciating land, for reasons as stated earlier. The metal parts and accessories of motor vehicles and machinery will rust away. Wood will rot eventually. Decay will also be present due to the elements of nature and through lack of physical care and attention.

- **Economic factors**

  Some assets will be put out of use due to some economic or commercial reasons although these assets are still in good physical condition. One major reason that usually accounts for this is technical obsolescence as a consequence of business innovation trends and technological breakthroughs in computer chip technology that greatly improves the speed of doing business and creating mass production capacity in manufacturing processes. The old plant and equipment becomes obsolete and no longer economical for improving business efficiency. These old assets may still have a productive use for other businesses. The assets will be disposed or sold to them because they cannot afford high investments for up-to-date equipment.

- **Time factor**

  Some commercial assets are tied to a time factor. An example is leasehold properties such as buildings which could be rented out under a lease agreement for ten years, have its legal life fixed in terms of years. Once the lease expires at the end of its term, it becomes worthless in commercial value. The asset will be de-registered from the statement of financial position as the asset goes back to its original owner. Instead of using the term depreciation, the term '*amortization*' is often used for this type of assets.

Specific issues relating to reporting of land and buildings

i. Reporting the split between land and building

One main argument says, as land is not subject to the process of depreciation, the asset must always be reported separately from buildings which are constructed on it. The split between them is necessary because the information on their asset values have to be precisely identified for two reasons:

a. The market value of these two identifiable assets are always different in principle as the basis of market valuation does not go in tangent or evolve in parallel.

b. Unlike land, buildings because of their finite lifespan are **depreciable assets**.

ii. Land and Buildings

Conventionally, land and buildings are usually reported as a global figure in the statement of financial position. Information using purchase contract notes can identify the acquisition costs of land and buildings separately. Land and buildings are therefore dealt separately even when they are acquired together. Land has an unlimited life and does not normally depreciate because its usefulness and revenue generating capacity remains intact over a prolonged time. Buildings do, however, eventually fall into a state of disrepair or become obsolete and therefore must be subject to a depreciation charge annually.

In principle, this means all industrial, commercial and administrative buildings are recognized as subject to annual depreciation charge with different depreciation rates throughout their estimated useful life. Any increase in the value of land on which the building is standing will have no consequential impact on the building's useful life. However, when a revaluation of the land and buildings take place the depreciation charge on the building must be based on the revalued amount.

Common misconceptions about depreciation

It is worth noting some misconceptions about the purpose and effects of depreciation.

a. One misconception is that the carrying amount of a reported asset in financial statements is equal to its net realizable value and that the object of charging depreciation on an asset is to reflect the fall in value of that particular asset over its useful life. This is a common, but an erroneous argument. The argument claims that freehold properties need not be depreciated in times when property values are rising. It is true that asset values increase over a period, i.e. its current value is greater than the carrying value in the financial statements. It is tempting that in such situations, it may not be necessary to depreciate the asset. The Standard maintains however, that this view is irrelevant, and that depreciation should still continue to be charged to each accounting period based on the depreciable amount, irrespective of a rise in value.

   It is also equally true that financial statements prepared under the '*historical cost convention*' often give a misleading view of its financial position particularly when a property's carrying amount is much higher its market value. In such cases, in order to circumvent this anomaly, it is open to a business entity to prepare modified financial statements incorporating a revaluation exerciseinto its books or even to prepare its accounts on the basis of current costs [not a common practice]. However, developments in accounting for financial instruments in recent years has improved accounting practice by changing the financial landscape for reporting financial assets and financial liabilities in the statement of financial position.

b. Another misconception is that depreciation is provided so that an asset can be replaced at the end of its useful life. This is an incorrect view.

Additional issues on depreciation

Two issues that you need to be aware about **what depreciation is not**:

i. Depreciation is not providing for loss of value of an asset. It is important to note that depreciation is a process of cost allocation not a process of asset valuation. It is an accrual technique which allocates the depreciation amount to accounting periods expected to benefit from the use of the asset. Therefore, assets that are increasing in value should still need to be depreciated.

ii. Depreciation does not result in the accumulation of cash or putting aside cash resources for the replacement of assets as they wear out. The balance in accumulated depreciation represents the total amount of the asset's cost that the entity has charged to expense. It is not a cash fund. Besides, any such fund set aside to purchase new non-current assets is entirely a separate matter and nothing do with the depreciation process.

Furthermore, IAS 16/MFRS 116 requires that depreciation should be recognized as **an expense** in the statement of comprehensive income. It is a normal practice to include depreciation charges in the expenditure incurred on a construction contract account which is carried forward and matched against future income arising from the contract under the provisions of IAS 11. The Standard also states that an entity is required to begin depreciating an item of PPE when it is available for use and to continue depreciating it until it is de-recognized even if it remains idle during the period.

Allocating Depreciation on PPEs

Before we move to a number of specific methods for calculating depreciation on an item of PPE, it is important that we understand the basic factors or concepts related to depreciation. To allocate depreciation on a PPE item, the following three issues about the depreciable asset are relevant:

- Cost
- Estimated useful life
- Estimated residual value

Earlier, our discussion dealt with the definition of cost as a known amount under initial measurement. The other two issues require some further explanation

Estimated useful life

IAS 16 stipulates the following factors to be considered when estimating the useful life of a depreciable asset:

- Expected usage of the asset
- Physical wear and tear, bearing in mind also the repair and maintenance record
- Obsolescence due to technological advances/improvements in production including change in market conditions affecting the product and service output as related to the asset,
- Legal and other restrictions on the use of the asset such as encumbrances placed on the asset, e.g. a loan secured against the building, owned by the entity.

Estimated useful life relates to the length of service expected from the usage or utility of the asset. Depending the nature of the asset used, expected useful life may take the form in terms of years or percentage, number of units of production output, or some other relevant measure such as usage or capacity of a factory machine.

Companies' base their estimates on their previous experiences or from known past records and in some cases, knowledge from trade publications. For an example, in aviation industry, commercial airlines such as Air Asia, MAS, Singapore Airlines uses a 15- years useful life to depreciate their passenger aircraft.

Estimated residual value

Commonly referred as scrap value or salvaged value of an asset. The amount of residual value should be estimated based on current age and conditions of similar assets, used in the same operating segment of the business and that it has reached the end of its useful live. The net sale proceeds that the entity will obtain from disposal of the asset is after deducting the estimated costs of disposal. In most cases, the residual value of an asset is likely to be immaterial.

A PPE's depreciable amount is therefore:

Depreciable amount = Cost – Estimated residual value

Review of estimated useful life and estimated residual value

EUL

The **estimated useful life** should be reviewed at the end of each reporting year and depreciation rates should be adjusted for the current and future periods if expectations vary significantly from original estimates. The effect of a change [reason, quantifying the estimate] should be disclosed in the accounting period in which the change occurs. When a completely new type of asset is acquired or due to an improvement expenditure significantly enhancing the asset's useful life [as a result of technological advancement or through creating a brand new product or service] it is still necessary to review estimated useful life even though this will be a difficult process.

ERV

Except for substantially valued items, the **estimated residual value** or scrap value of most items of PPE will be almost negligible as these assets would have reached a mature period of usage and utilization. At this stage, its future economic life could be a suspect if any revision of its estimated residual value would significantly change, thus any revision of residual value can become of lesser importance. In practical terms, residual values other than big or huge assets hardly have any material impact on the inflow of cash resources to the entity.

Furthermore, the residual value can be determined later when the asset is reaching its useful life but for purposes of calculating depreciation, it has to be estimated initially. So, this initial estimate is at best, a guessed figure or amount going by experience and knowledge of similar aged assets at that particular point in the operating segment of the business. At some time if the entity intends to scrap the asset, the disposal value is usually arrived at arm's length after negotiation with the interested buying party.

On the other hand of the spectrum, residual values can be enhanced if the entity decides to keep and use the asset for a longer period than its useful life. Usually in this circumstance, the entity will undertake **significant expenditure to enhance or improve its economic value** as well as spending more on repairs and maintenance. So, estimates of residual value could be revised accordingly.

Table Common policies on useful lives

PPE or Tangible fixed assets	Useful life in years	Corresponding annual rates
Freehold land.	Infinite	None
Buildings		
• Commercial	50	2 %
• Industrial	20–50	2-5 %
Plant and machinery	5- 8	12.5–20 %
Furniture, Fixtures and Fittings	5–10	10–20 %
Office equipment	5–10	10–20 %
Computer	3- 5	20 -33.3 %
Assets held under leases	Over lease period -	
Motor vehicles	≥5	20 %

These suggested depreciation rates are based on best estimates and depends on the operating industry in which such assets are deployed. Malaysian companies normally report their depreciation policies in the audited accounts and reports.

Methods of calculating depreciation charges

The depreciation charge of a PPE item is normally calculated using one of the following common methods:

- The straight line method (common and popular)
- The reducing balance method (selectively done based on usage)
- Based on actual usage or units of production (used in production or manufacturing)
- Sum of digits method (only by choice –quite rare in practice)

In actual accounting practice, the majority of entities tend to commonly adopt only one method or any combination of the methods suited to their circumstances and conditions of business. All these methods are acceptable under generally accepted accounting principles. An entity's management usually selects the method it considers to be appropriate and which best measures an asset's contribution to revenue and profits over its useful life.

Once a method is chosen as part of its accounting policy, the entity should apply it consistently over the useful life of the asset. Unless condition and usage of the asset warrants a significant change, then a revised estimate useful will be adopted by the entity's management. The effect of this change of accounting estimate will need to be disclosed

Each of these methods allocates different amounts of depreciation to each accounting period. However, they result in the same total amount of depreciation which is equal to the asset's depreciable amount, over the economic useful life of the asset.

Table Illustrating the Main Depreciation Methods

Time-based methods	**Methods based on activity level produced or consumed [or service level or level of use]**
Straight Line	Production output
Reducing balance	Service quantity
Sum of digits	
Depreciation charge or expense primarily determined regardless of the level of activity during the specified period.	Depreciation expense is the result of the multiplication of a constant depreciation rate per unit of activity times the number of units of activity consumed or produced during the period.

Illustrative Example

We compare all the three depreciation methods using the information in the following question:

A 3-ton lorry purchased for a haulage business cost RM 65, 000. The estimated useful life is expected to last for five years and then sold for scrap amounting to RM 5, 000. Usage over the five years is expected to be:

Year two hundred and fifty days

Year

Year

Year

Year

Required:

Calculate the depreciation charge to be provided for each year under:

a. The straight line method
b. The reducing balance method – using a rate of %
c. The usage or production [days] method
d. The sum of digits method

Prepare a depreciation schedule for each of the methods and explain its overall significance to the entity's management.

Solution

a. Straight line method

Under this method, an entity expenses an equal or fixed amount of depreciation for each year of the asset's estimated useful life. This method is used if the consumption of service potential relates more to the passage of time rather that the level of activity or if the asset is expected be productive equally in each year of usage or utility. The straight line method is the most popular and frequently used method for reasons of simplicity of application and also because it often reflects realistically the consumption of the asset's service potential.

In order to calculate the **depreciation charge** under the straight line method, the entity needs to determine the depreciable cost. The depreciable cost is the cost of the asset less its residual value [if any]. It represents the total depreciable amount subject to depreciation which is then divided by the useful life in years to arrive at the annual depreciation charge.

However, the entity is required to estimate the useful life of the asset in years. Alternatively, we also can determine an annual rate of depreciation. In this case, the rate is a 20 %(100/5 yrs)

Solution

In this example, the estimated residual value is given to be the scarp value.

$$\text{Annual depreciation charge or expense} = \frac{\text{Cost} - \text{Estimated residual value}}{\text{Useful life, in years}}$$

$$= \frac{65{,}000 - 5000}{5}$$

$$= \text{RM } 12{,}000 \text{ Depreciation each year for 5 years}$$

Journal entry to record the depreciation charge in year 1

Date	Account	Ref	Debit	Credit
17 July	Depreciation	GL.	12,000	
	Accumulated Depreciation	GL.		12,000
	(Being depreciation expense for the year on the lorry)			

Assets	=	Liabilities	+	Shareholders' Equity	
–5,000	=	0	+	–5,000.	[Depreciation expense]

Note the effect

Depreciation decreases the asset through accumulated depreciation and also decreases equity through the depreciation expense.

Depreciation schedule

Year	Depreciable Cost x	Depreciation Rate =	Annual Charge	Accumulated Depreciation	Asset Carrying Amount
1	60, 000	20 %	12, 000	12, 000	48, 000
2	60, 000	20 %	12, 000	24, 000	36, 000
3	60, 000	20 %	12, 000	36, 000	24, 000
4	60, 000	20 %	12, 000	48, 000	12, 000
5	60, 000	20 %	12, 000	60, 000	Nil

This depreciation schedules helps management to understand the impact of purchasing decisions on the financial statements over the years. See how the cost of the asset is allocated as annual depreciation charge. The entire cost is written off at the end of 5 years at nil value.

b. Reducing Balance Method

The reducing balance or diminishing balance method recognizes larger amounts of depreciation in the early years of an asset's life and smaller amounts in the later years. The process of charging depreciation under this method appears to be accelerated and is considered conceptually sound if the reducing pattern of depreciation expense more closely reflects the actual contribution that the asset makes to the revenue generating capacity. This method is logical when an asset is considered to provide superior performance in the early years of its useful life. The method works with maximum operating efficiency in the initial years but has an inclined tendency to incur more repairs and maintenance in later years.

This accelerating method is also most widely used accounting policy by entities. The method applies a constant or fixed % rate on the carrying amount [opening net book value] of the asset to arrive at the depreciation charge for the period. It is worth noting that the depreciation rate remains constant from year to year whereas the carrying amount to which the rate is applied diminishes [reduces] each year.

Annual depreciation charge = Carrying amount at beginning of year × % [Constant rate]

Carrying amount = Cost – Accumulated Depreciation

Journal entry to record the depreciation charge in year 1

Date	Account	Ref	Debit	Credit
17 July	Depreciation	GL	5, 000	
	Accumulated Depreciation	GL		5, 000
	(Being depreciation expense for the year on the lorry)			

Assets	=	Liabilities	+	Shareholders' Equity	
–5,000	=	0	+	–5,000.	[Depreciation expense]

In our example, the depreciation schedule under this method is as follows:

Year	Carrying Amount Beginning of year x	Depreciation Rate	Annual Depreciation Charge	Accumulated Depreciation	Carrying amount [NBV]
1	16, 000	40 %	6, 400	6, 400	9, 600
2	9, 600	40 %	3, 840	10, 240	5, 760
3	5, 760	40 %	2, 304	12, 544	3, 456
4	3, 456	40 %	1, 382	13, 926	2, 074
5	2, 074	-	1, 074	15, 000	1, 000

The reducing balance method avoids the entire problem of arriving at the residual value. This method differs from other methods in two ways:

i. First year depreciation is calculated on the asset's full acquisition cost at the accelerated rate of 40 %. Residual value is usually ignored initially in calculating the depreciation charge.

ii. Depreciation charge in the final year is an adjusted amount RM 1, 074 (plugged) needed to reduce the carrying amount to the residual value, which is RM 1, 000.

An alternative way of calculating the depreciation rate (r) is using a formula:

$$r = 100\left(1 - \sqrt[n]{\frac{s}{c}}\right)$$

Where n = useful life of the asset, s = the residual value or scrap value and c = cost of the asset

$$\text{Using the same figures, } r = 100\left(1 - \sqrt[5]{\frac{1,000}{16,000}}\right)$$

$$= 42.57\%$$

Depreciation charge is allocated as follows:

		RM
	Cost	16, 000
Year 1	Depreciation 42.57 % × 16, 000	(6, 811)
		9, 189**
Year 2	42.57 % × 9, 189 **	(3, 912)
		5, 277
Year 3	42.57 % × 5, 277	(2, 246)
		3, 031
Year 4	42.57 % × 3, 031	(1, 290)
		1, 741
Year 5	42.57 % × 1, 741	(741)
	Residual value (Scrap value).	1, 000

** The figure RM 9, 189 is described as the reducing or diminishing value. Hence, it is called 'reducing balance method'.

The depreciation rate derived from the formula appears to be 42.57 % but the previous exercise calculates this to be 40 %. Unlike the earlier version, the use of 42.57 % as annual depreciation rate correctly results in the residual amount of RM 1, 000. The previous depreciation schedule in year 5 needs to be adjusted by 'plugging' the amount, this being the only difference in the two methods. The depreciation charges differ by each year under both methods but in total the amount of depreciation to RM 15, 000, this is a matter of allocation.

Either method is equally acceptable as an accounting policy but the importance lies in the consistency of accounting treatment. The formula method to arrive at the depreciation rate of 42.57 % is commonly an adopted British accounting practice.

c. Units of Production Method

Under this method, useful life of the asset is expressed in terms of the total units of production or units of activity or usage expected from the asset rather than the passage of time. This method is more appropriately used in a manufacturing environment, suited to plant and machinery as production is based on units of output or in machine hours. This method is also suited for such assets used in delivery or transportation where the activity levels are based upon mileage or days on the road or hours driven by aircraft.

Entities estimate the total units of activity for the entire useful life of the asset and then divide these units into depreciable cost, thus resulting in a depreciation cost per unit. The depreciation cost per unit is then multiplied by the units of actual activity for the period to determine the annual depreciation charge.

Annual depreciation charge = Depreciation cost per unit × Units of production or activity for the period

$$\text{Depreciation cost per unit} = \frac{\text{Depreciation cost}}{\text{Total units of production or activity}}$$

In our example, the activity level is taken to represent usage in days. Total usage in days = 250 + 200 + 150 + 150 = 75 = 825 days

$$\text{Depreciation cost per day} = \frac{16{,}000 - 1{,}000}{825} = \text{RM } 18.18 \text{ per day}$$

Journal entry to record the depreciation charge for year 1

		RM		RM
Depreciation	Dr	4, 545		
Accumulated Depreciation			Cr	4, 545
(Being depreciation expense for the year)				

Assets	=	Liabilities	+	Shareholders' Equity	
–5,000	=	0	+	–5,000.	[Depreciation expense]

Asset Year	Usage Days ×	Depreciation Cost per unit	Annual Charge	Accumulated Depreciation	Carrying Amount [NBV]
1	250	18.18	4, 545	4, 545	11, 455
2	200	18.18	3, 636	8, 181	7, 819
3	150	18.18	2, 727	10, 908	5, 092
4	150	18.18	2, 727	13, 635	2, 365
5	75	18.18	1, 365	15, 000	1, 000

d. Sum of Digits Method

Under this method, the depreciation amount is allocated in the following manner. The method begins by adding up the years of expected useful life. The sum of digits method assumes more of the depreciable amount of the tangible asset should be allocated in the earlier years. Compared to the reducing balance method, the sum of digits method avoids extreme depreciation charges as can be seen in the annual depreciation expense going down by RM 1, 000 for each year. However, this method is rarely used in practice because of its mathematical novelty and moreover, it does not match close to reality. We need to determine the cost, estimate the useful and the residual value (if any) of the asset. Then count down from the number of years of useful life as follows:

Assume the same facts as before:

Say, given useful life of 5 years, this sums up to be 15 (5 +4 +3 + 2 + 1)

Depreciable amount = RM (16, 000 – 1, 000) = RM 15, 000

We calculate the annual depreciation charge for each year to be:

	RM
Year 1	$5/15 \times 15,000 = 5,000$
2	$4/15 \times 15,000 = 4,000$
3	$3/15 \times 15,000 = 3,000$
4	$2/15 \times 15,000 = 2,000$
5	$1/15 \times 15,000 = 1,000$

The journal entry for the depreciation charge will be repeated in the same manner and the impact on the accounting equation also gives the same effect as for the previous methods, the only difference is the magnitude in the calculated amounts.

Depreciation Methods Compared

Identify the circumstances where different methods of depreciation would be appropriate. The schedule of depreciation charges under different methods and their effect (impact) on profits are shown below:

Year	SLM	RBM		Production Units	Sum of Digits Method
	RM	RM	RM	RM	RM
1	3, 000	6, 400	6, 811	4, 545	5, 000
2	3, 000	3, 840	3, 912	3, 636	4, 000
3	3, 000	2, 304	2, 216	2, 727	3, 000
4	3, 000	1, 382	1, 290	2, 727	2, 000
5	3, 000	1, 074	741	1, 365	1, 000
	15, 000	15, 000	15, 000	15, 000	15, 000

The overall effect on profit for the entire five-year period is the same for all the methods. However, the allocation or distribution of depreciation charges for each year within the entire five-year period is obviously different. The profits of individual years will differ according to which depreciation method is adopted as an accounting policy. Comparing the depreciation charges between the straight line method and the reducing balance method, you tend to see the amount of charge is uniformly fixe each year under the straight line method whereas the reducing balance figures are not the same. The depreciation amount appears abnormally higher in the earlier years when compared to later years as the figures have a tapering effect. The 'extremes' suggest that the asset usage in early years are heavy, perhaps reflecting on the nature of use and consumption pattern of the asset, thus justifying the use of the method. This method appears more relevant and appropriate in the circumstances and conditions of the operating nature of the business. You may also note some variation of the two set of depreciation figures under the RBM due to calculation assumptions, one using the accelerating rate of 40 % and the other using a depreciation rate of 42.57 % based on the formula method. The sum of digits method is also similar to the reducing balance method because the amount of depreciation charge declines uniformly in stepped fashion. Because of the novelty, this method is rarely adopted in practice as preference is given more to the reducing balance method. On the other hand, manufacturing businesses owing to the nature of their type of activities, are more inclined in using production methods that suit them because the depreciation charge reflects more appropriately to their manufacturing requirements and usage of the asset.

Choice of Depreciation Methods

The choice of depreciation method adopted by an entity will clearly impact on its profit. So, the question is which depreciation method is appropriate or suitable that reflects on the pattern of consumption of economic benefits accruing to the entity from the use of the asset? In other words, the choice of the appropriate method should therefore be specific to each class of tangible fixed asset based upon entity's management understanding of the consumption pattern associated with the asset itself. In choosing a method, consideration should also be based on being rational and systematic. These conditions are met if the selected method of depreciation is decided at the date of acquisition and applied to all assets of one class or homogenous category.

Further, the Standard says, an entity should review the depreciation method at the end of each reporting period so that there is no significant change has occurred in the nature and pattern of consumption. Where this is the case, the entity should continue to apply the method consistently from one accounting period to the next accounting period. Consistency is important

Obviously for PPE assets with a constant or fixed pattern of consumption of economic benefits to be gained, the allocation basis should be done using the straight line method as this appears reasonably appropriate The reducing balance method which tends to accelerate the depreciation process fits best to those PPE assets that has the effect of generating more depreciation charge with increasing revenue earlier in their useful lives as compared to lesser amounts in later years. The units of production method such as the machine hour rate or some other actual output rate [based on the usage pattern], is a much better fit for those PPE assets that wears out because of physical use rather than obsolescence. These methods are used more in a manufacturing environment. The sum of digits method obviously is time based but it is not frequently resorted by entities as other methods are favored. Furthermore, the tax authorities rarely allow this method.

Survey results that emerged from the study of companies and their accounting policies on depreciation methods indicate that a significant majority of these companies use the straight line method of depreciation. The survey results also indicate that a significant number of these companies also use more than one method of depreciation. The reducing balance method is also another common and popular method used but selectively only few companies resort to using this accounting policy.

Table: Illustrating the Main Depreciation Methods

Time-based methods	**Methods based on activity level produced or consumed (or service level or level of use)**
Straight Line	Production output
Reducing balance	Service quantity
Sum of digits	
Depreciation charge or expense primarily determined regardless of the level of activity during the period	Depreciation expense is the result of the multiplication of a constant depreciation rate per unit of activity times the number of units of activity consumed or produced during the period

Accounting for Natural Resources

Land is normally stated at its acquisition cost and is not subject to any depreciation. Theoretically, land is not consumed through use, or wears out and the chances of it becoming obsolete are a distinct possibility. There are cases however, where land becomes a depreciable asset. In such cases, the land is acquired as a **natural resource** for industrial and commercial purposes. Examples of such cases are a quarry, a mine, an oil field or a natural gas well. It is important to note that the acquisition cost does not relate to the land surface but to the volume of non-renewable natural resources embedded beneath it. Timber extraction is another natural resource but it's a renewable resource [replanted] that can be exploited for generating revenue. Natural resources are a special type of PPE Being in the nature of wasting assets, natural resource assets are consumed for productive potential. For instance, the extraction of raw materials such as timber or minerals either to be used by the entity to make something into a finished product or sold in a raw state to other businesses.

Depletion

Depletion is a specific term used for the consumption of an asset of a wasting resource. As such, natural resources assets are expensed through depletion. Depletion expense is calculated in the same way as depreciation. In such cases, the calculation for depletion is determined normally on a unit consumption basis that is proportional to the output extracted in relation to the estimated life capacity of the deposits. The exploitation of natural resources such as timber extraction, mining operations, quarrying, extraction of oil for petroleum and natural gas come under this recognized heading of depletion. In all these cases, exploitation of the resource reduces the potential for further future exploitation.

Illustrative example

An oil lease, say may cost Petronas Carigali millions of ringgit with a capacity for extracting 15, 000 barrels of oil. The depletion rate is RM 25 per barrel. If 2, 000 barrels are extracted from the oil field next year.

The cost incurred for that period is RM 50, 000.

Journal entry to record the depletion expense:

	Debit	Credit
	RM	RM
Depletion expense	50, 000	
Accumulated depletion		50, 000
(Being depletion expense on oil extraction).		

You may note this topic is not mentioned as part of the syllabus requirement and therefore the topic can be ignored. The information is provided for illustrative purposes.

Impairment of Assets

An agreed principle in accounting practice is that assets normally should not be carried at above their realizable value. If the **carrying amount [net book value]** of an asset in the accounts is higher than its realistic or intrinsic value, measured as its *'recoverable amount'*, the asset is said to have suffered an **impairment loss.** The **asset's value** should therefore be reduced by the amount of the impairment loss. Consequently, the asset's carrying amount **is** then **written down** to its recoverable amount. **Recoverable amount** is higher of the asset's fair value less costs of disposal and value-in-use. The amount of the impairment loss is recognized immediately as an expense and is written-off in the profit or loss statement. Impairment losses could be triggered off by special events and are not normally caused by depreciation factors. Indications of a possible impairment of assets can trigger off due to several external or internal factors. For example, **a fall in the asset's market value** would be more significant than would normally be expected from the passage of time over normal use.

A prime example of this triggered event happened in 2008 when the electronic giant, Toshiba had to abandon producing the HD-DVD format due to a severe drop in demand as major customers such as Wal-Mart, Warner Brothers and others stopped placing their orders causing heavy and substantial losses in sales revenue and investment in manufacturing facilities. Sony's Blu-ray became the new industry standard format. Toshiba experienced significant problems and issues prior to exiting from the HD-DVD market. So, this is how an asset is subject to impairment causing a significant loss in the value of the asset.

Another example emerging would be from an internal source where an entity's asset could be impaired due to adverse changes in the use to which the asset is put or the asset's economic performance has worsened.

IAS 36 – *Impairment of Assets***,** provides detailed guidance for carrying out impairment reviews, the exact determination of recoverable amount, and the many other aspects of impairment of assets including the related accounting treatments and disclosures. This topic is treated more extensively in our written textbook - volume 2 as it is beyond the scope of an introductory accounting course. Anyway, students at this stage of their studies are expected to be aware of the basic concepts of impairment of assets. During the financial crisis, for various economic reasons many companies apparently have reported impairment losses in billions and the impact of these losses may have had a material effect on the financial performance of these entities.

Example to illustrate

Suppose, as a result of an impairment review at the end of the reporting period, the carrying amount of a factory's plant and machinery was RM 3 million, the fair value less cost of disposal was RM 2.5 million and the value-in-use was RM 2.8 million.

Required

i. Determine the impairment loss arising from the review exercise

ii. Show both the journal and ledger account entries.

Solution

First, we estimate the recoverable amount to be RM 2. 8 million [based on higher of the two amounts]. The factory's management would then recognize an impairment loss of RM 0.2 million.

		RM
Carrying amount [CA] of the asset		3.0
Recoverable amount [RA] is **higher** of		
i. Fair value less costs of disposal	2.5	
ii. Value in use	2.8	(2.8)
Impairment loss [CA > RA] =		0.2

An impairment loss is reported as an expense (just as depreciation charge) in the statement of profit or loss.

Journal entry to record the impairment loss	Debit	Credit
Impairment loss – plant and machinery	0. 2 m	
Accumulated impairment losses		0.2 m
(Being impairment loss on factory's machinery)		

IAS 36 allows for the reversal of impairment losses under certain restricting conditions but since this is beyond the scope of your syllabus, the topic can be ignored. It is included here to give students some background knowledge about what it is all about. However, the topic will be extensively dealt in our forthcoming textbook on **Financial Reporting.**

Accounting for Disposal of Assets

Tangible fixed assets or PPE eventually cease to serve an entity's business needs. This event usually can take place at any time during their useful life and in such circumstances the entity often disposes the asset. The asset may wear out or become obsolete or physically damaged through improper handling and maintenance.

Companies dispose PPE in three ways:

i. By retiring the asset – usually scrapping or discarding it as a fully depreciated asset with nil or zero net book value. In such cases the asset physically is no longer asset.

ii. By outright sale – sold to another party for some money consideration where a gain or a loss on disposal is reported in the profit or loss statement.

iii. By exchange – say, existing equipment is traded-in for new equipment where the old equipment is removed from the books of account and the new equipment is recorded as an asset.

We will deal with outright sale of PPE items although the other forms of disposal do not frequently occur. Some assets due to natural disasters, floods, fire, etc. are lost and cannot be salvaged which in such cases are written off at a loss in the accounts although they are rare events.

Accounting issues on Disposal

Fully depreciated assets

What happens if a fully depreciated asset is still used in the business? In this case, the asset and its accumulated depreciation continue to be reported in the statement of financial position without any further adjustment for depreciation charge. In order to verify the usage of the fully depreciated asset and its continued physical existence, common accounting practice is to state the asset's carrying amount in the balance sheet to be equivalent to RM 1 only. Upon its eventual retirement the company removes the asset from its books of account.

Partially depreciated assets

When long-lived assets are sold before the expiry of their useful lives, the difference between their carrying amounts [net book value] and the disposal or sale proceeds [or selling price] either results in a gain or a loss. This gain or loss from the sale or disposal of the asset is reported separately in the profit or loss statement and treated accordingly in the cash flow statement. Gains increase net income in the same way as revenue and losses decrease net income exactly as expenses do.

We need to match the sale proceeds with the asset's carrying amount before determining the gain or the loss on disposal:

		RM
i.e.	Sale or disposal proceeds	x
	Less: Carrying amount [net book value]	
	Cost	x
	Less: Accumulated depreciation	(x)
	Accumulated impairment losses [if any]	(x)
	Carrying amount	x
	Gain/(Loss).	x/(x)

If the sale proceeds exceed the carrying amount of the asset, a gain on disposal is reported. If the sale proceed is lower than the carrying amount of the asset, a loss on disposal is reported.

Entities have a choice in the accounting policy to be adopted for the treatment of depreciation charge or expense. This policy should be decided at the commencement when the asset was acquired and brought into use. In practice, most companies tend not to depreciate in the year of disposal but full depreciation is charged in the year of acquisition. Where this accounting policy is adopted consistently, no issue arises as the reporting of gains or losses on sale of asset will be the same regardless of accounting policy. Some companies charge and record depreciation up to the date of sale or disposal when the asset is removed from the accounting books. Either accounting treatment is acceptable in practice so long as the policy adopted is consistently applied. To account for disposal, the asset and its related accumulated depreciation and accumulated impairment losses [if any] should be removed from the books of account in the general ledger.

Example to illustrate

Suppose, an entity disposes an item of plant and equipment for RM 9 600 that cost RM 22, 750 on acquisition. The asset's accumulated depreciation is RM 13, 650. No impairment loss was reported previously in the books.

Required

a. Show the gain or loss from the sale of the asset
b. Show the accounting entries in the ledger accounts.
c. Show how the relevant entries are treated in the statement of cash flow.

Solution

a. Disposal of asset

First determine what is the carrying amount of the asset at the date of disposal before comparing it with the disposal proceeds to find the gain or loss on sale of the asset.

		RM
Disposal proceeds		9, 600
Less:		
Cost	22, 750	
Accumulated depreciation	13, 650	
Carrying amount.		(9, 100)
Gain on disposal		500

b. Ledger accounts (All in RM)

Plant and Equipment – at Cost

Balance b/f	x	Transfer to Asset Disposal A/c	22, 750
		Balance c/f	x

Accumulated Depreciation – Plant & Equipment

Transfer to Asset Disposal A/c	18,650	Balance b/f	x
Balance c/f	x		

Asset Disposal Account

Cost	22, 750	Accumulated depreciation	18, 650
Gain on disposal	500	Bank: proceeds from sale	9, 600

The gain (profit) on disposal of plant and equipment will be reported in the statement of profit or loss.

c. Entries in Cash Flow Statement

Only two entries on asset disposal are disclosed in the cash flow statement.

Extract:

Statement of Cash Flows

	RM
Cash Flows from Operating Activities	
Adjustments for non-cash items	
Gain from disposal of plant and equipment	500
Cash Flows from Investing Activities	
Proceeds from sale of plant and equipment	9, 600

Tutorial notes

i. Gain or profit on disposal is added back under operating activities. Loss is subtracted.
ii. Sale proceeds is a cash flow to be included under investing activities.

De-recognition of PPE

According to IAS Sixteen, PPE should be de-recognized [removed from books] either on disposal or when no future economic benefits are expected from the asset. In other words, the asset is effectively scrapped and therefore no longer exists physically. In the case of disposals, the usual accounting treatment [using the cost or revaluation model] has already been dealt earlier. The net profit or loss on disposal is included in the statement of comprehensive income. The sale proceeds should not be recognized as revenue but is shown in the statement of cash flow as an investing activity. [see below]

Where assets are measured using the revaluation model, any remaining balance in the revaluation reserve relating to the asset disposed of is transferred directly to retained earnings. No recycling of this balance into the statement of other comprehensive is permitted.

Reporting PPE Transactions on the Statement of Cash Flow

Basically three main types of transactions relating to non-current assets are reported on the statement of cash flow:

1. Acquisitions of non-current assets including PPE and others
2. Disposals or sale of assets and
3. Depreciation including amortization and depletion

Acquisitions and sale of PPE and intangible assets (disposal proceeds) are investing activities. As entities invest in PPE, the payments for PPE is a relates to **investing activities** that appear in the cash flow statement. The sale proceeds from disposal is a cash flow item as cash is realized when the asset is sold. The profit or loss on disposal is reported in the statement of comprehensive income under **'other income'** but because this is only a computed amount, it is normally **adjusted as a non-cash item** and accordingly, it is classified under **operating activities** in the statement of cash flow.

The required entries relating to PPE transactions are shown in the following statement of cash flows:

Cash Flow Statement [Indirect Method] for the year ended 31 December 2016

Extract

	RM	RM
Cash Flows from Operating Activities		
Profit before taxation		
Adjustments for non-cash items:		
Depreciation and amortization	x	
Profit from disposal of PPE	(x)	
Net Cash from Operating Activities		x

Cash Flows from Investing Activities		
Purchase of PPE	(x)	
Proceeds from sale of PPE	x	
Purchase of intangible assets	(x)	
Other investing activities		
Net Cash from Investing Activities		x/(x)
Cash Flows from Financing Activities -		
Net Increase/(Decrease) in Cash and Cash Equivalents		x/(x)

Reporting of Balances and Movement in Non-Current Tangible assets

The disclosure notes to the financial statements should be reporting the balances and movements in tangible fixed assets, by identifying:

i. The cost or gross value of the tangible fixed assets [for each major class of depreciable assets]; and

ii. The corresponding changes in accumulated depreciation and accumulated impairment losses.

Both these requirements are normally reported in a single statement. Such a statement is shown in table below:

Extract

Cost or Valuation	Land and Buildings	Plant and Machinery	Office Equipment	Assets under Leases	Motor Vehicles Total
Balance b/f					
Additions					
Revaluation					
Disposals					
Assets reclassified as held for sale					
Exchange differences					
Balance c/f					

Accumulated Depreciation and Impairment Losses†
Balance b/f
Depreciation charge for the year
Retirements/transfers
Disposals
Impairment†
Assets reclassified as held for sale
Exchange differences
Balance c/f

Net Book Value

At year end date (current year)

At year end date (last year)

The carrying amount is the net book value as shown in the total column which is net amount reported in the statement of financial position of the company.

† Impairment losses is listed here for information purposes only but it is beyond the scope of this course.

IAS 16 Disclosure requirements

The accounting standard has a long list of disclosure requirements for each class of PPE. For each major class of depreciable asset, the following details are required to be disclosed.

a. Measurement basis used for determining the gross carrying amount
b. Depreciation methods used
c. Useful lives or the depreciation rates used
d. Total depreciation allocated for the period
e. The gross carrying amount and the accumulated depreciation [aggregated with accumulated impairment losses] at the beginning and end of the period; and
f. Reconciliation of the carrying amount at the beginning and end of the period showing:
    i. Additions
    ii. Disposals
    iii. Acquisitions through business combinations
    iv. Increases or decreases resulting from revaluations and from impairment losses recognized or reversed directly in equity

v. Impairment losses recognized in profit or loss

vi. Impairment losses reversed in profit or loss

vi. Depreciation

vii. Net exchange differences arising from translation of the financial statements from the functional currency into the presentation home currency including the translation of a foreign operation into presentation currency of the reporting entity; and

ix. Others

The financial statements are also required to state the following:

a. Any recoverable amounts of property, plant and equipment
b. Any restrictions of title including existence and amounts and items pledged as security for liabilities
c. Accounting policy for the estimated costs of restoring the site
d. Amounts of expenditures on account of items in the course of construction
e. Amount of capital commitments on acquisitions

Additional disclosures are also encouraged by the standard where information can exemplify the user's understanding.

Chapter Summary

1. **Non-current assets** are long-lived assets that have finite or limited useful lives. Property, plant and equipment (PPE) are **tangible fixed assets** owned and controlled by the business entity as revenue generating assets. As these assets extend over more than one accounting period and through the passage of time and business usage, wears out over time. As such, it becomes necessary to **allocate (or apportion) the depreciable amount** of the assets **on a systematic and rational basis over its economic useful life** as the asset is consumed in the business. The only exception is **land** that is held on freehold which does not undergo depreciation because of unlimited useful life.

2. **Allocating depreciation on PPE**

   Three issues are crucial when determining the allocation of depreciation. Cost, estimated useful live, and estimated residual value. **Cost** is a known amount under initial measurement when the asset was acquired. In **estimating the useful life** of an asset, a number of factors to be considered are (i) expected usage, (ii) physical tear and wear of the asset, (iii) obsolescence due to technological advances or improvements in production that affects the product and service output of the asset, and (iv) legal encumbrances on the use of the asset that restricts the usage or capacity of the asset. The **residual value** (or scrap value) of the asset in most cases are negligible as the asset would have reached its mature period of usage and therefore its future economic substance can become of lesser importance. Only **residual values of huge assets may have some material impact on the inflow of cash resources.** Residual value of an asset can be enhanced if the entity decides to keep and use the asset for a longer period if substantial expenditure on repairs and maintenance can be undertaken to improve its economic value, thus revising its residual value.

3. **Methods for calculating depreciation**

   The depreciation charge or expense of a PPE can be calculated using a number of methods commonly used by business entities. The main methods are (i) Straight line, (ii) Reducing balance, (iii) Actual usage or Units of production. Companies tend to use one or more methods in combination suited to their circumstances and conditions of business. The **entity's management selects the method that it considers as most appropriate measure on the asset's contribution to revenue and profits**. The sum of digits method is least favored among the methods because the RBM is a better option that closely suits the requirements of the nature and purpose of the business. Detailed examples are provided in text that explain how depreciation charges are calculated under these respective methods. Management of the entity decides on the relevant **accounting policy** to be adopted with regards to depreciation of PPE items. Accounting policy adopted by the entity normally considers the **appropriateness and choice of the depreciation method that suitably reflects on the pattern of consumption of economic benefits from the use of the asset.**

4. **Accounting for disposal and retirement of assets**

   Tangible fixed assets or PPE eventually cease to serve the organization's business needs. At this point, a business entity can **dispose PPE in three ways**: (i) by retiring the asset with no further use and discarding it as a fully depreciated asset, (ii) by outright sale to another party for a profit or loss, and (iii) by exchange on trade-in for a new asset where the old asset is removed from the books of account. In all such cases, the **disposal of assets are fully accounted** for in the accounting records. In the case of **fully depreciated assets that are retired, the company removes the asset** from the books of account whereas on **partially depreciated assets**, the **disposals will report gains or losses in the profit or loss statement with cash flow implications in the statement of cash flow.**

5. **Disclosure requirements**

   The accounting standard **requires disclosure for each major class of PPE** (depreciable assets) the **measurement basis used** for determining the gross carrying amount of asset, depreciation methods used useful lives or depreciation rates, total depreciation allocated for the accounting period, the gross carrying amount and the accumulated useful depreciation and impairment losses at the beginning and end of period. **Reconciliation** of **the carrying amount at the beginning and end of the period** with regard to additions, disposals, increases or decreases resulting from revaluations, impairment losses recognized in profit or loss including any losses reversed in profit or loss, depreciation. **The financial statements are also required to state** any recoverable amounts of PPE, any restrictions of title, items pledged as security for liabilities, accounting policy for the estimated costs of restoring site, amount of capital commitments on acquisitions, including amounts of expenditures on items in the course of construction.

Key Terms

Accumulated depreciation
Accounting policy
Asset disposal account
Accelerated depreciation method
Amortization
Asset's carrying amount
Capital expenditure
Accumulated impairment losses
Non-current assets
Assets held under leases
Sum of Digits depreciation
Units of production method of depreciation
Tangible fixed assets
Net book value (carrying amount)

Change in an accounting estimate

Cost

Depletion

Depreciation

De-recognition of assets

Estimated residual value

Gain or loss on disposal of asset

Impairment

Limited useful life

Obsolescence

Reducing balance method depreciation

Straight line method depreciation

Recoverable amount of an asset

Fair value less disposal cost of an asset

Value-in-use of an asset

Depreciable cost of an asset

Estimated useful life

Enhancements

Freehold land and building

Indefinite life

Natural resources

Property, plant and equipment (PPE)

Revenue expenditure

Review Questions

1. PPE items are reported in the statement of financial position at their *'carrying amounts' or 'net book values.'* How do you arrive at the asset's carrying amount or the net book value?
2. IAS 16 requires the depreciable amount of a depreciable asset to be allocated on a systematic and rational basis to each accounting period during the useful life of the asset.
   a. Define depreciable amount
   b. Explain and justify the rationale for providing depreciation
   c. Briefly discuss the factors that trigger depreciation
3. What accounting concepts or principles are applied to the process of depreciation? Explain why?
4. There are three major issues that need to be considered before allocating depreciation on depreciable assets.
   a. State what are these issues?
   b. Briefly discuss why these issues or factors are important in the allocation process of depreciation on PPE
5. Explain why IAS 16 requires the annual year-end review of an asset's:-
   a. Estimated useful life; and
   b. Estimated residual value.
6. The depreciation charge of a PPE item is normally calculated using an appropriate method of depreciation that reflects best on the asset's usage and purpose.
   a. You are required to state and briefly describe four common methods of depreciation that an entity may select or choose to apply on its PPE.
   b. Compare and contrast these methods of depreciation.
7. Discuss with reasons, in what circumstances the reducing balance method is more appropriate than the straight line method?
8. The straight line method of depreciation appears to be the most popular and common method adopted by big and small entities. Explain with reason, why this depreciation method is a preferred choice?

9. The choice of depreciation method adopted is a matter of accounting policy that may have an impact on profits reported by companies in their financial statements.,. Describe some of the reasons for the choice of depreciation method.
10. Distinguish between depletion and depreciation in the context of natural resources
11. a. How does an impairment loss arises on an item of PPE.? Define what is the recoverable amount of an asset?
    b. Identify at least two factors that trigger the impairment of PPE
    c. How an impairment loss is reported in the accounts?
12. An asset ceases to serve an entity's needs when it reaches its economic useful life which at this point, the owner-entity basically has three ways to dispose it.
13. a. State the three ways in which the asset can be disposed.
    b. What do you understand by the term *'De-recognition'*?
14. How the gain or loss on disposal of an asset is determined?
15. Explain how you deal with the accounting issues on disposal with regard to:
    a. Fully depreciated assets?
    b. Partially depreciated assets?
16. How the disposal of an asset is reported in the statement of cash flow?
17. PPE items are reported in the statement of financial position at their *'carrying amounts' or 'net book values.'* How do you arrive at the asset's carrying amount or the net book value?
18. IAS 16 requires the depreciable amount of a depreciable asset to be allocated on a systematic and rational basis to each accounting period during the useful life of the asset.
    a. Define depreciable amount
    b. Explain and justify the rationale for providing depreciation
    c. Briefly discuss the factors that trigger depreciation
19. What accounting concepts or principles are applied to the process of depreciation? Explain why?
20. There are three major issues that need to be considered before allocating depreciation on depreciable assets.
    a. State what are these issues?
    b. Briefly discuss why these issues or factors are important in the allocation process of depreciation on PPE
21. Explain why IAS 16 requires the annual year-end review of an asset's:-
    a. Estimated useful life; and
    b. Estimated residual value.
22. The depreciation charge of a PPE item is normally calculated using an appropriate method of depreciation that reflects best on the asset's usage and purpose.
    a. You are required to state and briefly describe four common methods of depreciation that an entity may select or choose to apply on its PPE.
    b. Compare and contrast these methods of depreciation.
23. Discuss with reasons, in what circumstances the reducing balance method is more appropriate than the straight line method?

24. The straight line method of depreciation appears to be the most popular and common method adopted by big and small entities. Explain with reason, why this depreciation method is a preferred choice?
25. The choice of depreciation method adopted is a matter of accounting policy that may have an impact on profits reported by companies in their financial statements.,. Describe some of the reasons for the choice of depreciation method.
26. Distinguish between depletion and depreciation in the context of natural resources.
27. a. How does an impairment loss arises on an item of PPE.? Define what is the recoverable amount of an asset?
    b. Identify at least two factors that trigger the impairment of PPE
    c. How an impairment loss is reported in the accounts?
28. An asset ceases to serve an entity's needs when it reaches its economic useful life which at this point, the owner-entity basically has three ways to dispose it.
29. a. State the three ways in which the asset can be disposed.
    b. What do you understand by the term *'De-recognition'*?
30. How the gain or loss on disposal of an asset is determined?
31. Explain how you deal with the accounting issues on disposal with regard to
    a. Fully depreciated assets?
    b. Partially depreciated assets?
32. How the disposal of an asset is reported in the statement of cash flow?

Multiple Choice Questions

Select the right answer with only one possible answer.

Q1. The most appropriate method of depreciation for land is

- a. The straight line method
- b. The reducing balance method
- c. Either methods of (a) or (b) is equally acceptable
- d. None of the above

Q2. Depreciation will result in

- a. A decrease in both assets and reported profits
- b. An increase in cash
- c. A decrease in equity
- d. A decrease in liabilities
- e. An increase in assets and a decrease reported profits

Q3. Which of the following items would not be considered a PPE?

- a. Plant and machinery
- b. Patents and trademarks
- c. Research and development
- d. Oil well
- e. Software development

f. Leased assets

g. Building

a. 2 and 3

b. 3 and 5

c. 2, 3, 4 and 5

d. 2, 3, and 5

e. 2, 3, 5, and 6

Q4. Examples of tangible fixed assets include land, buildings, equipment and vehicles

a. True

b. False

Q5. Business entities can use only one method of depreciation for all of its depreciable assets

a. True

b. False

Q6. When using the reducing (or accelerating) balance method in calculating the annual depreciation charge, the depreciation rate is multiplied by the

a. Purchased cost of the asset

b. Depreciable amount

c. Carrying amount (net book value) at the beginning of the year

d. Fair value of the asset at the beginning of the year

e. The recoverable amount of the asset after impairment loss.

Q7. The process of allocating the cost of natural resources to expense as they are consumed each year is called

a. Depreciation

b. Amortization

c. Depletion

d. Exhaustion cost

e. None of the above

Q8. Which statement is false?

a. Depreciation is a process of allocating the cost of PPE over its useful life.

b. Depreciation is based on the matching principle because it matches the cost of the asset with the revenue generated over the asset's useful life

c. The cost of an asset minus accumulated depreciation equals the asset's net book value

d. Depreciation creates a fund to replace the asset at the end of its useful life

Q9. A company acquired a small lorry for RM 48, 000 on 1 January 2020. The lorry is estimated to have a useful life of 5 years with a scrap value worth RM 3, 000. The company's accounting policy on depreciation for vehicles is based on a straight-line method. What is the annual depreciation expense on the lorry for the year ended 31 December 2020?

a. RM 8, 500 b. RM 9, 600 e. RM 12, 000

c. RM 9, 000 d. RM 9, 500

Q10. Assuming in Q9, the lorry was used only for 4 years and on 1 January 2025, the company disposed the vehicle for RM 8, 500. What profit or loss would be reported in its accounts.?

a. RM 3, 500 gain
b. RM 3, 500 loss
c. RM 4, 800 gain
d. RM 4, 000 loss
e. RM 8, 500 gain

Q11. A company sold plant and equipment that originally cost RM 225, 000 for RM 95, 000, when the accumulated depreciation stood at RM 75, 000. What profit or loss on sale would the company be reporting in its profit or loss statement?

a. RM 55, 000 loss
b. RM 95, 000 gain
c. RM 55, 000 gain
d. No gain No loss
e. RM 150, 000 loss

Q12. A company bought plant and equipment for RM 150, 000 on 1 July 2020, to be used in its manufacturing process. The asset has a useful life of 8 years and an estimated residual value of RM 10, 000. What is the depreciation charge on the plant and equipment for the year ended 30 June 2021, assuming the company uses the reducing balancing method as its accounting policy for this type of depreciable asset? (Use the formula method to estimate the depreciation charge)

a. 38, 707
b. 42, 500
c. 43, 080
d. 30, 707
e. 21, 888

The essence of risk management lies in maximising the areas where he has some control over the outcome while minimising the areas he has absolutely no control over the outcome and the linkage between effects and cause is hidden from us.

– Peter Bernstein, 1996

Appendix

Useful Definitions on Depreciation

Depreciation is the systematic allocation of the depreciable amount of an asset over its estimated useful life. Depreciation for the accounting period is charged to net profit or loss either directly or indirectly.

Accumulated depreciation is the cumulative amount of depreciation charged since the initial recognition and measurement of an asset.

Depreciable assets are assets which:

- Are expected to be used for more than one accounting period
- Have a limited useful life
- Are held by an entity for use in the production or supply of goods and services, for rental to others, or for administrative purposes

Useful life is one of two things,

- The period over which a depreciable asset is expected to be used by the entity, or
- The number of production or similar units expected to be obtained from the asset by the entity.

The **depreciable amount** of a depreciable asset is the historical cost or other amount substituted for cost in the financial statements, less the estimated residual value.

The **depreciation method** used should reflect the pattern in which the asset's economic benefits are consumed by the entity.

The **depreciation charge** for each period should be recognized as **an expense** unless it is included in the carrying amount of another asset.

Chapter 11

Learning Outcomes

Understand the choice of two valuation models for PPE: the cost model and the revaluation model

Understand the purpose of a revaluation exercise on a non-current asset.

Understand the accounting for a revaluation surplus or deficit

Able to record the revaluation of a non-current asset in ledger accounts

Able to record the revaluation of a non-current asset in the statement of profit or loss and other comprehensive income and in the statement of financial position.

Able to calculate the profit or loss on disposal of a revalued asset

Able to calculate depreciation on a revalued non-current asset including the transfer of excess depreciation between the revaluation surplus and retained earnings

Revaluation and Derecognition of Tangible Fixed Assets

IAS 16/MFRS 116 permits entities the choice of two possible valuation models for PPE:

- **The cost model**

  Carry an asset at cost less accumulated depreciation and accumulated impairment losses: **or**

- **The revaluation model**

  Carry an asset at its fair value at the revaluation date less subsequent accumulated depreciation and accumulated impairment losses.

The Standard stipulates clearly that the **revaluation model** is available only if the **fair value** of the asset can be measured reliably.

Establishing Guidelines for Revaluations

The standard requires each model to be applied consistently to all PPE of the same *"class"*. A class of assets is defined to be a grouping of assets that have a similar nature or function within the entity's operating business. Properties are typically considered an example of one class of tangible assets, and another example would comprise plant and machinery.

If the revaluation model is adopted as an accounting policy, revaluations on a rolling basis is allowed provided the revaluations are kept up to date and should be applied to all assets in the entire class or category. If an entity re-value buildings then it must revalue all land and buildings in that class of assets at the same time and should be completed in a short period of time. Selective revaluation option for certain assets in that class of asset is not allowed by the standard.

The standard does not specify how frequently the assets need to be revalued. However, in practice, some entities revalue their properties at least every five years once or earlier depending on the entity's need or circumstances and the nature of business it is involved. In other words, revaluations are required to be carried out with sufficient regularity so that the carrying amount of the asset does not differ materially compared to that which would be determined using the current fair value at the reporting date.

In the case of plant and equipment, fair value can be based on available quotes on market value. Where a market value is not available it can be substituted by using replacement cost. Market values are not easily available for types of plant and equipment which are sold only rarely. Given the specialized nature of these assets, they are normally sold as part of an ongoing business. So the arm's length negotiation is applied when necessary.

The frequency of valuation depends on the volatility of the fair values of individual items of property, plant and equipment. The more volatile the fair value, the more frequently revaluations should be carried out. This is more of market forces dictating the pricing on fair values. Entities will have the option of deciding if the asset in question requires a revaluation exercise or not. It's a costly affair. Where the current fair value is substantially different from the carrying amount of the asset then a revaluation exercise would prove inevitable and so, should be carried out.

Accounting for Revaluations

Basis of valuation

When the revaluation model is used, assets are carried at their *"fair values"*. In the case of land and buildings, the market value usually represents fair value, assuming existing use and line of business. Such valuations are usually carried out by professional property value consultants.

Definition of fair value

A new definition is given by IFRS as below:

Fair value is the price that would be received to sell an asset or paid to transfer a liability in an orderly transaction between market participants at the measurement date.

The old version of the definition has been changed from 'between knowledgeable, willing buyer and willing seller on an arm's length transaction' to orderly transaction between market participants.

Computation of gains or losses

We can determine if there is a gain [surplus] or loss [deficit] on a revaluation by doing a simple calculation to compare:

Carrying amount of the non-current asset at the revaluation date	x
Valuation of non-current asset at fair value	x
Difference is either a gain or a loss on revaluation	x/(x)

When a revaluation takes place, the depreciation for the period up to the date of revaluation should be deducted from the carrying amount before computing the revaluation surplus or loss.

Accounting treatment

i. Revaluation surplus or gain

Gains or surplus represents an increase in the fair value [market value] of the asset. How is this recognized in the accounts? IAS Sixteen requires the increase or the gain to be recognized in equity under the heading of a revaluation reserve account as *'revaluation surplus'* unless the increase is reversing a previous decrease which was recognized as an expense in the statement of other comprehensive income. To the extent that this offset is made, the increase is recognized as income, any excess amount [remaining portion after offsetting] is then directly credited to equity as revaluation surplus.

The revaluation surplus is classified as an unrealized gain which subsequently becomes realized when the asset is disposed of [or derecognized].

Let's see how the double entry is done below:

Double entry

Dr	Non-current asset cost
	Difference between valuation at FV and Original cost or valuation.
Dr	Accumulated depreciation
	With any historical cost accumulated depreciation
Cr	Revaluation reserve
	Gain or surplus on revaluation

Example: Revaluation surplus

Capital Ideas carried in it's books, a piece of freehold land at RM 600, 000. Capital Ideas reduced the carrying amount from RM 450, 000 when three years ago the company experienced a slump in property values. The revaluation loss was treated as expense in the statement of other comprehensive income. However, in the current year property prices have increased due a surge in demand for land and the company's land is worth RM 730, 000 at the end of the reporting period.

Required

a. Prepare the required journal entries; and

b. Show the revaluation in the current year by updating the ledger accounts.

Solution

Working:		**RM' 000**
Carrying amount of the land at the revaluation date	450	
Valuation at fair value	730	
Surplus on revaluation	280	[Land value goes up this amount]
Less: Loss on revaluation reported 3 years ago (600 – 450).	(150)	
Transfer to equity – remaining revaluation surplus	130	

a. Journal entries to record the transaction

	RM' 000. Dr	RM' 000 Cr
Freehold land [Statement of financial position]	280	
Profit or loss [Statement of other comprehensive income].		150
Revaluation surplus (equity).		130
(Being adjustments resulting from a revaluation exercise.)		

b. Ledger Accounts (RM' 000)

Freehold Land

Balance b/f	450*		
Surplus on revaluation	280	Balance c/f	730

*The previous decrease in value on revaluation would have been adjusted three years ago. The reported figure in the balance brought forward is the current carrying amount.

Revaluation Reserve [Equity]

		Balance b/f	-
Balance c/f	130	Surplus on revaluation	130

Note: The surplus will be shown under **other comprehensive income**.

ii. Revaluation deficit or loss

The case is similar in treatment for a **decrease in value or loss on revaluation.** Any decrease should be recognized as an expense in the statement of other comprehensive income. The only exception to this rule is where a revaluation surplus already exists relating to a previous revaluation of that asset. To that extent, a revaluation loss can be **recognized in equity.** Any decrease in **excess or greater** than the previous revaluation surplus on that asset must be recycled as an expense in the statement of other comprehensive income.

Double entry

Dr Revaluation reserve [to maximum of original gain]

Dr Profit or loss [Statement of other comprehensive income]

Cr Asset [loss on revaluation]

Example: Revaluation decrease or loss

Using the previous example let us simply swap round the amounts given above:

The carrying amount (at valuation) previously reported was RM 730, 000 revalued. Again due to adverse economic factors, the value of the land has fallen to RM 575, 000

Required

a. Journal entries to record the changes in value of the freehold land.

b. Show the ledger accounts to account for the decrease in value.

Solution

See how the net loss on revaluation arises

	RM' 000	
Carrying amount of the land at the revaluation date	730	
Valuation at fair value	575	
Loss on revaluation	(155)	(Value goes down by this amount)
Equity: offset loss on revaluation (maximum of original gain).	130	
Transfer to other comprehensive account (net loss on revaluation).	(25)	

a. **Journal entries to record the transaction**	**RM' 000 Dr**	**RM' 000 Cr**
Profit or loss [Statement of other comprehensive income]	25	
Revaluation reserve (to maximum of original gain).	130	
Freehold land (loss on revaluation).		155
[Being adjustments resulting from a revaluation exercise]		

b. Ledger Accounts (RM' 000)

Freehold Land (at valuation)

Balance b/f	730	Loss on revaluation	155
	___	Balance c/f	575

The previous increase in value on revaluation would have been adjusted three years ago. The reported figure in the balance brought forward is now adjusted downward to RM 575, 000 which is the current carrying amount after adjustment.

Revaluation Reserve [Equity]

Loss on revaluation (maximum).	130	Balance b/f	130
Balance c/f	-		___

Note: The debit to the revaluation loss will be shown under other comprehensive income. The loss will be reflected as RM 130, 000 under revaluation reserve and RM 25, 000 loss under retained earnings, both entries within equity.

What happens when a revalued asset is depreciated?

Revaluation changes the depreciable amount of an asset, so subsequent depreciation charges are affected. An upward revaluation will increase the annual depreciation charge. Under the realization concept, normally a revaluation surplus is only realized when the asset is subsequently sold but when it is being depreciated, part of that surplus is being realized as the asset is used or consumed. The amount of the surplus portion realized is the difference between depreciation charged on the revalued amount and the lower depreciation amount which would have been charged based on the historical cost of the asset. This excess depreciation is a realized portion which can be transferred to retained earnings in equity but not recycled through the profit or loss statement.

IAS 16 **allows [but does not require]** entities to make a transfer of the 'excess depreciation' from the revaluation reserve directly to retained earnings as a movement within equity. Note carefully, **that it is company accounting policy to make a transfer of excess depreciation.**

The asset must continue to be depreciated following the revaluation. After the revaluation the depreciable amount would have changed. **The revalued amount is the depreciable amount which should now be depreciated over the asset's remaining useful economic life.**

Example: Revaluation and depreciation

Roxy Company bought an asset for RM 250, 000 on 1 January 2018. The asset was depreciated with a useful life of 5 years. On January 2020, the asset was revalued to RM 210, 000. The expected useful life has remained unchanged with three years remaining.

Required

a. Account for the revaluation of the asset.

b. Calculate depreciation charge from year 2020 onwards

c. Show the required accounting entries for [i] and [ii] above.

d. Show the related ledger accounts to record the adjusting entries.

c. Show the transfers as a movement in the statement of equity

Solution

a. Account for revaluation

We need to determine first the carrying amount of the asset on January 2020

	RM' 000
Cost on acquisition	250
Less Accumulated Depreciation	
RM 250,000 × 2/5.	(100)
Carrying amount	150
FV of asset at revaluation date	210
Surplus on revaluation	60

Asset value increases by RM 60, 000 which is credited to revaluation reserve in equity.

Journal entry:	Dr	Cr
	RM	RM
Asset account	60, 000	
Revaluation reserve.		60, 000
(Being adjustments to record the surplus on revaluation)		

b. Treatment for depreciation from January onwards

IAS 16 requires the calculation of depreciation charge should be determined using the asset's revalued amount over the asset's remaining useful economic life. So, the depreciation charge for the next three years will be RM 210, 000/3 years = RM 70, 000. Compared to depreciation on cost of RM 250, 000/5 years = RM 50, 000

Excess depreciation is (70–50) = RM 20, 000. So, for each year over the remaining three years, the excess depreciation of RM 20, 000 can be treated as the **realized** portion of the surplus.

Accounting entries as follows:	**RM**	**RM**
	Dr	**Cr**
Depreciation charge (year 3 onwards)	70,000	
Accumulated depreciation		70, 000
Revaluation reserve	20, 000	
Retained earnings.		20, 000

(Being treatment of depreciation charge on revalued amount and excess depreciation in equity)

Note: This annual transfer takes place as a movement in equity only, not a recycled item to be treated in statement of other comprehensive income.

c. Ledger accounts (RM' 000)

Asset Account

Balance b/f	250	Amount derecognized	100
Surplus on revaluation	60	Balance c/f	210

Accumulated Depreciation

Asset account - Amount derecognized	100	Balance b/f	100
Balance c/f	70	Depreciation charge for the year	70

Note: The previous accumulated depreciation amount is **derecognized.** From year 3 onwards, the new depreciation charge is based on the revalued asset value and calculated over the remaining useful life of three years.

Revaluation Reserve

Transfer to retained earnings	20	Surplus on revaluation	60
Balance c/f	40		

Retained Earnings

		Balance b/f	x
Balance c/f	x	Transfer from revaluation reserve re: excess depreciation	20

iv. Extract

Statement of Changes in Equity

	Revaluation Reserve	Retained Earnings	Total
Balance at the beginning of year	-	x	x
Profit for the year after tax		x	x
Surplus on revaluation	60		x
Transfer to retained earnings	(20) →	(20)	-
	40	x	x

Note: Other relevant items such as contributed share capital, other specified reserves and dividends on movement are not shown in equity statement.

De-recognition of PPE

According to IAS 16, PPE should be **de-recognized** [removed from books] either on disposal or when no future economic benefits are expected from the asset. In other words, the asset is effectively scrapped and therefore no longer exists physically. In the case of disposals, the usual accounting treatment [using the cost or revaluation model] has already been dealt with in the earlier and later sections. The net profit or loss on disposal is included in the statement of comprehensive income. The sales proceeds should not be recognized as revenue but shown as part of the asset disposal account. However, the cash proceeds from sale should be disclosed in the statement of cash flow under investing activities.

Where assets are measured using the revaluation model, any remaining balance in the revaluation reserve relating to the asset disposed is transferred directly to retained earnings. **No recycling** of this balance into the statement of other comprehensive income is permitted.

Chapter Summary

1. **The accounting standard permits entities the choice of two possible valuation models for PPE:** The cost model and the revaluation model. The cost model reports the asset at cost less accumulated depreciation and accumulated impairment losses and the revaluation model carries the asset at a fair value less accumulated depreciation and accumulated impairment losses. The revaluation model is available only if the fair value of the asset can be measured reliably. When using the revaluation model, certain guidelines need to be complied, one of which the model should be applied consistently to all PPE of the same class. Properties are an example of one class of tangible fixed assets, and another example could be plant and machinery. If an entity revalues a building, then it must revalue all land and buildings in that class of assets at the same time and it must be completed fairly soon.

2. **Accounting for revaluations**

   When the revaluation model is applied, assets are carried at "fair values". In the case of land and buildings, the market value represents fair value. Fair value is the price that would be received to sell an asset or paid to transfer a liability in an orderly transaction between market participants at the measurement date. A gain (surplus) or loss (deficit) on a revaluation is arrived:

	RM
CA of the asset at the date of revaluation date.	x
Valuation of the asset at fair value.	x
Difference is either a gain or a loss on revaluation	x/(x)

Depreciation for the period up the date of revaluation should be deducted from the carrying amount before determining the revaluation surplus or loss.

Surplus or gain on revaluation

IAS 16/MFRS 116 requires the increase (gain) to be recognized in equity under the revaluation reserve account as revaluation a surplus. Unless the increase is reversing the previous decrease which was recognized as an expense in the statement of other comprehensive income. To the extent this offset is made, the increase is recognized as income, any excess amount (remaining portion after offsetting) is then directly credited to equity as revaluation surplus. The revaluation surplus is an unrealized gain which subsequently becomes realized when the asset is disposed or sold (or derecognized).

Decrease or loss on revaluation

The case is similar in treatment for a decrease in value or loss on revaluation. Any decrease should be recognized as an expense in the statement of comprehensive income. Where a revaluation surplus exists relating to a previous revaluation of that asset (exception to the rule), to that extent, a revaluation decrease or loss can be recognized in equity. Any decrease in excess or greater than the previous revaluation surplus on that asset must be recycled as an expense in the statement of other comprehensive income.

3. **Treatment of depreciation for a revalued asset**

Revaluation changes the depreciable amount of an asset as subsequent depreciation charges are affected. An upward revaluation will increase the annual depreciation charge or expense. Under the realization concept, normally a revaluation surplus is only realized when the asset is subsequently sold but when it depreciated, part of that surplus is being realized as the asset is used or consumed. The amount of the surplus portion realized is the difference between depreciation charged on the revalued amount and the lower depreciation amount which would have been charged based the historical cost of the asset. This excess depreciation is a realized portion which can be transferred to retained earnings in equity but not recycled through the profit or loss statement. The standard allows (but does not require) entities to make a transfer of the excess depreciation from the revaluation reserve directly to retained earnings as a movement within equity. This choice of treatment is up to the company's policy.

4. **De-recognition of PPE**

The accounting standard specifies that PPE should be derecognized or removed from books either on disposal or when no future tangible economic benefits are expected from the asset. This means the asset is effectively scrapped and therefore no longer exists physically. Where assets are measured using the revaluation model, any remaining balance in the revaluation reserve relating to the asset disposed must be transferred directly to retained earnings. No recycling of this balance is permitted into the statement of other comprehensive income.

Key Terms

Accounting for revaluations

Fair value

The cost model

Gain (or surplus) on revaluation

Retained earnings

Recycling of balance

The revaluation model

Loss (or decrease) on revaluation

Carrying amount of the asset

Equity

Revaluation reserve

De-recognition of PPE

Excess depreciation

Review Questions

1. MFRS 116/IAS 16 permits two accounting models to be used by business entities for valuation of PPEs. Explain what are these models.
2. State what conditions should the revaluation model be used?
3. Briefly discuss a three guidelines specified by the accounting standard for revaluation of tangible fixed assets.
4. Give the new definition of 'fair value" by the IFRS. Explain how different is this from the previous definition?
5. How do you determine the gain or loss on revaluation of a tangible fixed asset?
6. When a revaluation takes place, what adjustment is required to be done before computing the revaluation surplus or loss?
7. Explain the accounting treatment for a gain or surplus on revaluation of an asset in accordance with the provisions of IAS 16/MFRS 116 using the revaluation model.
8. Discuss what happens when a revalued asset is depreciated?
9. Explain how depreciation is calculated on a newly revalued asset?
10. What is excess depreciation and how it is treated in the accounts?
11. Explain the term, De-recognition of PPE.
12. How would you treat an asset disposal in the accounts.? Show the extract for the required entries relating to a disposal of an asset in the cash flow statement.
13. Under the revaluation model, how do you deal with remaining balance in the revaluation reserve upon disposal of the asset or when it is de-recognized?
14. Show the required entries relating to excess depreciation and the transfers between the accounts in the statement of changes in equity.
15. Justify why the revaluation model has increasingly become an accepted norm in accounting practice given that the cost model in some situations fails to account for increases in asset values?

Multiple Choice Questions

Q1. Which accounting model would you select if there is a substantial change in the value of the assets that reflect on current market trend.

a. The cost model

b. The revaluation model

c. Neither of the models specified in (a) and (b)

Q2. When the revaluation model is adopted, what would be the main criteria applied

a. The management of the entity decided on a new accounting policy.

b. The revaluation model is adopted primarily on the basis of fair value which can be measured reliably and objectively it reflects the current market value of the asset.

c. The historical cost attached to the asset does not reflect the true value of the asset.

d. The company's bank felt the asset values being reported for PPE do no justify credit facilities to be availed to the company.

a. 1, 2, and 4 c. 1, 2, and 3 e. 1, 2, 3, and 4

b. 2 and 3 only d. 2, 3, and 4

Q3. Revaluation surplus represents an increase in FV of the asset and the gain is reported

a. As equity under revaluation reserve

b. As capital reserve

c. As an item in the statement of other comprehensive income

d. none of the above

Q4. Any decrease in value or loss on revaluation should be recognized as an expense in the statement of other comprehensive income

a. False b. True

Q5. The only exception to this rule in Q4

a. Where a revaluation surplus exists relating to a previous revaluation of that asset, to that extent, a revaluation decrease or loss can be recognized in equity.

b. Any decrease in excess or greater than the previous revaluation surplus on that asset must be recycled as an expense in the statement of other comprehensive income.

c. The accounting standard says treat the entire loss as an expense in the statement of other comprehensive income.

a. 1 b. 1 and 2 only c. 3 d. None of the above.

Q6. Which of the following statements is false?

a. Revaluation changes the depreciable amount of an asset as subsequent charges are affected.

b. Annual depreciation expense or charge will increase if there is an upward revaluation in asset value.

c. A revaluation surplus is only realized when the asset is subsequently sold or disposed.

d. Excess depreciation is a realized portion which can be transferred to retained earnings in equity but not recycled through the profit or loss statement.

e. Excess depreciation is a realized portion as the asset is consumed and therefore it must be recycled through the profit and loss statement.

Lenin is said to have declared that the best way to destroy the Capitalist System was to debauch the currency. By a continuing process of inflation, governments can confiscate, secretly and unobserved, an important part of the wealth of their citizens. By this method they not only confiscate, but they confiscate arbitrarily; and, while the process impoverishes many, it actually enriches some. The sight of this arbitrary rearrangement of riches strikes not only at security, but at confidence in the equity of the existing distribution of wealth.

— John Maynard Keynes

Chapter 12

Learning Objectives

After you have studied Section One, you should

Know the difference between tangible and intangible non-current assets
Be able to identify the three main categories if intangible assets
Understand the general characteristic of intangible assets
Understand the definition and the recognition and measurement criteria for intangible assets
Identify the definition and treatment of research cost and development cost in accordance with MFRS/IFRS
Be able to calculate amounts to be capitalized as development expenditure or to be expensed from given information
Be able to explain the purpose of amortization and calculate and account for the amortization charge
Know the guidelines for determining amortization policy
Understand the concept and definition of goodwill
Know what is purchased goodwill and how its value is arrived at
Know what IFRS 3 covers the accounting treatment of goodwill acquired in a business combination.
Know and understand the specific types of intangible assets such as computer software systems, patents and trademarks, brands, copyrights, franchises and licenses, etc.
Know how these type of specific intangible assets is accounted for?
Learn the accounting policies for intangible assets that are disclosed in the financial statements.
Know the difference between the two valuation models for intangible assets, their rules for implementing the revaluation model and their accounting treatment.
Know and understand the reporting changes in the value of intangible assets (excluding goodwill) and impairment test when amortization policy is not applied.

Intangible Assets

1. Scope

Earlier in section on **non-current assets**, we introduced intangible assets as one of the significant components of non-current assets that gets reported in the statement of financial position of entities. Given below in the diagram is a list of non-current assets that are mainly **categorized as intangible assets** in the financial statements of entities. These intangible assets are invariably reported by entities in their financial statements, only those that are relevant and specific to their activities usually get reported in their books of account.

1.1 Main Categories of Intangibles

We can broadly classify intangible assets into three main categories as follows:

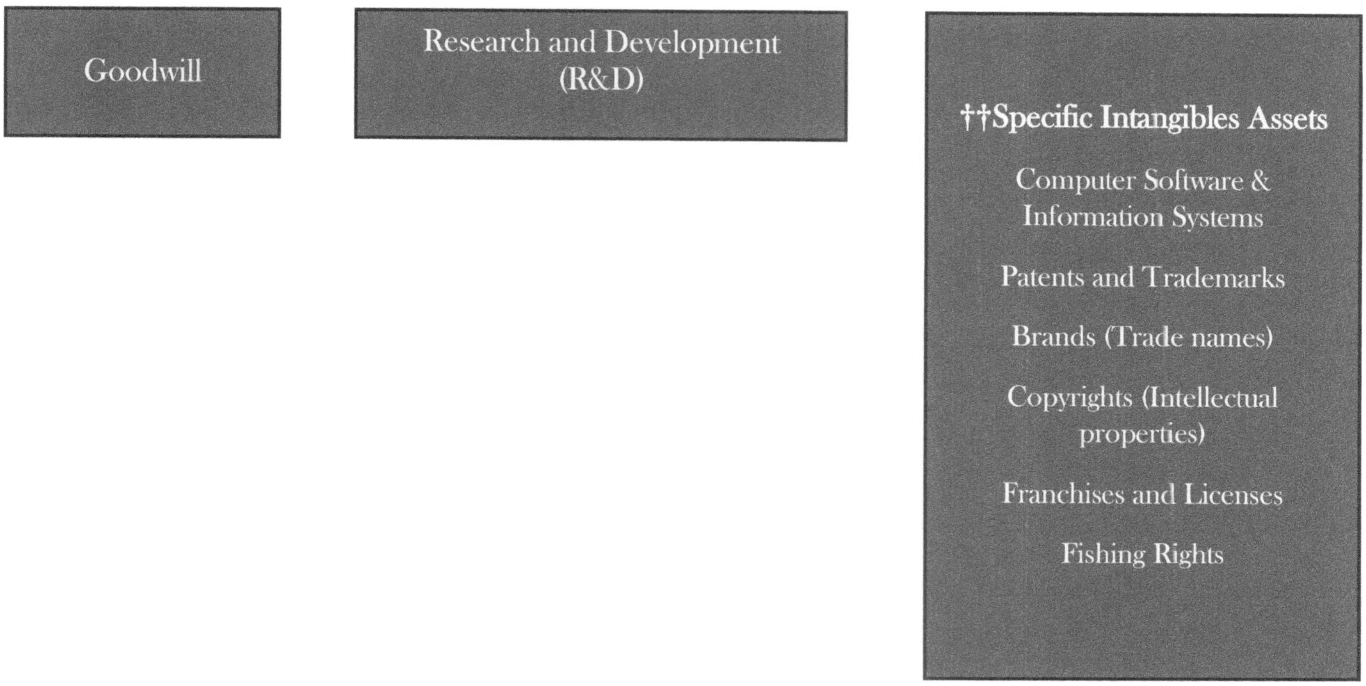

Figure 12.1

We deal with several of these assets in detail and others briefly because the topics are beyond the scope of this introductory accounting course. We discuss also the accounting issues as some of these topics normally feature in your examinations. Each of these intangibles is unique by nature and function. Entities use these intangibles as part of their business operations. Today's information era and knowledge-based economy relies increasingly on intangibles as evidence suggests that a significant investment of financial resources is devoted to these types of assets. The reporting of these assets requires accuracy and disclosure if financial statements were to give a true and fair view of the business. Finance professionals like accountants and financial analysts view t**hese assets to represent as a primary source of value creation** by a business entity in certain operating segments such as retail, cosmetics, software development or biotechnology products. For example, the development of brands or the sale of intellectual property rights and patent rights may be seen to represent a significant component of these business activities.

The amortization policy is based on the useful life of these assets as some of these intangibles have a finite life and others appear to have indefinite life. Intangible assets with indefinite lives are not subject to the normal amortization process. See discussion later in the chapter.

IAS 38 *Intangible Assets* cover **recognition, measurement and disclosure requirements.** We discuss some **general characteristics** of intangible assets followed by the **definition** of an intangible asset under **IAS 38** before then dealing with the **recognition criteria** for capitalizing intangible assets.

Research and development costs (R&D), its importance for the survival and successes of businesses, will be covered with illustrations. **IAS 38** lays down stringent rules and conditional requirements for the accounting treatment on capitalization. **Goodwill** is discussed in some detail in conjunction with **IFRS 3** *Business Combinations*. **IFRS 3** covers the accounting treatment of goodwill acquired in a business combination. We look into the main provisions of this standard. †† Accounting for other **specific intangibles** will be covered with some brief explanations on their special attributes. Since **computer software** is gaining an increasing trend in business applications and wide-spread uses, some in-depth treatment will be featured among the main topics in this Chapter. A brief discussion is then dealt on the rule for treating **internally generated intangible assets**.

Useful life and amortization policy is explained with reference to changes in value of intangible assets. The amortization policy is based on the useful life of these assets as some of these intangibles have a finite life and others appear to have indefinite life. See for more discussion later in the Chapter. The treatment on **disposals and retirements** of intangible assets are also dealt in the same way or exactly as for PPE.

The Chapter is long. Nearly in all these cases, relevant examples are illustrated to show the accounting aspects and their reporting requirements.

1.2 General Characteristics of Intangible Assets

In chapter 9, we mentioned **intangible assets** are long-lived assets that are usually considered to **have no physical substance** but can be characterized to be **associated with legal rights and attributes.** Generally, the definition of intangibles is based on the following four criteria:-

- **No physical substance** or rather lacking it
- The asset should be clearly **identifiable**
- The reporting entity claiming it as an asset **must have control over the asset** by treating it as a valuable economic resource: and
- There exists a defined **future economic benefits** derived from the asset.

These intangible assets are reported at substantial values in the statement of financial position. In fact, the carrying amounts of these assets may be represented significantly as high as 20% to 25% of non-current assets in some cases. They include computer software, motion picture films, fishing rights and have such attributes that carry special rights from patents, copyrights, trademarks, franchises, established reputable brands (trade names), and goodwill.

Entities in high–tech industries significantly carry valuable assets, particularly those that depend on research and development (R&D), another known sizable intangible asset. There are many companies involved in legal battles and industrial espionage to protect their patents, trademarks and copyrights over various smartphones and their mobile technologies including those products and services emerging from cyberspace technologies. For example, Sony spends huge amount of resources [$] in research and development, using innovative processes and designs, including computer technological advances such as wireless technology in order to stay competitively ahead of the market for their electronic and electrical products and services. Another example is Nestlé's intangible assets comprising mostly of reputable brands, patents, trade narks and copyrights that are substantially worth billions in the statement of financial position. These claim are justified if you go through some of the published accounts of these big entities such as Pfizer, Nestle, Proctor and Gamble, etc.

Before going further, we need to be aware that the **valuation** and **reporting** of intangibles in financial statements is **controversial** and in some accounting circles, has been a source of debate for a number of years before the accounting profession came up with the much improved version of the accounting standard dealing with intangible assets and GAAPs to streamline mainly very difficult issues such as to define objectively and value future economic benefits derived from these intangible assets **(Stolowy et al, 2010).**

There are three major issues involved in the reporting of intangible assets. These issues are represented in the diagram below and will be dealt in **Sections 2** and **3** of this chapter.

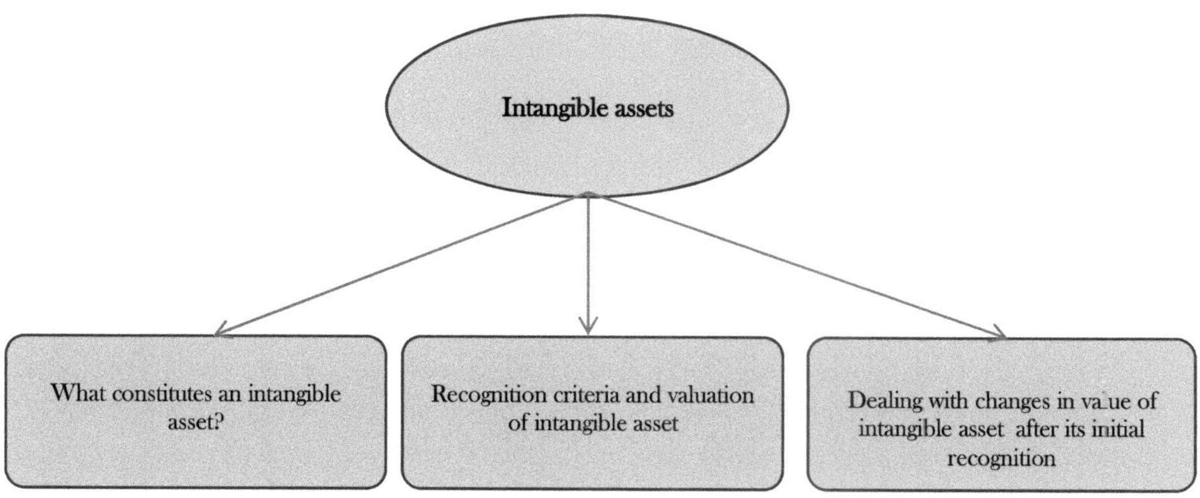

Figure 12.2 Intangible assets issues -

2. IAS 38/MFRS 138: Definition of an Intangible Asset

The standard lays down the rules for deciding whether or not an intangible asset may be recognized in the financial statements of an entity.

An **intangible asset** is defined by IAS 38 as **an identifiable non-monetary asset without physical substance**.

The asset must be:

a. **Controlled** by the entity as a result of events in the past, and
b. Something from which the entity **expects future economic benefits to flow**.

Examples of items that might be recognized as intangible assets were listed earlier in the scope section. Unless the item fully meets the definition in the standard, the item should not be recognized as an intangible asset. The standard offers detailed guidelines on the matter.

The prime consideration in this definition is **'what constitutes an intangible asset?'**

Let's look at the diagrams below which illustrate the necessary **conditions** emerging from the definition as given in the standard. These conditions or elements must be present if an intangible asset is to be recognized in the entity's accounts.

<table>
<tr><th colspan="3">Recognition Criteria (Conditions)</th></tr>
<tr>
<td>1. An intangible asset must be identifiable.

For non-physical items, there may be a problem with 'identification'. An example is 'Goodwill'.

For instance, if an intangible asset is acquired separately through purchase, there is evidence to suggest a transfer of a legal right, this would clearly establish the asset's identity.

Furthermore, if an intangible asset may be identifiable if it is separable, i.e. if it could be either sold or leased out

separable, i.e. if it could be either sold or leased out separately.</td>
<td>2. It must be under the control of the entity as a result of past event.

The entity must be able to enjoy the future economic benefits from the asset exclusively. A legally enforceable right is evidence of such control although not always a necessary condition.

Examples:
i. Control over technical knowledge or know-how only exists if it is protected by a legal right.
ii. The benefits and costs of skills training to employees most unlikely to be recognized as an intangible asset because an entity does not control the future actions of it's employees.</td>
<td>3. Future economic benefits are expected to flow from ownership of the asset.

Economic benefits can derive from sale of products or services or cost savings from reduction or curtailing of expenses.

An intangible asset must be measured at cost when recognized initially, if and only if both the following conditions are met:
i. If it is probable that the future economic benefits that are attributable to the asset will flow to the entity.
ii. The cost can be measured reliably.</td>
</tr>
<tr><td colspan="3">Entity's management should exercise judgement and discretion in assessing the viability relating to the flow of economic benefits to the entity. External evidence appears more reliable:
1. If an intangible asset is acquired separately, its cost can be measured reliably as its purchase price including any incidental costs of purchase, and any costs incurred in getting the asset ready for use.
2. An intangible asset acquired as part of a business combination (an acquisition or takeover) the cost of the intangible asset is its fair value at the date of acquisition.
IFRS 3 asserts that the fair value of intangible assets acquired in a business combination can be measured with sufficient reliability to be recognized separately from goodwill</td></tr>
</table>

According to **IFRS 3, quoted market prices** in an active market provide the most reliable estimate of the fair value of an intangible asset. If no active market exists for an intangible asset, its fair value is the amount that the entity would have paid for the asset, at the acquisition date, in an orderly transaction between market participants, on the basis of the best information available. In determining the amount, an entity should consider the outcome of recent transactions for similar assets. There are techniques for estimating the fair values of unique intangible assets such as brand names and these may be used to measure intangible asset acquired in a business combination.

Figure: 12.3

3. Recognition and Valuation of Intangible Assets

3.1 Consideration of Accounting Principles

How should intangible assets be treated in the accounts of an entity? Two contrasting accounting principles with regard to the recognition of intangible assets are explained below:-

Choice of accounting principles

Matching Principle

Intangible assets should be recognized capitalized initially under this convention for capitalization and then to be amortized should be over the estimated useful lives during which economic benefits are derived.

Prudence Principle

Under this convention, intangible assets are not since there is some degree of uncertainty on the economic benefits to be derived, and as such be expensed in the period when incurred.

However, it must be noted that the choice in accounting treatment of intangible assets is the outcome of a trade-off between relevance and reliability on one hand or prudence and conservatism on the other hand.

Accounting standards in the context of local GAAP in Malaysia tend to prescribe the recognition criteria for all the three main categories of intangible assets individually [R&D costs, goodwill and other specific intangibles]. The annual audited accounts and reports of companies listed in the KLSE or Bursa Malaysia may serve as an evidence to reveal the extent of accounting practice and policies adopted in the treatment of intangible assets prevalent amongst Malaysian companies.

Needless to repeat what has already been mentioned earlier; the recognition of an intangible asset should strictly follows the **IAS 38 definition and the recognition criteria**. The entity should clearly demonstrate that the item meets this **requirement unambiguously.**

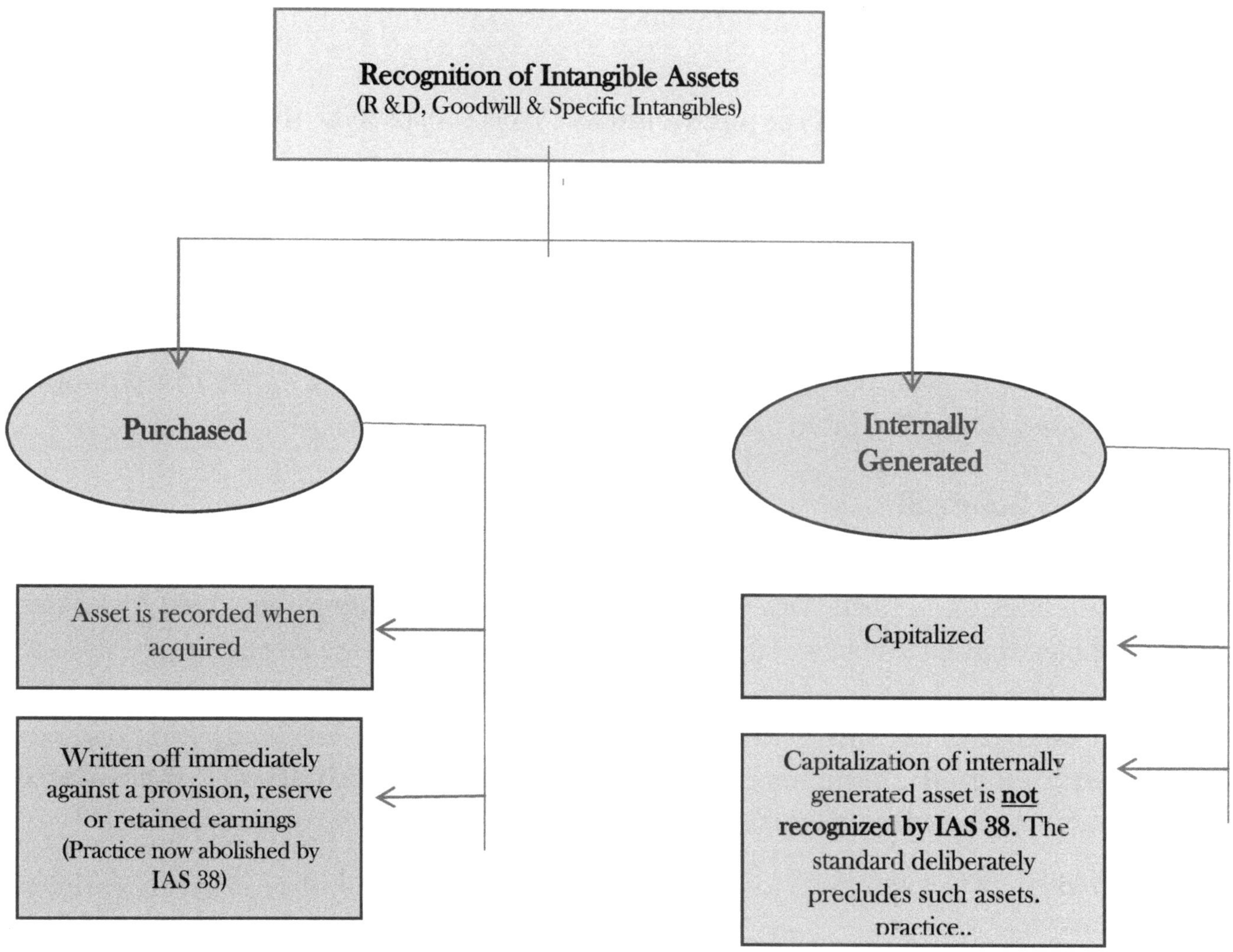

Source: Stolowy et al (2010)

Figure: 12.4 Recognition of Intangible Assets (Adapted)

3.2 Categories of Intangible Assets

A detailed description of the three main categories of intangible assets are outlined in **Sections 4 to 8**

4. Goodwill

4.1 Nature and Function of Goodwill

So, what is goodwill and how it is created? Goodwill is **inherently** present or exits in most businesses but there is no consideration given in monetary terms. In other words, it has **no objective valuation.** This is the **general view.**

Goodwill obviously **lacks physical substance** (that is why it is intangible) but it is automatically created owing to the **outcome of good relationships** between an established business and its customers. Evidently by building up on the **reputation and image** of the business for high standards of service and for high quality products, customers often recognize and experience this intangibility.

Another element is the **degree of responsiveness** that is very prompt as queries and complaints from customers are dealt with utmost speed and attention. This factor is further reinforced on customer relations, particularly when **staff's personality and attitude** towards customers' results in repeated sales. However, some degree of **uncertainty** exists as goodwill often changes frequently from time to time. For instance, one simple act of bad customer relations, say in handling orders from a value customer might damage goodwill and one act of expert handling of a customer's complaint resulting in good relations might create and improve goodwill. We can put all these different attributes or special features to represent what is goodwill?

4.2 Purchased Goodwill

As stated earlier above, there is an exception to the rule that goodwill has no objective valuation. This is when a business is **sold** with the purchaser **willing to pay** for goodwill for acquiring this new business that has abnormal potential earning power to create a comparative advantage in the market. This is what we refer to as **'purchased goodwill'**. Purchased goodwill usually happens in a **business combination** when the acquirer company in a group acquires another company at a premium. This premium ends up by being shown as '**Goodwill on Consolidation**'. Business combination comes under the provisions of **IFRS 3** which we will cover later.

How goodwill is then calculated (see diagram below) and recognized for accounting purposes in a group context?

Goodwill is **defined** as:
The difference between the purchase price of an acquired business and the fair value of its net tangible assets (identifiable assets less identifiable liabilities).

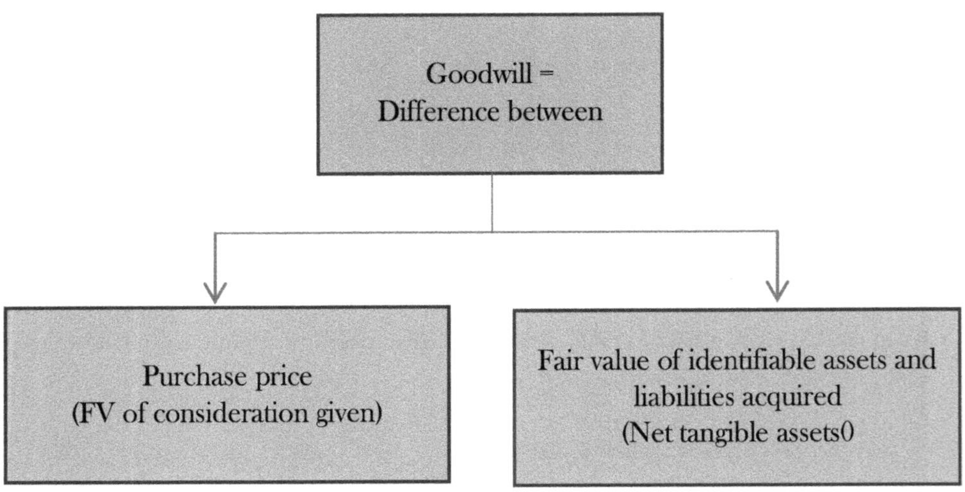

Figure: 12.5 Calculation of Goodwill

Note three important issues here:

1. **Purchased goodwill** is shown in the consolidated statement of financial position because it has been paid for as part of the purchase consideration in the acquisition of the new business. It has no tangible substance, and so it is an **intangible non-current asset.**
2. **Purchased goodwill** arising on consolidation is retained in the statement of financial position as an intangible asset under **IFRS 3.** The standard requires that goodwill must be reviewed annually for **impairment.** The concept of **amortization** does not operate for goodwill. (See below)
3. **IAS 38** prohibits the recognition of internally generated goodwill. Thus, the only goodwill that you see being reported in the financial statements is goodwill that results from business combinations or mergers and acquisitions as stipulated in **IFRS 3.**

4.3 Internally Generated Goodwill

Internally generated goodwill may not be recognized as an asset. **IFRS 3 deliberately precludes recognition of internally generated goodwill** because it requires, for initial recognition, the cost of the asset, rather than its fair value because **'cost'** is capable of being measured reliably and that it should be identifiable and controlled. Therefore, an asset which is not reliably measurable in an objective manner should not be recognized as asset.

4.4 IFRS 3 Business Combinations

IFRS 3 covers the accounting treatment of goodwill acquired in a business combination.

The standard also states:

Goodwill: Future economic benefits arising from assets that are not capable of being individually identified and separately recognized.

Goodwill acquired in a business combination is **recognized as an asset** and is initially measured at **cost. Cost** is the excess of the cost of the combination (purchase price) over the acquirer's interest in the net fair value of the acquiree's identifiable assets, liabilities including any contingent liabilities.

After initial recognition goodwill acquired in a business combination is measured **at cost less any accumulated impairment losses.** Given the inherent nature of goodwill, it remains intact and unlike tangible non-current assets, it does not go through wear and tear or consumption through usage, therefore it is **not amortized**. Instead it is **tested** for impairment at least annually, in accordance with **IAS 36** *Impairment of assets.* [See **Section 4.6** below for more details]

4.5 Negative Goodwill

It is rare for negative goodwill to arise under normal circumstances but it arises when the acquirer's interest in the net fair value of the acquiree's net assets **exceeds** the cost of the combination. It ends up as a dangling credit in the books.

> **IFRS 3** refers to **negative goodwill** as the excess of acquirer's interest in the net fair value (FV) of the acquiree's identifiable assets, liabilities and contingent liabilities over cost. [FV – Cost].

Negative goodwill can arise under the following circumstances:-

i. Due to some unforced **errors** in estimating or measuring the fair value attributed to either
   a. the cost of the combination (purchase consideration given); or
   b. the identifiable net assets of the acquired business..
ii. As a result of a **bargain purchase**.

So, what to do with the dangling credit?

An entity should first **reassess** the amounts at which it has estimated or measured both the cost element of the combination and the identifiable net assets of the acquired business The exercise should identify any error. Any negative goodwill remaining should be **recognized i**mmediately in the statement of profit or loss as prudence would have it.

4.6 Impairment of Goodwill

The standard says that goodwill should be subjected to an annual impairment review. This process is covered by **MFRS 136/IAS 36.** However, this topic is not dealt here since it is not part of the required syllabus.

4.7 Disclosure requirements in the notes to the financial statement

IFRS 3 require the following **disclosures** which include a **reconciliation** of the carrying amount of goodwill at the beginning and end of the accounting period, showing separately:

i. The gross amount and accumulated impairment losses at the beginning of the period
ii. Additional goodwill recognized during the period
iii. Impairment losses recognized during the period
iv. Ant net exchange differences arising during the period, and
v. The gross amount and accumulated impairment losses at the end of the period

Review Questions

1. Outline the main characteristics of goodwill which distinguish it from other intangible assets?
2. To what extent do you consider that these characteristics should influence the accounting treatment of goodwill? State your reasons.
3. a. Discuss briefly the general nature and function of goodwill.

   b. Explain what is a business combination under IFRS 3?

   Questions on IFRS 3 may not be required by students to answer as IFRS 3 is not examined at your level of studies.
4. State how goodwill is calculated in a business combination? Explain why purchased goodwill is capitalized in the financial statements?
5. Explain what you understand by 'Goodwill on Consolidation'?
6. Explain why IFRS 3 deliberately precludes the recognition of internally generated goodwill to be accounted as an asset?
7. What are the main issues involved with goodwill acquired in a business combination under IFRS 3 provisions. Discuss the accounting treatment of goodwill in the financial statements. Explain why goodwill is not subject to a policy of amortization.
8. State with reasons why goodwill needs to be tested and accounted for impairment?
9. i. What is negative goodwill?

   ii. Why and how does negative goodwill arise?

   iii. How do deal with the issue when there is negative goodwill in the accounts?

   iv. Discuss the accounting treatment of negative goodwill in the financial statements.
10. State and list what are the disclosure requirements for goodwill in the financial statements according to **IFRS 3?**

Problem Question

1. Oreo Cookies Bhd specializes in manufacturing confectionary products and one of its famous brand is 'Oreo Black Snack'. Oreo Cookies acquired Jacobs Biscuits Sdn Bhd for M 25 million For a cash consideration by creating a rights issue to finance the purchase of the business. The fair value of Jacobs Biscuits Sdn Bhd's net assets at the date acquisition were RM 22.5 million.

   Required

   a. **Show how the calculation is done for the cost of goodwill purchased by Oreo Cookies Bhd**

   b. Explain how the goodwill will be treated in Oreo's financial statements?

   c. What further action will be required by Oreo Cookies in future years to maintain the goodwill asset in the financial statements?

2. Cinta Rasa Sayang Bhd, a chain of hotels in Malaysia, paid a cash consideration of RM 36 million to acquire another hotel, 'Pelangi Lodge' in Penang Island. At the date of acquisition, Pelangi Lodge reported the following audited financial data:

Summarized Statement of Financial Position of Pelangi Lodge

	RM' million
Non-current assets	18
Current assets	20
	38
Less: Current liabilities.	(23)
Net assets	**15**
Represented by:	
Share capital	10
Reserves	2
Shareholders' equity	12
Long term liabilities	3
	15

Pelangi Lodge's auditors confirmed the company's net assets had a fair value of RM 13.8 million when the negotiations for the transaction concluded between the two parties.

Required:

a. **Calculate the amount attributed to goodwill.**

b. **Show the journal entries for the acquisition to be recorded in Cinta Rasa Sayang's books.**

c. **IAS 38 specifies that the goodwill reported in the consolidated statement of financial position should be reviewed annually, usually at the end of each reporting period.**

   i. **State and explain briefly what is the nature and purpose of this review?**

   ii. **Six months after the acquisition of Pelangi Lodge, how do you deal with the accounting treatment if the carrying amount of the goodwill exceeds its recoverable amount say, by RM 300,000?**

   iii. **Show the required entries for the adjustment on impairment loss.**

5. Accounting for Research and Development (R & D)

Companies with on-going substantial research and development activities have to decide whether the related expenditures incurred be treated as assets or expenses? The split between the research phase and the development phase of a project undertaken by an entity is an important decision to be made for financial reporting purposes. Companies like Sony, Samsung, Toyota or Siemens have huge commitments for R&D activities in their operating business, so their accounting policies in dealing with this significant cost item has a material impact on their finances.

5.1 Definition of Research under IAS 38

Research is 'original and planned investigation undertaken with the prospect of gaining new scientific or technical knowledge and understanding'.

Examples of research costs

i. Activities aimed at obtaining new knowledge
ii. The search for, evaluation and final selection of, application of research findings or other knowledge
iii. The search for, alternatives for materials, devices, products, processes, systems or services; and
iv. The formulation, design, evaluation, and final selection of possible alternatives for new or improved materials, devices, products, processes, systems or services

5.2 Distinguishing between Pure and Applied Research

The distinction between pure research and applied research within the classification of research and development requires **different accounting treatment** given the nature and purpose: of such research activity.

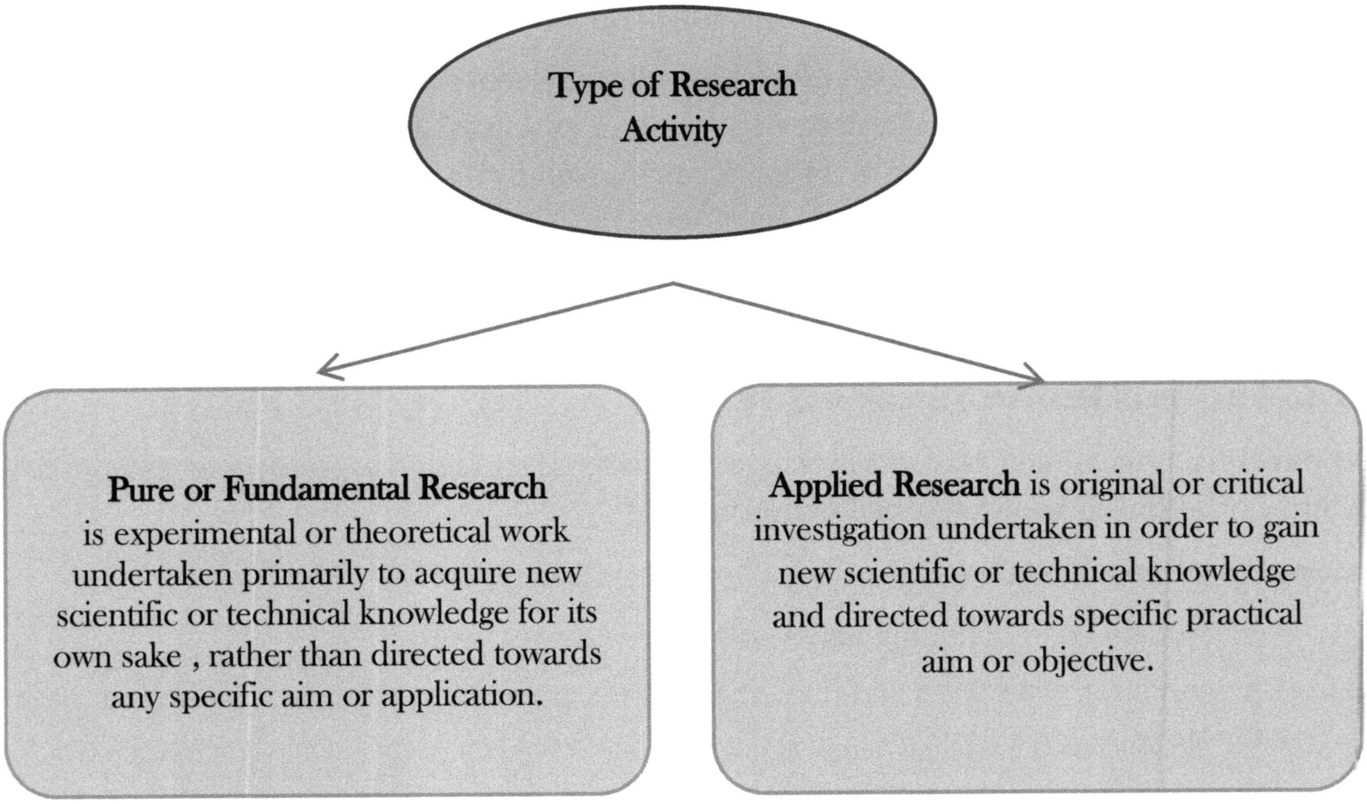

Figure: 12.6

5.3 Definition of Development under IAS 38

Development is 'the application of research findings or other knowledge to a plan or design for the production of new or substantially improved materials, devices, products, processes, systems or services before the start of commercial production or use'.

Examples of development activities

i. The design, construction and testing of pre-production or pre-use prototypes and models;

ii. The design of tools, jigs, moulds, and dies involving new technology;

iii. The design, construction, and operation of a pilot plant that is not of a scale economically feasible for commercial production; and

iv. The design, construction and testing of a chosen alternative for new or improved materials, devices, products, processes, systems or services

5.4 Accounting for R & D Expense or Costs

Research activities by definition do not meet the criteria for recognition under **IAS 38** because at the research phase of a product, there is some degree of uncertainty that future economic benefits will probably flow to the entity from the project. Under **IAS 38,** costs associated with **research phase** are always **expensed** whereas costs in the **development phase** are **capitalized** under certain restricting conditions provided the entity can clearly demonstrate that it can satisfy the specified criteria under the standard. **[See Section 5.3]**

According to **prudence concept** of accounting, research and development costs are to be expensed when incurred. Without exception, the prudence principle certainly requires research costs to be written off as an expense. No intangible asset arising from research or from the research phase of an internal project shall be recognized. **IAS 38** stipulates that **expenditure incurred on research** shall be **recognized as an expense** in the statement of comprehensive income when they are inc**urred.** However, according to the standard if specified criteria are met and the circumstances warrant it, some development and applied research costs may be capitalized and recorded or reported as an intangible asset. **[See Section 5.3 for more explanatory details]**

5.5 Specified Criteria for Capitalization of Development Costs

In contrast with research costs, development costs are incurred progressively at a later phase of the project, and the probability of success should become more apparent. According to **IAS 38,** 'an intangible asset arising from development or from the development phase of an internal project shall be recognized if, and only if, an entity can demonstrate **all** of the following specified conditions are met:-

a. The technical feasibility of completing the intangible asset so that it will be available for use or sale;
b. Its intention to complete the intangible asset and use or sell it;
c. Its ability to use or sell the intangible asset;
d. How the intangible asset will generate probable future economic benefits. Amomg other things, the entity should demonstrate the existence of a market for the ouput of the intangible asset or the intangible asset itself or if it is to be used internally, the usefulness of the intangible asset;
e. Its ability to measure the expenditure attributable to the intangible asset during its development reliably;
f. The availability of adequate technical, financial and other resources to complete the development and to use or sell the intangible asset.

The underlined wording '*shall*' is important here. Essentially it might be construed by the reader that capitalization of **R&D** is automatic if **all** the six specified conditions are met. Given that some of these criteria are extremely subjective, it is easy to claim that a condition has not been met or has been met. So, scrutiny and caution are absolutely necessary on the part of the reporting entity to ensure accuracy and accountability in this area of accounting.

5.6 Controversy over Capitalization of R&D

The issues involved on capitalization of R&D costs are debatable. The subject over the *capitalization of R&D has been a controversial topic among many users of financial statements. Banks, financial analysts and some quarters of the accounting fraternity including some other stakeholders as well who take an extreme prudent approach, appear to have claimed that the capitalization of R&D is a serious drawback of the prudence convention, because by shifting a substantial portion of the expenditure to treat it as an asset in the balance sheet gives rise to a distortion of the bottom-line performance, thus pushing the profits upwards cosmetically. The argument is that a true and fair view of the financial performance is grossly misrepresented.

One argument supporting the capitalization policy appears to suggest that R&D expenses create a positive outcome which should be related to future accounting periods when economic benefits will flow to the entity. The amortization policy adopted also tends to reflect positively on the treatment. This is in line with the matching concept. So in all probability, R&D expenses should be capitalized or accrued and not expensed immediately in the statement of comprehensive income.

One further **counter argument** claims that future economic benefits potentially arising from R&D activity are not sufficiently objective as there is too much of uncertainty and subjectivity surrounding its flow to the entity. The argument maintains that the R&D expenditure incurred at the time hardly justifies capitalization. The prudence convention therefore, dictates in favor of expensing R&D costs as incurred.

5.7 Other internally generated intangible assets

The standard strictly prohibits the recognition of internally generated assets such as brands, mastheads, publishing titles including customer lists and similar items as intangible assets. Nearly in all these cases, they objectively fail to meet the definition and recognition criteria. Furthermore, these items are often indistinguishable from internally generated goodwill on the same basis that was discussed earlier.

Example

Keith Farmer is developing a new production process with no definite plan how it is going to be used or sold as it is early days now. During 2018, expenditure incurred was RM 125,000 of which RM 25,000 was incurred before 30 June 2018 and the remaining RM 100,000 was incurred between 1 July 2018 and 1 December 2018. Keith Farmer demonstrated that the development phase has progressed and at 1 July 2016 meets the recognition criteria as an intangible asset. The recoverable amount of the know-how embodied in the process is estimated to be RM 65,000.

Required

a. **How should the expenditure be treated?**

b. Keith Farmer claimed the development phase has made significant progress so that the expenditure incurred on the process can be treated as an intangible asset.

   State on what possible grounds this decision was arrived at? Your answer should be in accordance with IAS 38 rules on capitalization of development costs. Comment on the recoverable amount of RM 65,000

Answer

a. At the end of 2016, the production process is recognized as an intangible asset at the cost of RM 100,000. This is the development expenditure incurred since the date when the recognition criteria were met, that is 1 July 2016. The RM 25,000 expenditure incurred up to 30 June 2016 (or before 1 July 2016) is expensed because the recognition criteria were not met. It will never form part of the development cost (of the production process) recognized in the statement of financial position classified under intangible assets.

b. Keith has confirmed the production process has reached a critical stage for it to be recognized as development costs. In accordance with **IAS 38**, the project is treated as an intangible asset on the basis of its **technical feasibility** and amongst other related factors. Furthermore, the management would have verified demand conditions for the process in the market environment by confirming the asset can **generate probable future economic benefits.** The marketing manager after conducting a market survey would have confirmed that a market exist for the **use** of the process in production on condition that the **process is completed**. The asset could be **sold** in the market. The cost incurred to date was **measured reliably** during the development phase and **resources were available** until the process was completed successfully.

   The recoverable amount of the know-how embodied in the process, estimated at RM 65,000 has no bearing because the asset has been capitalized and the **incidence of impairment will not arise here at the initial measurement stage.** Impairment review will take place at the end of next reporting period at which point, the asset would be tested for impairment in accordance with **IAS 36** rules on impairment of assets.

5.8 Illustrative Exercise

Reporting in the Financial Statements

Show figures on R&D Activity

Examples

1. Because of uncertainties regarding future economic benefits, all of R&D expenses are expensed.
2. Reporting R&D expenses as a separate function, item or line than breaks it down between part expensed and, by deduction, the part capitalized.

3. Capitalizes the development part of R&D when appropriate and reports expensing the research costs as part of operating expenses. Other classification for expensing R&D is given under the heading 'selling, general and administrative expenses'.

Accounting Policies

1. **Bayer (Germany)**

   Annual report 2008 – Pharmaceuticals, Chemicals

   R&D expenses: According to IAS 38 (Intangible assets), research costs cannot be capitalized: development costs must be capitalized if, and only if, specific narrowly defined conditions are fulfilled. Development costs must be capitalized if it is sufficiently certain that the future economic benefits to the company will also cover the respective development costs. Since development projects are often subject to regulatory approval procedures and other uncertainties, the conditions for the capitalization of costs incurred before receipt of approvals are not normally satisfied.

2. **Sandvik (Sweden)**

   Annual report 2008 – Engineering Group in Tooling and Materials Technology.

   Note 4: Research, development and quality assurance.

(in SEK millions)	2008	2007
Expenditure for		
Research and development	2,347	2,195
Quality assurance	464	544
Total	**2,811**	**2,739**
of which expensed	2,478	2,362
of which expensed relating to R&D	2,014	1,818

Research and quality assurance expenditures are expensed as incurred. Expenditure for development is reported as an intangible asset if it meets the criteria for recognition as an asset in the statement of financial position.

3. **Saint Gobain (France) Annual report 2008 – Production, processing and distribution of glass, high performance materials**

   Note 1: Accounting Principles and Policies

   Research costs are expensed as incurred. Development costs meeting the recognition criteria under IAS 38 are included in intangible assets and amortized over their estimated useful lives (not to exceed five years) from the date when the products to which they relate are first marketed.

6 Computer Software and Information Systems

6.1 Accounting for Computer Software Costs

Accounting for computer software and information systems costs in today's business practiceenvironment is more simplified as indicated by the flowchart shown in **Figure 12.7.** The most critical issue is deciding on the accounting treatment of **internally developed software** for internal use by the developing entity itself

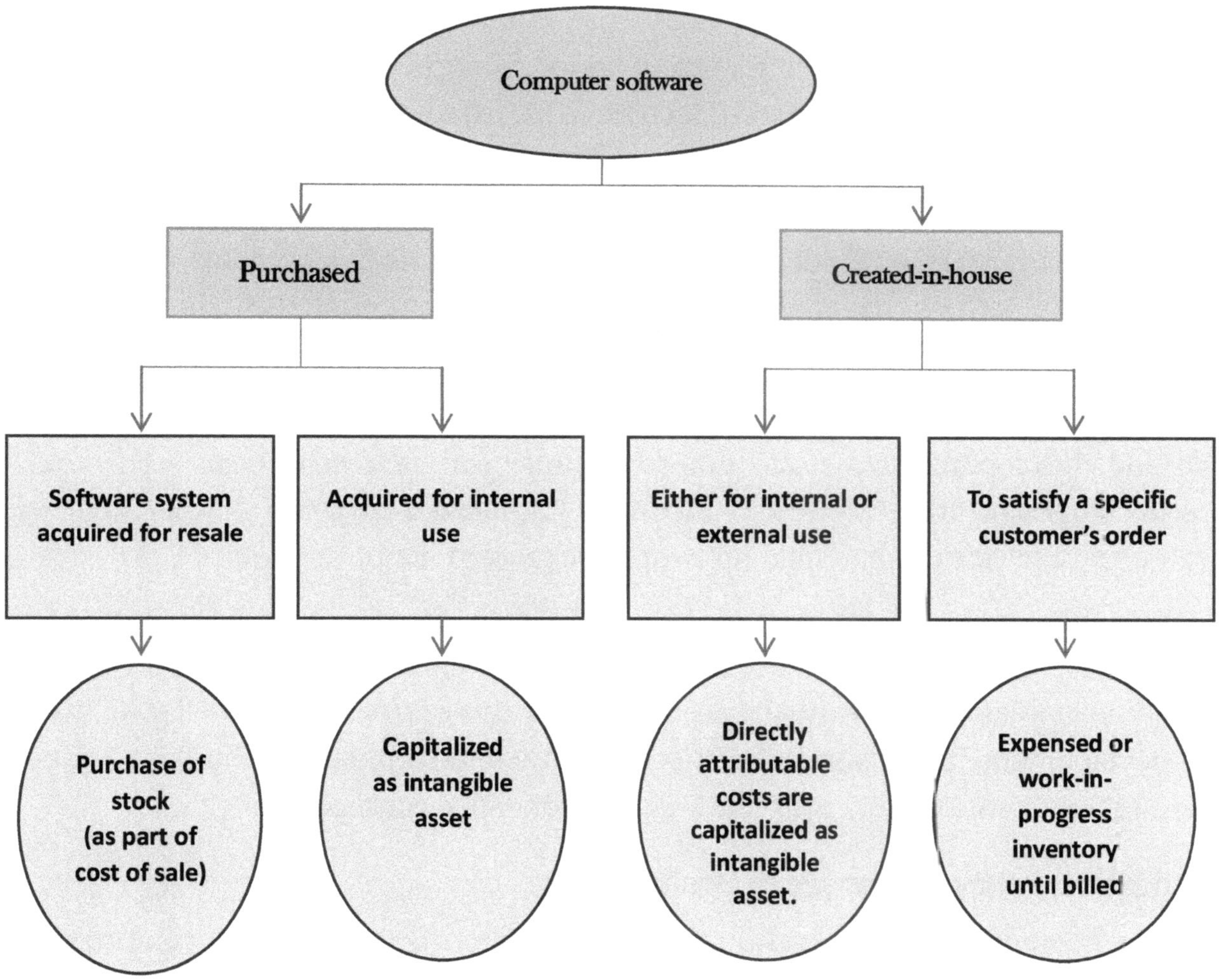

Source: Stolowy et al (2010)

Figure 12.7 Accounting for Computer Software (Adapted)

6.2 Accounting Issues

i. Capitalizing or Expensing

Some real case examples of **accounting policies** adopted by international companies (that have a global presence) for reporting computer software are illustrated as follows:

1. Internally generated software amounting to € 20 million incurred during the development phase were capitalized as intangible asset
2. Software development expenses are accounted for as assets for clearly identified projects whose technical and sales risks are reasonably controlled and on which a return is certain. Only projects with a total development cost exceeding € 1 million are recognized. Development expenses cease being accounted for as assets when the product is rolled out as part of the overall marketing stage. Maintenance and continuation expenses are expenses as soon as they are incurred. The amounts accounted for assets are amortized using the straight-line method over the maximum of three years and they are tested for impairment at the end of each reporting period. Amortization for the period is recognized in the statement of comprehensive income as an expense by type.
3. The company capitalizes costs associated with software developed or obtained for internal use when both the preliminary project stage is completed and the company's management had authorized further funding of the project which it deems probable will be completed and used to perform the function intended. Capitalization of such costs ceases no later than the point at which the project is substantially complete and ready for its intended purpose.

Research and development costs and other computer software maintenance costs related to software development are expensed as incurred. Capitalized software development costs are amortized using the straight-line method over the expected life of the product.

These companies are based in Europe, Asia and North America that have used accounting principles consistent with the local accounting standards and GAAPs, all of which comply with **IFRS.** These examples demonstrate the accounting aspects of treating costs relating to computer software development (and its associated activities) where capitalization policy is appropriate and where expensing such costs is in line with the prudence concept.

ii. Amortization Policy – Changes in Useful life

Useful life of computer software costs that are capitalized is subjective as computer software development is relatively short-lived given the dynamic nature of the information technology industry, and may not be like other intangible assets. This is because computer technology and information systems tend to evolve rapidly to avoid susceptibility to obsolescence and competition in the industry. **Technological obsolescence** is therefore a crucial element for most companies whose activity is largely dependent on computer software development. So, the amortization periods may not extend in some extreme cases beyond three years and in other cases, typically it may extend to five years. These changes in useful life or periods of amortization if modified to reflect changing circumstances may have an impact on the timing of revenue recognition.

Review Questions

R&D

1. Why it is necessary to split between research and development phases as an important decision?
2. Define research and identify one example of research costs.
3. Distinguish between pure and applied research.
4. Explain briefly the accounting treatment for research costs.
5. Define development under **IAS 38** and identify at least two development activities.
6. What is the accounting treatment for research and development cost in accordance with **IAS 38** requirements? Explain the reasons for such treatment.
7. Briefly discuss what underlying accounting concept is applied to the treatment of R & D costs?
8. Identify all the specific criteria that should be used stringently for capitalization of development costs.
9. Briefly explain the controversy over the capitalization of development costs. What arguments are advanced for the support of these controversial issues?

Computer Software

10. Explain why computer software and information systems costs increasingly have become an important issue for business entities?
11. Discuss the difference between purchased and internally generated software information systems.
12. Explain the accounting treatment for computer software systems costs with reference to Question 11.
13. What accounting issues are involved between capitalization and expensing of costs relating to computer software and information systems? Briefly state the main issue in your discussion.
14. What is the term 'amortization' means?
15. How should the amortization policy be adapted to changes in useful life of an intangible asset?

7. Specific Intangible Assets

Under this category several specific intangible assets are dealt and explained in turn. Each type of 1intangible asset is unique, and reporting these assets can vary from one asset to another. Computer software and information systems were covered earlier in **Section 6. Section 7** will now cover other specific intangible assets by type and description.

Three possibilities listed below determine how the asset is acquired?

1. By outright purchase
2. Through a business combination (merger or acquisition of another company), or
3. Internally generated or developed

These methods can impact how the intangible asset is recognized and measured?

7.1 Patents

Patents are granted by a government agency or an official authority bestowing the holder or inventor of a product or manufacturing process the exclusive rights to use or sell the invention or rights to it. The invention can be a specific product or process. For example, Sony's blue ray format Malaysia's pharmaceutical product 'Polleney –Essence of Black Fish with American Ginseng' is a registered patent. The duration of the protection offered by a patent varies between countries but it may extend to several years from 5 years to 20 years or exceeding 20 years depending from where the patent is legally registered. Malaysian patents have known to have a duration of 7-10 years. 17 years in USA, UK and France. Patents cannot be renewed but a new patent on the basis of modifications or technical improvements to the original invention can be legally enforced to extend its effective life. Like any other asset, a patent can be bought for a consideration if the reporting entity has a potential use for it, say for its core business or manufacturing process or its components assembly plant.

Illustrative Example

Petronas, Malaysia's National Oil and Gas Company acquired a patent which cost RM 330,000 on 30 September 2016 and its expected useful life is ten years. The company's chief accountant decided to amortize the patent over its economic useful life. The company's financial year ends on 31 March 2017.

Required

Show how the company will record the acquisition and amortization for this patent in its books?

You are required to shown only the journal entries.

Journal entries to record the transactions

Date	Account	Ref	Debit	Credit
2016				
30 Sept	Patents	GL	330,000	
	Bank	CB		330,000
	(Being acquisition of a patent)			
2017				
31 March	Amortization expense – Patents	GL	16,500*	
	Accumulated amortization - Patents	GL		16,500
	(Being amortization expense for the period)			

* Provided on time-apportionment basis (330,000 × 10% × 6/12)

The entries to be recorded in the ledger accounts will be exactly the same as for PPE items.

Assets	=	Liabilities	+ Shareholders' Equity	
- 16,500	=	0	+ - 16,500	[Amortization expense]

Accounting effect

Amortization for an intangible decrease both asset and equity exactly as depreciation does for a PPE.

7.2 Trademarks (Trade Names)

Trademarks and trade names such as established brand names give distinctive identification (symbol, logo, design, slogan or word, emblem, etc.) to a manufactured product or service that distinguishes from other similar family of products or services. Examples of famous trademarks or brand names are **'Nestlé's** milk product with the slogan 'Good food and Good life', and **Nike's**' 'swoosh' symbol which is the trademark for its sport products. Similarly, the logo associated with **Coco Cola's** 'Dynamic Ribbon', and Singapore's pharmaceutical product, **Polleney**'s slogan – 'Essence of Black Fish with American Ginseng' are all registered trademarks. Distinctive identification of products or services, is usually marked with symbols ™ or ®.

Legal protection for trademarks is usually granted by registration by a governing body or an authorized office or agency of a government. Registered trademarks may have a definite useful life, (10 years or 20 years) usually determined by a written contract and which can be renewed and extended for the same period under some specified conditions so that the entity's business is not disrupted. The useful life of trademarks for the purpose of amortization policy may not necessarily follow its legal useful life, it can be determined for s shorter period. Compared with patents and trademarks, The registration process is not expensive in terms of costs unless the entity acquires a brand name through a business combination or from outside parties which in all such cases, the acquisition cost may prove more expensive. As an intangible asset, a trademark or brand name goes through exactly the same process like a PPE item.

7.3 Licenses

Government and other business entities offer **licenses** to individual businesses, allowing them to use properties or legal rights owned by them for an agreed fee and upon agreed duration. **Fishing rights** in a particular location when it is allowed to operate by an entity is an example of a licensed agreement. A **licensed agreement** is granted specifically under a patent or a trademark.

7.4 Copyrights

Copyrights provide exclusive rights to the publication, production and sale of the rights for an intellectual creation such a book or other literary achievements, works of art and music composition, film and other dramatic work, etc. Copyrights increasingly now in a competitive environment also protect computer programs and information systems such as **Microsoft's** Windows® and Excel. Usually, copyright's protection is granted by a government agency to extend up to remaining life of the author (publisher of a book, or music composer, artist or a programmer) with an additional 50 years. The cost of obtaining a copyright from the government is low but it may prove exorbitant in term of costs if an existing copyright is purchased from an owner or when a particular copyright is acquired in a the business combination.

7.5 Franchises

All over the world, **franchised businesses** have grown big to become a common business contractual arrangement for an agreed stated fee that grant privileges and rights to a franchisee (individual entrepreneurs or businesses) to produce and sell certain products or services, usin certain trademarks, patents or licenses under specified conditions with or without organizational support from the franchisor. The arrangement may extend to geographical regions or international territories and may carry certain rights or privileges to modify or do specific things identified under the franchise agreement for the product or service offering usually to suit local conditions, customs and tastes. Many established franchises are in the food or retail industry such as **Kentucky Fried Chicken**, **McDonalds, Pizza Hut, Secret Recipe, 7-eleven** and many more that you think of. **Kumon Maths,** a Japanese concept of learning mathematics among school going children is an established franchise in the services sector. Other service sector franchises includes hotel chains like **Days Inn,** etc. The fact that franchised businesses are successfully run on-stop with management's ability to continue renewing the agreement, the **useful lives** of many franchises are apparently **indefinite.** For this reason, **franchised costs** are therefore **not subject to any amortization process**. The fee paid to the franchisor is usually a large sum of money in many cases. The plant and equipment and other administrative facilities that are used in the franchised business usually originates from the franchisor under leasing arrangements. The duration and terms of the franchise agreement are specified in the contract. One of the things about franchised business is that both the franchisor and the franchisee agree to a mutual and specific performance to uphold to the letter of the franchise contract. However, where the parties violate the spirit of the agreement, the contract can be broken with or without legal proceedings under the presiding judicial authority in force at that time.

7.6 Deferred Expenditure

Preliminary expenses

These are expenses incurred during the process when an entity is being incorporated or establishing a new business legally. These are **preliminary (organization set-up) costs** associated with the formation of a newly private limited company or public company in Malaysia (known as Sendirian Bhd or Berhad respectively) These costs include registration or incorporation fee, stamp duty for the authorized share capital, professional and legal expenses relating to the creation of a memorandum and articles of association (By-laws) and filing fee with the Companies Commission of Malaysia (Persuruhanjaya Syarikat Malaysia).

Pre-operating expenses include company secretarial expenses, accounting and auditor's fee, the annual filing fee upon incorporation, etc. All these costs are recognized and treated as an asset prior to the commencement of business operations. The local GAAPs in Malaysia allows this choice in accounting practice but such expenses must be written–off immediately in the statement of comprehensive income, once the business starts generating revenue, that is usually upon the commencement of business operations usually evidenced by the first cash proceeds from revenue. Alternatively, such expenses are **amortized** over a short period and the debits are shown in the statement of profit or loss.

IAS 38 prohibits both these deferred expenditures to be recognized as an intangible asset on the grounds that it fails to meet the **definition and recognition criteria** (future economic benefits are not certain and the costs cannot be measured reliably) of an intangible asset.

However, where an entity strictly complies with the provisions of IAS 38, both preliminary and pre-operating expenses will be expensed as incurred. The anomaly seen here is that there is no revenue to match these costs. A Malaysian company normally **amortize** these expenses over a fairly a short period until revenue from business accrues or flows into the company. Under this accounting treatment, while the company remains dormant, losses are reported in the financial statements for each year until the commencement of business operations.

8. Measurement of Intangible Assets Subsequent to Initial Recognition

IAS 38 allows two methods of valuation for intangible assets after they have been first recognized. According to the standard, intangible assets should be initially measured at cost, but subsequently they can be carried at **cost** or at a **revalued amount.**

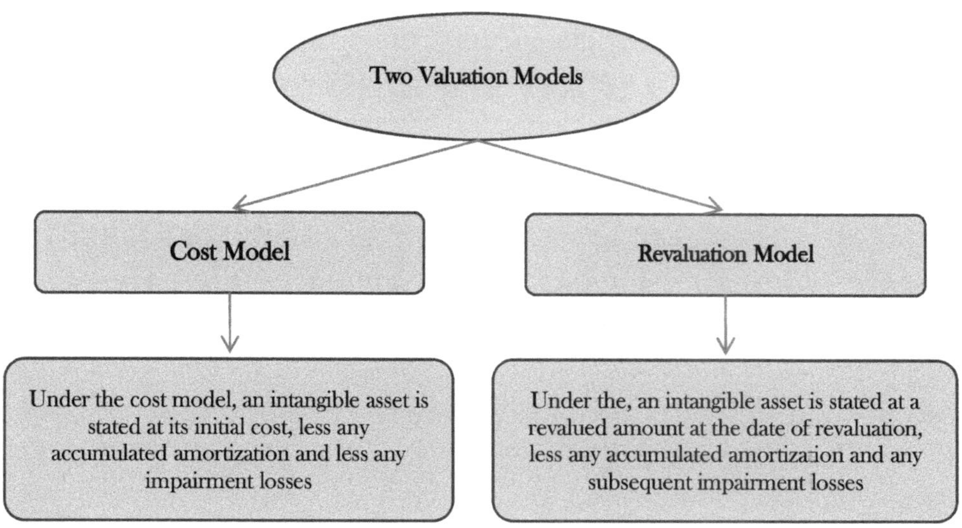

Figure 12.8 Valuation Models

Few important rules about implementing the **revaluation model:**

- An active market must exist in that type of asset so that the fair value can be measured reliably.
- To prevent selective revaluations, the entire class of intangible assets of that type must be revalued at the same time.
- If there is no active market for an intangible asset in a class of revalued assets that cannot be revalued, the asset is to be reported at cost less any accumulated amortization and impairment losses.
- Revaluation should be carried out with such regularity that the reported carrying amount is consistently determined using fair value at the end of the reporting period.

The revaluation model cannot for all practical considerations be applied to an intangible asset because an intangible asset is recorded at its acquisition cost during initial recognition. The standard states that it is unlikely for any subsequent expenditure to be recognized in the carrying amount of an intangible asset. While the choice of cost model or revaluation model is made available for intangible assets, the standard also says the revaluation model will be very rarely adopted in practice by any entity.. Furthermore, the standard also says there will not usually be an active market for an intangible asset. For example, although publishing rights, copyrights and film rights can be sold in a market, each as a unique sale value. In such cases, revaluation to fair value would be certainly inappropriate. However, a fair value may be obtainable for assets such as fishing rights or taxicab licenses.

8.1 Accounting Rules for Revaluation

i. When an intangible asset is revalued upwards to a fair value, the amount of the revaluation surplus should be credited directly to equity under the revaluation reserve account. However, if a revaluation surplus is a reversal of a revaluation decrease that was previously charged against income, any remaining surplus (if any) after the reversal, should be credited as a revaluation surplus directly under equity's revaluation reserve account.
ii. Where the carrying amount of an intangible asset revalued downwards, the amount of the revaluation decrease (a deficit)) should be charged as an expense against income, unless the asset has been previously revalued upwards. A revaluation decrease or deficit should be first charged against any previous revaluation surplus relating to that asset.

The accounting rules apply exactly as with the PPE revaluation exercises dealt in Chapter 11.

Despite the availability in the choice of both valuation models for intangible assets, **IAS 38** takes the view that the **revaluation model** is extremely rare in practice as most entities adopt the traditional cost model.

Example

A company acquired an intangible asset which was measured at fair value. As there was an active market for this type of asset, the asset was revalued upwards by RM 4,000 in 2018. A revaluation surplus of RM 4,000 was recorded under a revaluation reserve account. At the end of year 2020, the asset was revalued again, this time the fair value decreased by RM 5,000.

Required

Show the accounting treatment for the downward revaluation.

Solution

The downward valuation of RM 5,000 should first be set-off against the revaluation surplus of RM 4,000. The revaluation surplus will be reduced to RM nil and a charge of RM 1,000 will be recognized as a loss on revaluation in the statement of other comprehensive income.

Notes

When a revaluation model is adopted, and an intangible asset is revalued upwards, the revaluation surplus may be transferred to retained earnings when the surplus is eventually realized upon disposal or sale of the asset. The surplus may also be realized over time as the asset is used by the entity. The amount of the surplus realized each year is the difference between the amortization charge for the asset based on the revalued amount of the asset and the amortization that would be charged on the basis of the asset's historical cost (which is based on the initial acquisition cost). the realized portion of the surplus (excess amortization) in such case be transferred directly to retained earnings from revaluation reserve **within equity**, but not recycled through the statement of profit or loss. Refresh your memory on this topic in Chapter 11.

9. Reporting Changes in the Value of Intangible Assets

After the recognition criteria, **IAS 38** deals with changes in the value of intangible assets (excluding goodwill) with particular emphasis on useful lives and amortization policy.

9.1 Useful life

The standard distinguishes between intangible assets with finite or indefinite useful lives.

Finite useful life

Intangible assets with finite lives can be measured reliably, therefore amortization is charged on these intangible assets. The amortization amount of an intangible asset with a finite useful life will be allocated on a systematic basis over its useful life. Amortization is usually calculated using the straight-line method. Intangibles with finite lives are also subjected to impairment.

Indefinite useful life

Intangible assets with indefinite lives are **not subject to any amortization** because they indefinite lives and therefore allocation on a systematic basis is not possible. Instead, these intangibles are tested for impairment for any possible loss of value and if any, a loss is reported when it is realized. Goodwill is a prime example of an intangible asset with an indefinite life.

The standard states that an entity is required:

a. **To review at the end of each reporting year to assess** its useful life as indefinite; and
b. **To test** both categories of an intangible assets (with finite and an indefinite useful life) **for impairment** by comparing its recoverable amount with its carrying amount in accordance with **IAS 36** [*Impairment of assets*]. The carrying amount refers to the acquisition cost of the intangible asset less any accumulated impairment losses if any previously reported.

Therefore, an entity should **assess** the useful life of an intangible asset, which may be finite or infinite life An intangible asset has an indefinite useful life when there is **no foreseeable time limit** to the period over which the asset is expected to generate cash flows for the entity.

Many factors can determine the useful life of an intangible asset, including:

i. Expected usage
ii. Product life-cycles
iii. Technical, technological, commercial other types of obsolescence
iv. Industry influence
v. Competition rivalry with expected actions
vi. Level of maintenance required
vii. Restrictive covenants on the use of the asset such as expiry dates of related leases.

The useful life of an intangible asset normally do not exceed the period of any contractual or legal rights but a shorter period may be adopted over which the entity expects to use the asset

9.2 Amortization Policy

Intangible assets with a finite useful life should be amortized over its expected useful life. Some uidelines given below can be useful to determine the policy on the amortization process.

- Amortization commences only when the asset is made available for use
- Amortization ceases at the earlier of the date:
  i. That the asset is classified as held for sale (refer to **IFRS 5 Non-current assets held for sale and discontinued operations; and**
  ii. The asset is **derecognized.**

- The amortization method adopted should reflect the pattern on how future economic benefits are consumed. For example, the straight line method is more appropriate if the pattern of usage or consumption cannot be predicted reliably.
- The amortization charge should be recognized in profit or loss

The **residual value** of an intangible asset is problematic as in most cases it is practically assumed to be **zero**. Unless or otherwise if an external party is committed to acquire the asset at the end of its useful life or if there is an active market for that type of asset. In these circumstances the expected residual value can be measured.

The standard requires the amortization policy (both the period and method) for the intangible asset to be **reviewed** at the end of each reporting period.

Putting the foregoing points together, the diagram represented by **Figure 12.9** (as shown below) summarizes the **changes in value** of intangible assets according to **IAS 38 provisions**.

One exception to be noted here is that the changes in value of **Goodwill** is not dealt in the same way as all other intangible assets. **IFRS 3** apply the following provisions to **Goodwill:**

- Amortization is not applicable
- Impairment test is to be done annually, usually at the end of the reporting period, based on **IAS 36** rules
- Goodwill is not subject to reversal of impairment loss. [This condition do not apply to other intangible assets]

9.3 Accounting for Impairment of an Intangible Assets

Earlier in **Section 9.1 impairment test** for both finite and indefinite (not infinite) intangible assets was briefly described. The standard stipulates that impairment testing is required as it applies to intangible assets [as it does for plant, equipment and property]. All intangible assets with the notable exceptions such as goodwill, certain special types of trademarks, copyrights and licenses which have indefinite lives are therefore not subject to any amortization. However, all categories of intangible assets are **subject to a write-down** when their value decreases due to impairment factors. Such a **decline in the value** of an asset **represents an impairment** loss which is reported in the financial statements.

Let's look at an **illustrative example** below:

ABC Group reported goodwill at a carrying amount of RM 3,750,000 in its consolidated statement of financial position in 2014. Three years later on 31 March 2017, market demand conditions have deteriorated to a point when an impairment review exercise indicated that the goodwill amount which was based on a fair value at the date of acquisition is now worth at a recoverable amount of RM 2,250,000.

Required

Show what accounting entries will be recorded by ABC Group in its consolidated financial statements?

Answer

Rule:

Impairment loss occurs whenever the carrying amount (CA) of the asset exceeds its recoverable amount (RA).

Therefore, impairment loss {CA > RA] = RM 3,750,000 – RM 2,250,000 = RM 1,500,000

ABC Group will record an impairment loss of RM 1,500,000 and adjust the consolidated accounts by writing down the carrying amount of the goodwill as follows:

Journal entry:

	Debit	**Credit**
Impairment loss on Goodwill	RM 1,500,000	
Goodwill		RM 1,500,000
(Being adjustment for impairment loss on goodwill)		

Accounting effect

↓ **Asset value** ↓ **Shareholders' Equity** (Impairment loss) [↓ value goes down]

Both Goodwill and Equity **decrease** through loss on retained earnings. Once goodwill is impaired, it cannot be reversed unlike other tangible assets. **IFRS 3** prohibits any reversal of the impairment loss.

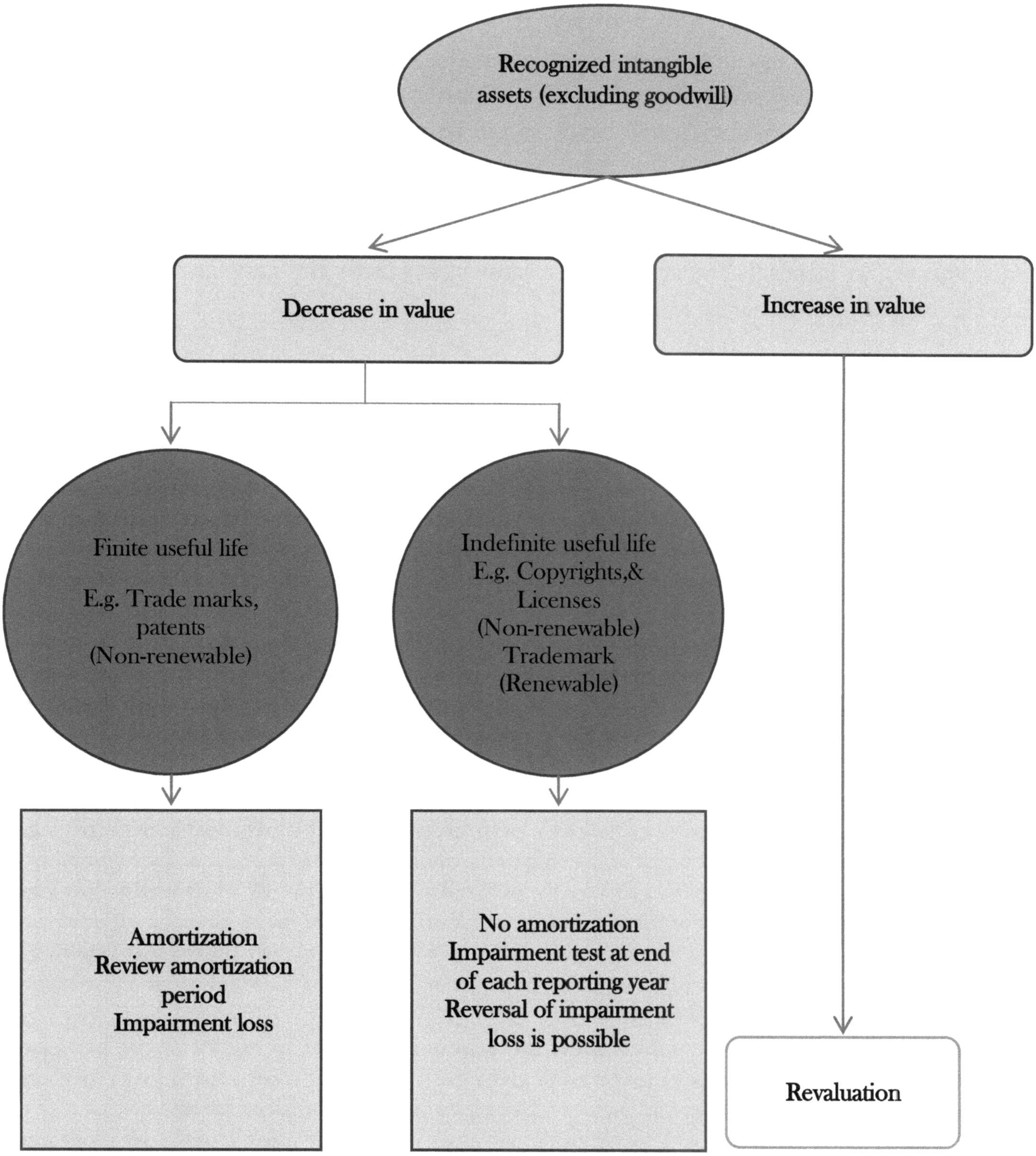

Source: Stolowy et al, (2010)

Figure 12.9 Reporting Changes in Value of Intangible Assets (Adapted)

10. Disposals/Retirement of Intangible Assets

An intangible asset that has no further expected economic benefits from its future use or asset can be disposed or sold, they should be retired by eliminating them from the statement of financial position. The carrying amount (if any balance) will be **reported at a loss** in the statement of comprehensive income in (SOCI) in the case of a retired asset. In the case of a disposal**, the gain or loss** arising from the **difference between the net disposal proceeds and the carrying amount o**f the asset should be taken to profit or loss (SOCI) as a gain (income) or loss (expense) on disposal. The accounting treatment is exactly the same as for disposal of a tangible fixed asset or non-current asset.

Chapter Summary

Summary points for Chapter 12 is rather long and wide because of a variety of intangible assets that need to be dealt adequately. Good to glance through the summary points as they can facilitate your revision of key topics in this area.

1. **Intangible assets** are broadly classified into goodwill, research and development (R&D), and specific intangible patents and trademarks, copyrights (intellectual properties), franchises and licenses. This class of intangible assets have **no physical substance**, but **clearly identifiable** and the reporting entity must **exercise control** over the assets as they **have future economic benefits** to be derived from their substance as useful resource for the business.
2. The choice of accounting treatment of intangible assets is a trade-off between relevance and reliability on one hand or prudence on the hand. The **matching principle** requires these assets to be **capitalized** and then **amortized** over their estimated useful lives to derive economic benefits. **Under prudence**, intangible assets are **not capitalized** particularly when there is **uncertainty over the economic benefits to be derived** and therefore should be **expensed** in the period when incurred.
3. **Internally generated intangibles are not recognized by IAS 38/MFRS 138** as the standard deliberately precludes such assets from capitalization because it has no cost that can be measured reliably, identifiable and controlled. **Purchased goodwill** in a business combination **happens when a group acquires another company at a premium** which is goodwill on consolidation, the **difference between the FV of consolidation given (purchase price) and FV of identifiable assets and liabilities acquired.** It has no tangible substance but has the potential earning power to create a comparative advantage in the market. The **asset is retained in the statement of financial position** and must be **reviewed annually for impairment**. The concept of **amortization does not apply for goodwill.**

   Negative goodwill is rare but **it arises when the acquirer's interest in the FV of the net assets acquired exceeds the purchase consideration given** due to unforced errors in estimating the FV and could be the result of a bargain purchase. The question **what to do with the dangling credit?** If scrutiny of the cost elements of the combination and the identifiable net assets are not ascertained, **it must be recognized immediately in the statement of profit or loss** as prudence would have it.
4. The text defines and makes a distinction between **pure and applied research** as different accounting treatment is given depending upon the nature and purpose of research activity. Owing to some degree of uncertainty about future economic benefits, **expenditure incurred on research activities is expensed (written-off) in the statement of profit or loss** whereas **costs associated with the development phase are capitalized under restricting conditions** provided the entity can clearly satisfy the specified criteria under the requirements

of IAS 38. **Capitalization is allowed if** the reporting entity can clearly demonstrate **all the specified conditions can be met objectively**. Refer to the text for details of the criteria. The text also **discusses controversy** over the capitalization policy of the standard. Some **useful example**s are given **relating to accounting policies** of certain global companies **on reporting** their R&D activities.

5. Computer software and information systems that are **directly purchased** or **created-in-house** - where the **accounting issue relates to capitalization or expensing. Software systems acquired for resale constitute part of the cost of sale** as normal inventory whereas **purchased software systems acquired ( ) for internal use or in-house application are capitalize**d as intangible asset **subject to amortizatio**n. Those **computer software systems created in-house** either for internal or external use, **their attributable costs are capitalized as intangible asset subject to amortization.** Where **computer software created** in-house t**o satisfy a specific customer's order,** it is treated as **an expense or treated as work-in-progress** inventory **for later billing. Amortization policy is a contentious issue** with computer software development as this tends to be short-lived owing to the dynamic nature of information technology industry that evolves rapidly. **Technological obsolescence and competition** in the industry may **affect the amortization periods** and in most cases may not extend beyond three years. However, changes in useful life or periods of amortization may **have an impact on timing of revenue recognition**.
6. **Specific intangible assets** such as patents, trademarks or trade names (e.g. brands) licenses (e.g. fishing rights), copyrights (intellectual properties), and franchises are unique by nature and tend to vary from one another given their useful purpose. All these assets are legally protected and their useful lives differ in periods and the amortization process governing each type of intangible asset is time related and the manner in which they were acquired. The important thing to note is that these assets confer economic benefits to the business entity. Their accounting treatment goes exactly the same process like a PPE item. However, **franchises businesses** that usually have indefinite useful lives **are not subject to any amortization process on the franchised costs**. The plant and equipment and other administrative facilities used in the business originates from the franchisor usually under leasing arrangements.
7. **Deferred expenditure** in the form of preliminary expenses and pre-operating expenses do not come within the provisions of IAS 38 as the standard prohibits deferred expenditure to be recognized as an intangible asset on the grounds that it fails to meet the definition and recognition criteria of an intangible asset. **Preliminary expenses** relate to organization set-up costs associated with the formation of a newly private or public company in Malaysia whereas **pre-operating expenses** are incurred after incorporation. **Such costs are recognized and treated as an asset prior to the commencement of business operation**. Local **GAAPs in Malaysia allows this choice in accounting practice** but must be written-off immediately in the statement of comprehensive income once the business starts generating revenue. While such expenses are allowed to be written-off, the anomaly here is that there is **no revenue to match these costs**. Companies generally amortize such expenses over a short period until revenue is generated by the company. While the company remains dormant, **losses are reported** in the financial statements **for each period** until when business operations kick off.
8. **IAS 38** allows **two methods of valuation for intangible assets** after they have been initially measured at cost but subsequently they can be reported at cost or at a revalued amount. The standard states that it unlikely to be practical for **any subsequent expenditure to be recognized as the carrying amount** of an intangible asset and therefore the **revaluation model is rarely adopted in practice** by any entity. The standard also says that **an active market** may not exist in some cases for an intangible asset and for this reason **revaluation to fair value or market value would be certainly inappropriate**. Fishing rights or taxicab licenses could be an exception.

9. The standard distinguishes between intangible assets with finite or indefinite useful lives. **Amortization** amount on an intangible asset with **finite useful life** will be allocated on a systematic basis over its useful life. usually calculated on a a straight line method. Intangible assets with finite lives are also **subject to impairment. Amortization** on intangible asset with **indefinite life is not normally provided**. Instead, this asset must be **tested for impairment** for any possible loss of value and such **a loss is reported when realized**. Goodwill is a prime example. The standard requires amortization policy (period and method) for an intangible asset to be reviewed at the end of each reporting period. **Useful lives and recoverable amounts** to be assessed as part this review process. Refer to **Figure 2.9** for changes in value of intangible assets

Key Terms

Amortization
Amortization policy
Cost measured reliably
Control of the asset
Fair value
FV of consideration given
Future economic benefits
Purchased goodwill
Intangible assets are identifiable
Initial recognition
Recognition criteria
Valuation of intangible assets
Specified criteria for capitalization of development
Cost
Changes in useful life
Technical feasibility
Trademarks
Copyrights
Deferred expenditure
Pre-operating expenses
Revaluation model
Reporting changes in value of intangible assets
Market prices
Matching principle
Prudence
Internally generated intangible assets
FV of identifiable assets and liabilities
Negative goodwill
Business combination
Impairment
Pure or fundamental research
Applied research
Research and development (R&D)
Accounting policy on R&D
Computer software and information systems
Technological obsolescence
Patents
Licenses
Franchises
Preliminary expenses
Cost model
Specific intangible assets

Review Questions

1. a. Identify and list the different types of specific intangible assets.
   b. There are three ways in which these assets can be acquired. Describe them.
2. Explain how each of these specific intangible assets are treated in accounts in terms of recognition and measurement? Give examples of each.
3. Discuss how deferred expenditure is treated in the accounts under local GAAPs.

4. Explain why IAS 38 do not recognize deferred expenditure as an intangible asset?
5. Explain the two valuation models that can be adopted for intangible assets.
6. State and explain the rules involved about implementing the revaluation model.
7. Discuss the accounting rules under the revaluation model.
8. a. Explain what reporting changes can affect the value of intangible assets?
   b. What other requirements that the standard stipulates when changes in the useful life of intangible assets with finite or indefinite useful lives?
9. List and identify the factors that determine the useful of an intangible asset.
10. Explain the guidelines relating to amortization policy on intangible assets.
11. One exception is that changes in value of goodwill is not dealt in the same way as all other intangible assets. IFRS 3 provisions apply to goodwill.

    Sate what are these provisions?
12. Show what accounting entries will be recorded by a parent company in its consolidated financial statements with regard to an impairment loss on goodwill in a group context? Give an illustrative example to show how impairment loss in the value goodwill on consolidation arises? Use your own set of figures. Show the journal entries to reflect on this adjustment.

    You are also required to show the accounting effect of impairment loss on *asset value*, and *shareholders' equity* in group context.
13. An intangible asset that has no further expected benefits from its future use or the asset can be disposed or sold. The asset is normally retired or de-registered.

    Show what accounting entries that need to be reflected in

    i. the statement of comprehensive income in the case of a retired asset?

    ii. the statement of comprehensive income in the case of a disposal?
14. What does the IFRS 3 says about the accounting treatment of goodwill in a business combination?

Multiple Choice Questions

Some questions to be prepared. Not done yet. O/S

My nomination of the most significant financial innovation of the last 25 years: the financial futures - the futures exchange style trading of financial instruments.

— Merton Miller (1986)

Chapter 13

Learning Objectives

After you have studied this chapter, you should be able to:

Understand the accrual concept of accounting as opposed to the cash basis of accounting
Understand why accrual accounting gives a better measurement of performance.
Understand what are other accounting concepts that underlie the accrual basis of accounting
Understand the adjusting process for updating the final accounts
Adjust expense accounts for accruals and prepayments
Understand the revenue recognition principle
Adjust for any accrued revenue items
Account for the accruals, prepayments and accrued revenue in the statement of financial position
Account for the amounts of accrued expense and accrued revenue in statement of comprehensive income
Prepare the extended trial balance to show all related adjustments for accrued expenses and prepayments.

Accounting for Accruals and Prepayments

1. Scope

In this chapter, the concept of accrual accounting in financial accounting is emphasized as opposed to the cash basis of accounting. Accrual accounting is used because it gives a better measure of performance than the cash basis. With some illustrative examples, we compare and contrast the two bases of accounting. We also justify why the use of cash accounting fails and at the same time explain why accrual accounting superiorly gives a better edge over cash accounting. We also discuss other conventions or concepts such as the matching principle, revenue recognition principle and time-period concept that appear to reinforce accrual accounting. We then deal with the accounting aspects with regard to adjustments for accruals and prepayments and show how the reporting is dealt in the financial statements. Finally, we show case the extended trial balance (worksheet) where all the required final adjustments on accrued expenses and prepayments including accrued revenues are reflected using the double entry system.

1.1 Cash and Profits

If you check every financial statements of reporting entities, you may observe that cash and profits never or very seldom agree because of timing differences due to:

i. Collection and payments of cash; and
ii. Items such as sales or expenses would be accounted for but debtors may settle later in line with the credit policy and same time, you may incur expenses for the period but payments are deferred to a later period and may not necessarily be in the same accounting period.

You may utilize the cash or part of your realized profits to settle your creditors and make payments to discharge your utility bills such as electricity and telephone, including staff salaries, etc. Your proceeds from your trade debtors (accounts receivables) would have been collected but you may have certain liabilities due for payments or expenses still outstanding and not paid or have incurred some prepaid expenses before utilizing them in the next period. If you think of all these financial events or transactions taking place at different times, you may realize the reality of doing business almost makes it impossible to match profits with cash to be equal under the **accrual accounting concept.** However, it is possible to reconcile the profits to cash and this may pose a bit of a problem in accounting sense, but accountants have developed the cash flow statement which gives accurately in much detail the reconciliation between profits and cash and cash equivalents. Much of this is about accrual accounting.

1.2 Accrual Accounting as Opposed to Cash Basis of Accounting

Shareholders expect a return on their investments in the form of dividends and capital gains (to be realized if the value of their shares have appreciated or increased). Banks also expect borrowers to settle their debt by servicing their scheduled capital repayments with interest payments. Accounting therefore provides useful information in the form of financial statements to these stakeholders to make informed decisions. We also discuss other conventions or concepts that appear to reinforce accrual accounting

The question is how this information is made available to stakeholders? Accounting is based on either the:

- Accrual basis; or the
- Cash basis.

Let's understand what these bases of accounting mean:

Accruals basis of accounting

Under this **accrual concept of accounting**, the transactions or events taking place can have an impact on the entity's assets and liabilities as well as the financial performance in the period. The timing of cash flows relating to these events or transactions may occur either within the accounting period or in some near or future period. For example, accountants normally record these transactions or events as they occur, such as the sale of a product or when service is performed for the customer or the entity incurs some expenses. However, cash is not received or paid on these transactions or events until they are deferred for settlement at a later period, nevertheless record of sales or service and expenses are accounted for so long as these financial transactions or events relate to the accounting period. Accounting for accruals is also based on **matching principle** where revenue generation takes place only upon related or incidental expenditure.

Cash basis of accounting

Under the cash basis of accounting, only cash transactions are recorded. These cash transactions are cash receipts (inflows) and cash payments (outflows). Cash receipts represent revenue, and cash payments are treated generally as expenses*. Profit is recognized when receipts are in excess of payments and similarly a loss is recognized when expenses exceeds receipts. In practice, the cash basis of accounting is rarely adopted by business entities. Furthermore, the accounting standards promulgates accrual accounting as the basis for financial reporting as it reflects business reality.

*Expenses may include other payments relating to capital expenditure, etc.

Differences between Accruals Accounting and Cash Accounting

To illustrate the difference between the two bases of accounting, let's look at the following two hypothetical financial transactions:

A company invoices a customer for a sale of goods amounting to RM 2,250 on a 30day credit period. The inventory cost of these goods is RM 1,575. The customer (trade debtor) will settle the account only after 30 days but first takes delivery of the goods now.

The accrual basis would recognize RM 2,250 as sales revenue because the company has the right to some future economic benefits in the form of an accounts receivable (classified as a current asset) which previously did not exist before the sale took place. The payment from the customer after 30 days' time is merely an exchange of an asset (accounts receivable) for another asset (cash) which obviously has no impact on the company's revenue. However, under cash accounting there is no exchange of cash taking place at the point of sale and accordingly has no impact on revenue and as such the sale is not recorded. It is only when cash is eventually received or realized from the customer that a sale transaction is recorded under the cash accounting basis.

Obviously, the use of cash accounting actually fails to capture the economic substance of the transaction. Two consequences emerge from this anomaly in the use of cash accounting.

i. The accounts receivable of RM 2,250 is a legal claim by the company to receive cash in the foreseeable future, which is clearly an asset, therefore it should appear in the statement of financial position. Without recording economic events, assets are understated.

ii. The creation of assets by lawful means also results in the increase of equity, and should therefore be recognized as revenue. Without recognition of revenue, the company's sale is understated.

Similarly, let's assume that the same company had incurred expenses for utilizes such as electricity (RM 900), water (RM 150), and telephone (RM 2,350) and at the same time had incurred outstanding interest on borrowings amounting to RM 3,300 for the accounting year ended on 31 December 2016. None of these accrued expenses were discharged or paid until the following year end.

Accrual accounting would recognize these expenses in the statement of profit or loss as these transactions have resulted in the flow of economic benefits for the company in the reporting period. These expenses therefore would be recorded regardless of when payments are made. The discharge of these accrued liabilities has a cash flow impact only after the financial year end for the company.

The use of cash accounting basis would not account for any of these expenses during the accounting period, thus, failing to recognize the **economic substance** of these transactions or events. It is only when cash is eventually paid will cash basis accounting record the transactions amounting to RM 6,700 in total. What is observed here is that cash accounting would treat all payments as expenses with the consequential understatement of liabilities and understating expenses?

From the above discussion, two facts are driven home:

i. The accrual basis of accounting is virtually adopted and complied by all business entities as a requirement of the financial reporting standards.
ii. Cash accounting violates the requirements of accounting standards by omitting useful, relevant and accurate information to users of financial statements. The use of cash accounting basis fails to faithfully represent the economic substance and reality of company's transactions as and when they occur regardless of the timing of payments or receipts.

Cash flows are an important source for the survival mode of any businesses but for measuring financial performance and financial position, accrual accounting gives us a better understanding and appraisal of how businesses have actually performed both qualitatively and quantitatively during the financial period.

1.3 Accruals Accounting and Other Accounting Conventions

Some lengthy discussion was devoted to explaining accrual accounting but you need to be aware of other conventional accounting concepts which underpin the use of accrual accounting.

The Matching Concept

Matching as a concept explains the relationship between revenues and expenses. According the Conceptual Framework, there is a direct association between the costs incurred and the earning of specific items of revenue or income. Unlike assets, expenses do not offer future benefits to an entity. This process is commonly referred to as the matching of costs with revenues. Profit or loss is however, primarily determined by the changes in assets and liabilities and is not the direct result of matching of revenue and costs although conventionally the matching concept facilitates the process. The use of matching concept to illustrate the analysis attributed to the change in the composition of assets and liabilities in determining profit or loss is beyond the scope of this text but you get the drift.

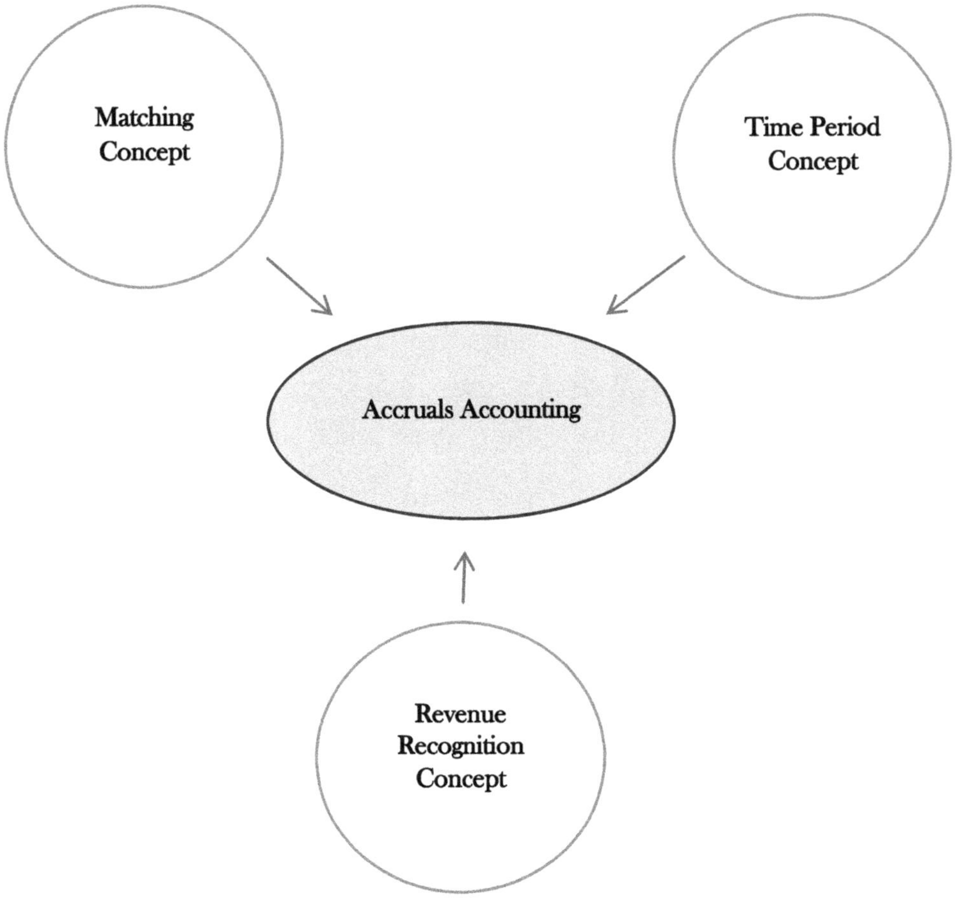

Figure 13 1 Illustrates these concepts with a brief explanation that follows

The Time Period Concept or Assumption

Businesses operate on a **going concern basis** which means that they have no intentions to scale down or liquidate their activities but instead continues in operational existence for the foreseeable future. To know how well a business has performed, the reporting of economic events or transactions need regular progress reporting. Accountants, therefore prepare financial statements for specified periods to appraise the company's performance. The **time-period concept** is adopted conventionally to communicate accounting information to all intended users of financial statements on a regular basis or at intervals. According to **IAS 1** (*Presentation of Financial Statements),* requires an entity to present a complete set of financial statements with comparative information as appropriate at least on an annual basis. The annual report containing the audited accounts and reports serves this very useful purpose. Apart from annual reports, entities also prepare financial statements on interim basis such as quarterly abridged reports to comply with listing requirements of Bursa Malaysia or KLSE, or a half-yearly report as appropriate for a specific purpose to address board requirements or intended relevant parties. Accrual accounting provides the basis for the time-period reports as discussed above.

The Revenue Recognition Principle

When should revenue be actually recognized? Revenue is recognized only when you **'earn'.** The following examples may illustrate this point:

i. Movies or music from DVDs
ii. A notebook or a laptop or a smartphone such as Samsung or Nokia
iii. Fashion clothes or garments from Dorothy Perkins or Marks & Spencer; and services
iv. 'The Economist' or "Her World'
v. University tuition fees or a haircut

So, when do business people in shopping malls or departmental stores that provide these goods or services earn their revenue or money? A sale is immediately recognized when cash is exchanged for the supply of consumer goods or when a service is rendered but in some cases such as university tuition fees, **revenue recognition** is a contentious issue because university's revenue policy usually determines at which point tuition fees earned is to be recognized as revenue. In practice, revenue recognition is based on the nature and condition of business involved, the time taken or duration to complete a contract or a project or at which point when services are to be rendered.

IAS 18-*Revenue* provides useful guidance on the **revenue recognition principle.**

Sale of goods

According to the standard, generally for the sale of goods, revenue is recognized based the following principles:

- When there is a transfer of risks and rewards of ownership of goods is to the customer by the owner;
- The owner retains neither effective control over the goods sold nor has continuing managerial involvement to the extent usually associated with ownership;
- The revenue earned can be measured reliably;
- It is probable that the economic benefits associated with the transaction will flow to the entity (or owner); and
- The costs incurred or expected to be incurred in respect of the transaction can be measured reliably.

So, for consumer sales transactions, the standard clearly indicates that it is usually at the **point of sale** when cash is exchanged for goods that you purchased. The same criteria also apply for goods over the counter.

Services rendered

Similar principles apply. For example, a customer pays immediately when a haircut is completed, so revenue is earned when the service is rendered to a customer' satisfaction. However, there is a difference when the services you render is not consumed immediately but is more time bound. Revenue is recognized as **'earned'** by reference to a **'stage of completion'** of the transaction usually at the end of the reporting period. For example, construction contracts on mega projects take few years to complete, how revenue is recognized then? You do not usually wait until the entire construction project is completed before you see your earnings. This is because cash flows are an important source for the survival of companies in the construction sector, thus **the percentage (%) of completion method** (based on the requirements of IAS 10) is applied to revenue recognition policy. Revenue is therefore recognized in stages when substantial progress is made on the project before work-in-progress is certified and progress payments are released. **Profit taking** in contracts is based on this accounting treatment approach as it reflects the business reality in the construction industry. For contracts of short duration, revenue recognition is based on the '**completion method'** usually within the reporting period when earnings or profits are recognized in the statement of profit or loss.

So, to sum up, **when should you recognize revenue?** This is after it has been earned and not before. In most cases, revenue is earned when a business entity delivers goods or services to a customer.

The annual audited financial statements must disclose the reporting entity's revenue recognition policy in the notes to its accounts, accompanying the financial statements.

1.4 Adjustments to Final Accounts

Virtually, all business entities are required to present the final version of their financial statements. Up to this point, all the books of accounts of an entity would have been updated except for some final adjustments usually at the year-end which would be required before the final accounts are drawn up and made ready for presentation to the shareholders. Shareholders and stakeholders simply want to know how well the company is performing. The financial statements report this information, and therefore all accounts must be up-to-date.

The adjusting process requires the updating of the final accounts so that:

i. All revenue and expense items disclosed in the statement of profit or loss and other comprehensive income are complete, accurate and valid as they relate to the reporting period of twelve months; and

ii. The assets and liabilities including shareholders' equity correctly represent the financial position of the entity at the balance sheet date and there are no material misstatements that would overstate or understate the assets or liabilities or any items relating to equity.

This **adjusting process** begins with the unadjusted trial balance and usually involves a number of accounts to be updated using the double entry system. The trial balance once it is adjusted by putting through these sundry adjustments, it is then ready for preparing the financial statements. Most of the items such as share capital, cash account, accounts payable, other capital items in the unadjusted trial balance may not require any further adjustments as these have been dealt routinely through the day-to-day transactions which continuously provide the necessary entries for these accounts.

So, which accounts require updating through these adjustments? Usually they fall under these categories below

- Accrued expenses and certain sundry creditors for late transactions
- Accrued revenue items such as rent income
- Prepaid expenses such as insurance, etc.
- Unearned revenue
- Adjustments for depreciation on PPE
- Interest on loans or other borrowings as they are time-bound.

The Chapter focuses on the first 4 topics only. Adjustments for depreciation on PPE are done in Chapter 9 and interest on loans will be covered in the next textbook, *"Financial Reporting and Contemporary Practice'.*

Accrued Expenses

Business entities incur expenses before they pay cash. **Accrued expense** refers to a liability that arises from an operating expense that has not been discharged or paid at the balance sheet date but the expense incurred actually relates to the reporting period.

Some examples of accrued expenses are:

i. Utility bills such electricity, telephone,

ii. Interest expense on a loan

iii. Staff salaries

iv. Consumables

v. Packing materials

vi. Rent, etc.

Let's look at the illustrative examples below:

Ex ample 1

A rent of RM 36,000 per year is payable in arrears at the end of every three months. The rent was not always paid on due dates

A schedule of rent due and rent paid is shown below:

	Rent	
Amount(RM)	Due	Paid
9,000	31 March 2021	31 March 2021
9,000	30 June 2021	3 July 2021
9,000	30 September 2021	3 October 2021
9,000	31 December 2021	6 January 2022

Quarterly rent is $3/12 \times$ RM 36,000 = RM 9,000. The rent account appeared as

Rent			
31 March	Cash	9,000	
3 July	do	9,000	
3 Oct	do	9,000	

The rent due on 31 December 2021 was paid on 6 January 2022, payment will be recorded in the books for the year 2022 as part of the double entry. Obviously the year's rent is RM 36,000 which should be recognized as the total expense for rent in the statement of profit or loss for year ended 31 December 2021. However, only RM 27,000 was paid and RM 9,000 for rent in the last quarter of 2021 still remains outstanding at the financial year-end date.

So an accrual adjustment is required for this liability. The journal entry for this accrued rent is

Journal entry

Date	Account	Folio	Debit	Credit
31.12.2021	Rent	GL	9,000	
	Accrual	GL		9,000
	(Being adjustment of rent for last quarter of 2021)			

The rent account is now updated by putting through the accrual adjustment as follows:

Rent

2021		RM	2021		RM
31 March	Cash	9,000	31 Dec	Profit or Loss	Profit or Loss
3 July	do	9,000			
3 Oct	do	9,000			
31 Dec	Accrual c/d	9,000			
		36,000			36,000
			2022		
			1 Jan	Accrual b/d	9,000 ←

There are two ways of treating the accrual adjustment.

i. One way is to show RM 9,000 rent owing for 2021, but paid in 2022 by carrying the amount down to 2022 as shown above in the rent account.
ii. Another way is to credit the amount owing to an accruals account separately which is reflected as a liability under current liabilities. See the accruals account below:

Accruals

2021		RM	2021		RM
31 Dec	Accrual c/d	9,000	31 Dec	Rent for last quarter	9,000 ←
		9,000			**9,000**
			2022		
			1 Jan	Accrual b/d	9,000

Remember other types of accrued expenses will also be recorded in this account as well but there is none assumed here. The accrual c/d in the rent account is not shown rather as a balance but to explain what the balance is for – an **accrued expense**.

Both ways are acceptable in accounting practice. However, for trial balance purposes, the accrual carried down (c/d) balance in the rent account must be shown as part of the balances for accruals account in the trial balance. Other types of accrued expenses may occur which will be recorded in the accruals account if the second way in accounting is adopted as an option.

Prepaid Expenses

Entities incur expenses in advance although they do not relate to the current accounting period. A prime example of this type of expense is **insurance.** In accounting terminology, this is referred as **prepaid expense (or prepayment).** Therefore, prepaid expenses are assets because they provide a future economic benefit for the business entity. Let's look at the illustrative examples on insurance and packing materials:

Example 1

The increased new insurance cover for an entity for a year is RM 11.700, payable at the rate of RM 2,925 per month for each quarter starting from 1 April 2020 to 31 to 31 March 2021. However, payments made by the company appeared to be irregular.

The company's financial year end is 31 December 2021. The record for prepaid insurance in the last quarter ending 31March 2020 showed an amount of RM 2,625. A schedule of insurance due and insurance paid by the company is shown below:

Insurance

Amount (RM)	Due	Paid
2,925	1 April 2020	1 April 2020
2,925	1 July 2020	RM 5,850
2,925	1 October 2020	31 August 2020
2,925	1 January 2021	15 Dec 2020

One way of facilitating your understanding is to use a diagram like the one below:

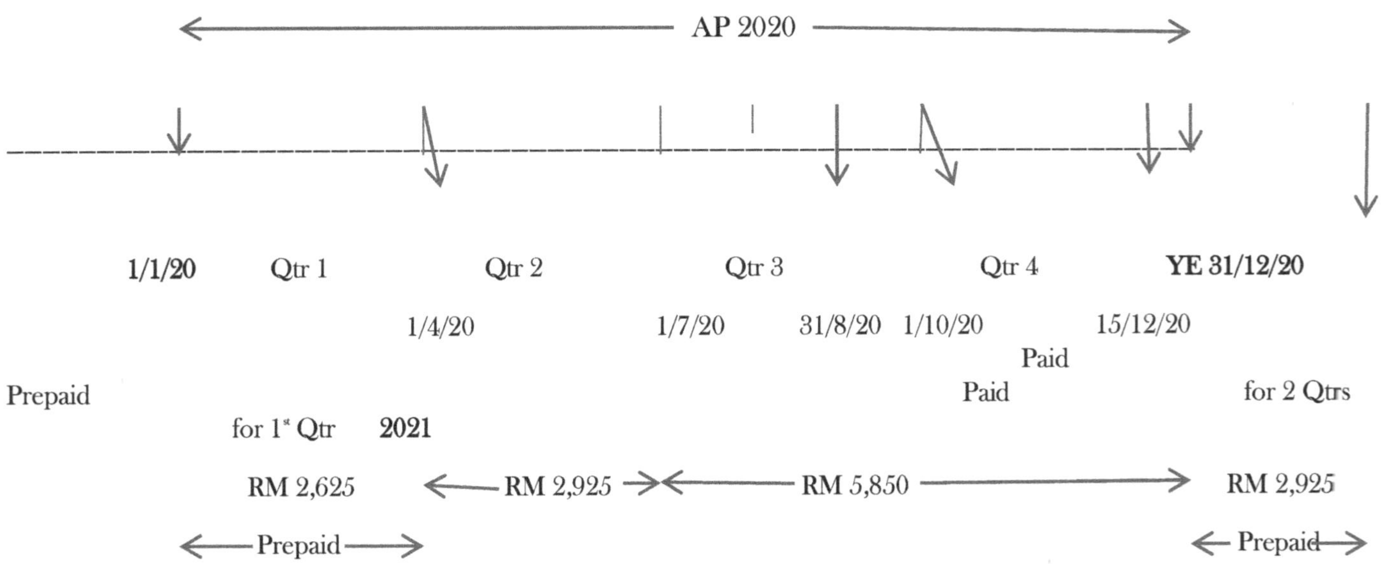

Just a note for students, you can use this diagram as a guide for an accrual adjustment but you need to adapt it because accrued expenses work as a mirrored image of prepayments.

Just a note for students, you can use this diagram as a guide for an accrual adjustment but you need to adapt it because accrued expenses work as a mirrored image of prepayments. The insurance account for the year ended 31 December 2020 will be shown in the general ledger:

Insurance

2020	RM	2020	RM
1/1 Prepaid b/d	2,625		
1/4 Bank	2,925		
31/8 Bank	5,850		
15/12 Bank	2,925		

At this stage the insurance account is unadjusted yet for the year end prepayment.

Now the last payment of RM 2,925 is not for the year 2020, it relates to the first quarter payment for insurance due in year 2021. You also note the prepaid amount of RM 2,625 for the first quarter of 2020 was brought down (b/d) from last year's prepaid insurance account. For a period of 12 months the **cost of insurance** for the year 2020 is RM 11,400 and this is, therefore, the exact amount that needs to be transferred to the statement of profit or loss. However, note the trial balance will be adjusted for prepayments

If this figure of RM 11,400 (including the prepaid amount b/d from 2020) is entered, then the prepaid amount of RM 2,925 must be adjusted to balance the insurance account. As at 31December 2020 this is an economic benefit paid for but not used up; it is a current asset and therefore needs to be carried down (c/d) as such to 2021 as a debit balance. It is a **prepaid expense.** However, the trial balance will be adjusted for prepayments.

The insurance account can be completed:

Insurance

2020		RM	2021		RM
1/1	Prepaid b/d	2,625	31/12	Profit or Loss	11,400
1/4	Bank	2,925	31/12	Prepaid c/d	2,925
31/8	Bank	5,850			
15/12	Bank	2,925			
		14,325			**14,325**
2021					
1/1	Prepaid b/d	2,925 ←			

Just as for accruals, there are two ways of treating the prepayment adjustment.

i. One way is to use the same insurance account to show the posting of payment of RM 2,925 for 2020, but adjust the prepaid amount to be carried down to 2021 by crediting the insurance account as shown above.

ii. Another way is to debit the prepaid amount directly to a prepayment account separately which will be classified as an asset under current assets. Both ways are acceptable in accounting practice. Now see below how the prepayment account is done:

Prepayments

2020		**RM**	**2020**		**RM**
1/1	Prepaid insurance b/d	2,625	31/12	Transfer to Insurance a/c	2,625
15/12	Bank:				
	Insurance prepaid for first Qtr2021	2,925			
			31/12	Prepaid c/d	2,925
		5,550			**5,550**
2021					
1/1	Prepaid b/d	2,925			

Prepayments will simultaneously also happen when items other than insurance are bought and used in business particularly if they are not fully used up or utilized in the reporting period. For instance, packing materials or other forms of consumables which are not entirely used up over the period in which they are purchased for consumption in the business. The stocks of these unused items in hand at the end of the period will be there waiting to be used in the following year. Since money was spent on these stock items, they are a form of prepayment and therefore needs to be carried forward as prepaid asset to the next period when they will be consumed.

Example 2

(**r**elates to packing materials)

A company purchased packing materials amounting to RM 4,800 for the year 2020. A physical sock-take on 31 December 2021 showed the estimated value of stock in hand to be RM 960. The company's financial year-end is 31 December 2020 From the given information, it can be seen that in 2020 the packing materials consumed by the company appeared to have been RM 4,800 – RM 960 = RM 3,840. The company will still have a stock of RM 960 packing materials at the year-end date (SOFP) to be carried forward to 2021. The RM 960 unused stock of packing materials is carried forward as a form of prepayment to be classified as a current asset in the statement of financial position.

Packing Materials

2020		**RM**	**2020**		**RM**
31/12	Bank	4, 800	31/12	Profit or Loss	3, 840
			31/12	Stock c/d	960
		4, 800			4, 800
2021					
1/1	Stock b/d	960			

The stock of packing materials is not included as part of the stock in trade or inventory of unsold goods in hand in the statement of financial position, but is included as part of other prepayments of expenses. In reality, it was paid in advance.

Let's do another example that combines both accrued expenses and prepayments. A rather long but not a difficult question to which the answer requires some careful planning as it tests comprehensively on your understanding of the final adjustments relating to both accruals and prepayments, including the postings to update the ledger accounts and finally presenting the financial statements to show how these items are reported

Example 3

Syarikat MRCB's financial year end is 31 December 2021. The company has incurred the following expenses, none of which have been paid for at the date of statement of financial position. These are year-end recurring expense items that usually occur for which payments are normally discharged in early part of January 2022. The accountant records these expenses as accruals in the statement of financial position.

Rent due for the month of December 2021– RM 4,500. Up to November 2021, the monthly rent was RM4,000 and from December onwards, the rent was increased upon yearly review.

a. The salary of one employee for the month of December 2021 whose payment was delayed because of extended leave - RM 2,750.
b. Utilities – Telephone RM 3,900, Electricity and Water 3,600
c. Closing stock of consumables at year-end was valued at RM1,350
d. Closing stock of unused packing materials at year-end was RM 2,790.
e. Sundry creditors – (i) Consumables RM 90 (ii) Packing materials RM 1, 890

The following balances were extracted from the unadjusted trial balance as at 31 December 2021.

Extracts

Other Creditors and Accruals –

Balances b/f 1.1.2021

Rent - RM 4,000

Utilities –Telephone RM 3,775

Electricity & water RM 3, 480

Sundry creditors: Consumables RM 1, 105

Packing materials RM 1,445

Prepaid expenses:

Balances b/f 1.1.2021

Packing materials RM 2,850

Expense accounts:

Salaries, allowances and bonuses RM 225,700

Rent RM 48,000 (includes rent payment for December 2020)

Telephone and internet charges RM 59,775

Electricity and water charges RM 54, 480

Consumables RM 7,660

Packing materials RM 25,315

Required

a. **Show journal entries to reverse the opening accruals**

b. **Show the closing journal entries for the accrued expenses for the year ended 31 December 2021.**

c. **Update the ledger accounts and show the closing balances for the year 2021**

d. **State the adjusted final amounts of all:**

   i. **Expenses to be charged in the statement of profit or loss**

   ii. **Accrued expenses to be shown in statement of financial position**

(Only for the items you have adjusted)

Answer

a) Journal entries for the reversal of opening accruals

Date	Account	Folio	Dr	Cr
31 Dec	Sundry creditors and accruals		13,805	
	Rent			4,000
	Telephone			3,775
	Electricity and water			3,480
	Sundry creditors: Consumables			1,105
	Packing materials			1,445
	Stocks b/f Consumables		990	
	Packing materials		2,350	
	Prepaid expenses			3,340
	(Being reversal of opening creditors and accruals			

b) Journal entries for accrued expenses at the year end

Date	Account	Folio	Dr	Cr
31 Dec	Rent		4,500	
	Salaries, allowances and bonuses		2,750	
	Electricity and water		3,600	
	Telephone		3,900	
	Consumables		900	
	Packing materials		1,890	
	Prepayments – Closing stock of consumables		1,350	
Closing stock of packing materials				2,790
Consumables - stocks c/f				1,350
Packing materials – stocks c/f				2,790
Sundry creditors and accruals				17.540

(Being adjustments for year-end accrued and prepaid expenses)

c) Ledger Accounts

Other creditors and accruals **Prepayments**

Rent account

Paid (Jan to Nov) 990	48,000	Accrual b/f	4,000
		Profit or Loss (44,000 + 4,500)	**48,500**
Balance c/f 1,350	**4,500**		
	52,500		**52,500**

Prepaid consumables

Stock b/f	990		
consumables	1,350	Transfer to Consumables	
		Stock c/f	
	2,340		2,340

Telephone & internet charges

Paid (Jan to Nov)	59,775	Accrual b/f	3,775
		Profit or Loss (44,000 + 4,500)	**59,900**
Balance c/f 1,350	**3,900**		
	63,675		63,675

Prepaid packing materials

Stock b/f	2,350		
consumables	2,790	Transfer to Consumables	
		Stock c/f	
	5,140		5,140

Telephone & internet charges

Paid (Jan to Nov)	59,775	Accrual b/f	3,775
		Profit or Loss (44,000 + 4,500)	**59,900**
Balance c/f 1,350	**3,900**		
	63,675		63,675

Prepaid packing materials

Stock b/f	2,350		
consumables	2,790	Transfer to Consumables	
		Stock c/f	
	5,140		5,140

Electricity & water charges

2,550		Accrual b/f	3,480
Paid (Jan to Nov)	54,480	Profit or Loss (51,000 + 3,600)	**54,600**
Balance c/f 900	**3,600**		
	58,080		58,080

Sundry creditors

Transfers:		Bal b/f	
Consumables	1,105	Transfers:	
Materials	1,445	- Consumables	
		- Materials	
		Stock c/f	
Balance c/f	**2,790**		
	5,340		

Salaries, allowances & bonuses

Paid (Jan to Nov)	225,700	Accrual b/f	
		Profit or Loss (225,700 + 2,750)	**228,450**
Balance c/f	**2,750**		
	228,450		228,450

[Closing balances are in bold]

Consumables

Stock b/f	990	Creditor b/f	1,105
Paid (Jan to Nov)	7,660	Profit or Loss (Consumed)	**7,095**
Creditor c/f	**900**	Stock c/f	**1,350**
	9,550		9,550

Packing materials

Stock b/f	2,350	Creditor b/f	1,445
Paid (Jan to Nov)	25,315	Profit or Loss (Consumed)	**25,320**
Creditor c/f	**1,890**	Stock c/f	**2,790**
	29,555		29,555

d) (i) Statement of Profit or Loss for the year ended 31 December 2021

Extract

Administrative Expenses

Salaries, allowances & bonuses	228,450
Rent	48,500
Electricity & water charges	54,600
Telephone & internet charges	59,900
Consumables	7,095
Packing materials	25,320

(ii) Statement of Financial Position as at 31 December 2021

Extract

Current Assets

Prepayments –		
Unused stock of consumables	1,350	
Unused stock of packing materials	2,790	4,140

Less: **Current Liabilities**

Other creditors and accruals		
Rent	4,500	
Telephone	3,900	
Electricity & water	3,600	
Salary	2,750	
Consumables	900	
Packing materials	1,890	17,540

Some Notes

i. The question tested your understanding and knowledge of accrued expenses and sundry creditors involved in updating the final accounts.

ii. The example is illustrated to test you on multiple adjusting entries related to accruals. and to some extent on minor adjustments for prepayments.

iii. Accruals for such items like audit fee, company secretarial fee & disbursements are not dealt here as part of the final adjusting entries. Usually in practice, these adjustments are handled by the auditors once the audited financial statements are agreed by the Board of Directors. So ignore them.

iv. An additional entry which is always the last final adjustment to put through is the income tax expense in the statement of comprehensive income and the corresponding income tax payable shown as a liability in the statement of financial position. This part of the adjustment is deliberately left out because it is beyond the scope of your syllabus requirement. This advance topic will be dealt in your forthcoming textbook, 'Financial Reporting and Contemporary Practice' when you are in the final year of your degree program. So, ignore taxation.

Accrued Revenue (Deferred income)

Business entities sometimes may involve in other activities that can generate additional income for the business. For instance, the entity may use its own investment properties to earn revenue by renting out commercially to outside parties. A business entity therefore needs to account for accrued revenue from rent before they receive the cash. Revenue that is recognized but not yet collected or received by the end of the reporting period is called **accrued revenue.** Rent receivable is treated as other debtor in the accounts.

Let's look at the following **example:**

A manufacturing company has a large warehouse space than its present requirements, so it rents part of it to another company for RM 2,500 per month on a lease that started on 1 January 2021. The lease rental is receivable for every three months in arrears from the tenant.

The following details were given for the year ended 31 December 2021.

Rent		
Amount RM	**Due**	**Received**
7,500	31 March 2021	5 April 2021
7,500	30 June 2021	5 July 2021
7,500	30 September 2021	7 October 2021
7,500	31 December 2019	7 January 2022

The account for 2021 will appear as:

Rent Receivable

2021	**RM**	**2021**		**RM**
		5/4	Bank	7,500
		5/7	Bank	7,500
		7/10	Bank	7,500

Any rent received, will be reported(credited) to the profit or loss statement as revenue. The actual amount earned as revenue for the 12 months (covering 4 Quarters) in year 2021 is RM 30,000. However, since the rent of RM 7,500 for the last quarter of 2022 was received only on 7 January 2022, an adjustment for rent receivable will be credited to the account and then carried down as a debit balance owing to the company. The RM 7,500 owing is shown as a sundry asset to be classified under current assets on 31 December. 2021. When this rent is received on 7 January 2022, the posting of the credit entry in the rent receivable account will contra off the opening debit entry. All entries are done in one single account.

The rent receivable account can now be completed:

Rent Receivable

2021		**RM**	**2021**		**RM**
31/12	Profit or Loss	30,000	5/4	Bank	7,500
			5/7	Bank	7,500
			7/10	Bank	7,500
			31/12	Accrued income c/d	7,500
		30,000			30,000
2022			2022		
1/1	Accrued income b/d	7,500	7/1	Bank	7,500

Alternatively, the accrued c/d of RM 7,500 can be transferred to a sundry debtor's account as the amount owing by the tenant on lease is an asset.

Unearned Income

Some business entities receive cash from customers before earning the revenue. This creates a liability termed as **unearned income** or deferred income. Only when the services are rendered or the job is completed does the **entity recognizes revenue being earned**.

Let's see an **example**

A company performs a cleaning and maintenance service to all office buildings and premises on a contract. It invoices the customers at the end of each month only when the job or service is completed. A new customer has engaged the company's cleaning services for an agreed monthly rate of RM 850, commencing immediately. The company collects the first payment on 15 December 2021 and records the transaction as follows:

Journal entry

Date	Account	Folio	Debit	Credit
15/12/2021	Bank	GL	850	
	Unearned Income from Service	GL		850
	(Being cash received in advance for cleaning services.)			

Unearned Income from Cleaning Service

				2021		
				15/12	Bank	850

Any unearned income or revenue derived from a cleaning and maintenance contract is a liability as the company has a legal obligation to perform services for the new customer it has contracted. The unadjusted trial balance as at 31 December 2021 will indicate unearned revenue with a RM 850 credit balance. However, according to company's revenue recognition policy, it must have performed the cleaning service during the last 15 days of the month, thus invoicing the new customer only one-half of the contracted amount which is RM 850 x 50% = RM 425. Therefore, the following adjustment will be made:

Journal entry

Date	Account	Folio	Debit	Credit
31/12/2021	Unearned Income from Cleaning Service	GL	425	
	Revenue from Cleaning Services	GL		425
	(Recognition of earned income for cleaning services.)			

Obviously, this adjustment recognizes that income has been earned from cleaning services performed and the transfer of RM 425 to revenue account reduces the liability from the total amount received RM 850. Thus, revenue from cleaning service increases reported income for 2021. Let's see what effect these journal postings have on the accounts.

Unearned Income Cleaning Service

2021		**RM**	**2021**		**RM**
31/12	Revenue a/c	425	15/12	Bank	850
31/12	Revenue a/c	425			
		850			850
2021			2021		
			1/1	Balance b/d	425

Revenue from Cleaning Services

2021		**RM**	**2021**		**RM**
31/12	Revenue a/c	100, 125	1/12	Balance b/d	96,500*
			31/12	Bank	3,600*
			31/12	Unearned income a/c	**425**
		100,125			100,125

* These represent the company's revenue from other services.

The important thing to remember is that any revenue collected in advance is accounted for this way. **Unearned revenue**s in contractual terms represent a legal obligation to perform services or specified jobs and as such they are not revenue or income to be recognized immediately but are a liability to be accounted for initially. The revenue recognition principle applies here strictly.

Chapter Summary

1. The **adjusting process** we have seen in the foregoing pages for **accruals and prepayments**, apart from other routine adjustments are normally reported for preparing the final accounts before presentation, basically they are critical to ensuring that the financial statements are updated completely and accurately on all material aspects, possibly without any misstatements or omissions. At the same time, the adjusted final accounts for these items are in a position to give a better measure of financial performance. To sum up, all these adjusting entries through accruals and prepayments consequently affect at least both the following accounts:
   - Revenue or Expense;
   - Current asset (prepayments) or Current liability (accruals)

   Refer to the Chart given in Figure 13.2 for the timing of these adjusting entries that usually takes place toward the end of the financial reporting period.
2. **Accrual basis of accounting** is a preferred option as opposed to the **Cash basis of accounting** and the standard require this practice to be adopted compulsorily in financial reporting. Other **accounting concepts** (*matching, revenue*

recognition and time period) and **conventions** appear to **reinforce** *accrual accounting*. We demonstrated through some illustrated examples as to why the accrual basis of accounting is **superior** as opposed to cash basis because it captures the **economic substance of the reported transactions or events**. **Revenue** is recognized only when you earn regardless of when payments are received. **Expenses adjusted** on accrual basis in the statement of profit or loss, result in the flow of economic benefits for the company Besides, the discharge of accrued liabilities (recorded expenses regardless of when payments are made) has a cash flow impact only after the financial year end for the company. Cash accounting **violates** the requirements of accounting standards by omitting useful, relevant and accurate information to users of financial statements.

3. **IAS 18** provides useful guidance on the **revenue recognition principle** for **sale of goods** and **services rendered.**

   The relevant section in the chapter highlights some of these principles as related to sales of goods and services rendered. It is worth noting them for better understanding. In another instance, **revenue is recognized as earned** by reference to a s**tage of completion** of the transaction at the end of the reporting period in the case of construction contracts. For mega projects that extend for more years, **earnings or profit taking** are recognized in the **statement of comprehensive income** on the **basis of percentage (%) of completion method** as per the requirements of **IAS 10.** As cash flows are important source for the survival of business entities, you do not wait until the entire construction project is completed before you recognize your revenue.

Key Terms

Accruals
Accrual basis of accounting
Accrued revenue
Adjusted trial balance
Cash basis of accounting
Matching principle
Revenue recognition principle
Time period assumption
Prepayments
Sale of goods
Services rendered
Adjusting entry
Unadjusted trial balance
Unearned revenue

Review Questions

1. Why do profits and cash seldom agree? Explain some some of the circumstances that cause this difference.
2. Accounting is based on either (i) the accrual basis or (ii) the cash basis
   a. Define these two bases of accounting
   b. Explain the main difference between these accounting conventions. Provide examples to support your explanation.
   c. What is the adopted view of the accounting standard in practice with regards to these two basis of accounting?
3. Give reasons why the accrual basis of accounting is a preferred option for providing a better measure of performance. You may compare and contrast between the two bases of accounting.
4. Briefly explain the following accounting conventions as they linked to the accrual basis of accounting. Illustrate with examples for your explanations.
   a. The matching principle
   b. Time period assumption
   c. The revenue recognition principle

5. IAS 18/ MFRS 118 on Revenue provides useful guidance on the revenue recognition principle. State these operating rules for these two items and provide some relevant examples.
   a. Sales of good
   b. Services rendered
6. Explain how the revenue recognition principle is applied in the following cases?
   i. Movies or music in digital form. (DVDs were used in the recent past).
   ii. Sale of a car
   iii A notebook or a laptop or a smartphone such as Samsung, Readme or Nokia
   iv. Fashion clothes or garments from Dorothy Perkins or Marks & Spencer
   v. The 'Economist' or 'Her World'.
   v. University tuition fees or a haircut
7. Explain why some final adjustments are required to the financial statements before a final version of the accounts are drawn up?
8. The adjusting process requires updating of the final accounts. Identify the nature of these final accounts and justify the reasons or rationale for doing so.
9. State the other categories of accounts that require updating through the final adjusting process at the year end.
10. Explain what are accrued expenses and prepaid expenses? How are these items treated in the statement of financial position? Provide examples.
11. What is the difference between accrued revenue and unearned revenue (or income)? State the accounting treatment for these two items and where they are shown in the financial statements.

Multiple Choice Questions

1. The company's accountant due to a busy working schedule had omitted an accrual adjustment to record staff salaries of three unpaid employees amounting to RM 18, 500 at year end. This oversight has the effect of
   a. Understate net profit by RM 18, 500
   b. Overstate net profit by RM 18, 500
   c. Understate assets by RM 18, 500
   d. Net effect on net profit is nil
   e. Overstate current liabilities by RM 18, 500
2. On 1 September 2021, a company purchased a one - year insurance policy coverage for RM 9, 000 that commences immediately. What is the amount of insurance expense and prepaid insurance amount that should appear in the statement of profit or loss and under current assets respectively for the year ended 31 December 2021? How much of prepaid in
   a. RM 3, 000 and RM 6,000
   b. RM 4, 000 and RM 5, 000
   c. RM 12, 000 and RM Nil
   d. RM Nil and RM 12, 000
   e. RM 6, 000 and RM 6, 000

3. If there is a prepaid insurance account brought forward balance of RM 4, 500 from last year, what would be the insurance expense amount to be recognized in the statement of profit or loss, assuming the same facts apply as in Q 2? The prepayment carried forward will be the same for the year end with no change.

   a. RM 8, 500

   b. RM 7, 500

   c. RM 8, 000

   d. RM 6, 000

   e. RM 12, 000

4. Consumable supplies account had a debit balance of RM 1, 200. At the year end, a physical stock take showed consumables supplies amounting to RM 350 still available. The required adjusting entry is:

   a. Dr. Consumables supplies RM 350; Cr Consumables expense RM 350

   b. Dr. Consumable expense RM 850; Cr Consumables supplies RM 850

   c. Dr. Consumables expense RM 850; Cr. Consumables supplies RM 350

   d. Dr. Consumables supplies RM 850; Cr. Consumable expense RM 850

   e. Dr. Consumables expense RM 350; Cr. Consumable supplies RM 350

5. APS Consulting received from a client, a sum of RM 9, 000 for consulting services to be rendered over 6 months equally commencing from 1 October 2021 to 31 March 2022. APS credited this money to Unearned Consulting Fees. APS Consulting's financial year end is 31 December 2021. What would be the adjusting entry on 31 December 2021?

   a. Dr. Unearned Consulting Fees for RM 6, 000

   b. Dr. Unearned Consulting Fees for RM 4, 500

   c. Cr. Consulting Fees Earned RM 6, 000

   d. Dr. Consulting Fees Earned RM 4, 500

   e. Cr. Cash for RM 9, 000

6. Audit fee amounted to RM 3,000, Accounting fee incurred for RM 4, 500, Outstanding salaries and wages not paid until after the year end, Utility bills relating to electricity, telephone and water supplies totaled RM 2, 400 were discharged after the financial year end. Earlier, the client already paid in advance on account RM 900.

7. What would be the adjusting entry for accrued charges at the year end?

   a. RM 9, 000

   b. RM 7, 500

   c. RM 9, 900

   d. RM 2, 400

   e. RM 900

8. Some adjusting entries at the end of its accounting period were unintentionally omitted from the final accounts. The company had failed to record RM 1, 850 of insurance coverage that had expired. This RM 1, 850 had been initially debited to the prepaid insurance account. The company also failed to recognize accrued salary expense of RM 1, 200. As a consequence of these two oversights, the financial statements for the reporting period will

   a. Understate assets by RM 1, 850

   b. Understate expenses by RM 3, 050

c. Overstate profits by RM 2, 050

d. Overstate liabilities by 1, 200

e. The Company ignored the treatment of these items in the financial statements.

Problem Solving Questions

9. Sam and Chong started their business operations in its first year. The earnings reported from the business revenue account is RM 60, 000. Their customers paid cash RM 48, 000 on account. Sam and Chong incurred operating expenses of RM 42,500 but had not settled RM 3, 500 of these expenses at the year end. Sam and Chong prepaid some expenses RM 3, 350 that would relate to next year's accounts.

   Required:

   Calculate the first year's net profit under the cash basis and the accrual basis of accounting.

10. Young and Beauty Company reported net profit RM 42, 000 and net sales of RM 393, 000 for the current year Competitors in the operating segment earn on average a profit margin of 15 %.

    Required:

    Calculate the company's net profit margin and comment on the result. Competitors in the operating segment earn on average a profit margin of 15 %.

Chapter 14

Learning Objectives:

After you have studied this chapter, you should be able to:
Define irrecoverable debts and doubtful debts
Understand why irrecoverable and doubtful debts arise
Understand the purpose of an aged receivables analysis
Understand the purpose of credit limits
Be able to prepare accounting entries to write-off an irrecoverable debt
Be able to record an irrecoverable debt recovered
Identify the impact of irrecoverable debts on statement of profit or loss and on the statement of financial position
Be able to prepare the accounting entries to create and adjust an allowance for receivables
Understand why it is necessary to create an allowance for receivables
Illustrate how to include movements in the allowance for receivables in the statement of profit or loss and how the
closing balance of allowance should appear in the statement of financial position
Understand credit controls with regard to collection of overdue receivable accounts
Know the difference between write-off method and allowance method
Understand the implications of using financial ratios in debt management

Accounting for Irrecoverable Debts and Allowances for Receivables

1. Scope

In this chapter, we are concerned about a company's trade receivables being unable to be converted into cash on time due to collection problems. **Irrecoverable debts** become an issue for most companies and the value of these assets must be **written down to its recoverable amount** which creates a cause for concern. As such, in extreme cases where evidence suggests that trade receivables prove uncollectible; the company has no choice but to **write-off such debts as loss events or make necessary allowances (or provisions) for doubtful receivables** on the basis of prudence. The **aging analysis** of trade receivables forms an important analytical tool and basis **for determining the allowances as required to be**

charged as an expense in the statement of profit or loss. We cover the **allowance method** which is the preferred way for providing the required allowances on trade receivables or accounts receivables with a brief discussion on its merits. Before we look at some illustrative examples of accounting for doubtful receivables and irrecoverable debts, we do a case study on aging analysis of account receivables of a company and the accompanying **accounting policy** **t**hat deals with this aspect of it. A brief discussion is then devoted towards the **direct write-off method** for accounting doubtful receivables and explain why this **short-cut method is an unacceptable accounting practice**. This is followed by detailed illustrative case examples to test your understanding of the methods involved in accounting for irrecoverable and doubtful receivables. The **incremental approach** to the allowance method is also discussed with an example to show where the variance is in the approach. **Credit control** is an important application tool used by management to reduce the incidence of bad and doubtful receivables as this can eat into the company's profits. We discuss several **measures of credit control policy**. What happens if a customer settles an old debt which was written off previously? We show the necessary adjustments using three methods and explain the circumstances when each is applied.

The chapter is not complete without paying sufficient attention on **how to accelerate cash flows from collections of receivables** by discussing two ways for achieving the purpose. Finally, we explain **key financial ratios** that are relevant in the **management of receivables** that have a direct impact on liquidity and collection periods.

2. Trade Receivables

Trade receivables or **accounts receivables** arise from credit sales and are amounts owed by trade customers to the business entity. Receivables are the mainstay of any business because significant amount of capital is tied up in this current asset. The accounting aspects of trade receivables have been covered adequately in Chapter 5, and any reference can be made there for more detailed information on the topic. However, this chapter is more confined to accounting issues relating to the recoverability of receivables (doubtful debts) and their collection.

When a business entity makes a sale or provides a service on credit, the transaction goes through some simple steps. For example, if Mydin sells goods on credit to Samy. Samy takes delivery of the goods and receive an invoice from Mydin. The invoice will be processed through Mydin's accounting system and it will state how much must be paid for the goods and the credit period or deadline for settlement or payment due, e.g. 30 or 45 days. Mydin now has an account receivable or commonly called 'a trade debtor'– the amount of debt legally payable to Mydin by Samy.

The total value of trade receivables for a business at any one point of time represents the amount of sales which have not been paid yet or remains outstanding for collections. The credit policy and the efficiency with which the business administers its accounts receivables determine the speed at which the recoverability process is optimal. In accounting, an accounts receivable is reported at its **recoverable amount** in the statement of financial position. Recoverable amount is taken to mean **'net realizable value'**.

Recall from Chapter 5 how the entry to record sales revenue on credit is done via the sales day book or sale journal.

SDB – Journal entry (amount assumed)

Date	Account	Folio	Debit	Credit
31.12.2021	Accounts Receivable	GL	1,850	
	Sales Revenue	GL		1,850
(Sales on credit per invoice no: 205, on 5/12/16)				

When some sales are done on a cash basis the company would collect cash for all its receivables. The record entry for cash sales is as follows:

Dr Bank		RM 1,200	
	Cr Cash sales		RM 1,200

The company has no further action after this transaction other than updating the accounting records. Sales transactions on credit however go beyond this stage. There are follow-ups on administrative procedures such as:

i. Collections;
ii. Recovery of trade receivables in the case of defaulting customers;
iii. Monitoring credit policy; new customers and reviewing old cases; and
iv. Updating the accounting records and sales ledgers to keep track of receivables.

2.1 Irrecoverable Receivables

However, cash sales do not happen always. If you note the history of accounts receivables you will realize that in the majority of cases, collections will not pose a major problem as business goes on as usual for these trade debtors. Unfortunately, some trade debtors will begin to default on payments due to unavoidable constraints or difficulties experienced in the business environment. In such cases, how do we account for irrecoverable receivables? Irrecoverable receivables is treated as an expense because it is a loss transaction or event just like other operating expenses such as rent, utilities, salaries and advertising and sales promotions. Companies treat irrecoverable receivables as bad debts expense to be written-off in the statement of profit or loss; an expense that is already **impaired** where the recovery is virtually zero – uncollectible at all resulting in **a**

loss transaction. The individual accounts of these receivables (bad debts) in the sales ledger will be written-off without trace with consequential adjustments to the sales ledger control in the general ledger.

2.2 Allowance for Doubtful Receivables

There is always a case for risk of default in payments by customers as some of these accounts receivables become doubtful for collection and recovery. In accounting reality, it is difficult to ascertain which of these customers or trade debtors would default on their credit terms. **Credit control** works but it cannot be guaranteed to provide a good measure of results all the time as the administration process on credit policy is a continuous one. To account for these eventualities, the accounting profession developed the *allowance method* to be used and in certain limited cases, the *write-off method* is also applied to account for doubtful receivables. See **Figure 14.1**below:

Change of Terminology

The terminology used today has changed to reflect on current trends and is made more international.

What used to be called previously "Provision for doubtful debts" is now being replaced by "Allowance for doubtful receivables." Accounts receivables used to be referred as "trade debtors" in those days when I was studying chartered accountancy. However, in essence nothing has really has changed as these designated accounts still play similar functions and purposes.

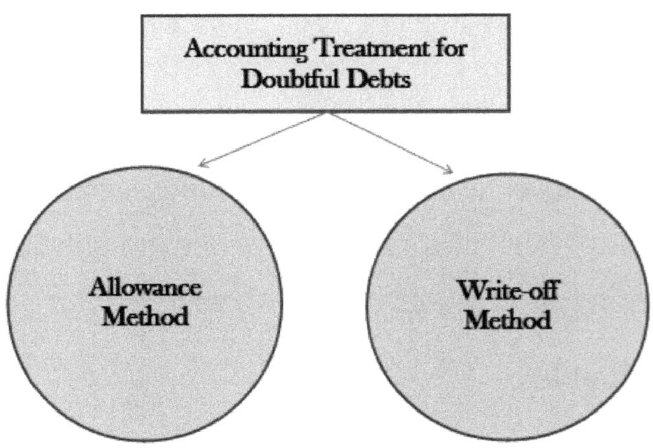

2.3 Allowance Method

The allowance method provides a much better way to account for doubtful receivables or debts. The allowance is set up in order to include a realistic value for receivables in the statement of financial position, without actually write-off the debt. The balance is left in the receivables or sales ledger so that collection procedures continue, but the receivables in the balance sheet (SOFP) are valued as though the amount is not to be recovered. The trial balance is therefore shows:

	Dr RM	Cr RM
Accounts receivables	36, 575, 230	
Allowances for receivables		731, 505

(See below how this reported in the accounts.

What this indicates is that the business already has an allowance, charged as an expense to the statement of profit or loss in previous years. The question is how this allowance arises in the first place?

IAS 39: Financial Instruments -*Recognition and Measurement*, stipulates that **loans and receivables,** like any other financial assets, are impaired if, and only if, there is objective evidence of impairment as a result of one or more **'loss events'** that occurred after their initial recognition. The following loss events are based on observable data on loans and receivables:

- Significant financial difficulty of a specific debtor with the possible risk of bankruptcy or going into liquidation;
- A breach of contract by a specific debtor resulting in a default or inability to pay both interest and capital repayments;
- A number of delayed payments with adverse changes in the position of debtors;
- Debtors in general defaulting due to adverse economic conditions and other adverse changes or circumstances in industry environment and conditions.

Based on the entity's collection experience and information of debtors' past track record, the allowance method allows for collection losses based on best estimates and by using the information available from these sources. Under this method, there is less need to observe which customers or debtors will fail to pay. So, most companies adopt this method to account for their delinquent accounts by recording the estimated amount as irrecoverable debts or setting up an allowance for doubtful receivables. This account is a contra to the accounts receivables (see below). The estimated allowance basically indicates that the entity will not be able to realize the collection of these doubtful debts or receivables by being more prudent. The following illustration shows how the accounts receivable is reported in the statement of financial position under current assets:

As at 31 December 2021 (amount assumed)		
	RM	
Accounts receivable	36, 575,230	
Less: Allowance for doubtful receivables	(731,505)	[Amount unlikely to be collected]
Accounts receivable, net	35, 843,725	

This is a disclosure note to the financial statements. Only the net figure is reported in the statement of financial position. This note shows what the trade debtors owe the company RM 36,575, 230, but the expected collection is only RM 35,843,725.

Alternatively, if preparing a company's SOFP for publication, receivables are reported this way:

Accounts receivables, less allowance of RM 731, 505	RM 35, 843,725

You can addback to determine the full amount of the receivables. – Net receivables RM 35,843,725 plus the allowance of RM 731,505.

What gets reported in the statement of comprehensive income?

So far the discussion is confined towards SOFP presentation and disclosure but what gets reported in the statement of comprehensive income? Remember that it is only the increase or decrease in the allowance that goes into the statement of profit or loss. More of this will be elaborated in later **sections** of this Chapter.

2.4 Aging Analysis

One of the best methods to estimate irrecoverable and doubtful debts is to use the aging analysis based on the company's history of collections from customers. Using information gathered on possible 'loss events' as suggested by IAS 39 as this aids the analytical process further. Companies use this common and popular method for estimating delinquent receivables as this approach focuses on the most relevant accounts receivables at the cut-off SOFP date. The aging analysis takes into account individual receivables from specific customer accounts by analyzing how long they have been outstanding with reference to their historical business status or aging of accounts The aging of receivables are typically classified into age groups such *as 'not due yet'*, '30 days overdue', *'31-60 days overdue,'* and *'over 60 days overdue,'* Management would then consider those accounts which are not yet due may have a 1% chance of not going into bad debts, and those that have been overdue for 30 days are more likely be uncollectible, say, 2% or3%, and so forth. Past experience may also suggest that a fairly fixed percentage of trade receivables proves to be uncollectible each year.

The allowance for each classified age debt group is thus determined using the **vertical analysis approach**, the totals of these allowances forms the basis of estimates that the entity will need to provide at the reporting year-end. **Figure 14.2,** using a table below illustrates a simple hypothetical version of the aging method of calculating allowances for irrecoverable receivables.

Figure 14.2: Aging Analysis of Accounts Receivables

Receivables (RM)	Not due yet	Days	< 30 Days	31-60 60 days	Over Total
Customer X	650	650			
Customer Y	500	300	800		
Customer Z	550	350	750	200	1,850
Totals	12,500	6,500	4,500	3,000	26,500
Estimated % irrecoverable	1%	5%	10%	18%	
Required allowance	125	325	450	540	1,440

Based on the above aging analysis, the total amount of allowance to be desired is RM 1,440 for receivables totaling RM 26,500. This allowance represents approximately 5.4% (RM 1,440 of RM 26,500) of the receivables expected to be doubtful or impaired. Of course, it is really not prudent enough at this stage of the analysis to decide on the 5.4% and then use RM 1,440 as a provision for the allowance. The actual estimate really depends on the age groups and the individual percentage (%) allocated to each age group.

Again, bearing in mind that there is a possible limitation on this type of aging analysis which is perhaps not complete unless we exercise more caution by looking at specific information such as '**Loss Events**' associated with specific customers. In this case, Customer X is clearly a likely case going for bankruptcy or liquidation because of the defaulting system of payments and cash flow problems. Let's take a closer look at the table and you are not aware of the impending 'loss event' about Customer X at this stage. The aging analysis disregards this critical fact and only provides an allowance based on the following calculation: RM 134 [550 x 1% + 350 x 5% + 750 x 10% + 200 x 18%] when possibly the entire RM 1,850 is considered a bad debt (or impaired). The analysis, of course is not complete unless you **assess each customer's receivable row by row horizontally rather than by age group vertically.** Probably you would take into account specific information about each customer in your objective assessment of receivables whether impaired or not. By becoming more aware of the knowledge that Customer X's likelihood to be a '**loss event**' and the probability of this happening is 90%. In that case you set up an allowance of RM 1,665 (90% of RM 1,850) **specifically** for Customer X (Specific bad debts are tax allowable by Inland Revenue Board.)

However, in actual practice these calculations are based by taking into consideration the aging factor of receivables for a customer and specific information on a **customer's credit**

worthiness before determining the required allowance to be set-up at the reporting year-end. While calculations are inherently subjective to assumptions, the analysis of bad and doubtful receivables calls for careful **and prudent judgment of individual customer's account.** You **cannot avoid some moral hazards** that may emerge out of this process as information may appear asymmetrical.

2.5 Illustrative case study

Let's look into the case of one company that reports its position on trade receivables and allowance for doubtful receivables. The following is an extract taken from its annual accounts and report which is used for our hypothetical discussion.

Notes to the Financial Statements for the year ended 31 December 2021

(Extract)

Accounting Policy:

Allowances for doubtful receivables represent the Company's estimates of losses that could arise from the failure or inability of customers to make payments when due. These estimates are based on the ageing of customers' balances, specific credit circumstances and the Company's historical bad receivables experience.

Trade Receivables

(RM millions)	**2021**	**2020**
Not due yet	12, 325	11, 520
< 30 days overdue	1, 120	960
31-60 days overdue	360	295
days overdue	115	136
91-120 days overdue	90	105
>120 days overdue	630	615
Total trade receivables	14, 640	13, 631
Less: Allowance for doubtful receivables	(438)	(425)
Net trade receivables	14, 202	13, 206

Based on the historic trend and expected performance of the customers, the Company takes the view that the above allowance for doubtful receivables adequately covers the risk of default.

Movement of allowances for doubtful receivables (RM '000)	**2021**	**2020**
Balance as at 1.1.2021	425	465
Receivables write-off	(102)	(145)
Allowance for receivables during the year	115	105
Balance as at 31.12.2021	438	425

Note:

The aging analysis shown above is not an integrated part of the required note normally disclosed in the financial statements. The data is shown only for presentation purposes, thus contributing to our discussion.

The Company's accounting policy on allowances for receivables is explained below. The provision for allowance on doubtful receivables amounting to RM 438,000 represents the amount that the Company will not be able to collect. The net amount of the receivables RM 14,202,000 is the amount that the Company expects to collect within the next twelve months and realize in cash receipts. The net amount is the figure that will be reported in the statement of financial position classified under current assets. If you look at the bottom of these figures, there is a disclosure on the movement on allowance for doubtful receivables. The movement reflects on the opening balance which represents last year's ending balance, the write-off of receivables during the year and the amount of allowance considered as reasonably appropriate for the year and the necessary allowance at the reporting year-end. A closer examination of the allowance reveals that out of RM 425,000 at the start of the year, RM 102,000 of receivables were considered for write-offs which left a total outstanding balance of RM 323,000 before providing the necessary top-up allowance for receivables of RM 115,000 as a bad debt expense at the reporting date. The ending balance of **RM438, 000 is the total allowance which is set-off against the total trade receivables**. The total allowance is based on the company's ageing list of receivables, specific credit circumstances of customers and using past trends on bad debts experience.

Now, let's put all these accounting data using the ledger accounts to record the transactions of this Company. The reported figures are all in RM' 000 and is for the year ended 31 December 2021.

Accounts Receivables

	14, 202	
425	══	

Allowance for Doubtful Receivables

Write-off	102	Balance b/d	
Balance c/d	438	Irrecoverable receivables for the year	115

Irrecoverable Receivables (Expense)

Allowance for receivables	115	

Net receivables, RM 14,202,000 [14,640 -438]

The allowance for doubtful receivables account operates very similarly to the accumulated depreciation account for a PPE item.

2.6 Write off of Irrecoverable Receivables (Bad Debts)

How does a business entity deal with the issue of irrecoverable receivables or bad debts? **Irrecoverable bad debts are usually written off as an expense in the statement of profit or loss** because they are uncollectible as collection and recovery procedures would have failed for various documented reasons.

Let's use an example to illustrate the write-off of irrecoverable debts using another company's specific customer balances for our purposes. We use T-accounts to simplify the write-off process.

XYZ Company had these accounts receivables reported on 31 December 2021. Assume the amounts are in RM'000.

Sales Ledger

Accounts Receivable Large

8	

Accounts Receivable Small

5	

Accounts Receivable Tiny

1	

Accounts ReceivableOthers

106	

General Ledger

Allowance for Doubtful Receivables

	25

Total Accounts Receivable = RM 120 **Allowance = RM 25**

Accounts Receivables (Net) = RM 95

Sometime before the year-end in 2021, the Company's Credit Division determined that the Company is unable to collect from these trade debtors – Large, Small and Tiny. The Company's accountant then decided to write-off these receivables after obtaining sufficient evidence from the status report of these customers. The following adjusting journal entries were made:

Amounts in RM'000

Date	Account	Folio	Debit	Credit
31.12.2021	Allowance for doubtful receivables	GL	14	
	Small	SL		5
	Tiny	SL		1
(Being write-off of irrecoverable debts for the year)				

After the write-off, the Company's accounts showed these amounts:

Accounts Receivable Large

8	Write-off	8

Allowance for Doubtful Receivables

Write-off receivables	25
Large	8
Small	5
Tiny	1
Balance c/d	11

Accounts Receivable Small

5	Write-off	5

Accounts Receivable Tiny

1	Write-off	1

Accounts Receivable Others

106		-

Total Accounts Receivable = RM 106 **Allowance = RM 11**

Accounts Receivables. Net = RM 95

2.7 Consequence of Write-Off of Accounts Receivables as Bad Debts

The affected accounts' receivables are **reduced to nil balances as the amounts will not be collected** from these customers'. At this point, the accounts' receivables cease to be an asset because it is now no longer probable that the economic benefits associated with the transactions will flow to the Company [IAS 18, paragraph 14(a)]. The allowance previously set aside is now **'utilized'** by the write-off. The write-off of receivables has no effect on current assets, and no effect on net accounts receivable. Do you notice why the net accounts receivable has not changed, it still remains the same at RM 95. There is also no effect on the net operating income as no expense was charged out by these write-offs. Why is this so? It is because the allowance for doubtful receivables has been initially provided for in the previous accounting periods. The adjustment to the allowance is merely a realization now of an already expired expense. The **increase or decrease in the provision for allowance on doubtful receivables is a continuous adjusting process as more expense is expected in each reporting year as the allowance is utilized for write-offs and at same time the allowance is also replaced by further top-ups**. Putting this way, we say, *"out with the old and in with the new"*.

3. Write-off Method

This is another method to account for doubtful receivables. The practice takes a very conservative approach by waiting before actually determining the position of a specific customer's receivable until it becomes uncollectible despite taking appropriate measures for recovery. At this point, the accountant then writes-off the customer's account and records the adjustment as an irrecoverable debt expense. Using the same previous example as before, the adjusting entries would appear as follows:

Amounts in RM'000

Date	Account	Folio	Debit	Credit
31.12.2021	Irrecoverable receivables expense	GL	14	
	A/c Receivable -Large		SL	
	A/c Receivable -Small	SL		5
	A/c Receivable -Tiny	SL		1
(Being write-off of irrecoverable debts for the year)				

The write-off method is not an acceptable accounting practice because the Company deliberately tends to be extremely 'over' prudent with the write-off policy on doubtful debts. It fails to take into account the possibility of impairment of the receivables at the cut-off (or SOFP) date. The consequence of doing so results in the **over-statement of the asset position relating to accounts receivables**. The amounts are **not reported at their recoverable amount, thus violating IAS 16 provisions on impairment.**

However, this method has a useful purpose for income tax computations because the Inland Revenue Board does not accept the provisioning method of allowances since the taxable position of companies is always determined by actual receipt basis which defers with financial reporting principles. This method has implications for **temporary differences** between net income for financial reporting purposes and the adjusted taxable income for income tax purposes.

However, **most companies virtually adopt the allowance method in preference to the write-off method.** The main advantage for the direct write-off method is that it has far fewer accounting formalities involved to be complied when compared to the allowance method.

4. Testing Your Understanding.

Now that we have covered most of what are required to be known, we will attempt a comprehensive question which puts all the accounting issues together so as to gain a better understanding of the principles underpinning this topic.

Illustrative Examples

a) Cash Discount

Sometimes, an invoice issued to a customer will state that a **cash discount** is available if full payment is received by certain date. The offer is to encourage prompt settlement of the invoice by the customer. Let's assume an invoice for RM4, 750 on goods sold was issued o n 1 June 2021 Leong Sales Service to Sammy Enterprise stated that a 2% discount is allowed if the invoice is paid within 21 days – three weeks of the normal period of credit of 30 days. Let's suppose that Sammy Enterprise takes the offer up and pays on 21 June.

Required:

1. **Show the accounts receivable account of Sammy Enterprise in Leong's Sales Ledger.**
2. **What accounting entries are required to be recorded in the General Ledger?**

Answer:

i. The following entries will be recorded in Sammy Enterprise's account when the payment is made on this date as shown below:

Sammy Enterprise

2021	**RM**		**2021**		**RM**
1 June	Sales	4, 750	21 June	Bank	4, 655
			21 June	Discount allowed	
		4, 750			4, 750

ii. Accounting entries:

The discount is 2% of RM 4, 750 which works out to be RM 95. The receipt of RM 4,655 will be recorded on the debit side of Leong Sal es Service's cash book and the discount allowed to Sammy on the debit side of discounts allowed account (General Ledger). Both amounts will be credited to the accounts receivables account in the General Ledger as follows:

Dr	Cash Book (Bank account)	RM	4, 655
Dr	Discounts allowed	RM	95
Cr	Accounts receivables	RM	4,750

The note stated is not part of the answer but just some explanation on the commercial practice of discounts:

Nowadays, the practice of allowing discounts is not as common as it used to be although prompt settlement of invoices is encouraged. One reason for not encouraging this commercial practice is that it's more expensive and does not benefit sellers in the case of traders like Leong Sales Service. If Leong earns 6% per annum interest on his bank deposit account, the business will receive only about RM 16 of this 6% of RM 4,655 x 21/365 days.

b) What happens if Customer Fails to Pay

Using the same example as above, Sammy Enterprise (SE) fails to pay by the due date. At this point, Leong Sales Service (LSS) should take necessary procedures for the recovery of the debt from SE by monitoring and collecting the overdue receivable account. These recovery procedures should be effective, fair and legal. It may be that LSS should engage the services of a debt collector and possible resort to legal proceedings against SE. As these procedures are beyond the scope for discussion in this chapter although some basics of credit control need to be understood here. Some relevant notes on credit control will be covered later in the chapter. LSS has to accept the fact that if all attempts fail, the amount due from SE will be not collectible and therefore becomes a bad debt. This is possibly due to several reasons, this might be a case that SE has gone out of business or declared bankrupt or SE has absconded without trace. At this point, LSS probably realizes that the accounts receivable of RM 4,750 is no longer an asset because the economic benefits associated with this transaction in all probability will not be realized as a cash flow to LSS.

Required:

i. What action should LSS take to recognize this "loss event"?

ii. What journal entry is required to record this loss event? Explain the implications of this treatment in LSS books of account.

Answer

i. The action for this loss event is for LSS to write-off the accounts receivable account of SE as an irrecoverable debt. This adjustment will be recorded in the SE's account in the sales receivable ledger

ii. The required journal entry is as follows:

Dr Irrecoverable debts RM 4, 750

Cr Sales receivable control RM 4, 750

(Amount due from customer Sammy Enterprise written-off as irrecoverable)

Implications:

Both account entries are posted in the General Ledger while the corresponding entry is made in the sales ledger. As a result of this adjustment, the accounts receivable of SE as recorded in the sales ledger now ceases to be an asset when the debit entry is transferred to the irrecoverable debts account as an expense.

One important implication that emerges from writing-off irrecoverable bad debts is the consequential adverse impact on profit which can be quite significant for the entity. Let's assume Leong SS sells goods at a constant gross profit margin of 25%, the effect of the irrecoverable amount due can be analyzed in the following trading account shown in the table below:

	RM
Sales	4, 750
Less:	
Cost of sales (75% of 4,750)	(3, 563)
Gross profit	1, 187
Less:	
Irrecoverable debts write-off	(4, 750)
Loss	(3,563)

To turn this loss into a profit position, Leong SS must generate an additional sales of RM 14,252 to make it break-even (25% of RM 14,252 = RM 3, 563) first before creating more new sales at a slightly higher GP margin, say 30%.

c) **Creating an Allowance for Receivables**

The following information on Leong Sales Service's (LSS) business is given:

Financial year-end is 31 December 2021

Trade receivables or accounts receivables at the balance sheet date is RM 585,500

Total receivables written off as irrecoverable debts during the year 2020 was RM 160, 215

The irrecoverable debt of Sammy Enterprise (SE) has been recognized and included as part of the total amount for the year 2021

Leong SS feels it may be prudent to provide for an additional charge for irrecoverable receivables or doubtful debts based on the total of accounts receivables at the financial year end. Past experience would suggest that a fairly fixed percentage (%) of trade receivables proves to be uncollectible each year, particularly for the kind of trading business engaged by LSS. Some scrutiny using an ageing analysis of customers' receivables and related specific information has been part of this process. Suppose LSS's past experience indicates that on average 3% of accounts receivables proves to be uncollectible. This works out to be 3% x RM 585,500 = RM 17,565. Leong SS intends to write-off about RM 17,565 of this amount in 2021. It is appropriate therefore to charge this amount as an expense in the year 2021 in which the related sales occurred (using the matching principle) although LSS would not be able to determine specifically which of these receivables are uncollectible until 2021.

The opening balance brought forward in the allowance for doubtful debts account is RM 15,028 which represented 3% of trade receivables totaled RM 500,933 as at 31 December 2021

Required:

i. What will be reported as the total receivable expense for the year 2021?

ii. State the amount of trade receivables that will be included and reported in current assets of the statement of financial position as at end of 2021.

iii. Prepare the required ledger accounts to record all the entries

Answer:

i. The total amount charged as an expense in the statement of profit or loss for the year 2016 is as follows:

Irrecoverable debts written off	160, 215 (Specific debts)
Less:	
Last year's allowance for receivables	(15, 028) (General provision)
Add:	
End of year allowance for receivable	17, 565 (General provision)
Receivables expense for 2021	162, 752

It is important to note that the allowance of RM 15, 028 is reversed out for 2021 so that the irrecoverable debts which was anticipated and charged in 2021 are not charged again in 2021.

ii. Amount included and reported in current assets in the statement of financial position as at 31 December 2021 is as follows:

Accounts receivables	585, 500
Less:	
Allowance for receivables	(17, 565)
Accounts receivables, net	567, 935

iii. The Underlying Ledger Accounts:

Accounts Receivable Control Account

2021	RM	2021	RM
31 Dec Balance	585,500		

Irrecoverable Debts Account

2021	RM	2021	RM
31 Dec Write-off of irrecoverable debts	160, 215	31 Dec Allowance for receivables (Old)	15, 028
31 Dec Allowance for receivables (New)	17, 565	31 Dec Profit or Loss Statement	162, 752
	177, 780		**177, 780**

Allowance for Doubtful Receivables

2021	RM	2021	RM
31 Dec Irrecoverable debts (Old)	15, 028	1 Jan Balance b/d	15, 028
31 Dec Balance c/d	17, 565	31 Dec Irrecoverable debts (New)	17, 565
	32, 593		32, 593
		2022	
		1 Jan Balance b/d	17, 565

Notes:

You will note that the allowance for doubtful receivables has just two entries for the year. At the end of each accounting period the old allowance is taken out and the new allowance is put in. In each case, the corresponding entry is made in the irrecoverable debts account (or receivables). This being an expense account is closed off with the transfer to the statement of profit or loss.

Relatively speaking, the above method appears easy to understand particularly if you are new to this approach. It is safe and a reliable method to arrive at the correct figures.

The expense charged to the statement of profit or loss will always be:

Irrecoverable debts or receivables written off	x
Less: Last year's allowance for receivables (old)	(x)
Add: Current year's allowances for receivables (new)	x)
	x

The figure in the statement of financial position will always be:

Accounts receivables	x
Less: Current year's allowances for receivables	(x)
	x

The computation of these figures was already given earlier in the Chapter but for ease of convenience, this is repeated here for student's benefit.

The Incremental Approach

The incremental approach is an alternative method of updating the allowance for accounts receivables at the end of each accounting period. This method has the advantage of fewer entries to be made in the ledger accounts but involves a bit of difficulty in knowing what you are doing. basically reporting changes in the movement by accounting for increases or decreases during the year on an incremental basis. Using this method, the opening allowance for doubtful receivables is changed to give the end of year allowance. The required change in the allowance results in either an increase or a decrease. This is just a variation in the accounting approach.

Let's use this approach and see where the change is required in the allowance for doubtful receivable Using the same previous data, the irrecoverable debts expense charged in the statement of profit or loss for 2021 will be:

	RM	
Irrecoverable debts written off	160, 215	
Increase in allowance for receivables		
[17, 565 – 15, 028]	2, 537	[The required change]
Receivables expense	162, 752	

There will be no change in the reported figure for accounts receivables included under current assets in the statement of financial position:

	RM	
Accounts receivables	585, 500	
Less:		
Allowance for receivables	(17, 565)	As before
Accounts receivables, net	567, 935	

The entries in the ledger accounts are shown below:

Irrecoverable Debts

2021	RM	2021	RM
31 Dec Write-off of irrecoverable debts	160, 215	31 Dec Profit or Loss Statement	162, 752
31 Dec Increase in Allowance for receivables	2, 537		
	162, 752		162, 752

Allowance for Doubtful Receivables

2021	RM	2021	RM

31 Dec Balance c/d	17, 565	1 Jan Balance c/d	15, 028
		Irrecoverable debts	2, 537
			17, 565
	17, 565		17, 565
		2021	
		1 Jan Balance b/d	17, 565

Where the change results in a decrease in the allowance for doubtful receivables, the decrease would have been debited and the irrecoverable debts account would have been credited. Students can attempt this exercise on their own since the required change is to be made on the opposite side of both accounts. Just a single journal entry is necessary to complete both the accounts.

5. What if a Customer Settles an Old Debt?

Leong SS is surprised to receive some good news when a full payment of RM 4, 750 from Sammy Enterprise in 2021 along with a letter apologizing for the delay. Having written off SE's debt in 2020, what should be done now to record this payment? There are three ways of handling this adjustment in the accounts for this kind of transaction:

Method 1

	RM
Dr Bank	4, 750
Cr Irrecoverable debts	4, 750

Method 2:

Dr Bank	4, 750
Cr Accounts receivables	4, 750 [Also Cr SE's account in Sales Ledger)
Dr Accounts receivable	4, 750 [Also Dr SE's account in Sales Ledger]
Cr Irrecoverable debts	4, 750

Method 1 is more appropriate where a full or part payment is received at the end of bankruptcy or insolvency proceedings or from a debt collection agency.

Method 2 reverses the irrecoverable debt write off. This applies to SE's case. **Method 2** is more appropriate when full payment is unexpectedly received from the customer. Refer to **Section 3**

(b) for write-off of SE's account as an irrecoverable debt on 31 December 2020. This adjustment now in 2021 puts back SE's accounts receivable account (write back) and at same time the SE's account is closed off (contra adjustment)) as full settlement is made to LSS. SE may continue to be a valued customer.

Method 3

This method for write-off as recommended in **Section 1.7** of this Chapter is not applicable here as there was no prior provision for allowance for doubtful debts set up for SE's irrecoverable debt in 2020 by LSS's accounting system. **Method 3** would not have resulted in a clear write-off of SE's debt as an expense in the statement of profit or loss but instead SE's debt would have been used up (or utilized) by the allowance if it was set up in previous accounting periods. We have no information whether LSS had such earlier provisioning of allowance for doubtful debts or receivables.

Hence, what can we learn from this situation? Leong SS was a bit too hasty in writing off the receivable in the first place when it is still considered a doubtful debt and not an irrecoverable debt as assumed when SE failed to pay the debt. LSS should also review its collection procedures carefully.

6. How to Achieve Fast Cash Flows from Customers?

Which company does not want speedy collections from customers? Quicker or rapid cash flows help to finance growth and expansion of business by creating new products or services, fund research and development activities so that the business has a competitive advantage in the market place. Some companies doing business on credit terms may find themselves in difficult cash flow situations to finance some of their business activities by engaging in factoring their receivables to obtain ready cash at high expense. Retailing businesses on the other hand, may find it easier to doing business using credit card sales.

Two common strategies could be suggested here that can help to generate cash flows speedily.

1. **Using Credit Cards or Debit Cards**

   A business normally sells goods and services and allows the customer to settle payments using Credit cards such as MasterCard, or VISA or American Express or Carte Blanche or in some cases Debit cards used for prompt settlement. While this payment strategy helps to generate fast cash flows and increased sales, it comes with a cost attached, say at least 2% to 3% of the total payment due from sale of a transaction. Debit cards do not charge but cash is dispensed immediately on the spot via the customer's bank account.

   Let's see how a typical transaction is done using one of these Credit Cards. For an example, Sony sells one of its Blue Ray Home Movie Theatre set for RM 10,800 and the customer pays with an AE Card.

Entries:	**Dr**	**Cr**
Bank	10, 475	
Charge for processing transaction (3%)	325	
Sales		10, 800

(Being sale of Home Movie Theatre BR 64 by AE Credit Card – gets credited to Bank A/c)

Sony Shop processes the cash transaction using its AE credit card machine linked to its AE server. which automatically credits Sony's account for a discounted portion of RM 10, 476 of the RM 10,800 sale price. 3% goes to American Express as processing fee as an operating expense. That reduces Sony's net profit as it bears the cost for using this facility to speed up cash flows from collections for its business.

2. Factoring Services

Factoring services are available to ease the burden of collections as customers would only settle payments on account strictly based on agreed credit terms. Most entities may find this waiting time for collections rather slow as their operating activities require immediate funding or much earlier than the anticipated timing of cash flows. These companies make large sales to various customer or other entity companies on credit, debiting their accounts receivables and crediting their sales revenue. The credit terms could be longer than 30 days or 45 days or in some cases even 60 days. As working capital is severely tied up in these trade receivables, financing obviously becomes an issue. These companies might then sell their accounts receivables to a *factor* to solve their immediate cash flow needs.

A factor company serves this need by earning revenue or commission from **advancing a discounted price for the receivables** placed in their collection with a responsibility to receiving hopefully full amount from the respective customers. The benefit to the factor's client company is the immediate receipt of cash with a service cost attached that could be quite expensive when compared to retaining the receivables in the entity's own books and then collecting the full amount or in some cases ending up as doubtful receivables. One of the major disadvantages of placing receivables with a factor service is that the entity may **lose effective control over the collection process** but legally still has a responsibility for incurring any irrecoverable debts that may emerge after the factoring. For these onerous reasons, some companies prefer to engage less costly means of raising cash perhaps using short-term borrowings or bank overdrafts from banks.

Now, let's illustrate how factoring works with accounts receivable; assume the entity sells its most active accounts receivables amounting to RM 250,000 for immediate cash flow needs of RM 237,500, discounted at 5% The entity would then record the transaction as follows:

Entries:	**Dr**	**Cr**
	RM	**RM**
Cash	237, 500	
Financing cost (5%)	12, 500	
Accounts receivable		250, 000

(Being sale of accounts receivable to a factor)

Just like interest expense, the financing cost is an operating expense. You may however notice the financing cost is 5% of the total sale value of the accounts receivable which the company had to forgo in terms of opportunity cost in order to avail immediate cash for the business rather than just waiting for 30 to 60 days to collect the full amount. This a costly decision particularly if companies are forced to do this in circumstances when the timing of cash flows is causing some financial distress to their businesses.

7. Credit Control

Business entities normally accept the reality if certain accounts receivables can result in eventual non-payment of debts from customers. This is the inevitable part of the process and cost of doing business. The process allows the provisioning for allowance on such incidence of recoverability but what is the threshold of tolerance here if credit control and credit policy goes a bit weary? From our earlier discussion, we saw that irrecoverable debts can severely damage profit and hence, cash flow. Therefore it becomes imperative for any business to maintain some form of credit control. One of the important measures it can take is to reduce the incidence of irrecoverable debts to a minimum level. Credit control must start very early upon the initiation of the first credit sales to a customer. The following three control measures can act as a good foundation for credit control:

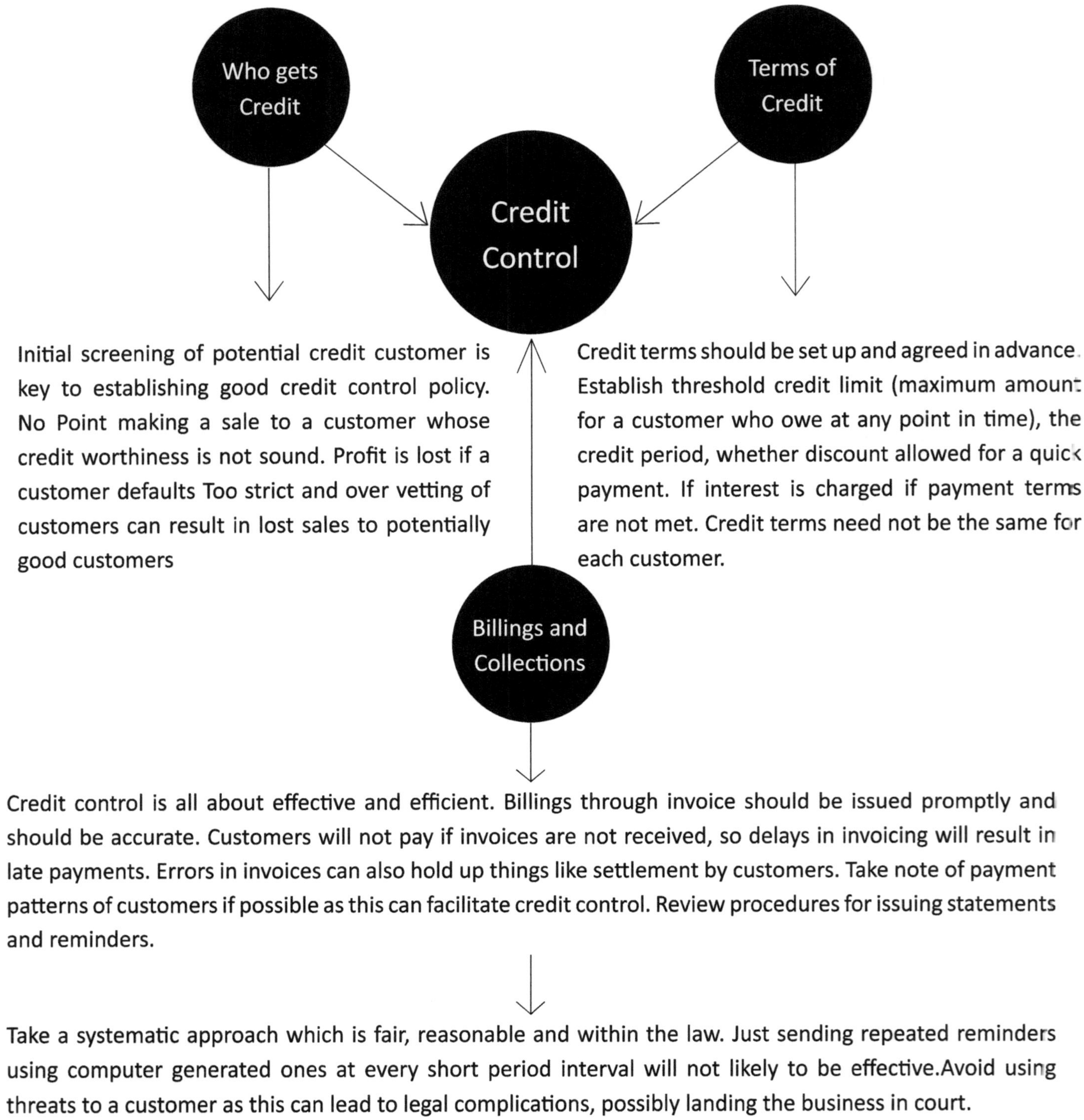

Credit control is all about being effective and efficient. Billings through invoice should be issued promptly and should be accurate. Customers will not pay if invoices are not received, so delays in invoicing will result in late payments. Errors in invoices can also hold up things like settlement by customers. Take note of payment patterns of customers if possible as this can facilitate credit control. Review procedures for issuing statements and reminders.

Collection of Overdue Accounts

Take a systematic approach which is fair, reasonable and within the law. Just sending repeated reminders using computer generated ones at every short period interval will not likely to be effective. Avoid using threats to a customer as this can lead to legal complications, possibly landing the business in court.

8. Using Financial Ratios to Make Decisions

In accounting, the use and purpose of financial ratios is to provide relevant information to users for making useful decisions in business. A bank considering lending money to a potential customer needs to assess the borrower's capacity to repay the loan with interest payments. If a borrower with a higher level of debt in their books will have less chance of securing credit facilities from a bank because of the probability of high risk in default of repayments. To analyze a company's financial position, lenders use ratios calculated on various key figures in the financial statements.

You may find two key ratios useful in financing or investment decisions:

i. Current ratio; and
ii. Turnover in number of days' sales receivables.

Both these ratios can be used by decision makers particularly investors, bankers or others to measure liquidity and efficiency respectively.

Current Ratio

The current ratio is one of the most commonly and widely used ratios used in interpreting the liquidity position of a company – that is whether the company has adequate cash resources to meet its liabilities in the short-term.

The ratio is expressed as:

$$\frac{\textbf{Current assets}}{\textbf{Current liabilities}}$$

Let's use some hypothetical figures to compute this ratio: The current assets and current liabilities of a certain company are taken from its statement of financial position.

	2021	**2020**
Current ratio = Current assets/Current liabilities		
(Assume in RM Million).	20.5/12.5	18.75/14.55
	= **1.64**	= **1.29**

Interpreting the current ratios

The current ratio basically measures the ability of the company to pay-off the liabilities as and when it falls due with its current assets. A high current ratio is preferably a good indicator of liquidity and the company finds it very useful as it is able to use the available resources from current assets to finance its current liabilities. This position is said to be technically solvent which means that the company has more than adequate financial resources to meet its contingencies within the next 12 months. An increasing current ratio from period to period is a positive indication of improvement that the company is financially sound and healthy. The ratios computed for 2021 is 1.64 times and for 2020 is 1.29 times, both these ratios showing an increasing trend appear to suggest the company probably has virtually no problem in settling its liabilities as and when it falls due. Most successful companies operate with current ratios between 1.5 and 2.0, depending on the industry or business segment in which it operates. It is good to compare current ratios with other similar companies in same type of business to see it is relatively better or worse. On the other hand, low current ratio is a concern for worry as it may suggest liquidity problems as financing working capital may need to be beefed up. The situation is a relative one; it has to be viewed in the context of operating activities and cash flows. See more in Chapter 25 on current ratio.

In the context of current assets, accounts receivable is highly a significant asset constituting it, one which contributes in size to the current ratio. Where the current ratio appears positive as discussed above, it can be assumed safely that all receivables are collectible with probable fewer incidences of doubtful receivables.

Efficiency Ratio: Control of Receivables

Collecting receivables becomes more important after a business makes a credit sale. Accounts receivable collection period is one of efficiency ratios that measure the average length of time (in number of days or times) it takes for a company's customer to pay. The receivable turnover is calculated as follows:

$$\frac{\text{Average accounts receivables*}}{\text{Sales}} \times 365 \text{ days} \quad (1)$$

or

$$\text{Receivables Turnover (times)} = \frac{\text{Sales}}{\text{Average accounts receivables}}$$

$$\text{Days} = 365/\text{Receivables Turnover}$$

- Average = (Opening + Closing Balance)/2

Receivable collection period indicates how long it takes on average to collect receivables. A shorter period is obviously preferred as receivables are converted into cash more quickly. The longer the collection period, the cash collected is less to pay off liabilities and may be slow to expand or grow the business. Using hypothetical figures, let's determine the receivable turnover; The sales revenue is based on the reported figure in the statement of profit or loss and the receivables are taken from the statement of financial position (using this year's opening balance and the current year's closing balance). Average receivables are the simple average of the opening and closing balances.

$$\text{Receivable Turnover} = \frac{\text{Average Receivables}}{\text{Sales}} \times 365 \text{ days}$$

2021	2020
$\frac{14,135 \times 365}{92,993}$	$\frac{13,372 \times 365}{81,042}$
$= 55.5$ days	$= 60.2$ days

Average receivables $= (3,631 + 14,640)/2$

For 2021 $= 14,135$

Average receivables $= (14,112 + 13,631)/2$

For 2020 $= 13,372$

Students can work out using the second formula

At best, the receivables collection period (or turnover) is only an approximate.

i. The value attributed to receivables in the balance sheet (SOFP) might be high or low compared with the normal level of sales the company usually does.
ii. Sales revenue reported in the statement of profit or loss is net of sales taxes but the receivables in the statement of financial position are inclusive of sales tax. We are not strictly comparing like with like.

Interpreting the receivables collection periods

It takes the company an average of 55 days to collect its receivables in 2016 compared to 60 days in 2015. Customers took a bit longer in 2015 to pay their accounts. Why is this so? But the collection period is relatively shorter for 2016 approximately by 5 days. However, it is necessary to evaluate the company's collection period of 55 days and compare it with the credit terms that it offers customers when sales are made. It is also important to be aware of the average number of days that creditors allow the company to settle their liabilities without penalty interests if delayed. Even if the company offers a 30 day or 45 days credit period on sales, the company's collection period of 55 days appears longer than the credit policy allows. Given the fact that some customers tend to delay payments and some even fail to settle for a much longer period, this creates some kind of mismatching particularly with some creditors who expect payment of their accounts payable within 30 days, thus creating gaps in cash flows to meet obligations. The position obviously indicates rather lack of efficient management of trade receivables which adversely leads to the incidence of possible bad or doubtful receivables which in turn eats into the company's profits if it goes unchecked. The consequence of this is that the company may be forced to borrow cash on short term interest rates that could prove expensive in order to settle outstanding creditor's accounts.

A collection period significantly in excess of the normal credit terms of payment within 30 days suggests poor management of funds of a business. Some companies however offer generous credit terms to win good customers and again in some cases, exporting customers may have to carry large amounts of receivables, and so their average collection period might be well in excess of the 30 days or even more.

The trend of the collection period over time is probably a better guide. If the collection period is not controlled over the short term, this is highly indicative of poorly managed credit control policy. Companies need to watch their collection periods closely. If collections slow down, the business usually finds it necessary to borrow short term funds or find other sources of financing such as selling receivables to a factor at discounted price.

Examples of Accounts Receivable Collection Period

Using companies within the same business segment or industry as examples **(Figure 14.3)**, we compare the collection periods of each company, we observe the following trend:

The differences in collection period reflect the differences in the nature and type of business these companies operate. Supermarkets operate on carry and cash basis and therefore hardly have any accounts receivable at all. Food manufacturers, on the other hand tend to have a longer collection period whereas other manufacturers of food and drinks appear to have relative shorter periods. The collection periods however are fairly constant from the previous year for all four companies.

Figure 14.3: Food Industry – Receivables Collection Period.

	Type of Company	**Collection Period in Days**	
		2016	**2015**
1.	Supermarket	6	5
2.	Food Manufacturer	82	79
3.	Cooking Oil Refiner	29	31
4.	Can/Bottled Drinks Producer loss	30	33

Chapter Summary

1. Chapter 14 is all about **accounting for irrecoverable debts and allowances for trade receivables**. It is an inevitable facet of business phenomenon today that every entity in business **incurs debts at some point due to collection problems** in recovering these debts on. Customers may face business failure when cash flows become sluggish perhaps due to slow-down in the economy or the business is not performing as expected or customers' going bankrupt. These **lost events create irrecoverable debts which need to be written-off as an expense** in the accounts. Companies use the **allowance method to make provisions for doubtful debts** based on prudence and experience and knowledge of customers' past track record of payments.
2. There are two methods in accounting for the incidence of bad or doubtful receivables that become irrecoverable particularly when **recovery procedures fail to convert debts into cash**. The **allowance method** provides an effective way to account for doubtful receivables or debts. The allowance created is based on a realistic value for receivables in the statement of financial position – amounts that are recoverable without actually writing-off the debt. Collection effort will still continue until cash is realized. The **increase or decrease in allowance is charged as an expense or as a credit in the statement of profit or loss**. The accounts receivables will be shown net of allowance in the statement of financial position. The **write-off method** deals with issue of irrecoverable bad debts when they become uncollectible or recovery procedures would have failed for various reasons. **Irrecoverable debts are usually written-off as an expense in the statement of profit or loss**. The ledger entries are all kept separate for accounts receivables, allowance for doubtful receivables and irrecoverable receivables. The increase or decrease in provision for allowance on doubtful receivables is a continuous adjusting process as more expense is expected in each reporting period as the allowance is utilized for write-offs and at the same time the allowance is also replaced by further top-ups.
3. The write-off method is not an acceptable accounting practice as it takes a conservative approach where the company deliberately tends to be **'over' prudent with the write-off policy**. It fails to take into account the possibility of **impairment of the receivables** at the cut-off date (SOFP date). This approach results in overstatement of the asset position relating to accounts receivables as the amounts are not reported at their recoverable amount, thus violating IAS 16/MFRS 116 provisions on impairment. However, most **companies actually adopt the allowance method** in preference to the write-off method. However, the write-off method has fewer accounting formalities to be observed.
4. Illustrative examples in the chapter deals with **what happens if customers fail to settle the accoun**t and how this loss event is recorded in the accounts with implications for the entity. Accounting entries relating to **creating allowance for receivables is also illustrated** with an example with the underlying ledger entries shown. The use of **aging analysis** becomes all too important when a company decides to use the allowance method, taking an **incremental approach to deal with the loss events**. Again an illustrative example on **what if a customer settles an old debt** is also demonstrated using three different methods.
5. The ultimate question in the management of receivables is concerned with **'how to achieve speedier cash flows** from customers. The text discusses the **use of credit or debit cards as common strategies** while the use of **factoring services** requires commission as a means for paying the required service. The factoring of debts involves some **financing cost** in the form of discounting by an agreed %. The entity has **access to immediate cash** net of this discount %. See texts for an illustrative example.
6. **Credit control policy** is instituted when debt management of receivables becomes imperative in order to reduce the incidence of irrecoverable debts to a minimum level. Credit control measures deals primarily on (i) **who gets credit**, a screening process of potential credit customers, (ii) **terms of credit**, establishing threshold credit limit and period for different customers, and (iii) **billings and collections**; effective and efficient billings and taking a systematic approach on collection of overdue accounts.

7. **Using financial ratios** to provide useful information on customers' position by making useful decisions about the **risk** involved on **default payments** by customers. Key ratios being used are the **current ratio** and **receivables collection period**. Current ratio indicates the liquidity position of a customer and receivables turnover period relates to collection period it takes on average for a customer to settle. Where liquidity ratio appears positive above the benchmark, it may suggest receivables are collectible within credit terms with fewer cases of doubtful receivables. A shorter collection period is a preferred measure for receivables to be converted into cash more quickly, thus avoiding delays in discharging liabilities.

Key Terms

Accounts receivables
Accounts receivable control account
Aging analysis
Allowance for doubtful receivables
Allowance method
Bad or doubtful debts
Billings and collections
Credit control
Collection of overdue accounts
Credit or debit cards
Financial ratios
Accounts eceivables turnover or receivable collection period
Trade debtors
Incremental approach on allowance
Accounting policy
Irrecoverable receivables (Bad debts)
Write-off method
Recoverable amount of debt
Current ratio
Credit control policy
Terms of credit
Factoring services

Review Questions

1. Describe what is a trade receivable or an accounts receivable?
2. What accounting principle is applied to accounts receivable as reported in the statement of financial position?
3. Compared to cash sales, sales done on credit terms have more administrative procedures. State what are these?
4. i. How does an irrecoverable debt arise?
   ii. What is the accounting treatment for irrecoverable debt in the financial statements?
5. i. Explain the accounting treatment for doubtful receivables.
   ii. What are "Loss Events"?
   iii. Identify in what circumstances these "Loss Events" arise? Give 3 types of loss events.
6. i. State the two methods of accounting for doubtful receivables
   ii. Briefly describe each of these methods.
7. Discuss why the allowance method is a preferred method to account for doubtful receivables? State the main advantage for using this method
8. How is accounts receivable reported and disclosed in the statement of financial position. Use any estimated amounts as an example.

9. One of the best methods to estimate irrecoverable and doubtful debts is to use the 'aging analyses'.
   i. Explain the reasons for using the aging analysis
   ii. Using a simple aging analysis as an example, explain how you would arrive at the required estimated amount for the allowance on doubtful receivables.

   (Read through the given explanatory notes for aging analysis as a relevant guide to handle this question requirement)
10. Explain and justify why the write-off method is an unacceptable method in accounting for recognition of doubtful and bad debts?
11. i. Explain the importance of credit control policy to an organization.
    ii. Briefly identify the type of measures necessary to maintain an effective credit control policy. (No detailed explanation is required)
12. With an example, show how if a customer settles an old debt in full? Assume the company had earlier written off the debt. Explain only two methods and justify the circumstance when it is used.
13. Describe briefly two ways of speeding up cash flows from collections of receivables.
14. Explain the importance of using financial ratios in the management of receivables. Briefly describe two such key ratios with illustrative examples.

Multiple Choice Questions

Q1. A company's accounts receivable balance reported at 31 December 2020 is RM 1, 250, 000. Its allowance for doubtful accounts receivables on same date stood at RM 5, 500 before year-end adjustment. The company reported a net sales of RM 5 million. Using the aging analysis on receivables, it estimates that 3 % of outstanding accounts receivable are uncollectible. Determine what amount of bad debts would be written-off as irrecoverable debts in the statement of profit or loss?

a. RM 43, 000 b. RM 5, 500 c. RM 32, 000
d. RM 37, 500 e. RM 150, 000

Q2. A company's accounts receivable ledger balance at the year-end date showed RM 475, 000 and its allowance for doubtful debts account has a debit balance of RM 2, 800 before any adjustment. It estimates on a prudent basis that 4 % of outstanding accounts receivables are uncollectible. It reported a sales turnover of RM 2, 785,000 (net) in its statement of comprehensive income for the financial year just ended. Determine the amount of bad and doubtful debts expense that would be reported in the statement of comprehensive income for the year?

a. RM 16, 200 b. RM 19, 000 c. RM 21, 800
d. RM 63, 400 e. RM 2, 800

Q3. Given question 2 as above, what will be the amount of accounts receivable that will be reported in the statement of financial position?

a. RM 475, 000 b. RM 472, 200 c. RM 456, 000
d. RM 63, 400 e. RM 458, 800

Q4. The company's statement of financial position at the year-end showed current assets to be RM 2, 225, 000 and current liabilities as RM 1, 025, 000. Calculate its current ratio.

a. 2: 1
b. 1.97: 1
c. 2.5: 1
d. 2.17: 1

Q5. Determine the accounts receivable turnover in Q2 above. The company's opening balance on accounts receivable was RM 469, 000 (net).

a. 5.05 times

b. 3.95 times

c. 4.95 times

d. 5.9 times

e. 4.25 times

Q6. What will be the company's collection period in days?

a. 62 days

b. 91 days

c. 45 days

d. 60 days

e. 36 days

Q7. Comment on the results calculated for Q4, Q5 and Q6.

Chapter 15

Learning Objectives

After you have studied this chapter, you should be able to:

Understand the essential nature of hire-purchase transactions
Understand the accounting concept "Substance over Form' that governs the reporting of HP transactions.
Understand the parties involved in an hire-purchase transaction
Learn and understand the accounting treatment for hire-purchase transactions
Learn and understand the technicalities of drawing up hire-purchase accounts in the books of a business entity
Know the reporting and presentation of HP transactions in the financial statements including the disclosure notes..
Know the accounting treatment for part exchange of an asset as part payment in a HP transaction.

Accounting for Hire-Purchase Transactions

1. Scope

Hire-purchase transactions are normally **arranged to finance the purchase of assets** when circumstances do not allow for the outright purchase of the asset in cash immediately. Basically, a buyer, a vendor and the finance company are involved in this type of transaction. This is clearly demonstrated in the given example where the essential nature of the hire-purchase transaction and the roles played by these parties are described. The accounting concept **"Substance over Form"** basically governs hire-purchase transactions. The relevant sections in the Chapter explain the accounting treatment using the principle underling the concept and the reporting of hire-purchase transactions including the required disclosures in the financial statements. The Chapter also deals with what happens to a hire-purchase transaction if an asset is exchanged for part payment? The implication is explained with a reference to an example highlighting the accounting entries that would be required as a result of this arrangement.

2. Essential Nature of Hire-Purchase Transactions

Hire-purchase has become a **common** and established **method of financing the purchase of vehicles**, and all sorts of plant and equipment. Most types of vehicles, particularly cars are bought using hire-purchase financing schemes and evidence suggest the majority of Malaysian car-owners resort to this frequent method of financing.

Goods and services are bought and paid either by cash or credit at the time of purchase but a transaction bought by hire-purchase contract is different from normal sales. Customers may not have immediate funds sufficient to finance the purchase of a vehicle or other forms of capital goods of their liking. Therefore, they **resort to a finance company** in order to borrow the required amount by **availing a loan to pay the vendor** who is supplying the vehicle on hire-purchase terms. The vendor (seller) and the finance company in most cases are linked together by a business arrangement or it could be the same entity undertaking both activities of selling and hire-purchase financing.

The essential differences between a normal sale and a hire-purchase transaction are:

i. The asset is **not legally owned by the purchaser until the final installment payment is made** to the finance company. The finance company providing the hire-purchase still retains the legal ownership of the asset during the period of hire.

ii. The purchaser agrees to pay for the hired item by installments over a period of time. This period may extend for two or three years and in some cases could be even for longer periods given the size and magnitude of the transaction.

iii. The **hire-purchase price** for the item **is based on the cash price** usually fixed by the market but the price will include an interest charge at prevailing rates for the duration of the hire-purchase agreement.

iv. The **ownership** of the asset on hire-purchase **does not legally pass** to the purchaser **unti**l the following two conditions are met:

   a. the **final installment is paid**; and

   b. a legal option to buy the asset is agreed by the purchaser.

Furthermore, in the event that the purchaser decides to discontinue paying the installments at some point, the purchaser is legally bound to return the item back to vendor's possession. The purchaser in that case would not be able to obtain any refund of installments already paid.

On the other hand, if **the purchaser for any reason is unable to continue paying the agreed installments**, the **vendor has the right to legally repossess the asset.** The vendor would retain all the installments already paid.

3. Law of Hire-Purchase

The Hire Purchase Act governs all hire-purchase transactions. The law relating to hire-purchase is complex and is outside the scope of this Chapter. However, the basic provisions are all explained and interpreted in the Chapter.

4. Hire-Purchase Transaction – How it is administered?

In substance, hire-purchase transactions are illustrated in the following example:

Anthony Goonting SB whose year-end is 31 December, buys one of the latest models of Mercedes Benz from Audrey Sales and Service on 1 July 2021 for RM 250,000.

Goonting has only RM 25,000, so he takes a loan to finance the remaining portion for the purchase of the car from MB Finance SB, under the Hire-Purchase Agreement which contains the transaction detail:

	RM	
Price of car	250, 000	
Deposit	(25, 000)	
Amount on hire-purchase	225, 000	(Effectively as HP Loan)
Interest @ 28% for 5 years	63, 000	
Total amount due on hire-purchase	288, 000	

The hire-purchase loan plus interest is repayable in 60 monthly installments of RM 4, 800 each commencing on 1 August 2021.

Anthony Goonting contends that he has bought a Mercedes Benz for RM 250, 000, making an immediate down payment of RM 25, 000 as deposit and the balance plus interest over 60 installments, the first installment commencing on 1 August 2021.

From Audrey Sales and Service's point of view, the company has sold the car and been paid immediately in full. (RM 25, 000 by Goonting and RM 225, 000 by MB Finance SB]

From MB Finance SB's point of view, they have financed RM 225, 000 by way of loan and will be repaid with interest RM 63, 000 each year over a 5- year period.

Required

a. **Prepare journal entries to reflect the hire-purchase transactions on 1 July 2021**

b. **Show the transactions in the General Ledger accounts for six months up to 31 December 2021 in the books of the Anthony Goonting SB (Purchaser)**

5. Accounting for Hire-Purchase Transactions

The accounting convention – *"Substance over Form"* basically governs the reporting of hire-purchase transactions.

The asset under hire-purchase is said to be **legally owned by the vendor**. However, the **substance of the transaction** appears to override this consideration by **treating ownership of the asset** as though it **is legally vested in the hands of the purchaser** which means ownership is transferred upon the signing of the agreement. There are two compelling reasons for this, the first being; **the asset is exclusively used by the purchaser with** all the attended **risks and rewards of ownership** such as insurance and maintenance are the responsibility of the purchaser. Secondly, the asset was bought on hire-purchase terms so that the asset would be owned by the purchaser. Thus, the *form* of the transaction is that **legal ownership eventually passes upon the payment of the final installment**. In law, installments are effectively hire charges. **The installments are effectively repayments of the loan.** The ***substance* of the transaction is reflected in the accounting treatment** as evidenced in the way the transaction is reported in the accounts even though the legal form is different. In law, the ownership of goods subject to hire-purchase is transferred by the vendor to the finance company. Only upon payment of the final installment, legal ownership of the asset passes to the purchaser. **Accountants tend to take the view that legal ownership being retained by the finance company is actually seen to be a form of security until all outstanding installments are repaid**.

Accounting lays emphasis on the *'substance of a transaction'* and therefore treats an asset bought on hire-purchase as though it is legally owned by the purchaser.

For accounting purposes, the total purchase price is split into two components:

i. **Cash price**: this amount is debited to the asset account; and
ii. **Interest**: this is the cost of borrowing availed as a loan to finance the purchase and is charged as an expense in each accounting period as hire-purchase interest. This interest accrues over time - each installment should be charged only with the interest accrued for that relevant period.

Let's put all these in a proper context using the above example:

	RM	
Price of car	250, 000	Treated as an asset in accounts
Deposit	(25, 000)	Advanced by purchaser
Amount on hire-purchase	225, 000	Loan availed
Interest @ 28% for 5 years	63, 000	Hire-purchase interest suspense
Total amount due on hire-purchase	288, 000	

Answer

1. Journal Entries as at 1 July 2021

		RM
Dr: Motor vehicle	250, 000	
Cr: Hire Purchase Creditor's Account		250, 000
(Being Mercedes Benz bought on hire-purchase terms)		
Dr: Hire=purchase Creditor's Account	25, 000	
Cr: Bank		25, 000
(Being deposit for the car paid to Audrey SS via MB Finance)		
Dr: Hire-Purchase Interest Suspense A/c	63, 000	
Cr: Hire-Purchase Creditor A/c		63, 000
(HP Interest charges @ 28% for 5 years)		

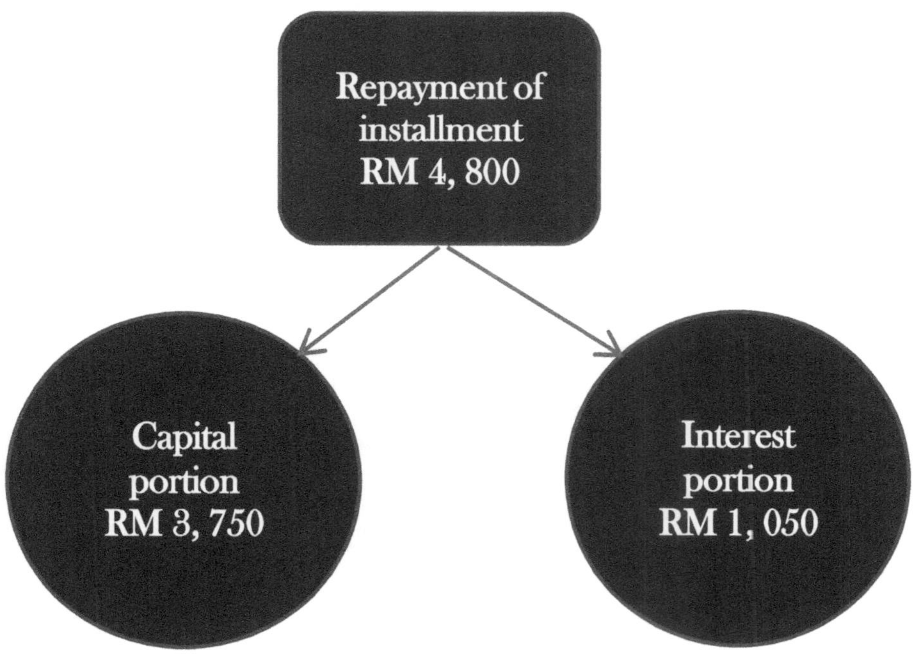

Figure 15.1 Repayment of Hire-Purchase Installment

Installment repayment on hire-purchase is split between capital and interest portions.

2. Workings

Monthly installment:	RM 288, 000/60 = RM 4, 800	
Interest	RM 63, 000/60 = 1, 050	**Shown in Figure 15.1**
Capital:	RM 225, 000/60 = 3, 750	

Now, let's update the transactions for six months up to 31 December 2021 in the **General Ledger and Cash Book maintained by Anthony's business.**

Ledger Accounts in the books of Anthony Goonting SB (Purchaser)

Car Account (Mercedes Benz)

2021	RM		
I July MB Finance SB (i)	250,000		

Hire-Purchase Creditor = MB Finance SB

2021	RM	2021	RM
1 July Cash deposit (i)	25, 000	1 July Car (i)	250, 000
1 Aug to		Interest Suspense A/c (iii)	63, 000
31Dec Bank: 5 installments			
@ RM 4,800 (ii)	24, 000		
31Dec Balance c/d (iv)	264, 000		
	313, 000		313, 000
		2022	
		1 Jan Balance b/d (iv)	264, 000

Hire-Purchase Interest Suspense A/c

2021		RM	2021		RM
1 July	HP Creditor –MB Finance (iii)	63, 000	31 Dec	Profit or Loss Statement (v) (5 installments @ RM 1, 050)	5, 250
			31 Dec	Balance c/d (vi)	57, 750
		63, 000			63, 000
2022		**RM**			
1 Jan	Balance b/d (vi)	57, 750			

Cash Book (Bank)

	2021		RM
	I July	Audrey Sales & Service (Deposit for car) (i)	25, 000
		1 Aug to 31 Dec MB Finance (ii)	24, 000
		5 Installments @ RM 4, 800	

Notes

i. The amount of loan availed is RM 225, 000 being RM 250, 000 less the Deposit RM 25,000

ii. The 5 installments of RM 4, 800 each are paid monthly commencing 1 August 2021. Probably by standing instructions to the bank via direct debits.

iii. The interest on HP loan is credited to the HP Creditor's A/c and by debiting the HP Interest Suspense Account.

iv. At the financial year end, RM 264, 000 remains outstanding

v. The **HP interest** for the 5 installments up to 31 December 2021 is calculated at RM 1, 050 per month for 5 installments amounting to RM 5, 250, **is charged as an expense** in the statement of comprehensive income.

vi. The outstanding balance of RM 57, 750 in the HP Interest Suspense Account represents the **interest expense** for the remaining years 2021 to 2025 and will be released annually as an expense in the statement of profit or loss of these years

2021 to 2025: 12/60 x 63, 000 = RM 12, 600 in each of these years and

2025: 7 installments @ RM 1, 050 = RM 7, 350.

vii. **HP Liability is always shown net of HP Interest Suspense A/c** in the statement of financial position because that is the **capital commitment** that remains outstanding. over the HP period. The **HP interest suspense a/c is a deferred expense account** which is released to the statement of comprehensive income each year during the period of the HP agreement.

viii. HP Liability is disclosed and presented in the statement of financial position as follows:

Current Liabilities:

Current portion of HP liability ≤ 12 months

Long Term Liabilities:

HP Liability > 2 – 5 years (as in our example.)

(Notes to the accounts normally show breakdown figures)

6. Depreciation of Assets Bought on Hire-Purchase

Assets bought on hire-purchase are depreciated in the usual way. Depreciation is based on the cash price. The interest element is completely ignored in depreciation calculations. In our example, the car capitalized as an asset in Anthony Goonting's books, will be depreciated using an appropriate rate of 20% per annum which is not an uncommon practice.

7. Reporting of Hire-Purchase Transactions in Financial Statements

Statement of Financial Position: as at 31 December 2021

Extract

Non-Current Assets	
Property, plant and equipment:	**RM**
Motor vehicle - At Cost	250, 000
- Accumulated Depreciation	(25, 000)
	225, 000
Current Liabilities	
Hire-purchase liability [(4, 800 × 12) =57, 600 – (12 × 1, 050)]	45, 000
Long Term Liability	
HP Liability [264, 000 – 57, 600] = 206, 400 – [1, 050 × (55 - 12)]	161, 250

Notes to the accounts:

Hire-purchase liability as at 31 December 2021	264, 000
Less: Hire-purchase interest suspense	(57, 750)
Outstanding HP commitment	206, 250
Repayable:	
Current portion ≤ 1 year	45, 000
Between 2 – 3 years	90, 000
Between 4 - 5 years	71, 250
	206, 250

Statement of Comprehensive Income for the year ended 31 December 2020

Extract

Gross profit	xxx
Less: Operating Expenses	
Depreciation	25, 000
Operating profit	xxx
Less: Finance costs – HP Interest	(5, 250)
Profit for the year before tax	xxx

8. Hire-Purchase Transaction with an Exchanged Asset as Part Payment

Sometimes, **a hire-purchase transaction is entered without payment of a deposit** but instead **an asset is exchanged for part consideration**. The parties usually agree to this arrangement. The exchanged asset is another used vehicle whose commercial value is negotiated and agreed upon by the finance company.

An example of this type of transaction is illustrated in the following case:

Zenith Traders wants a new vehicle for use in the business to transport goods to its customers. One of its current fleet of vans has been in use for 4 years in the trade. The company now requires a bigger van. Zenith Traders approach a vendor to negotiate the new van that is already on sight in the vendor's show room. After some preliminary negotiations, both parties agreed to a deal. The same finance company, MB Finance SB will be used for the hire-purchase transaction.

The hire-purchase agreement which was signed on 1 September 2021, highlights the following details relating to the new vehicle as follows:

Cash price	89, 500
Less: Van traded in for part exchange	(10, 500)
Amount availed as loan	79, 000
Add: Interest charges @ 28% for 5 years	20, 500
Total amount due on hire-purchase	99, 500

The HP loan plus interest is repayable in 60 monthly installments commencing 1 October 2021.

The old van traded in was acquired on 30 September 2017 for RM 60,000. It was depreciated at the rate of 20% per annum on a straight line basis. The policy adopted by the company; in year of acquisition, full depreciation is charged and in the year of disposal no depreciation is charged.

Zenith Traders' financial year end is 31 March 2022.

Required

a. Show the journal entries to be recorded for the hire-purchase transaction on 1 September 2021

b. How would you treat the exchange of the company's asset for the new vehicle in accounting?

Prepare the necessary accounts to reflect the required adjustments.

Answer

a. Journal Entries as at 1 September 2021

	RM	RM
Dr: Motor vehicles account	89, 500	
Cr: Hire-purchase creditor – MB Finance		89, 500
(Cash price of new van bought on hire-purchase is capitalized)		
Dr: Hire-purchase creditor's a/c	10, 500	
Cr: Asset disposal a/c		10, 500
(Old van traded in as part exchange for the new van: old van is now de-registered)		
Dr: Hire-purchase interest suspense a/c	20, 500	
Cr: Hire-purchase creditor a/c		20, 500
(HP interest charges @ 28% for 5 years)		

b. Part Exchange of Asset for the new Van

In lieu of payment, Zenith Traders traded in its old vehicle for a consideration of RM 10, 500.

This is effectively a cash down payment or deposit paid to the finance company although no cash transaction took place. The amount RM 10, 500 is to be treated as disposal proceeds for the old van. As the old van is no longer an asset in Zenith Traders books, it is de-registered and the profit or loss arising on the disposal (on exchange) is reported in the financial statements.

For accounting purposes, the disposal is shown as follows:

Disposal proceeds			10, 500
Less:			
Carrying amount of the assets at the date of disposal			
		RM	
At cost		60, 000	
Less: Accumulated depreciation			
YE 31.3.2018 @ 20% SL	12, 000	(Full depreciation in year of acquisition)	
YE 31.3.2019 @ 20%	12, 000		
YE 31.3.2020 @ 20%	12, 000		
YE 31.3.2021	12, 000		
YE 31.3.2022	Nil	(No depreciation charge in year of disposal)	
		(48, 000)	
Net book value @ 31.3. 2022			(12, 000)
Loss on disposal			(1, 500)

The company should report a loss on disposal of asset for the year ended 31 March 2022 in its Statement of Comprehensive Income.

Journal entries:

Dr: Asset Disposal A/c	60, 000
Cr: Motor Vehicles A/c – at cost	60, 000
Dr: Accumulated Depreciation A/c	48, 000
Cr: Asset Disposal A/c	48, 000

(Transfers to asset disposal a/c upon the exchange of old van for the new van)

Asset Disposal Account

2021			**2021**		
1 Sept	Motor Vehicles A/c	60, 000	1 Sept	Accum Depreciation	48, 000
			1 Sept	HP Creditor's A/c (Disposal proceeds on exchange of asset)	10, 500
			1 Sept	Loss to SOCI	1, 500

Tutorial note

The required ledger accounts of this hire-purchase transaction although not a question requirement, the recorded accounts in General Ledger will proceed exactly in the same way as shown in the previous example. Students can perform this exercise on their own to complete the accounting exercise so that their knowledge and understanding is more thorough as part of an additional assignment.

9. The Seller's Books (Vendor)

This Chapter does not cover the recording of hire-purchase transactions in the books of the seller or vendor. The scope of this topic is beyond the student's syllabus requirements. The accounting entries in the books of the finance company are usually found in a more advanced text.

Chapter Summary

1. Hire-purchase transactions on assets is a **common form of financing scheme** for entities who lack finance for outright purchase of assets. The vendor supplies the asset and the financing company provides the necessary funds as **a loan to the purchaser with a financing cost**, called hire-purchase interest. Hire-purchases transactions are governed by a legal contract. Motor vehicles are predominantly bought using hire-purchase finance. The **ownership of asset on hire-purchase does not legally pass to the purchaser until the final installment is paid** with an option to acquire the asset if agreed by the purchaser. Where the purchaser is unable to continue paying with the agreed installments, the finance company has the right to legally repossess the asset. The finance company would retain all the installments already paid.
2. Accounting for hire-purchase transaction is **governed by 'substance over form'**. In substance, the asset is treated as legally owned by purchaser and therefore it is **capitalized** in the books of account by the purchaser. The total hire-purchase price is split into two components with **the cash price debited as a tangible fixed asset** under PPE (motor vehicle account) and **the interest portion** being a financing cost, **is charged as an expense** (hire-purchase interest) **in each accounting period**. The interest portion is debited to HP interest suspense account and the corresponding credit entry goes to HP creditor's account. The **HP liability is always shown net of HP interest suspense account in the statement of financial position** because it represents the **capital commitment outstanding** over the HP term period. **HP liability is disclosed in the statement of financial position with current portion (≤ 12 months) under current liabilities and outstanding repayments ≥ 12 months under long-term liability**. The HP interest suspense is deferred expense account which is released in the statement of comprehensive income over the HP period.

   Depreciation of assets bought under HP is treated in the usual way and is based on the cash price of the asset.
3. Sometimes under special arrangement with the vendor, **an asset can be exchanged as part payment for a deposit** on the hire-purchase transaction. The transaction will be treated in the same usual way as for accounting purposes. In the books of the purchaser, **the trade- in- value of the exchanged asset would be treated as disposal proceed**s with **a gain or loss on the asset being reported in the statement of comprehensive income**. The exchanged asset will be deregistered.

Key Terms

Asset account	Asset disposal account
Cash price	Capital commitment
Hire-purchase agreement	Disclosure requirements

Hire-purchase creditor

Hire-purchase interest suspense account

Hire-purchase interest

The Hire-Purchase Act

Legal ownership of the asset

Exchange of asset

Finance company (financier)

Vendor or supplier

Substance over form

Deposit

HP installment

Review Questions

1. Describe the circumstances under which a business entity might buy an asset on hire-purchase terms instead of paying for it outright in cash. What is the main advantage and one main disadvantage of using Hire- purchase financing scheme?
2. Identify the parties in a hire-purchase transaction and state the roles they play in the transaction.
3. One of the concepts of accounting is 'Substance over Form'. Describe how a hire-purchase transaction reported in the statement of financial position is governed using the principles underlying this concept?
4. List out the accounting entries for a hire-purchase transaction in the books of a business entity buying
5. Show how hire-purchase transactions are reflected in the financial statements of a business entity buying on HP terms. You are required to state the disclosure requirements that are reported in the accounts.
6. a. Explain what happens if a hire-purchase transaction is financed by part exchange of an asset in lieu of a cash deposit or down-payment?

   b. Explain what further accounting is required in the books of a business entity relating to an exchange of asset as part payment?
7. Discuss the consequences when the purchaser on hire-purchase terms defaults in payments?

Multiple Choice Questions

Q1. State which of the following statements is true?

i. Hire-purchase transaction is an outright purchase of an asset.

ii. Hire-purchase transaction is effectively a loan with a financing cost.

iii. Legal ownership eventually passes to purchaser upon final installment

iv. The asset on hire-purchase is exclusively used with all attended risks and rewards of

.

a. (i),(iii) and (iv)

b. (i) and (ii)

c. ((ii), (iii) and (iv)

d. (ii) and (iii)

e. Only (i)

Q2. *Substance over form* of a hire-purchase transaction treats the asset as though it is not legally owned by the purchaser.

a. True

b. False

c. None of the above

Q3. Cash price of an asset under HP terms is treated as cost of the asset. Interest on hire-purchase loan is the cost of borrowing.

a. Both these elements are two components making up the total purchase price for accounting purpose.

b. Cash price is treated as the cost of an asset and therefore is debited as an PPE item.

c. The entire interest portion is a financing cost that is released as an expense in the statement of comprehensive income in the year the HP contract is signed.

d. The interest on HP transaction is charged as an expense annually in the statement of comprehensive income.

e. HP liability is shown net of HP interest suspense account and HP creditor's account.

Which of the above following statements is true?

a. (i), (ii) and (iii)

b. (i), (ii) and (iv)

c. (i) and (ii) only

d. (i), (ii), (iii) and (iv)

e. (i), (ii), (iv) and (v)

Q4. You are given the following HP transactions:

Cash price of the asset is RM 250, 000

Down payment for the asset is 10 % of cash price

Interest is charged at 25 % for 5 years on the HP finance

Answer the following questions?

i. What is the amount availed on hire-purchase?

a. RM 281, 250

b. RM 231, 250

c. RM 225, 000

ii. What is the interest cost on the HP loan for the 5 years?

a. RM 56, 250

b. RM 46, 250

c. RM 59, 250

iii. What is the split between interest and capital repayment on a monthly installment basis?

	Interest charges	Capital repayment
	RM	**RM**
a.	937.50	3, 750
b.	940	3, 747.50
c.	938	3, 750
d.	939	3, 749
e.	950	3, 700

Q5. What balances will be reported in the year-end of the first year? Assume the HP agreement was signed on 1 July 2021 and the year-end is 30 September 2021. Use the given information in Q4.

	HP Creditor's account	HP Interest suspense account
	RM	RM
a.	53, 500	267, 185
b.	52, 900	267, 785
c.	53, 750	266, 935
d.	53, 437.50	267, 187.50
e.	52, 437.50	268, 187.50

Q6. Given Q5, what balance will be reported under HP Liability in the statement of financial position?

(Assume no split between current liabilities and long-term liability)

a. 215, 700

b. 214, 700

c. 213, 700

d. 212, 700

e. 216, 250

Chapter 16

Learning Objectives

After you have studied this chapter, you should be able to:

Understand the definition of 'provision', 'contingent liability' and 'constringent asset'
Understand the distinction between provisions, contingent liabilities or contingent assets
Be able to identify the different methods of accounting for provisions, contingent liabilities and contingent assets
Be able to calculate provisions and know the changes affecting provisions
Be able to account for movements in provisions
Understand and know the requirements of reporting provisions in the final accounts
Understand the restrictive disclosure requirements and treatment for contingent liabilities and contingent assets.

Provisions and Contingent liabilities and Contingent assets

1. Scope

The Chapter first introduces the concept of liability and provides two separate sections dealing with **provisions and contingencies.** When recognized in the financial statements provisions are classified as liabilities of uncertain timing and amount whereas contingencies are not assets or liabilities but they are potentially disclosure items in the notes to the financial statements. Fundamentally, they are important to understand their relevance in financial r4eporting as users are in better position to appraise the financial effects of transactions and events. A flowchart is given which brings out the reporting requirements as to the proper classification of contingencies and disclosure requirements in the financial statements. Apart from definitions, the differences between provisions, contingent liabilities and contingent assets are clearly spelt out. The different methods of accounting for provisions, contingent liabilities and contingent assets are identified with types ofexamples. Computational examples of calculating provisions are also illustrated. Movements in accounting for provisions are explained. Finally, the reporting of provisions and treatment of contingencies in financial statements are shown with an illustrative example of the type of accounting policy of a large company reported in an annual report and accounts.

2. Concept of Liability

Generally, we understand what a liability is as reported in the statement of financial position but let's first define what a liability is?

The *Conceptual Framework* for financial reporting defines *liability as a present obligation which will be settled through an outflow of resources embodying economic benefits. Liabilities are recognized in the statement of financial position when it is probable that such an outflow will occur and the amount of which can be measured reliably.*

Reporting in financial Statements

A liability in the short-term is reported in nominal amount whereas for long-term liability this is expressed in present value terms, taking into account the time-value of money. Liabilities are classified into current liabilities and long-term liabilities. Obligations falling due within one year of normal operating cycle of a company are current liabilities and any obligations falling due beyond that period of time are classified as long-term liabilities.

The following extract reflects basically what gets reported in the statement of financial position:

Statement of Financial Position (Balance Sheet)

Extract:

	2021	**2020**
Equity	**RM' 000**	**RM' 000**
Ordinary share capital		
Retained earnings		
Reserves		
Other components of equity		
Non-Current Liabilities		
Long term borrowings		
Pensions and other post-retirement benefits		
Deferred tax		
Long term provisions		

Each of these items is normally accompanied by explanatory notes to the financial statements with detailed break-downs, identifying the nature of liabilities by components. Remember referencing back and forth between the financial statements and the related notes is an integral part of reading the financial statements. Gaining an actual understanding of the major categories of liabilities reported in the statement of financial position becomes all too important.

We are not going into details of other non-current liabilities other than confining our discussion and treatment on provisions and contingencies which is what this Chapter is about.

3. Provisions

Objectives

IAS 37/MFRS 137 *Provisions, Contingent Liabilities and Contingent Assets* primary objective is to ensure that appropriate recognition criteria and measurement bases are applied to provisions, contingent liabilities and contingent assets and that sufficient information is disclosed in the notes to the financial statements so that users can understand and appraise their nature, timing and amount.

The standard aims to provide necessary guidance so that reporting of these disclosure items are adequately presented with relevant information.

Importance of IAS 37MFRS 137 in Financial Reporting

Before IAS 37, there was no accounting standard dealing with provisions. It was open for business entities to report these events and results in the most favorable light. Entities tend to make large one-off provisions in years where a high level of underlying profits are generated. These provisions, often known as 'big bath' provisions, were then available to shield expenditure in future years when perhaps the underlying profits were not healthy or as good. In other words, provisions were deliberately used for profit smoothing. Profit smoothing is not seen in good light as it is misleadingly manipulative. With the emergence of IAS 37, these malpractices in accounting have become of the past. The **key objective of IAS 37 is to ensure that provisions are made only where there are ostensibly valid grounds for them**. The rules were tightened. IAS 37 views a provision as a liability.

Key definitions:

IAS 37 defines a **provision is a liability of uncertain timing or amount**.

IAS 37 distinguished provisions from other liabilities such as accounts payables (trade creditors) and accruals. Provisions have **uncertainty about the timing of amount of the future expenditure** to be incurred. However, the degree of uncertainty in the case of other short-term liabilities is far more less than for provisions.

a. Recognition

Under **IAS 37** a provision should be **recognized** as a liability in the financial statements when

- An entity has a **present obligation** (legal or constructive) as a result of past event.
- It is **probable that a transfer of resources embodying economic benefits will be required to settle the obligation**
- A **reliable estimate** can be made of the amount of the obligation

What Obligation Means?

A legal obligation is fairly clear and requires no clarification. However, you need to understand what a **constructive obligation** is?

> IAS 37 defines a constructive obligation as:
>
> An obligation that derives from an entity's actions where:
>
> 1. By an established pattern of past practice, published policies or a sufficiently specific current statement that the entity has indicated to other parties that it will accept certain responsibilities; and
> 2. As a result, the entity has created a valid expectation on the part of those other parties that it will discharge those responsibilities,'

For an example, an oil and gas company may have an established practice of always putting right any environmental damage caused by drilling, even though it is not legally obliged to do so, in this way, it has created a valid expectation that it will do this and it will have to recognize the constructive obligation by making a provision each time it drills a new well.

Probable transfer of resources

A transfer of resources embodying economic benefits can be regarded as more **'probable'** if the event is **more likely to happen than not**. The probability of the event taking place is more than 50%. For example, if the company has entered into a warranty obligation then the probability of transfers of resources embodying economic benefits could be extremely small particularly in respect of one specific item. However, when considering the population as a whole the probability of some transfer of resources is quite likely to be higher, If the probability of transfer of resources is greater than 50%, then a **provision** should be created for the **expected amount**.

How provisions are measured?

> The amount recognized as a provision should be the best estimate of the expenditure required to settle the present obligation at the end of the reporting period.

Basis of measurement

1. The entity's management will use their best judgment to **determine the estimates** in the light of prior experience of similar transactions.
2. Where the provision being measured involves a large population of items, the amount of obligation is estimated by weighting all possible outcomes by their associated probabilities, resulting in an **expected value** (as best estimate).
3. An allowance is made for **uncertainty.**
4. Where the provision is based on a single item such as the outcome of a legal case or litigation, **provision** is made **in full for the most likely outcome**.

Some illustrative examples

Example 1 Creating a provision for warranty obligation

ST Industries sell products with a warranty under which customers are covered for the cost of repairs of any manufacturing defect that becomes apparent within the first six months of purchase. The company's past experience and future expectations indicate the following pattern of likely repairs.

% of items sold	Defects	Cost of repairs if all items suffered from these defects
		RM Million
80	None	-
15	Minor	1.2
5	Major	3.9

Required

i. What is the amount of provision required?

ii. Show the underlying ledger accounts

iii. How would these entries be reported in the financial statements?

Answer

i. Using expected values, the provision is estimated as follows:

[(0.8 × Nil) + (0.15 × 1.2) + (0.05 × 3.9)] = **RM 375, 000**

The required provision is RM 375, 000

ii. Underlying ledger accounts

Warranty Costs – repairs for defects

	RM' 000
Provision for repairs	375

Provision for Warranties

	RM' 000
Warranty –repairs (costs)	375

iii. Reporting in financial statements

Warranties are shown as an expense and normally included as part of the manufacturing costs in this case but in other cases it is disclosed separately as an operating expense. Provision for warranties is normally shown under non-current liabilities. However, a liability for warranty that is due for payment within a year is shown as a current liability in the statement of financial position.

Environmental clean-up cost

Where the effect of time-vale of money is material, the amount of provision should be the **present value of the expenditure** required to settle the obligation. An appropriate **discount rate or cost of capital** should be used. In this case, the discount rate should be a **pre-tax rate** that reflects current market assessments of the time-value of money. The discount rate(s) should not adjust for risks for which future cash flow estimates have been adjusted.

Example 2

A mining company knows from past experience when it ceases certain operations on a particular site in 5 years' time, it will have to incur environmental clean-up costs of RM 8 million.

	Provision required
	RM
PV of RM 8 million in 5 years' time,	
Say, the relevant discount rate in this case is 10%	
In year 1	
RM 8 million @ 0.621* (Using PV table)	4, 968, 000
In year 2	
RM 8 million @ 0,683 ** (Using PV table)	5, 464, 000
	496, 000

* The discount rate for 5 years @ 10%

** The discount rate for 4 years @ 10%

The increase in the 2nd year of RM 496, 000 will be charged to profit or loss. This is the unwinding of the discount which is accounted for as a finance cost.

The original provision of RM 4, 968,000 will be added to the cost of assets involved in the mining operation and depreciated over 5 years.

At the end of the 5th year, the provision for environmental cleanup cost will cumulatively amount to RM 8 million at which this point, the mining company will discharge the full amount to settle its obligation to pay-off the expenditure as part of its environmental cleanup process before it moves or relocates to a new mining site.

Now let's show the accounting entries:

a. i. The journal entries to record the transactions*

Journal entries

Dr; Mining asset account	4, 968, 000	
Cr: Provision – for environmental clean-up costs		4, 968, 000
(Being provision for environmental clean-up costs in year 1 discounted @ 10 % for 5 years)		
Dr: Finance cost	496, 000	
Cr: Provision – environmental clean-up cost		496, 000
(Being finance costs for year 2 - @DF 10 %)		
Dr: Finance cost	544, 000	
Cr: Provision – environmental clean-up cost		544, 000
(Being financing cost in year 3 for environmental clean-up costs @ DF 10 %)		

Working: RM 8 million @ 0.751 (using PV Table) –

RM 6, 008, 000 – RM 5, 464, 000 = RM 544, 000

For years 4 and 5, calculations done in same manner. Journal entries will be repeated likewise.

ii. Show the underlying ledger accounts

(You are required to prepare the ledger accounts only for the first 3 years)

G. Ledger

Mining Assets (RM, 000)

Provision	4, 968		
(Re: Environmental clean-up costs)			

Provision (Environmental clean-up costs (RM' 000)

		Mining asset account	4,968
		(Clean-up costs – year 1)	
		Year 2 – Finance cost	496
Balance c/d	6, 008	Year 3 - Finance cost	544

Finance costs (RM' 000)

Provision - Year 2	496		
Provision – year 3	544		

b. Show how these accounts will be presented in the financial statements

(You are required to prepare the ledger accounts only for the first 3 years)

Extract:

Statement of Financial Position

(For 3 year ending)	**RM' 000**
Non-current assets	
Property, plant and equipment	4, 968*
* not adjusted for depreciation	
Non- current liabilities	
Provision for liabilities (496 + 544)	1, 040

Statement of Comprehensive Income

For year ended (3rd year)

	RM' 000
Operating profit for the year	**xxx**
Less:	
Finance costs	544

Note

The mining assets' carrying amount would be included as part of the property, plant and equipment. Carrying amount is cost less accumulated depreciation and impairment losses. However, no adjustment is shown for depreciation on the mining assets.

c. Write-up of an accounting policy for disclosure on the company's environmental clean-up cost

The company's policy recognizes the need to provide for environmental clean-up costs when it ceases mining operations at the end of its expiry period. Accordingly, a provision is made in the accounts for the estimated costs in cleaning up of the environmental where its mining operations are located. Based on best estimates, a provision for RM 8 million is considered sufficient for the environmental clean-up costs. This estimated figure will be spent at the end of 5 years when mining operations are expected to cease. The environmental clean-up cost was arrived at after taking into consideration the time value of money using a discount rate of 10 % to determine the present value of the expected clean-up costs which is charged as a capitalized cost of the mining assets in its first year of operations. In subsequent four years consecutively, an annual provision will be added based on the present value calculations. The annual amount will be released as financing costs and charged to the statement of comprehensive income.

Prime examples of provisions

IAS 37 considers the following list as possible examples of items for which provisions may to be justified. Some illustrative examples were already covered earlier

i. Warranties
ii. Major repairs
iii. Environmental contamination
iv. Decommissioning or abandonment costs
v. Restructuring
vi. Onerous contracts

In nearly all these cases, the entity will have a clear policy for dealing with these types of issues as it affects in their particular circumstances. We are not discussing these issues in more detail here as they are beyond the scope of study at this level. However, provision for restructuring costs is a contentious issue on which IAS 37 has given more guidance specifying strict criteria in the standard to check on possible abuses of provisioning for restructuring. These issues will be covered in our next forthcoming textbook, *"Financial Reporting, A Contemporary Practice."*

Other related issues

Use of provisions

Changes in provisions

Future events

Future operating losses

Disclosure

Disclosures for provisions fall into two components:

i. Details of **change in the carrying value** of a provision should be disclosed with movement from the beginning to the end of the year

ii. Explanation as to the background of the provision and the uncertainties affecting the outcome.

Contingent Liabilities and Contingent Assets

The following flow chart is taken from **IAS 37** which provides a clear guidance on the summary requirements concerning provisions and contingent liabilities.

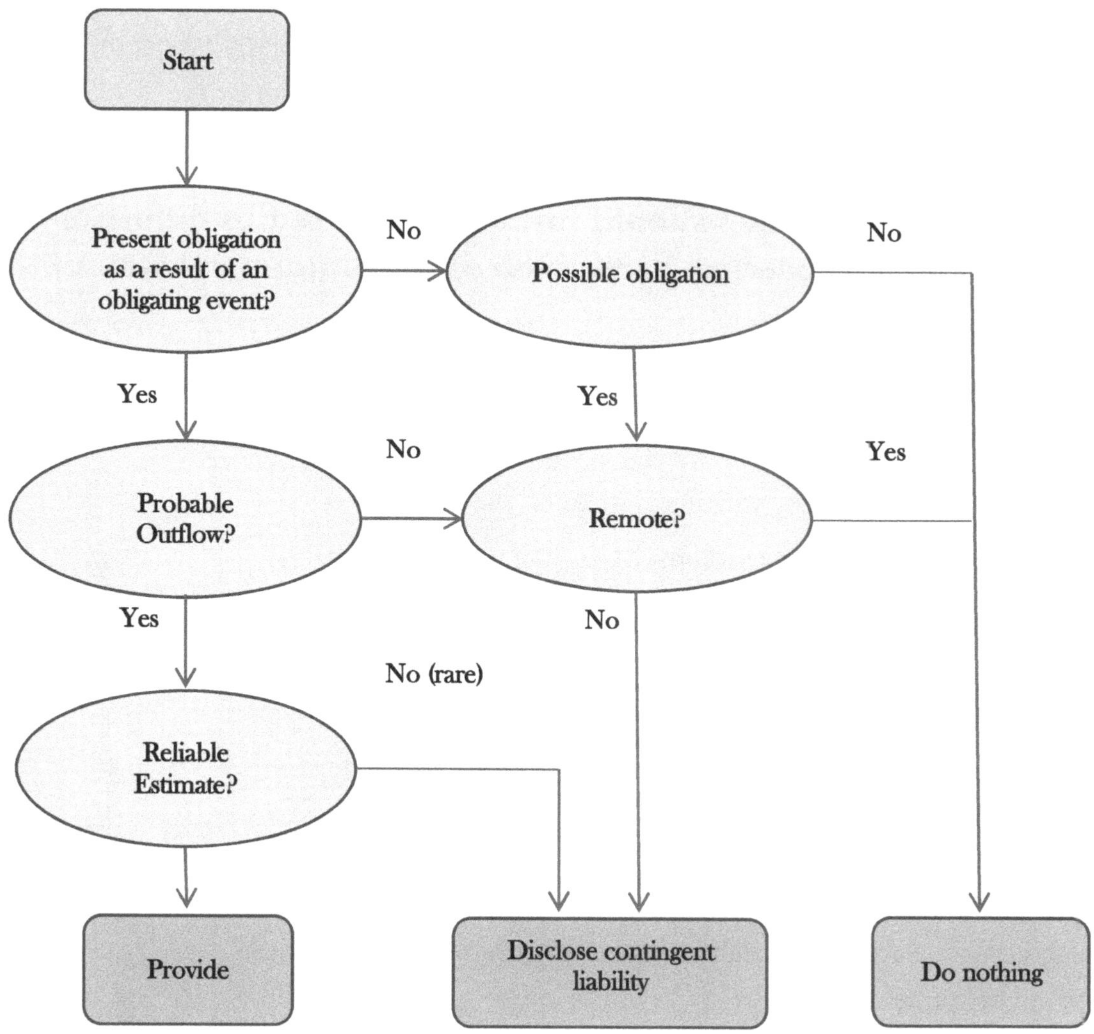

The most important rule to remember is that an entity should never recognize a contingent asset or liability in the accounts but they should be disclosed only as a note to the financial statements.

Figure 16.1

Definitions

IAS 37 defines a **contingent liability** as:

A **possible obligation** that arises from past events and whose existence will be confirmed only by the **occurrence or non-occurrence of one or more uncertain future events not wholly within the control of the entity;**

or

A **present obligation** that arises from past events but is not recognized because it is not probable that an outflow of resources embodying economic benefits will be required to settle the obligation; or the amount of the obligation cannot be measured with sufficient reliability

Rule of thumb

Probable means a probability of more than 50% that the event is likely to occur. If an obligation is probable, it is not a contingent liability. Instead a provision is required.

How is a contingent liability treated in financial statements?

Conventionally, contingent liabilities **should not be recognized in financial statements** but normally **they are disclosed as part of the notes in financial statements.**

What disclosure is required?

- A brief description of the nature of the contingent liability
- An estimate of its financial effect
- An indication of the uncertainties that exist
- The possibility of any reimbursement

Example of a disclosure note on contingent liability in the financial statements

Contingent Liability

	2021	2020
	RM' 000	RM' 000
Unsecured:		
Guarantees given to a financial institution with respect to facilities granted to the company	6, 340	4, 715

Other than what is reportedly disclosed above, at the date of this report there does not exist any contingent liabilities of the company which have arisen since the end of the financial year.

Contingent Assets

IAS 37 defines a contingent asset as:

A possible asset that arises from past events and whose existence will be confirmed by the occurrence or non-occurrence of one or more uncertain future events not wholly within control of the entity.

The important rule to remember is that **a contingent asset must never be recognized.** It is only when the realization of the related economic benefits is virtually certain that due recognition take place. At that point, **the asset becomes no longer a contingent asset.**

Illustrative example

An entity is engaged in a litigation (legal dispute). The outcome is not yet known. However, a number of possibilities arise.

Nature of Dispute	Action taken
1. The entity is expected to pay a sum of RM 115, 000 in damages.	A provision is recognized.
2. Possible damages are RM 115,000 but the entity is not expected to pay.	A contingent liability is disclosed.
3. The entity is expected to pay the damages but is unable to estimate the amount.	A contingent liability is disclosed.
4. The entity expects to receive damages in the sum of RM 115,000. Receipt of this amount is virtually certain.	An asset is recognized
5. The entity expects to probably receive damages of RM 115, 000.	A contingent asset is disclosed.
6. The entity assumes it may receive damages, but not probable.	No disclosure

What disclosure is required of a contingent asset?

The standard states that contingent assets must be only disclosed in the notes to the financial statements if they are **probable**. A brief description of the contingent asset should be provided along with an estimate of its likely financial effect.

An exception to the general rule

IAS 37 allows reporting entities to avoid disclosure requirements if such reporting of provisions, contingent liabilities and contingent assets would be expected to **seriously prejudice** the interest and position of the entity particularly in disputes with other parties. This concession is usually **rare** but if special circumstances warrants it, it be can be exercised provided details of the general nature of the provisions and contingencies together with a supporting explanation and reason is given for the non- disclosure.

Further Illustrative Example

Let's look at an illustrative case on the accounting treatment of provisions, and contingencies

Case 1

Cinta Sayang had given a corporate guarantee for the borrowings of another subsidiary, Didik-Sayang, whose financial position as at 31December 2021 appeared sound. However, in the following year, the financial performance of Didik-Sayang deteriorates badly as business worsens. At 31 December 2022 Didik Sayang files for voluntary liquidation in order to protect itself against the company's creditors.

Required

What are the implications for accounting treatment?

a. As at 31 December 2021
b. As at 31 December 2022

Suggested answer

a. As at 31 December 2021

The giving of corporate guarantee by Cinta Sayang is an obligating event that gives rise to a present and legal obligation. However, as at 31 December 2021 no transfer of resources is probable in settlement of the obligation. Accordingly, no provision is recognized. The corporate guarantee is disclosed as a contingent liability unless the probability of any likely transfer appears to be remote. (in which case no disclosure required)

b. As at 31 December 2022

As in above (a), there is a present obligation as a result of a past obligating event which is giving of the guarantee. As at 31 December 2022, it is probable that a transfer of resources will be required to settle the obligation. A provision is therefore **recognized** for the best estimate of the provision because at this date, information may become more apparent. The filing for voluntary liquidation is prima facie evidence that the parent company is under **legal and constructive obligation** to honour the guarantee.

The table below is taken from ACCA's article which shows the treatment for an entity depending on the likelihood of an event happening;

Likelihood	Outflow of resources (Entity has to pay out)	Inflow of resources Entity may receive income
Remote	Do nothing	Do nothing
Possible	Contingent liability	Do nothing
Probable	Provision	Contingent asset
Virtually certain	Provision	Asset

It can be seen that an entity could only recognize an asset from potential inflow if the **realization of income is virtually certain**.

Chapter Summary

1. The Chapter discusses provisions, contingent liabilities and contingent assets in the context of financial reporting. How these significant items are dealt in terms of accounting treatment and their disclosure in the financial statements. Under the requirements of IAS 37/MFRS 137, **contingent liabilities and contingent assets** are strictly **disclosure items** (under restricting conditions) to be reported in the notes to the financial statements whereas **provisions are liabilities of uncertain timing or amount** which are accounted for, using the double entry system.
2. A provision 8must **fulfill three criteria** requirements before it is recognized as a liability in the entity's accounts. The entity has **a present obligation** (legal or constructive) arising from past event and it is **probable that a transfer of resources embodying economic benefits to settle the obligation** and that the amount of the **obligation can be estimated reliably**. The standard clearly defines both legal and constructive obligation. The standard specifies at least 50 % probability for the transfer of resources before a provision is recognized in the accounts. The Chapter gives two illustrative examples where provisions are estimated - **warranty obligation** and **environmental clean-up costs** in reporting these items in the accounts.
3. The Chapter illustrates by giving a clear flow-chart that shows when a provision is recognized on the basis of a present obligation. The Chart also stipulates when **a contingent liability needs to be disclosed** in the financial statements. However, **a contingent asset is never recognized in the accounts** and **requires no disclosure** unless and until the **realization of economic benefits is virtually certain** (highly probable), then at this point, it is disclosed as a note in the financial statements with a **description along with an estimate of its likely effect**. The accounting standard obviously lays emphasis on the **prudence concept** for recognition and measurement of provisions and contingencies. **Calculations** are based on **best estimates** and the **use of probabilities and present value**.

Key Terms

Contingent asset

Contingent liability

Provision

Present obligation (legal or constructive)

Probable transfer of economic resources

Reliable estimate

Present value

Probability

Environmental clean-up costs

Warranty costs

Virtually certain.

Review Questions

1. Explain the concept of liability based on the *Conceptual Framework.*
2. a. Define a provision and state the conditions under which it is recognized in the financial statements. List some examples of provisions.
   b. Where is a provision disclosed in the accounts and explain how they are measured?
3. Explain what you understand by the following two terms? Give an example of each.
   i. Present obligation
   ii. Constructive obligation
4. Explain what is meant by probable transfer of economic resources?
5. Discuss how a warranty provision is arrived by using a numerical example.
6. a. Why do organizations in some business segments need to make a provision for environmental clean-up costs? Taking the example of a particular industry, show how a provision is estimated?
   b. Show the accounting entries in the underlying ledger accounts.
   c. Show how these accounts are presented in the financial statements?
7. Discuss the importance of an accounting policy disclosure in the case of environmental clean-up costs.
8. What are contingent liabilities and contingent assets.
9. Under what circumstances is a continent liability and a contingent asset need to be disclosed in the financial statements. Give an example of a contingent liability and a contingent asset.
10. Present obligation and possible obligation are terms used in IAS 37/MFRS 137. State the requirements in treating these terms in the financial statements with regard to provisions and contingent liabilities and contingent assets.
11. What are the disclosure requirements for a contingent liability and a contingent asset?
12. a. In the case of a litigation, a business entity need to consider the nature of a legal dispute. Explain the number of possibilities when a provision, a contingent liability or a contingent asset arises?
    b. What appropriate action is required when dealing with these possibilities? State the accounting treatment in each possibility.
13. Given the likelihood of a contingency happening is remote, what treatment is required in the accounts? Explain the rationale underlying the treatment.
14. Write short notes
    a. On how provisions are reported in the financial statements? Discuss measurement and disclosure requirements in your answer.
    b. On the difference between disclosure requirements on contingent liabilities and contingent assets. In your answer, explain the fundamental concept that underlies these disclosure requirements.

Multiple Choice Questions

Q1. Which of these statements about a provision is true?

a. A provision is based on the best estimate to settle a present obligation at the end of the reporting period

b. A provision is an uncertain amount and timing of a liability to be accounted under current liabilities.

c. The amount of provision recognized for the reporting period appears both in statement of comprehensive income and in the statement of financial position.

d. The entity is expected to settle a present obligation amounting to RM 125, 000

  i. (a), (b) and (d)

  ii. (a), and (c)

  iii. (a), (c), and (d)

  iv. All of the about.

  v. (b) and (d)

Q2. Which of the following statements is false?

IAS 37 considers the following list as examples of provisions:

i. Warranties

ii. Major repairs

iii. Environmental contamination

iv. Retention money held in a contract

v. Restructuring

vi. Onerous contracts

  a. (ii) and (iv)

  b. (vi) only

  c. (iv) only

  d. (i), (iii), (v), and (vi)

  e. All of the above except (iv)

Q3. A company is expected to settle a legal obligation based on a contract. The amount of provision to be recognized in the statement financial position is RM 25, 000. Using the probabilities of 60 %, 30 % and 10%, calculate the expected value of the provision.

a. RM 17, 500

b. RM 15, 000

c. RM 22, 500

d. RM 25, 000

e. RM 27,500

Q4. A quarry operation by an entity takes 3 years to complete. Environmental policy required by the Malaysian government stipulates a clean-up cost at the end of the quarry operation.

The company estimates the provision to be RM 1.2 million. The estimated costs at present value is discounted using a rate of 9 % which best reflects the cost of capital.

Using PV table @ 9 %

Year 1	0.650	at the end of 3 years
Year 2	0.708	
Year 3	0.772	

Required

Determine the estimated clean-up cost for year 1 and Year 2

Quarry asset	Provision account (as financing cost)
RM 780, 000 year 1	RM 69, 600 year 2

RM 849, 600 year 1	RM 76, 800 year 2
RM 926, 400 year 1	RM 82, 000 year 2
RM 1, 000, 000 year 1	RM 90, 000 year 2
RM 1, 200, 000 year 1	RM 76, 800 year 2

Q5. Conventionally, contingent liabilities should not be recognized in financial statements but they are disclosed. The following are disclosed in the notes to the financial statements:

i. A description of the nature of the contingent liability

ii. An estimate of its financial effect

iii. An indication of the uncertainties that exist

iv. No possibility of any reimbursement

v. Uncertainty in the amount of the liability to be disclosed

Which of these statements is not true?

a. (i), (ii), and (iii)

b. (iii), (iv) and (v)

c. (iv) and (v) only

d. (ii) and (iv) and (v)

e. (v) only

Q6. A contingent asset is only disclosed when

a. Its probability is virtually certain but only to the extent of 80 %

b. It is virtually certain and its estimated amount is provided as a liability in the financial statements.

c. It is virtually certain and therefore disclosed in the notes to the financial statements. Which of the above statements is true?

Bibliography

John Wild, Winston Kwok, Ken Shaw and Barbara Chiappetta, (2017) Financial Accounting, Information for Decisions, 3rd Edition, Asia Global Edition, McGraw Hill Education, Singapore.

Tan Liong Tong (2017) Financial Accounting and Reporting in Malaysia, Volume 1, 6th Edition, Wolters Kluwer, Kuala Lumpur.

Tan Liong Tong (2017) Financial Accounting and Reporting in Malaysia, Volume 2, 6th Edition, Wolters Kluwer, Kuala Lumpur.

Herve Stolowy, Michel Lebas and Yuan Ding (2010) Financial Accounting and Reporting, A Global Perspeeective, 3rd Edition, South-Western Cengage Learning, Singapore.

David Austen, Jacqueline Halls-Bryan and Peter Hallstone, (2015) Accounting for Cambridge International AS & A Level, First published,Oxford University Press,, Oxford, United Kingdom.

Walter Harrison Jr, Charles Horngren, C. William and Themin Suwardt (2014) Financial Accounting, International Financial Reporting Standards, 9th Edition, Global Edition, Pearson Education Limited, Harlow, England.

David Alexander & Christopher Nobes (2013) Financial Accounting, An International Introduction, 5th Edition, Pearson Education Limited Harlow, England.

Marshall B. Romney & Paul John Steinbart (2018) Accounting Information Systems, 14th Edition, Global Edition, Pearson Education Limited, Harlow, England.

Weygandt ,Kimmel and Kieso (2008) Financial Accounting, A Focus on Fundamentals, 6th Edition, International Student Version, John Wiley & Sons, (Asia) Pte Ltd, Singapore.

Alan Sangster (2016) Frank Wood's Business Accounting 2, 13th Edition, Pearson Education Limited, Harlow, England.

Ian Harrison and Michael Hillman (2013) Revision Guide Cambridge AS and A Level Accounting, Hodder Education, London, England.

Frank Wood and Alan Sangster (1998) Frank Wood's A Level Accounting, 2nd Edition, Financial times Pitman Publishing, London, England.

ACCA Platinum Approved (2018) Paper 3 Financial Accounting (International) Study Text, BPPLearning Media, London, England.

BPP ACCA Study Text (1988) Paper 2.8 Regulatory Framework of Accounting, First Edition, BPP Publishing Limited, London, England.

M. Drever, P. Stanton & S. McGoowan (2007) Contemporary Issues in Accounting, First Published, John Wiley & Sons, Milton Queensland, Australia.

K.R Subramaniym and John J. Wild (2009) Financial Statement Analysis, 10th Edition, McGraw Hill International Edition, Singapore.

Revsine, Collins and Johnson (2005) Financial Reporting and Analysis, 3rd Edition, Pearson Prentice Hall,, New Jersey.

A.H. Millichamp (1984) Foundation Accounting, An International Manual for Accounting students, DP Publications, Hampshire, England.

About the Authors

Panirselvam Ayadurai *is a chartered certified accountant by training who had spent a substantial period spanning almost 40 years of his professional career in public accounting both in Malaysia and England (1985-1992), prior to switching to a career in academia. He holds a PhD in finance and economics from an American University in San Francisco and a MBA from De Montfort University, England. He is a senior accounting technician having been a qualified member of The Association of Accounting Technicians, England since 1984., He was awarded an Advanced Diploma in management accounting by the Business School of CIMA. He gained his professional expertise in auditing, financial accounting and reporting, and taxation during his long career stints in several firms of chartered accountants in Kuala Lumpur and London. He was a licensed practicing company secretary for many years prior to switching to University lecturing. He is now a retired University lecturer and still finds himself academically active in his research areas. Mr. Panirselvam was attached to the business and management faculty for almost 8 years in AIMST University, with a lecturing portfolio in financial accounting and reporting, auditing, taxation, corporate governance and finance particularly in the area of investment and portfolio analysis and entrepreneurial finance. During his spare time, he contributes written articles to newspaper tabloids on contemporary issues in accounting and business finance. He is a reader in financial economics and has a passion for pure mathematics. He is married with 4 grown-up children and lives in Subang Jaya. He practices yoga and loves to watch Badminton.*

Gayatri Panirselvam *has significantly contributed useful academic research work for the publication of this book. She is also involved through a joint effort to write the second book on financial reporting which is currently in progress. She has BA (Hons) in accounting and finance from Teesside University, England. She has a MSc in international accounting from University Utara Malaysia. She also has an advanced diploma in Accounting from the Institute of Financial Accountants, UK. Gayatri is attached to Air Asia in a managerial capacity with a portfolio for reporting revenue and accounts receivable for the airline with other responsible divisional roles. She also teaches part-time in financial accounting amongst other related subjects. Gayatri is married to a civil engineer with 3 children and lives with her family in Penang. For a hobby, she finds time for cooking her traditional Indian cuisine and reads widely on aviation industry.*

www.ingramcontent.com/pod-product-compliance
Lightning Source LLC
LaVergne TN
LVHW070846210926
848482LV00016B/880